MICROSOFT®
FrontPage 2000

Mastering and Using

H. Albert Napier
Philip J. Judd

South-Western
EDUCATIONAL PUBLISHING
Thomson Learning™

Australia • Canada • Denmark • Japan • Mexico • New Zealand • Philippines
Puerto Rico • Singapore • South Africa • Spain • United Kingdom • United States

ISBN: 0-538-43152-0

1 2 3 4 5 6 7 BM 03 02 01 00

Managing Editor: Carol Volz
Project Manager/Editor: Cheryl L. Beck
Marketing Manager: Larry Qualls
Consulting Editor: Robin Romer, Pale Moon Productions
Production Services: GEX Publishing Services
Graphic Designer: Brenda Grannan, Grannan Graphics

I(T)P®

International Thomson Publishing

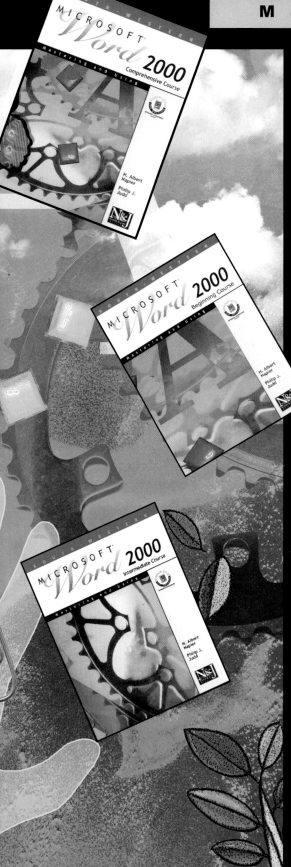

What's New in FrontPage 2000

- ► Personalized menus and toolbars

- ► Customizable menus and toolbars

- ► Format Painter

- ► Background spell checking as you work

- ► Customizable themes

- ► Pre-built web components, such as Category Component and Office Web Components

- ► Absolute and relative positioning of page elements

- ► Nested subwebs with different access rights

- ► Ability to create disk-based webs on a hard drive or a network drive

- ► Source control to reserve file so others cannot edit it

- ► Workflow reports to set up and assign responsibilities for pages to team members

- ► Compatibility with specific Web browser features and servers

- ► Roaming user profiles on server

Napier & Judd

In their over 48 years of combined experience, Al Napier and Phil Judd have developed a tested, realistic approach to mastering and using application software. As both academics and corporate trainers, Al and Phil have the unique ability to help students by teaching them the skills necessary to compete in today's complex business world.

H. Albert Napier, Ph.D. is the Director of the Center on the Management of Information Technology and Professor in the Jones Graduate School of Administration at Rice University. In addition, Al is a principal of Napier & Judd, Inc., a consulting company and corporate trainer in Houston, Texas, that has trained more than 90,000 people in computer applications.

Philip J. Judd is a former instructor in the Management Department and the Director of the Research and Instructional Computing Service at the University of Houston. Phil now dedicates himself to corporate training and consulting as a principal of Napier & Judd, Inc.

Philip J. Judd

H. Albert Napier,
Ph.D.

Preface

At South-Western Educational Publishing, we believe that technology will change the way people teach and learn. Today there are millions of people using personal computers in their everyday lives—both as tools at work and for recreational activities. As a result, the personal computer has revolutionized the ways in which people interact with each other. Personal productivity software and the Internet are two of the most influential applications used on personal computers today. Napier and Judd combine the following distinguishing features to allow people to do amazing things with their personal computers.

Distinguishing Features

All the textbooks in the *Mastering and Using* series share several key pedagogical features:

Case Project Approach. In their more than twenty years of business and corporate training and teaching experience, Napier and Judd have found that learners are more enthusiastic about learning a software application if they can see its real-world relevance. The textbook provides bountiful business-based profiles, exercises, and projects. It also emphasizes the skills most in demand by employers.

Comprehensive and Easy to Use. There is thorough coverage of new features. The narrative is clear and concise. Each unit or chapter thoroughly explains the concepts that underlie the skills and procedures. We explain not just the *how*, but the *why*.

Step-by-Step Instructions and Screen Illustrations. All examples in this text include step-by-step instructions that explain how to complete the specific task. Full-color screen illustrations are used extensively to provide the learner with a realistic picture of the software application feature.

Extensive Tips and Tricks. The author has placed informational boxes in the margin of the text. These boxes of information provide the learner with the following helpful tips:

► Quick Tip. Extra information provides shortcuts on how to perform common business-related functions.
► Caution Tip. This additional information explains how a mistake occurs and provides tips on how to avoid making similar mistakes in the future.
► Menu Tip. Additional explanation on how to use menu commands to perform application tasks.
► Mouse Tip. Further instructions on how to use the mouse to perform application tasks.

End-of-Chapter Materials. Each book in the *Mastering and Using* series places a heavy emphasis on providing learners with the opportunity to practice and reinforce the skills they are learning through extensive exercises. Each chapter has a summary, commands review, concepts review, skills review, and case projects so that the learner can master the material by doing. For more information on each of the end-of-chapter elements see page viii of the How to Use this Book section in this preface.

Appendices. Mastering and Using series contains an appendix to further help the learner prepare to be successful in the classroom or in the workplace. Appendix A teaches the learner how customize FrontPage to match their personal style and preferences. They review how to work with personalized menus and toolbars; display, hide, dock, and float toolbars; customize the menu bar and toolbars; and hide the Views bar.

Microsoft Office User Specialist (MOUS) Certification. The logo on the cover of this book indicates that these materials are officially certified by Microsoft Corporation. This certification is part of the MOUS program, which validates your skills as a knowledgeable user of Microsoft applications. Upon completing the lessons in the book, you will be prepared to take a test that could qualify you as either a core or expert user. To be certified, you will need to take an exam from a third-party testing company called an Authorization Certification Testing Center. Call **1-800-933-4493** to find the location of the testing center nearest you. Tests are conducted at different dates throughout the calendar year. To learn more about the entire line of training materials suitable for Microsoft Office certification, contact your South-Western Representative or call **1-800-824-5179.** Also visit our Web site at *www.swep.com.* To learn more about the MOUS program, you can visit Microsoft's Web site at *www.microsoft.com/train_cert/cert/.*

SCANS. In 1992, the U.S. Department of Labor and Education formed the Secretary's Commission on Achieving Necessary Skills, or SCANS, to study the kinds of competencies and skills that workers must have to succeed in today's marketplace. The results of the study were published in a document entitled *What Work Requires of Schools: A SCANS Report for America 2000.* The in-chapter and end-of-chapter exercises in this book are designed to meet the criteria outlined in the SCANS report and thus help prepare learners to be successful in today's workplace.

Instructional Support

All books in the *Mastering and Using* series are supplemented with the following items:

Instructor's Resource Package. This instructor's manual, packaged on an Electronic Instructor CD-ROM, contains lesson plans that begin with teaching materials and preparation suggestions, along with tips for implementing instruction and assessment ideas; a suggested syllabus for scheduling semester, block, and quarter classes; and SCANS workplace know how. The Electronic Instructor CD-ROM also contains:

► Student lesson plans	► PowerPoint presentations
► Data files	► Portfolio assessment/worksheets
► Solutions files	► Learning styles strategies
► Test questions	► Career worksheets
► Transparencies	► Tech prep strategies

Course Test Manager. Course Test Manger is a powerful testing and assessment package that engages instructors to create and print tests from testbanks designed specifically for South-Western titles. In addition, instructors with access to a networked computer lab (LAN) can administer, grade, and track tests online. Students also can take online practice tests, which generate customized study guides that indicate where in the text students can find more information on each question. To see a demo of Course Test Manager, visit *www.course.com.*

Learner Support

Data CD-ROM. To use this book, the learner must have the data CD-ROM (also referred to as the Data Disk). Data Files needed to complete exercises in the text are contained on this CD-ROM. These files can be copied to a hard drive or posted to a network drive.

How to Use This Book

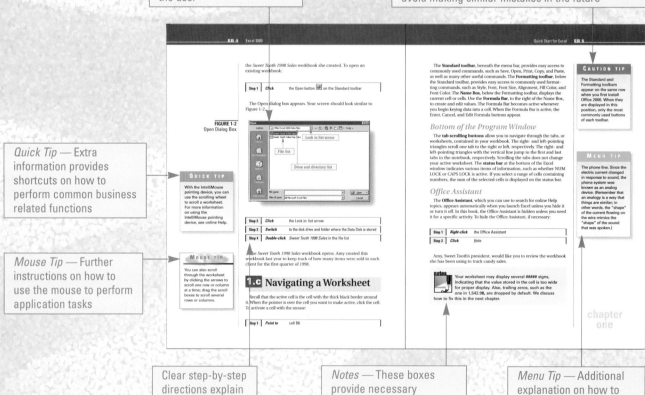

Learning Objectives — A quick reference of the major topics learned in the chapter

Case profile — Realistic scenarios that show the real world application of the material being covered

Chapter Overview — A concise summary of what will be learned in the chapter

Full color screen illustrations provide a realistic picture to the user

Caution Tip — This additional information explains how a mistake occurs and provides tips on how to avoid making similar mistakes in the future

Quick Tip — Extra information provides shortcuts on how to perform common business related functions

Mouse Tip — Further instructions on how to use the mouse to perform application tasks

Clear step-by-step directions explain how to complete the specific task

Notes — These boxes provide necessary information to assist you in completing the exercises

Menu Tip — Additional explanation on how to use menu commands to perform application tasks

End-of-Chapter Material

Concepts Review — Multiple choice and true or false questions help assess how well the reader has learned the chapter material

Summary — Reviews key topics discussed in the chapter

Commands Review — Provides a quick reference and reinforcement tool on multiple methods for performing actions discussed in the chapter

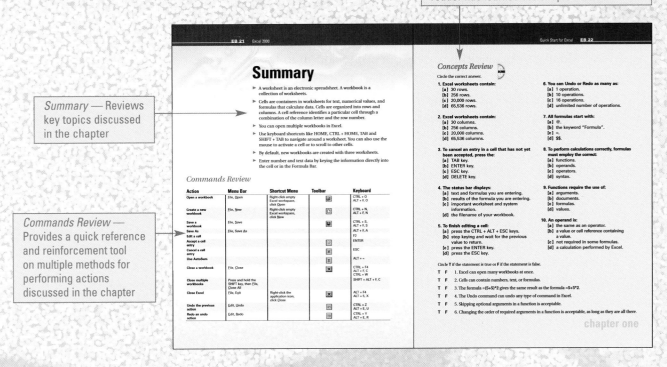

Skills Review — Hands-on exercises provide the ability to practice the skills just learned in the chapter

SCANS icon — Indicates that the exercise or project meets a SCANS competencies and prepares the learner to be successful in today's workplace

Case Projects — Asks the reader to synthesize the material they learned in the chapter and complete an office assignment

Internet Case Projects — Allow the reader to practice using the World Wide Web

MOUS Certification icon — indicates that the exercise or project meets Microsoft's certification objectives that prepare the learner for the MOUS exam

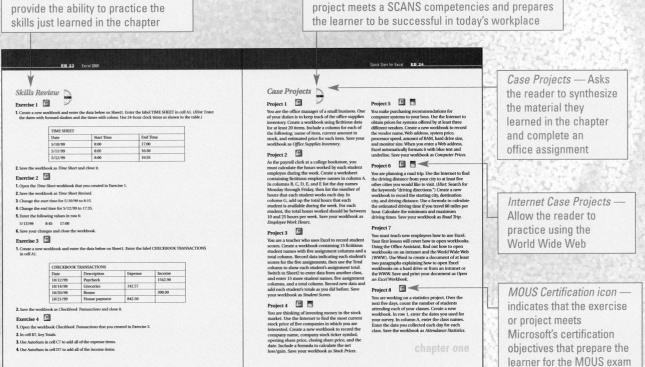

Acknowledgments

We would like to thank and express our appreciation to the many fine individuals who have contributed to the completion of this book.

No book is possible without the motivation and support of an editorial staff. Therefore, we wish to acknowledge with great appreciation the project team at South-Western Educational Publishing: Cheryl Beck, project manager; Mike Broussard, art and designer coordinator; Angela McDonald, production coordinator; Kathy Hampton, manufacturing coordinator, and Carol Volz, managing editor.

We are very appreciative of the personnel at Napier & Judd, Inc., who helped prepare this book. We acknowledge, with great appreciation, the assistance provided by Ollie Rivers and Nancy Onarheim in preparing and checking the many drafts of this book and the instructor's manual.

Contents

Quick Start for FrontPage 2000

Chapter Overview

This chapter gives you a quick overview of opening, viewing, modifying, saving, printing, and organizing web pages. To learn these skills, you open an existing web and then view it in different FrontPage views. You also modify and save a web page. In addition, this chapter shows you how to print the web page structure and how to organize your web pages. You will use these basic skills every time you create or edit a FrontPage web.

Case profile

Sarah's PartyWorld is a medium-sized business located in Kansas City, Missouri, that specializes in prepackaged, coordinated supplies and theme ideas for birthday celebrations, holiday parties, bridal and baby showers, and other special occasions. Sarah's PartyWorld currently has a simple web site. Sarah Whaley, the owner, hires you to design, create, and publish a new, more attractive, and complex web site for Sarah's PartyWorld. Your first task is to open the existing web site and to view, modify, save, print, and organize the web pages in FrontPage 2000.

LEARNING OBJECTIVES

- Define a FrontPage web
- Start FrontPage 2000
- Open an existing FrontPage web
- View a web page in Normal, HTML, and Preview tabs in Page view
- Modify and save changes to a web site
- View a web site in Reports, Hyperlinks, or Folders view
- View and print a web site structure in Navigation view
- Manage tasks
- Get Help in FrontPage 2000
- Close a FrontPage 2000 web

chapter one

1.a Defining a FrontPage Web

A **web site** usually consists of multiple, interrelated web pages covering a specific purpose or business. **Web pages** are separate documents stored as individual files. Using separate web pages instead of one large document makes it easier to manage a web site and provides for faster downloading of the pages. The individual pages at a web site are connected with **hyperlinks**, a text or image that is associated with a location (path and filename) on the same or another web page. An **external hyperlink** is text or an image that is associated with the path to a web page at a different site. An **internal hyperlink** is associated with another area in the same web page or another page in the same web.

FrontPage organizes the hyperlinked web pages of a web site into units called **FrontPage webs**. Each FrontPage web is stored in its own folder on your hard drive or on a server. Usually, hyperlinked web pages covering the same content are part of one FrontPage web. Groups of pages administered by the same person also might be included in the same FrontPage web.

Before you begin working on the new Sarah's PartyWorld web site, you want to open the existing FrontPage web and look at it in different FrontPage views.

QUICK TIP

Text hyperlinks usually appear in a different color and are underlined. To identify a text or image hyperlink, you can place your mouse pointer on the text or image. If the mouse pointer changes to a pointing hand pointer, the text or image is a hyperlink.

1.b Starting FrontPage 2000

Before you can begin to work with FrontPage, you need to open the application. Each time you open the application, you open a new, blank web page. To open the FrontPage application and a new, blank web page:

Step 1	*Click*	the Start button 🔲Start on the taskbar
Step 2	*Point to*	Programs
Step 3	*Click*	Microsoft FrontPage
Step 4	*Click*	the Page button 📄 on the Views bar, if necessary

The FrontPage application opens with a blank web page. Your screen should look similar to Figure 1-1, which identifies the specific components of the FrontPage application window.

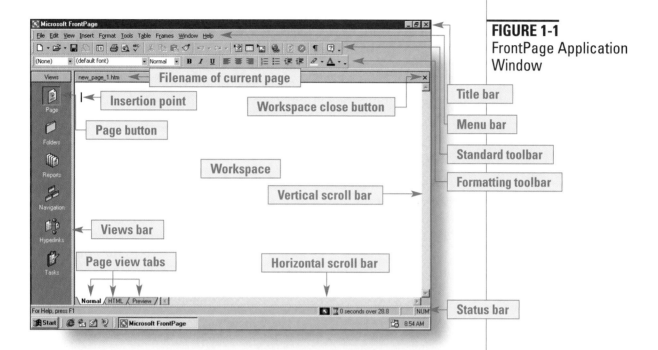

FIGURE 1-1
FrontPage Application Window

notes

FrontPage 2000 features personalized menus and toolbars, which "learn" the commands you use most often. When you first install FrontPage 2000 only the most frequently used commands appear immediately on a short version of the menus, and the remaining commands appear after a brief pause. Commands that you select move to the short menu, while those you don't use appear only on the full menu.

The Standard and Formatting toolbars may appear on the same row in FrontPage 2000. In this position, only the most commonly used buttons of each toolbar are visible. All the other default buttons appear on the More Buttons drop-down lists. As you use buttons from the More Buttons drop-down list, they move to the visible buttons on the toolbar, while the buttons you don't use move into the More Buttons drop-down list. If you arrange the Formatting toolbar below the Standard toolbar, all buttons are visible. Unless otherwise noted, the illustrations in this book show the full menus and the Formatting toolbar below the Standard toolbar. See Appendix A for more information about using and modifying the personalized menus and toolbars.

chapter
one

Menu Bar

The **menu bar**, located below the title bar, has ten drop-down menu commands that contain groups of additional, related commands. For example, the File menu contains commands for opening, closing, previewing, and printing web pages. You can use the mouse or the keyboard to select a command from the menu bar. The activities in this book instruct you to select menu bar commands with the mouse. The Commands Review section at the end of each chapter provides a summary of both mouse and keyboard techniques to select a menu command.

Standard Toolbar

The **Standard toolbar** is located under the menu bar and is made up of buttons that represent commonly used commands. For example, the Standard toolbar contains buttons for opening saving, previewing, and printing a web page. The Standard toolbar allows you to perform a command quickly by clicking the button that represents the command. You can customize the Standard toolbar (or any other toolbar) by adding or deleting buttons.

Formatting Toolbar

The **Formatting toolbar**, located under the Standard toolbar in Figure 1-1, contains buttons that represent commonly used formats. You can use buttons on the Formatting toolbar to modify web page text appearance; for example, you can change the font or text alignment.

Views Bar

The **Views bar**, located under the Formatting toolbar on the left side of the window, provides shortcuts you can use to view FrontPage webs. You use **Page view** to create or edit a web page. You organize web site files and folders in **Folders view**. **Reports view** provides a way to analyze and manage the content of a web site. **Navigation view** provides tools you use to design your web site structure. You can view and edit hyperlinks in **Hyperlinks view**. Finally, you can create and edit an electronic "To Do" list for the web site in **Tasks view**.

Workspace

The large area to the right of the Views bar is called the **workspace**. You key headings and text, insert bulleted and numbered lists, add pictures, and insert other web page components in the workspace as you create or edit a web page. You also view the web structure, hyperlinks relationships, and tasks in the workspace.

Insertion Point

The blinking vertical bar in the upper-left corner of the workspace is the insertion point. The **insertion point** marks the location where text is entered in a web page.

Scroll Bars

Scrolling changes the view of the current web page in the workspace. The **vertical scroll bar** appears at the right side of the workspace and scrolls the current web page up and down. The **horizontal scroll bar** appears below the workspace and scrolls the current web page left and right.

Page View Tabs

FrontPage has three ways to look at the current web page as you create or edit it in Page view: Normal, HTML, and Preview. The Normal, HTML, and Preview tabs are located to the left of the horizontal scroll bar in Page view. The Normal tab provides a **WYSIWYG** (What You See Is What You Get) view. You create and edit your web pages in the **Normal tab** much as you create and edit a word processing document. FrontPage inserts the appropriate HTML code as you create or edit a web page in the Normal tab. **HTML** is the abbreviation for HyperText Markup Language, the code or tags used to create web pages. You use the **HTML tab** to view or edit the actual HTML tags. The **Preview tab** shows how the current web page will look in a **web browser**, the software program used to view web pages.

Status Bar

The **status bar** appears at the bottom of the window above the taskbar and displays messages as you are working on a web page. For example, when you open a web page, the status bar displays a message telling you that the page is being opened and how long it takes for the page to download when someone accesses it with a web browser.

1.c Opening an Existing FrontPage Web

Because the existing Sarah's PartyWorld web site was created in an earlier version of FrontPage, Sarah suggests you use it to review the FrontPage 2000 views.

chapter
one

M ENU TIP

You can open an existing web by clicking the Open Web command on the File menu. You can open a recently reviewed web by pointing to Recent Webs on the File menu, and clicking the web folder name.

notes Before you begin each chapter, copy the Data Files from the CD-ROM to your hard drive. To repeat any activities or exercises that require FrontPage web Data Files, you must recopy the Data Files so that you are working with a copy of the original web.

You begin by opening the existing web site:

| Step 1 | *Click* | the Open button list arrow on the Standard toolbar |
| Step 2 | *Click* | Open Web |

The Open Web dialog box opens.

Step 3	*Click*	the Look in: list arrow
Step 4	*Switch*	to the disk drive and folder where the Data Files are stored
Step 5	*Open*	the Chapter_1 folder
Step 6	*Double-click*	the My_Webs folder

Your dialog box should look similar to Figure 1-2.

FIGURE 1-2
Open Web Dialog Box

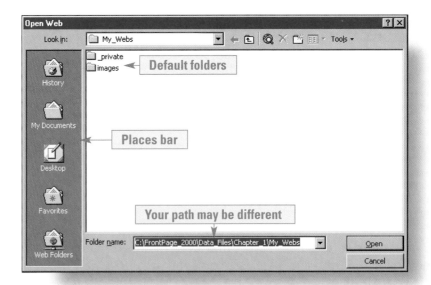

| Step 7 | *Click* | Open |

The Folder List may automatically open when you open the web. The **Folder List** is a list of all the folders, web pages, and image files for the open web. If the Folder List does not open automatically, you can display it with a button on the Standard toolbar.

Step 8	*Click*	the Folder List button 🔳 on the Standard toolbar, if necessary, to view the Folder List

Your screen should look similar to Figure 1-3.

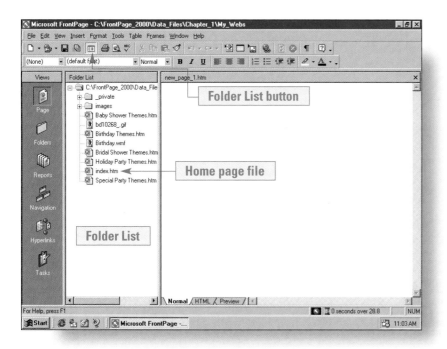

FIGURE 1-3
Folder List

notes

When you install FrontPage, a folder called "My Webs" is installed on the C:\ drive. FrontPage stores any new webs in this folder by default. Each web you create is stored in its own subfolder inside the My Webs folder. For the activities in this text, save your webs in the location specified by your instructor.

The individual web subfolders contain two additional subfolders created by FrontPage: the _private and images folders. The _private subfolder contains the files FrontPage uses to manage your web and should be left alone. The images subfolder can be used to store picture, sound, or video files included at the web site. Moving these files into the images folder makes the Folder List less cluttered and easier to read.

MENU TIP

You can display the Folder List by clicking the Folder List command on the View menu.

CAUTION TIP

Web servers, the computer software and hardware used to make web pages available to others, may use different rules for naming home pages. Most require you use either *default.htm* or *index.htm*. When you use FrontPage to publish a web site to a server, FrontPage automatically changes the home page name, if necessary. If you upload your web files manually instead of having FrontPage publish them for you, you may have to rename the home page file to *default.htm* or *index.htm*.

**chapter
one**

FIGURE 1-4
Enlarged Workspace in Normal Tab in Page View

Each web site has a primary page called the **home page**. The home page for the existing Sarah's PartyWorld web site is named *index.htm*. You want to view the home page for this web.

To view the home page:

Step 1	**Double-click** *index.htm* in the Folder List

The Sarah's PartyWorld home page opens in the workspace. You can hide the Folder List to enlarge the workspace.

Step 2	**Click** the Folder List button [image] on the Standard toolbar

Your screen should look similar to Figure 1-4.

Now you are ready to review the different FrontPage views.

C

1.d Viewing a Web Page in the Normal, HTML, and Preview Tabs in Page View

FrontPage has three ways to display the current web page in Page view. Figure 1-4 shows the existing Sarah's PartyWorld home page in the Normal tab. You use this view to create or edit a web page by keying and formatting text, inserting bulleted or numbered lists, and inserting graphic images. As you create or edit a web page, FrontPage automatically inserts the appropriate HTML tags that you can view and edit.

Viewing HTML Tags

HTML tags are special bracketed instructions that specify how a document should be displayed in a web browser. You can view these HTML tags by clicking the HTML tab. To view the HTML tags in the existing Sarah's PartyWorld home page:

Step 1	*Click*	the HTML tab

Your screen should look similar to Figure 1-5.

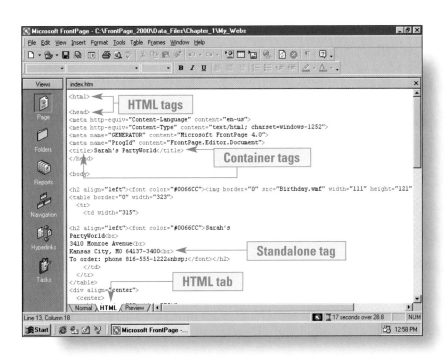

FIGURE 1-5
HTML Tab in Page View

HTML tags structure a web page document by defining the parts of the page, such as the title, headings, body, tables, and images. There are two types of HTML tags: **Container tags** surround and define a web page item, and **Standalone tags** insert a web page item. A web page title appears in the title bar of a web browser. The HTML tags that define a web page title are the Container tags <title> and </title>. The tag <title> appears at the beginning of the title text and the </title> tag appears at the end of the title text. An example of a Standalone tag is the <br> tag that inserts a line break at the end of a text line.

Previewing a Web Page

As you create or edit a web page, you should preview it to see how it will look in a web browser. The Preview tab allows you to see how the current web page looks in a web browser without having to open the page in a web browser.

To preview the current web page:

Step 1	*Click*	the Preview tab

Your screen should look similar to Figure 1-6.

FIGURE 1-6
Preview Tab in Page View

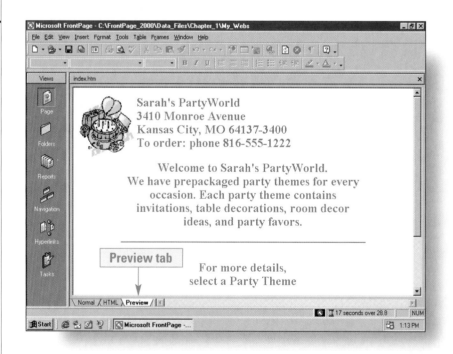

You return to the Normal tab in Page view.

| Step 2 | *Click* | the Normal tab |

Sarah asks you to quickly modify the home page by adding her e-mail address below the phone number in the text at the top of the page.

1.e Modifying and Saving Changes to a Web Site

You want to add Sarah's e-mail address as a **mailto: link**, a special hyperlink that automatically opens the viewer's e-mail message composition window when clicked. To do this you simply key the e-mail address and press the SPACEBAR. You first need to position the insertion point after the phone number text and then press the SHIFT + ENTER keys to insert a line break.

To position the insertion point and create the mailto: link:

Step 1	*Click*	at the end of the line following the phone number text (line four at the top of the page)
Step 2	*Press*	the SHIFT + ENTER keys
Step 3	*Key*	E-mail us at sarah@xeon.net
Step 4	*Press*	the SPACEBAR
Step 5	*Observe*	that the e-mail address becomes a different color and is underlined, indicating a hyperlink

To update the web page, you must save it.

| Step 6 | *Click* | the Save button 🖫 on the Standard toolbar |

The web page you just modified and saved is part of a **disk-based web**, a web stored on your local hard drive or network drive. If you want your modifications to a web to be available to others browsing the company intranet or the World Wide Web, you must publish the revised web to a web server creating a **server-based web**. Publishing a web is discussed in detail in later chapters.

Previewing and Printing a Web Page

You can preview a web page and print it in Page view. To preview the *index.htm* web page:

Step 1	*Click*	File
Step 2	*Click*	Print Preview

The *index.htm* file opens in Print Preview. Your screen should look similar to Figure 1-7.

FIGURE 1-7
Print Preview

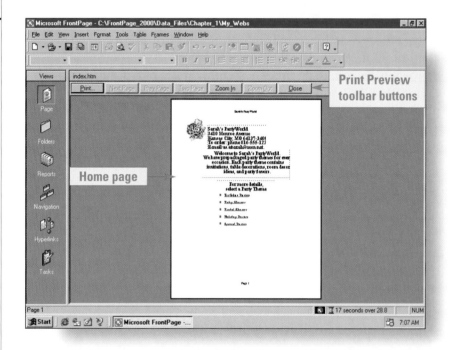

You can use buttons on the Print Preview toolbar to view the next, previous, or two pages of a multiple page file, zoom the page in or out, and print it. To print the page:

Step 1	*Click*	the Print button ⌗Print...⌗ on the Print Preview toolbar
Step 2	*Click*	OK

After modifying and saving the web page, you want to see the kinds of information FrontPage maintains about the web, the arrangement of the hyperlinks in the web, and a list of all the folders and files in the web. You can do this in Reports, Hyperlinks, and Folders views.

1.f Viewing a Web Site in Reports, Hyperlinks, or Folders View

FrontPage provides additional ways to view and manage a web. For example, you can view different reports about the status of a web, view a diagram of the hyperlinks in a web, and view a list of folders and files in the web. You do this by switching from Page view to the appropriate view with the shortcut buttons on the Views bar.

Using Reports View

Reports view provides information about the status of a web site. For example, you might want to know how many files are in the current web or if the current web includes broken hyperlinks. A **broken hyperlink** is one that no longer connects to a valid location. You can get answers to these and other web management questions in Reports view.

To view the current web in Reports view:

Step 1	**Click**	the Reports button 🗗 on the Views bar

The Site Summary report opens in Reports view. Your screen should look similar to Figure 1-8.

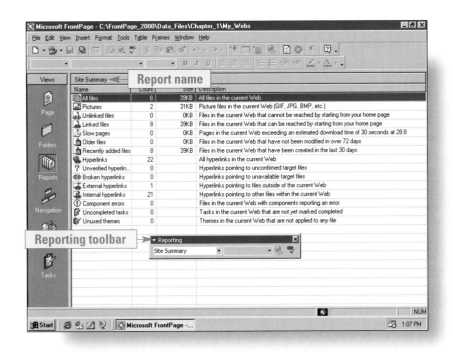

FIGURE 1-8
Site Summary Report

chapter
one

The Reporting toolbar may automatically appear when you switch to Reports view. If the Reporting toolbar does not automatically appear, you can display it.

Step 2	*Right-click*	the menu bar to display the toolbar shortcut menu
Step 3	*Click*	Reporting
Step 4	*Point to*	each button on the Reporting toolbar and view its ScreenTip

The Site Summary report itemizes the different detail reports available for the current web. You can view an individual report by selecting the report name from Report button drop-down list on the Reporting toolbar. You want to view a list of all the files in the current web. To view the list of files:

| Step 1 | *Click* | the Report button list arrow `Recently Added Files ▾` on the Reporting toolbar |
| Step 2 | *Click* | All Files |

A report listing all the web page and image files in the current web opens. Your screen should look similar to Figure 1-9.

FIGURE 1-9
All Files Report

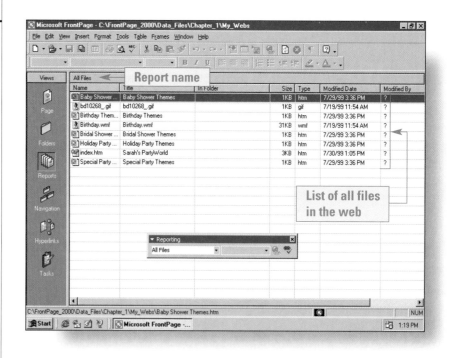

If you have a long list of files in a web, you may want to sort the list by filename, title, size, type, or date modified. You can do this by clicking the column heading buttons, such as Name or Title. You also can open and review a file listed in the All Files report by double-clicking the filename in the list or by right-clicking the filename in the list and clicking the <u>O</u>pen command. After reviewing the list of files, you want to close the Reporting toolbar and return to Page view.

| Step 1 | *Click* | the Close button ✖ on the Reporting toolbar |
| Step 2 | *Click* | the Page button 🗐 on the Views bar |

Using Hyperlinks View

Hyperlinks view allows you to see a diagram of the hyperlinks to and from the current page. You want to see all the hyperlinks to and from the home page. To view the hyperlinks diagram:

Step 1	*Verify*	that the *index.htm* page is open in Page view
Step 2	*Click*	the Hyperlinks button 🗐 on the Views bar
Step 3	*Hide*	the Folder List, if necessary

The diagram of the hyperlinks to and from the home page opens. Your screen should look similar to Figure 1-10.

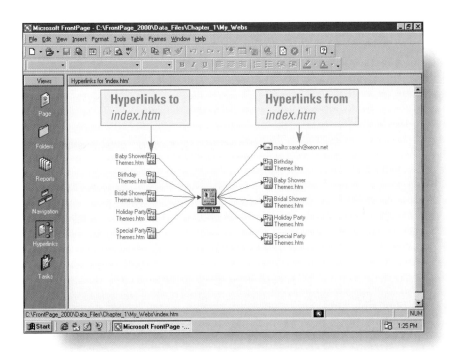

FIGURE 1-10
Home Page in Hyperlinks View

chapter
one

You can change the view to another page in the web by displaying the Folder List and selecting another page. To view the hyperlinks to and from the Bridal Shower Themes page and return to Page view:

Step 1	*Display*	the Folder List
Step 2	*Click*	Bridal Shower Themes in the Folder List to select it
Step 3	*Observe*	the diagram for the hyperlinks to and from the Bridal Shower Themes page
Step 4	*Click*	the Page button  on the Views bar

Using Folders View

To easily manage the folders and files in a FrontPage web, you must be able to see a list of all folders and files. One way to view a list of folders and files is to display the Folder List using the Folder List button on the Standard toolbar. Another way to view a list of folders and files for a web is in Folders view.

To display the current web in Folders view:

Step 1	*Click*	the Folders button  on the Views bar

Your screen should look similar to Figure 1-11.

FIGURE 1-11
Current Web in
Folders View

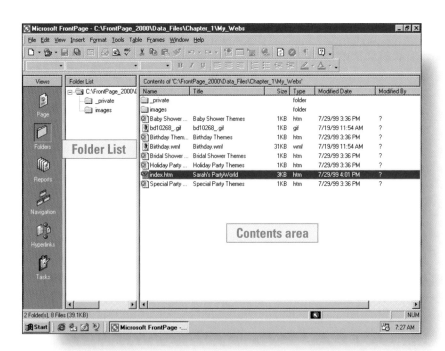

Changing a Filename and Updating Its Hyperlinks

You can manage the files in the current web in Folders view. For example, you can use a shortcut menu to open, rename, or delete a file. When you rename a file, you must also update any hyperlinks to that file. You decide to rename the *Special Party Themes.htm* page and then update the hyperlinks to and from the page. To rename the page and update the hyperlinks:

Step 1	***Right-click***	the *Special Party Themes* filename
Step 2	***Click***	<u>R</u>ename
Step 3	***Key***	*New Party Themes.htm*
Step 4	***Press***	the ENTER key

The Rename dialog box opens, reminding you one page has hyperlinks to this page and asking whether you want to update this page so that there will be no broken hyperlinks.

Step 5	***Click***	<u>Y</u>es to update the hyperlinks

Moving and Organizing Files Using Drag and Drop

You can also organize the files in the web quickly by using the drag-and-drop method to move files to different folders. Recall that the images folder is automatically added to each web so that you can store all image files in one location. This helps to reduce clutter in the file list if you have many image files in a web.

To select both image files and move them to the images folder using drag and drop:

Step 1	***Click***	the *bd10268_.gif* file to select it
Step 2	***Press & Hold***	the CTRL key
Step 3	***Click***	the *Birthday.wmf* file to select it
Step 4	***Release***	the CTRL key
Step 5	***Drag***	the selected files to the images folder in the Folder List

The image files are moved to the images folder and renamed to include the new location.

Viewing File Properties and Renaming the Page Title

You can view a file's properties with a shortcut menu in Folders view or the Folder List. **File properties** are the special attributes of a file, such as its filename and location. To view the properties for the *index.htm* file:

Step 1	*Right-click*	the *index.htm* file in the file list
Step 2	*Click*	Properties
Step 3	*Click*	the General tab, if necessary

The General tab in the index.htm Properties dialog box opens. Your dialog box should look similar to Figure 1-12.

FIGURE 1-12
Properties Dialog Box

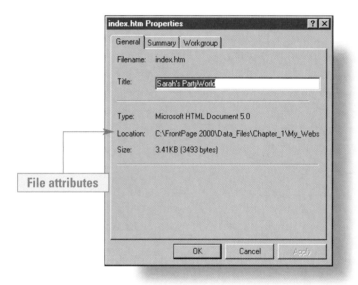

QUICK TIP

You can change the page title in the page Properties dialog box. Right-click the page whose title you want to change in the Folder List and click Properties. Click the General tab. Key the new title in the Title: text box. Click OK.

The General tab in the index.htm Properties dialog box provides information about the filename, file type, file size and location, and the web page's title. The Summary tab provides information about the date created and date last modified, as well as any special comments you want to add about the file. You can use the Workgroup tab to assign the file to a specific category or person, to indicate the review status, and to prevent the file from being published to a web server.

Step 4	*Click*	the Summary tab
Step 5	*Observe*	the options
Step 6	*Click*	the Workgroup tab
Step 7	*Observe*	the options

Step 8	*Click*	Cancel to close the dialog box
Step 9	*Click*	the Page button 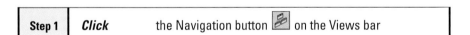 on the Views bar
Step 10	*Hide*	the Folder List, if necessary

You want to review the arrangement of the pages, or **web structure**, of the existing Sarah's PartyWorld web. You can do this in Navigation view.

1.g Viewing and Printing a Web Site Structure in Navigation View

A FrontPage web consists of interrelated pages that are organized in a tree-like structure. The home page appears at the top of the tree and the related pages branch out at different levels below the home page. You use Navigation view to review the web's tree structure. You can also modify that structure in Navigation view by adding, deleting, or moving pages to a new position in the tree.

To view the tree structure of the existing Sarah's PartyWorld web:

| Step 1 | *Click* | the Navigation button on the Views bar |

Your screen should look similar to Figure 1-13.

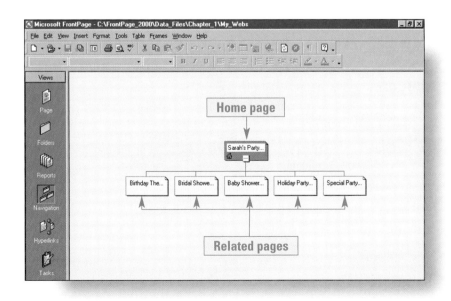

FIGURE 1-13
Tree Structure in Navigation View

chapter
one

The home page is at the top of the tree and the related pages become the next level of the tree. You can quickly organize pages in the tree by dragging them to a new location.

Moving and Organizing Files Using Drag and Drop

If a web has many pages, you may need to organize the pages by moving them to a new location in the tree structure. You can do this easily with drag and drop. You decide to move the Birthday Theme page after the Baby Shower Theme page in the second level of the tree. To move the page:

Step 1	*Drag*	the Birthday Theme page box to the right and drop it between the Baby Shower Theme page box and the Holiday Party Theme page box
Step 2	*Observe*	the new arrangement of pages in the tree

FrontPage provides a Navigation toolbar you can use to view the tree structure in different ways. To display the Navigation toolbar, if necessary:

Step 1	*Right-click*	the menu bar
Step 2	*Click*	Navigation
Step 3	*Review*	the toolbar buttons using ScreenTips

You can zoom the view of the tree structure using the Navigation toolbar. To enlarge the view to 150% and then reduce the view to 100%:

Step 1	*Click*	the Zoom button list arrow 100% ▼ on the Navigation toolbar
Step 2	*Click*	150%
Step 3	*Observe*	the tree structure
Step 4	*Click*	the Zoom button 100% ▼ on the Navigation toolbar
Step 5	*Click*	100%

You can view the tree structure in Portrait or Landscape orientation. **Portrait orientation** is a vertical view of the tree structure. **Landscape orientation** is a horizontal view of the tree structure. To change the orientation to Portrait and then back to Landscape:

Step 1	*Click*	the Portrait/Landscape button on the Navigation toolbar
Step 2	*Observe*	the Portrait orientation of the tree structure
Step 3	*Click*	the Portrait/Landscape button on the Navigation toolbar

The tree structure returns to Landscape orientation. You can expand or collapse the view of levels on the tree structure. To collapse and then expand the tree structure:

Step 1	*Click*	the Minus icon on the home page box to collapse the tree
Step 2	*Click*	the Plus icon on the home page box to expand the tree

Printing from Navigation View

You may need a printed copy of the tree structure for reference or web site documentation. You can both preview and print the tree structure in Navigation view.

To preview and print the tree structure:

Step 1	*Click*	File
Step 2	*Click*	Print Preview

The Print Preview window opens in the workspace.

Step 3	*Click*	the Print button [Print...] on the Print Preview toolbar
Step 4	*Click*	OK
Step 5	*Switch*	to Page view

Creating, editing, and maintaining a FrontPage web consists of many related tasks. To help manage a web effectively, you can create an electronic "To Do" list of outstanding items to be completed.

QUICK TIP

You can use drag and drop to organize web files by displaying the Folder List in Navigation view and dragging a file to a new location. You can also add new pages to the web in Navigation view by displaying the Folder List and then dragging a web page from the Folder List to the tree structure.

MENU TIP

You can also zoom the tree structure and switch between Portrait and Landscape orientation by right-clicking the Navigation view workspace to view a shortcut menu.

chapter
one

1.h Managing Tasks

When completing some actions, FrontPage can automatically add a task to the task list for you. For example, when FrontPage checks the spelling in a web, you can have it create a task for each page that contains misspelled words. You can also manually add tasks to the list. For example, you may need to verify the content of certain web pages, insert a new image on a page, or update broken hyperlinks before the pages are published to a web server.

Viewing and Sorting Tasks in Tasks View

You view the task list by clicking the Tasks button on the Views bar. To modify a task's options, right-click the task to open the Task Details dialog box, and then change the appropriate option. You start a task associated with a specific file by right-clicking the task and clicking the Start Task command. This opens the associated file so you can work on it; it also marks the task "in progress." When a task is finished, you can mark it complete with a command on the shortcut menu or have FrontPage do it for you when you save the associated file.

You can assign a task to other members of a workgroup. You can also prioritize and delete tasks. If you have a long list of tasks, you may want to sort the list. For example, to see all the High Priority tasks listed first, you can sort the task list by Priority. You sort tasks by clicking the appropriate column heading button: Status, Task, Assigned To, Priority, Associated With, Modified Date, and Description.

Viewing Task History

The Task History consists of new tasks, tasks in progress, and completed tasks. To view the Task History you can right-click the workspace in Tasks view and then click the Show Task History command. If the Task History is not turned on, you see only new tasks and tasks in progress in Tasks view. You can also turn on the Task History by pointing to Task on the Edit menu, and then clicking the Show History command.

Sometimes you may have a question about a FrontPage tool or feature. You can use online Help to get answers to these questions.

1.i Getting Help in FrontPage 2000

It is easy to get online Help when working in FrontPage. From the Help menu, you can open the Help window, convert the mouse pointer to a help pointer, and load the Microsoft Office web page. You can also use the Microsoft FrontPage Help button on the Standard toolbar or press the F1 key to open the Help window. To convert the mouse pointer to a help pointer, you can press the SHIFT + F1 keys. Then click the help pointer on a menu command or toolbar button to view its ScreenTip help.

Now you are ready to close the current web.

1.j Closing a FrontPage 2000 Web

When you have finished reviewing and modifying a web, you can close it. Because you have completed your review and modification of the existing Sarah's PartyWorld web, you will close the web and then exit FrontPage 2000.

To close the web:

Step 1	*Click*	File
Step 2	*Click*	Close Web
Step 3	*Click*	Yes to save file changes
Step 4	*Click*	the Close button ☒ on the title bar to exit FrontPage

Now that you're familiar with opening, organizing, and navigating FrontPage Webs, you're ready to begin creating the new web for Sarah's PartyWorld.

CAUTION TIP

FrontPage 2000 does not use the Office Assistant animated graphic help tool that is available in other Microsoft Office applications, such as Word, Excel, and PowerPoint.

chapter
one

Summary

- ▶ A FrontPage web is a group of multiple interrelated web pages that cover a specific purpose or business.

- ▶ The menu bar, located under the title bar, contains ten drop-down menu commands with groups of additional, related commands. The Standard and Formatting toolbars, located under the menu bar, contain buttons that represent commonly used commands.

- ▶ The Views bar, located on the left side of the FrontPage window, contains shortcut buttons used to view FrontPage webs in several different ways. The white area to the right of the Views bar is called the workspace.

- ▶ You create and edit an individual web page in Page view. Page view also has three tabs you can use to view a web page: Normal, HTML, and Preview. You use the Normal tab to create and edit web pages, much as you create and edit a word processing document. Use the HTML tab to view and edit the HTML tags automatically inserted into the web page by FrontPage. The Preview tab allows you to see what the current web page looks like in a web browser.

- ▶ You organize files and folders in Folders view. Reports view provides tools for analyzing and managing a web site. You can design and modify a web site structure in Navigation view. Hyperlinks view provides a way to view the hyperlinks to and from each page of a web site. Tasks view contains a list of "To Do" items for a web page or web site. FrontPage can add items to the Task list automatically as you create and edit web pages, or you can add items manually.

Commands Review

Action	Menu Bar	Shortcut Menu	Toolbar/Mouse	Keyboard
Open an existing web	File, Open Web File, Recent Webs		list arrow then click Open Web	ALT + F, W ALT + F, E
Open a web page	File, Open	Right-click the filename in the Folder List and click Open	then click Open or double-click the filename in the Folder List	ALT + F, O CTRL + O
Switch between multiple open web pages	Window, then click the filename			ALT + W CTRL + TAB (next) CTRL + SHIFT + TAB (previous)

Action	Menu Bar	Shortcut Menu	Toolbar/Mouse	Keyboard
Display the Folder List	View, Folder List			ALT + V, E
View a web page in Page view	View, Page			ALT + V, P
View a web page in Normal, HTML, or Preview tabs when in Page view			Click the Normal, HTML, or Preview tab in Page view	
View the Site Summary report in Reports view	View, Reports			ALT + V, R
View a detail report in Reports view			Recently Added Files Double-click the report line in the Site Summary report in Reports view	
View a web in Hyperlinks view	View, Hyperlinks			ALT + V, H
View a web in Folders view	View, Folders			ALT + V, F
View a web in Navigation view	View, Navigation			ALT + V, N
Zoom the page in Navigation view			100%	
View the tree structure in Navigation view in Portrait or Landscape orientation				
Preview and print a web page	File, Print Preview File, Print		Print...	ALT + F, V ALT + F, P CTRL + P
View a web task list	View, Tasks			ALT + V, K
Create a new Task item	Edit, Task, Add Task File, New, Task	Right-click a filename in the Folder List or in Folders view or right-click the file icon in Hyperlink or Navigation views and click Add Task Right-click the workspace in Tasks view and click New Task		ALT+ E, A, A ALT+ F, N, T
Start a task	Edit, Task, Start	Right-click the task item and click Start Task		ALT+ E, A, S
Sort the Tasks list			Click the column header button: Status, Task, Assigned To, Priority, Associated With, Modified Date, Description	
View the Task history (including completed tasks)	Edit, Task, Show History	Right-click the workspace in Tasks view and click Show Task History		ALT E + A, H
Insert a line break				SHIFT + ENTER
View file properties	File, Properties	Right-click the filename in the Folder List or the contents area in Folders view and click Properties		ALT + F, I
Display additional toolbars	View, Toolbars	Right-click any toolbar (including the menu bar) and click the toolbar name		ALT + V, T

chapter one

Action	Menu Bar	Shortcut Menu	Toolbar/Mouse	Keyboard
Open the Options dialog box	Tools, Options			ALT + T, O
Rename a web page		Right-click the filename in the Folder List or in the contents in Folders View and click Rename		
Save a web page	File, Save File, Save As		☒	ALT + F, S CTRL + S ALT + F, A
Close a web page	File, Close			ALT + F, C CTRL + F4
Close a web	File, Close web			ALT + F, L
Getting Help in FrontPage	Help		🔃	ALT + H F1 SHIFT + F1

Concepts Review

Circle the correct answer.

1. The Standard toolbar appears in the FrontPage application window below the:
[a] menu bar.
[b] status bar.
[c] Formatting toolbar.
[d] scroll bar.

2. When you finish modifying a web page you should:
[a] close it.
[b] hide the HTML tags.
[c] view it in Tasks view.
[d] save it.

3. Zooming a web in Navigation view:
[a] shows the HTML tags.
[b] allows you to view the hyperlinks.
[c] moves text to the bottom of the page.
[d] increases or decreases the viewing size of the tree structure.

4. The insertion point:
[a] is located under the Standard toolbar and contains shortcut buttons.
[b] indicates the location where text is keyed in a web page.
[c] provides features for changing text alignment and font.
[d] always appears at the bottom of the screen above the taskbar.

5. Which of the following may be required as the home page filename by a web server?
[a] *default.htm*
[b] *home.htm*
[c] *homepage.htm*
[d] *titlepage.htm*

6. Reports view provides:
[a] a diagram of the tree structure of a web site.
[b] information about the status of a web site.
[c] a diagram of the hyperlinks to and from a page.
[d] a list of "To Do" items for a web site.

7. Folders view allows you to easily:
[a] change the tree structure of a web by moving pages with the mouse.
[b] organize files and folders for a web.
[c] print a list of hyperlinks.
[d] edit the text in a web page.

8. You can view and change certain attributes for a file in:
[a] the Options dialog box.
[b] Tasks view.
[c] the Preview tab.
[d] the Properties dialog box.

9. The Normal tab provides a:
 [a] view of the HTML tags.
 [b] preview of the page as it looks in a web browser.
 [c] WYSIWYG view.
 [d] list of files and folders in the web.

10. FrontPage organizes interrelated web pages:
 [a] in Folders view.
 [b] in file properties.
 [c] as FrontPage webs.
 [d] in Navigation view.

Circle **T** if the statement is true or **F** if the statement is false.

T F   1. An external hyperlink is text or an image that is associated with the path to a different web page.

T F   2. The images subfolder is used to store the hyperlinks for a web.

T F   3. HTML is the abbreviation for HyperText Markup Language.

T F   4. The Task History consists only of completed tasks.

T F   5. The Views bar contains shortcut buttons to different FrontPage views.

T F   6. HTML container tags insert individual items, such as a line break.

T F   7. When you finish using FrontPage 2000, you should exit it.

T F   8. A broken hyperlink no longer links to a valid location.

T F   9. You cannot use drag and drop to move files in Folders view.

T F   10. The status bar appears at the top of the FrontPage 2000 window below the menu bar.

Glossary

Use online <u>H</u>elp to look up the following words in the FrontPage glossary. Then, using your word processing program, create a document listing each word and its glossary definition. Save and print the document.

1. Navigation view

2. page

3. Web browser

4. Normal tab

5. web

6. folder

7. home page

8. mailto

9. Folders view

10. World Wide Web

11. Hyperlinks view

12. Page view

13. Reports view

14. server

15. Tasks view

chapter one

notes   Exercises 1–8 use the same FrontPage web, My_Webs2. Because you are making changes to the web in some of the exercises, it is recommended that you complete all the exercises in the order that they are presented.

Skills Review

Exercise 1

1. Open the My_Webs2 FrontPage web located in the Chapter_1 folder on the Data Disk.

2. Display the Folder List.

3. Open the *index.htm* file in Page view.

4. Hide the Folder List.

5. View the *index.htm* in the HTML tab.

6. View the *index.htm* in the Preview tab.

7. View the *index.htm* in the Normal tab.

8. Preview and print the *index.htm* file.

9. Close the web.

Exercise 2

1. Open the My_Webs2 FrontPage web located in the Chapter_1 folder on the Data Disk.

2. Display the web in Folders view.

3. Drag the *smallnew.gif* image file to the images folder.

4. Rename the *products.htm* file to *catalog.htm* and update the hyperlinks.

5. Rename the *news.htm* file to *whatsnew.htm* and update the hyperlinks.

6. Close the web and save the changes.

Exercise 3

1. Open the My_Webs2 FrontPage web located in the Chapter_1 folder on the Data Disk.

2. Display the web in Reports view.

3. Display the Reporting toolbar, if necessary.

4. Display the All Files report.

5. Open the Properties dialog box for the *index.htm* file.

6. Change the Title: on the General tab to "Home Page."

7. View the Site Summary in Reports view.

8. Close the web and save the changes.

9. Close the Reporting toolbar.

Exercise 4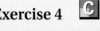

1. Open the My_Webs2 FrontPage web located in the Chapter_1 folder on the Data Disk using the Recent Webs command on the File menu.

2. View the web in Navigation view.

3. Change the orientation to Portrait.

4. Preview and print the tree structure.

5. Change the orientation back to Landscape.

6. Move the 70s-80s Disco page before the Golden Oldies page, using the mouse.

7. Preview and print the tree structure.

8. Display the Folder List.

9. Drag the *smallnew.gif* file from the images folder to the primary folder.

10. Switch to Page view.

11. Close the web.

Exercise 5

1. Open the My_Webs2 FrontPage web located in the Chapter_1 folder on the Data Disk.

2. View the web in Hyperlinks view.

3. Display the Folder List, if necessary, and select the *index.htm* filename.

4. View the hyperlinks to and from the *index.htm* page.

5. Expand the *whatsnew.htm* hyperlinks.

6. Collapse the *whatsnew.htm* hyperlinks.

7. Display the hyperlinks to and from the *catalog.htm* page.

8. Switch to Page view.

9. Close the web.

Exercise 6

1. Open the My_Webs2 FrontPage web located in the Chapter_1 folder on the Data Disk.

2. View the web in Tasks view.

3. Delete each task using the Delete command on the shortcut menu.

4. Switch to Page view.

5. Close the web.

Exercise 7

1. Open the My_Webs2 FrontPage web located in the Chapter_1 folder on the Data Disk.

2. Display the Folder List, if necessary, and view the *index.htm* page in Page view.

3. Scroll the page to view the contact information.

chapter one

4. Click at the end of the telephone number and press the BACKSPACE key to remove the entire phone number.

5. Key 864-555-2222 for the new telephone number.

6. Save the *index.htm* web page.

7. Preview and print the *index.htm* web page.

8. Close the web.

Exercise 8

1. Open the My_Webs2 FrontPage web located in the Chapter_1 folder on the Data Disk.

2. Display the Folder List, if necessary.

3. Open the *index.htm* web page in Page view.

4. Open the *catalog.htm* web page in Page view.

5. Open the *whatsnew.htm* web page in Page view.

6. Use the Window menu to view the *index.htm* page.

7. Use the CTRL + TAB keys to view the *whatsnew.htm* page.

8. Use the CTRL + SHIFT + TAB keys to view the *catalog.htm* page.

9. Close the *catalog.htm* page using the File menu.

10. Close the *index.htm* page using the Close button in the upper-right corner of the workspace.

11. Close FrontPage 2000 and the *whatsnew.htm* page.

Case Projects

SCANS

Project 1

Betty Brownlea, assistant to Sarah Whaley, is responsible for maintaining the existing Sarah's PartyWorld web site while you work on the new web site. She tells you that she prefers using keyboard shortcut keys when working in software applications like FrontPage 2000 and asks if you can print a list of the keyboard shortcuts for FrontPage. Open FrontPage 2000 and use the Microsoft FrontPage Help button on the Standard toolbar to open the Help dialog box. Use the Answer Wizard tab to search for a list of keyboard shortcuts. Print the entire list.

Project 2

Sarah and her network administrator, Bob Avila, are familiar with earlier versions of FrontPage and would like to know what new features are available in FrontPage 2000. Sarah invites you to lunch with her and Bob next Thursday and asks you to bring a list of new FrontPage features to discuss during lunch. Open FrontPage 2000 and use the Microsoft FrontPage Help command on the Help menu to open the Help dialog box. Use the Contents tab to find a list of new features. Using your word processing program, create a list and brief description of the new features. Print the document.

Project 3

Before you begin working on the new web site for Sarah's PartyWorld, you want to review some of the buttons on the various FrontPage 2000 toolbars. Open FrontPage 2000 with a blank web page. Use the What's This? command on the Help menu to convert the mouse pointer to a help pointer. Click the Publish Web button on the Standard toolbar with the help pointer to view its ScreenTip help. Click in the workspace to close the ScreenTip after your review. Press the SHIFT + F1 keys to convert the mouse pointer to a help pointer and click the Preview in Browser button on the Standard toolbar to review its ScreenTip help. Display the Navigation and Reporting toolbars and use the help pointer to review the ScreenTip help for each of the buttons. Using your word processing program, create a new document, and then for the Publish Web button, the Preview in Browser button and three other buttons from the Navigation and Reporting toolbars key the button name and a brief description of its function. Save and print the document.

Project 4

Connect to the Internet, launch your web browser, and load the home page for a search engine. Search for web sites of companies that offer products and services similar to those at Sarah's PartyWorld. Print at least three web pages for similar companies.

Project 5

As part of the documentation for the existing Sarah's PartyWorld web site, Betty Brownlea asks you to find the answers to the following questions.

1. How many files are there in the web?

2. How many picture files are there in the web?

3. How many external hyperlinks and internal hyperlinks are there in the web?

4. How many broken hyperlinks are there in the web?

5. How many uncompleted tasks are there in the web?

Open My_Webs in the Chapter_1 folder on the Data Disk and use Reports view to answer the questions. Using your word processing program, create a new document and then key each question and its answer. Save and print the document.

Project 6

Betty Brownlea wants to change the filenames for some of the web pages in the existing Sarah's PartyWorld web but she is concerned that changing the filenames will break the hyperlinks to the page. Using your word processing program, create a memo to Betty explaining how FrontPage handles this problem. Save and print the memo.

Project 7

You want to review any information about FrontPage 2000 at the Microsoft Office web site. Connect to the Internet and, using the Office on the Web command on the Help menu, launch your web browser and load the Microsoft Office home page. Follow links on the page to review FrontPage 2000. Print at least two web pages.

Project 8

You want to know what kind of support there is on the Web for FrontPage 2000. Connect to the Internet, launch your web browser, and use a search tool to locate several web sites that maintain support and information for FrontPage users. Print at least five web pages.

chapter one

Creating a Web Site

Chapter Overview

To assure that a new web site is attractive and informative and that it satisfies both management requirements and viewer needs, it is important to plan the web site's content and presentation. This chapter discusses ways to effectively plan a web site. After reviewing the goals, structure, and design for a new web site, you create a basic site using a FrontPage wizard. Then you prepare additional pages using a FrontPage template working in Page view. Finally, you insert a Word 2000 document into a web page.

LEARNING OBJECTIVES

- ▶ Develop a web site
- ▶ Use a wizard or template to create a web site
- ▶ Create and preview a new web page using a template or wizard
- ▶ Create a new page within Page view
- ▶ Add or import text into a web page

Case profile

The Sarah's PartyWorld web site development committee consists of Sarah Whaley, the owner, Bob Avila, the network administrator, and you. Based on an internal review of business activity, a review of the marketplace, and interviews with prospective clients, the committee developed a plan for the content, design, style, and layout of the new web site. You review the plan and then use FrontPage wizards and templates to create a sample web site based on that information.

chapter two

2.a Developing a Web Site

Businesses of every kind use web sites to advertise and sell their products and services to the millions of potential customers who browse the World Wide Web (WWW or Web) each day. Sarah, the owner of Sarah's PartyWorld, is impressed with the power of the Web to reach potential customers, and she wants to increase sales by more aggressively marketing and selling items online.

The web site development committee determined that the Web can provide a low-cost method of directly reaching consumers—not just in the Kansas City area, but around the world. The committee reviewed several recent market surveys that identify the typical Web user as an affluent, well-educated professional who accesses the Web more than 12 hours a week. The committee believes that Web users who fit this profile are potential customers for the company's party packages.

Sarah also expects that online marketing will allow the company to:

- Distribute its party planning packages quickly and inexpensively by selling directly to the consumer
- Add or remove products from the marketplace in a timely manner
- Target consumer groups
- Develop an ongoing dialogue with consumers by using the interactive capability of the Web
- Watch what online competitors are doing in the marketplace

Sarah's PartyWorld is currently Kansas City's largest retailer of party planning materials. Sarah advises that the company mission is to become the premier online retailer of party planning materials and services. With this mission in mind, you review the committee's goals for the web site.

Setting Goals for a Web Site

Creating an effective web site includes determining the goals for the web site. Along with advertising and selling products and services, web sites can also be used to gather data about prospective customers, provide customer support, build a positive company image, and entertain potential and current customers.

To help determine the goals for the new Sarah's PartyWorld web site, the committee began by asking a series of questions.

Will the web site:

- Advertise products and services?
- Allow customers to order products and services online?

chapter
two

- Provide online product support to customers?
- Build a company image?
- Collect information about current and potential customers?
- Provide links to related web pages?
- Provide general or industry information?

The committee's answers to these questions determine the overall purpose of the web site. As in many cases, the committee decided that the new Sarah's PartyWorld web site has more than one goal. The primary goal is to sell products and services online. The secondary goal is to establish the company image. Additional goals are to provide viewers with helpful and entertaining party ideas and links to other party-related web sites, and to establish a large potential customer database. To encourage viewers to submit their names, addresses, and e-mail information, they can register online for a chance to win a free holiday party package.

After determining the web site goals, the committee defines the web site structure.

Defining the Structure of a Web Site

Web sites should be structured so viewers can easily find important information. Information also must be presented in an interesting way to keep potential customers from leaving before they read the entire web page. Some web sites are designed with a single level of separate and unrelated pages to which viewers hyperlink directly from the home page. Although easy to use, this flat structure can be somewhat boring. Other web sites have multiple layers of hyperlinked pages. Such a complicated site can frustrate potential customers, as they link from page to page trying to find useful information. One way to achieve balance in the structure of a web site is to limit the number of linked pages and include as much important information as possible in the second or third level of linked pages.

The committee decides that a good way to balance the structure of the company's new web site is to create a home page at the top level with hyperlinks to four second-level pages: a party planner checklist, the primary product catalog, a general description page with information about the party packages, and the contest registration page. The third level consists individual pages for each major party theme and a page describing the company and its online policies. Other pages will be added as needed.

The basic structure for the new Sarah's PartyWorld web site should look similar to Figure 2-1.

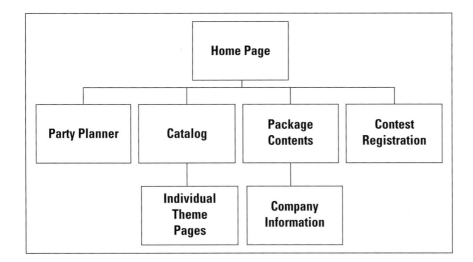

FIGURE 2-1
New Web Site Structure

Now that web site structure is defined, you can begin to design the individual pages.

Designing Effective Web Pages

When viewers browse the Web looking for information, they often decide whether or not to explore a web site based on the information immediately visible as a web page loads. To help viewers navigate easily through a web site, each page should include **navigational hyperlinks**, which are links to all the significant pages at the site. You also want to include a navigational hyperlink to the home page on every other page at the web site. If your pages are long, you can include a "Top of Page" navigational hyperlink at the bottom of the page so viewers can return to the top of the page without scrolling.

If a web page contains large graphic images that are slow to load, some viewers may simply stop the loading process and move to other web sites. In addition, some viewers may use a **text-only browser**—that is, a browser that doesn't read graphic images. For these reasons, you may want to limit the number of graphic images you use. In general, you want to include graphic images only when they are an important part of the web page design. For example, you want to include the company logo that identifies or "brands" all the pages at the new Sarah's PartyWorld web site.

Potential viewers of a web site can live anywhere in the world. You most likely will not know how they link to your web pages or what web browser they use. To accommodate all the potential viewers of your web site, you want to design the pages so that a variety of web browsers can read them. The committee has identified several items you will consider in designing the individual pages for the Sarah's PartyWorld web.

- The company logo and page title should appear on each web page.
- The company mission statement should appear on the home page.

chapter
two

- The same design theme must be used for all pages.
- Each page should contain navigational hyperlinks to other significant pages in the web.
- The company contact information—consisting of the mailing address, telephone number, and e-mail address—should be included on the home page.
- The webmaster e-mail address, copyright reference, and modified date should appear at the bottom of each page.

With the goals, structure, and design criteria in mind, you are ready to create a sample web using a FrontPage wizard.

2.b Using a Wizard or Template to Create a Web Site

A **wizard** is a series of dialog boxes that help you perform certain tasks by asking you a series of questions in a step-by-step process. A **template** is a model document that contains page settings, formats, and other elements. Using a wizard or template to create a new web saves time by automatically providing features you use to organize page content, such as navigational hyperlinks and a page layout with **tables**, grids consisting of columns and rows.

FrontPage contains a variety wizards and templates you can use to create web sites. Each wizard or template has a different goal or focus, such as building a corporate presence or providing customer support.

To view the wizards and templates:

Step 1	*Start*	FrontPage
Step 2	*Click*	File
Step 3	*Point to*	New
Step 4	*Click*	Web

The Web Sites tab in the New dialog box opens. Your dialog box should look similar to Figure 2-2.

MOUSE TIP

You can create a new web with the Web command on the New Page button list on the Standard toolbar.

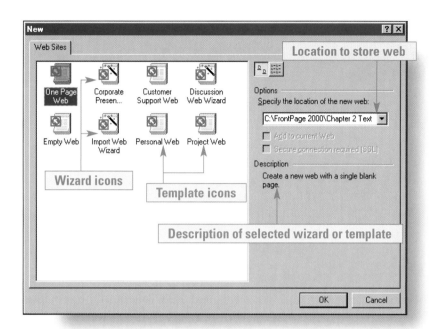

FIGURE 2-2
New Dialog Box

In this dialog box, you first select the desired wizard or template and then specify the web folder name and where the web is stored.

Because one of Sarah's PartyWorld web site goals is to establish a company image, you decide to try the Corporate Presence Wizard to create a sample web.

Step 5	*Click*	the Corporate Presence Wizard icon to select it
Step 6	*Key*	the path specified by your instructor and the web folder name Sample_Web in the Specify the location of the new web: text box
Step 7	*Click*	OK

In a few seconds, the first Corporate Presence Web Wizard dialog box opens. Your dialog box should look similar to Figure 2-3.

notes

The wizard dialog boxes remember the selections made the last time the wizard was used. The options selected when the wizard dialog boxes open on your screen may vary from those shown in the book.

Also, the number of wizard dialog boxes that open will vary, depending on the options you select as you go through the wizard process.

CAUTION TIP

To assure that your web can be published to a variety of web servers, you should limit your folder and filenames to no more than 32 characters. Another good reason to keep web folder and filenames short is the folder and filenames become part of the web URL, or path viewers can key in the Address bar of their browser to download a page.

Although many Window-based programs allow long, descriptive filenames that include spaces, if you upload a FrontPage web to a server via FTP, you cannot use spaces.

chapter
two

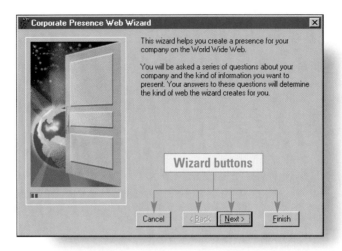

You can cancel the wizard, go to the next step, return to the previous step, or finish the wizard process with buttons at the bottom of the dialog box. You want to go to the next step.

Step 8	*Click*	Next>

The second wizard dialog box opens.

You select the type of pages to include in the web in this dialog box. A home page is required, but you can include or exclude the other listed pages by adding or removing the check mark from the check box to the left of the page name. You decide to include the Products/Services page for the primary catalog page and the Feedback Form page for the contest registration page in addition to the home page. To include the appropriate pages:

Step 1	*Click*	the What's New, Table of Contents, and Search Form check boxes to remove the check marks, if necessary
Step 2	*Click*	the Products/Services and Feedback Form check boxes to insert check marks, if necessary

Your dialog box should look similar to Figure 2-4.

FIGURE 2-4
Second Wizard Step

Pages
to add
to web

| Step 3 | *Click* | Next> |

The third wizard dialog box opens. You select certain topics to appear on the home page in this dialog box. Because most viewers will begin at the home page, it is a good idea to include something about your company here. Sarah's PartyWorld web design criterion includes a mission statement and contact information; you want to include both of those elements on the home page. To select the Mission Statement and Contact Information topics:

| Step 1 | *Click* | the Introduction and Company Profile check boxes to remove the check marks, if necessary |
| Step 2 | *Click* | the Mission Statement and Contact Information check boxes to insert a check mark, if necessary |

Your dialog box should look similar to Figure 2-5.

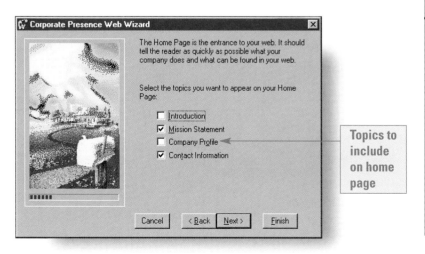

FIGURE 2-5
Third Wizard Step

Topics to
include
on home
page

chapter
two

| Step 3 | *Click* | Next> |

The fourth wizard dialog box opens. You want to create only one additional Products/Services page in addition to the main catalog page for a party theme page. To create one additional Products/Services pages:

Step 1	*Key*	1 in the Products text box
Step 2	*Press*	the TAB key
Step 3	*Key*	0 in the Services text box

Your dialog box should look similar to Figure 2-6.

FIGURE 2-6
Fourth Wizard Step

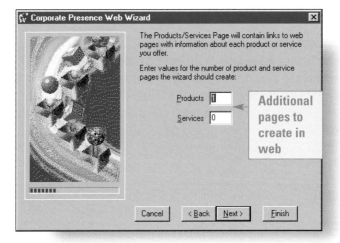

| Step 4 | *Click* | Next> |

The fifth wizard dialog box opens. Because you want to manually add detail items to the Products/Services pages, you remove all the check marks from the check boxes.

| Step 1 | *Remove* | the check mark from each check box, if necessary |

Your dialog box should look similar to Figure 2-7.

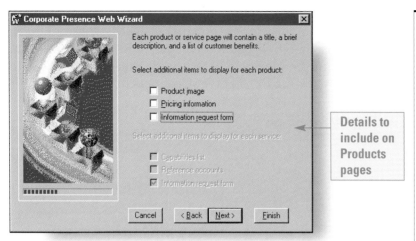

FIGURE 2-7
Fifth Wizard Step

Step 2	*Click*	Next>

The sixth wizard dialog box opens. You now select the elements to appear on the Feedback Form page. You want to include all the elements to capture as much information as possible about potential customers. To include all the elements:

Step 1	*Click*	each of the check boxes to insert a check mark, if necessary

Your screen should look similar to Figure 2-8.

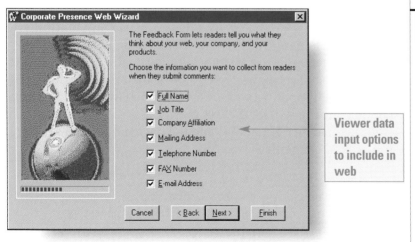

FIGURE 2-8
Sixth Wizard Step

Step 2	*Click*	Next>

chapter
two

The seventh wizard dialog box opens. Sarah plans to use the data you collect from the web site in both the Access 2000 and Excel 2000 applications; therefore, you want to select the format that separates individual information elements by tabs. This makes it easier to import the data into the other applications. To select a data format:

| Step 1 | *Click* | the Yes, use tab-delimited format option button, if necessary |

Your dialog box should look similar to Figure 2-9.

FIGURE 2-9
Seventh Wizard Step

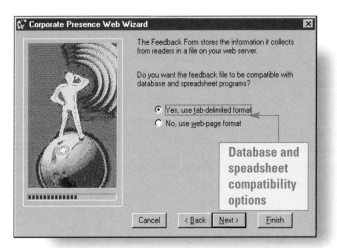

| Step 2 | *Click* | Next> |

The eighth wizard dialog box opens. You can automatically add important elements to each page in this dialog box. One of your design objectives is to have the company logo on each page. Another design objective is to have navigational hyperlinks to other pages at the site. Additionally, a well-designed web page should include contact information for the **webmaster** (the individual who manages a web site), a copyright notice, and the page modification date. To add the desired elements:

| Step 1 | *Click* | the lower Links to your main web pages check box to remove the check mark, if necessary |
| Step 2 | *Click* | the remaining check boxes to insert check marks, if necessary |

Your dialog box should look similar to Figure 2-10.

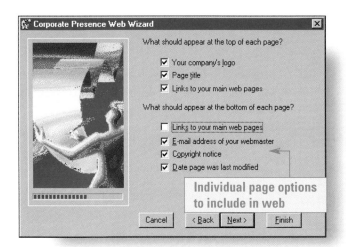

FIGURE 2-10
Eighth Wizard Step

| Step 3 | *Click* | Next> |

The ninth wizard dialog box opens. A **published** web site is one that is uploaded and stored on a web server. Some web authors add incomplete web pages to a published web site and mark them with text and an icon indicating the web page is "**under construction**." Other web authors think that only completed web pages should be added to a web site. Because Sarah's PartyWorld has an existing web site, the new web site will not be published until all pages are complete. Therefore, you do not need to use the "under construction" icon. To turn off the "under construction" icon:

| Step 1 | *Click* | the No option button |

Your dialog box should look similar to Figure 2-11.

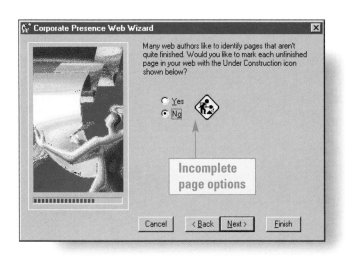

FIGURE 2-11
Ninth Wizard Step

chapter
two

Step 2	*Click*	Next>

The tenth wizard dialog box opens. You add your company name and address in this dialog box. To add the company information:

Step 1	*Key*	Sarah's PartyWorld in the first text box
Step 2	*Key*	PartyWorld in the second text box
Step 3	*Key*	3410 Monroe Avenue, Kansas City, MO 64137-3400 in the third text box

Your dialog box should look similar to Figure 2-12.

FIGURE 2-12
Tenth Wizard Step

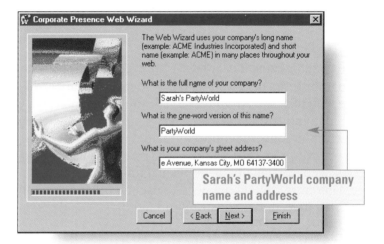

Step 4	*Click*	Next>

The eleventh wizard dialog box opens. You enter additional contact information in this dialog box. You want to include the telephone number and two e-mail addresses: one for the webmaster and one for general information. To include the information:

Step 1	*Key*	816-555-1222 in the first text box
Step 2	*Delete*	the text in the second text box, if necessary
Step 3	*Key*	webmaster@xeon.net in the third text box

| Step 4 | *Key* | sarah@xeon.net in the fourth text box |

Your dialog box should look similar to Figure 2-13.

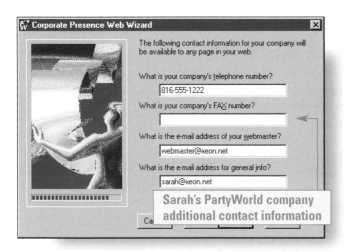

FIGURE 2-13
Eleventh Wizard Step

| Step 5 | *Click* | <u>N</u>ext> |

The twelfth wizard dialog box opens. Your dialog box should look similar to Figure 2-14.

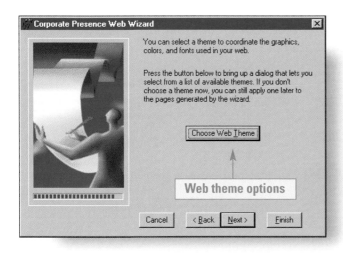

FIGURE 2-14
Twelfth Wizard Step

You can automatically apply a **theme** (a design scheme with coordinated graphics, colors, and fonts) to all the pages of the web by clicking the Choose Web <u>T</u>heme button and then selecting the theme

from a list of available themes. If you do not select a theme, FrontPage applies a default theme. You can also wait and apply a different theme later. You decide to apply a different theme at a later time.

Step 1	*Click*	Next>

You are almost finished with the wizard steps. If you want FrontPage to automatically create items for the task list you can select that option in the final wizard dialog box. You do not need task items for this sample web site. To eliminate the tasks items and finish the web:

Step 2	*Click*	the Show Tasks View after web is uploaded check box to remove the check mark, if necessary
Step 3	*Click*	Finish

The sample web containing four pages is complete. You can now view the pages.

Saving a FrontPage Web

The completed the sample web was saved in the location and Sample_Web folder you specified in the second wizard dialog box. Now you can add pages to the site by saving them to the same Sample_Web folder that contains the pages created using the wizard. You can view the Folder List to confirm that the sample web pages were saved. To verify the sample web pages were saved:

Step 1	*Click*	the Page button on the Views bar, if necessary
Step 2	*Click*	the Folder List button ▦ on the Standard toolbar, if necessary
Step 3	*Observe*	that the Sample_Web folder contains the _private and images default folders, the home page, the feedback pages, and two products pages
Step 4	*Open*	the *index.htm* home page in the Normal tab in Page view
Step 5	*Scroll*	the *index.htm* page and observe the elements added during the wizard process
Step 6	*View*	the *index.htm* page in the HTML and Preview tabs
Step 7	*Open*	and view the remaining pages in the web
Step 8	*Switch*	back to the *index.htm* page using the Window menu

The pages in the Sample_Web contain empty tables you can use to organize page content and partial **navigation bars**, sets of text or button hyperlinks to other pages in the web. The pages also contain a placeholder for the company logo graphic and notations that indicate where you should key certain text, such as the mission statement. You will modify these pages to insert the appropriate text, graphics, and navigational hyperlinks later. Right now, you want to add another page—the package contents page—to the web. You can quickly do this using a page template or wizard.

2.c Creating and Previewing a New Web Page Using a Template or Wizard

You can create a new page using either a page template or a page wizard. Sarah explains that each party package is available in three different content combinations and prices: Basic, Special, and Elite. You decide that the package contents page should have three columns of text describing the contents of the Basic, Special, and Elite packages. For speed and convenience, you want to try using a page template to create this page.

To create a page from the available page templates and wizards:

Step 1	*Click*	File
Step 2	*Point to*	New
Step 3	*Click*	Page
Step 4	*Click*	the General tab, if necessary

The General tab in the New dialog box opens with a list of available page templates and wizards. Your dialog box should look similar to Figure 2-15.

QUICK TIP

You can create your own page templates. For example, if your pages always have a company logo and description at the top of the page, you can create a template with those elements. When you use your template to create a new page, the logo and description are automatically placed on the page.

To create a page template, create a page with the settings and page elements you want, and then save the page with a template file type. The template is displayed with the other templates provided in FrontPage. For more information on creating and saving custom page templates, see online Help.

chapter
two

FIGURE 2-15
Page Templates and
Wizards

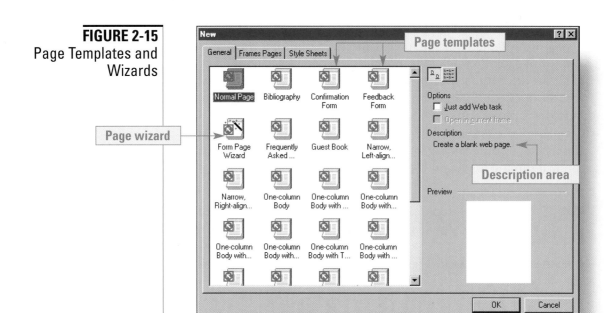

You can review a description of each page template or wizard by first
selecting it and then reading the description in the middle-right area
of the dialog box.

Step 5	*Click*	a template or wizard icon
Step 6	*Review*	the description
Step 7	*Continue*	to review several template or wizard descriptions
Step 8	*Double-click*	the Three Column Body icon

A new web page with a three-column layout opens in the Normal
tab in Page view.

Step 9	*View*	the new page in the HTML and Preview tabs
Step 10	*Switch*	to the Normal tab

You can change the page title in the Save As dialog box before you
save the page. To change the page title and save the page in the
Sample_Web folder:

Step 1	*Click*	the Save button 💾 on the Standard toolbar
Step 2	*Verify*	that the Sample_Web folder is open

Step 3	*Click*	Change
Step 4	*Key*	Package Descriptions
Step 5	*Click*	OK
Step 6	*Key*	*contents* in the File name: text box
Step 7	*Click*	Save
Step 8	*Observe*	the new file in the Folders List

You also want to add the party planner page to the web.

2.d Creating a New Page within Page View

You can also create a new page using the New Page button on the Standard toolbar. You decide to quickly add a page for the party planner using this method. Then all the second-level pages will be added to the web.

To add the party planner page:

Step 1	*Click*	the New Page button 🗋 on the Standard toolbar
Step 2	*Observe*	the new page opens in the Normal tab
Step 3	*Save*	the page as *planner* with the title Party Planner Checklist

Next, you want to add the party planner text to the party planner page.

2.e Adding or Importing Text into a Web Page

You can integrate Microsoft Office documents—such as Excel worksheets, PivotTables, charts, and Word documents—into a FrontPage web. You can insert either an existing Office file (such as a Word document) or a Microsoft Office component (such as a blank Excel worksheet) into a web page. A **Microsoft Office component** is a blank Excel worksheet, PivotTable, or Chart object viewers can use to analyze and manipulate data when viewing a web page.

You can also create hyperlinks to existing Excel workbooks, Word documents, and PowerPoint presentations on a web page. When viewers download the page into their web browser and click the hyperlink, the document opens in either the browser or a separate window and can be edited with the tools of the source (original) application.

Sarah tells you that the party planner text is available in a Word 2000 document. Rather than rekey the text into the *planner.htm* page, you decide to insert the Word document into the page. To insert the Word document into the *planner.htm* page:

Step 1	**Verify**	the *planner.htm* page is visible in the Normal tab in Page view and the insertion point is in the second column of the empty table
Step 2	**Click**	Insert
Step 3	**Click**	File

The Select File dialog box opens.

Step 4	**Switch**	to the Chapter_2 folder on the Data Disk
Step 5	**View**	Word 97-2000 (*doc) file types

Your screen should look similar to Figure 2-16.

FIGURE 2-16
Select File Dialog Box

Step 6	**Click**	the *Party_Planner_and_Checklist* document to select it
Step 7	**Click**	Open

The document is converted from text to HTML and inserted in the table. Because the original Word document consists of data organized in Word tables, the resulting text in the web page is also organized into tables. FrontPage adds table borders by default.

Step 8	*Scroll*	the *planner.htm* page to view the party planner text and checklist text arranged in tables
Step 9	*View*	the *planner.htm* page in the HTML and Preview tabs and then return to the Normal tab
Step 10	*Save*	the *planner.htm* page

You want to preview and print all the pages so that you can discuss the Sample_Web at the next committee meeting. To preview and print the web:

Step 1	*View*	the *index.htm* page in the Normal tab of Page view
Step 2	*Click*	File
Step 3	*Click*	Print Preview and review the page
Step 4	*Click*	the Print button [Print...] on the Print Preview toolbar
Step 5	*Continue*	to preview and print the remaining pages in the Sample_Web folder
Step 6	*Close*	the web

Now that you are familiar with using FrontPage wizards and templates to create a web and new web pages, you are ready to begin formatting your web pages.

chapter
two

Summary

▶ When developing a web site, you need to consider its goals, structure, and design.

▶ Navigational hyperlinks are links that viewers use to move from one page to another at a web site.

▶ A wizard is a series of dialog boxes that help you perform certain tasks by asking a series of questions in a step-by-step process.

▶ A template is a model document that contains page settings, formats, and other design elements.

▶ You can use wizards and templates to create a new FrontPage web and to add pages to an existing FrontPage web.

▶ When you create a new FrontPage web using a wizard or template, FrontPage saves the pages in the Web folder and location you specify.

▶ You can insert Microsoft Office documents and components into a FrontPage web.

▶ A webmaster is the individual who manages a web site.

▶ Publishing a web means to upload the web files to a web server.

▶ Navigation bars are sets of text or button hyperlinks to other pages in the web.

Commands Review

Action	Menu Bar	Shortcut Menu	Toolbar/Mouse	Keyboard
Create a new web	File, New, Web			ALT + F, N, W
Create a new page	File, New, Page	Right-click in the Folder List and click New Page	☐	ALT + F, N, P CTRL + N
Delete a page		Right-click a page in the the Folder List or Folders view and click Delete		Select a page in the Folder List or Folders view and press the DELETE key
Insert an Office document	Insert, File			ALT + I, F
Preview and print a web page	File, Print Preview File, Print		🖨	ALT + F, V ALT + P

Concepts Review

Circle the correct answer.

1. Creating an effective web site does *not* include:
[a] setting goals.
[b] determining the structure.
[c] using a different color scheme on each web page.
[d] using navigational links.

2. A text-only browser:
[a] helps viewers navigate through a web site.
[b] doesn't read graphic images.
[c] is a step-by-step process used to create a web site.
[d] reads graphic images.

3. A wizard is a:
[a] model document.
[b] step-by-step series of dialog boxes.
[c] tool to print a web page.
[d] way to view a web page.

4. One way to achieve balance in web site structure is to create:
[a] a single level of pages that link to the home page.
[b] ten to twelve levels of detail pages.
[c] only a home page.
[d] a home page with two or three additional levels of detail pages.

5. A template is a:
[a] series of step-by-step dialog boxes.
[b] model document that contains page settings, formats, and other elements.
[c] table consisting of columns and rows.
[d] way to manage an existing web site.

6. Which of the following methods does *not* create an individual web page?
[a] page wizard
[b] page template
[c] web wizard
[d] shortcut menu in the Folder List

7. Which of the following Microsoft Office *components* can be inserted into a web page?
[a] Excel worksheets and PowerPoint presentations
[b] Excel worksheets and Word documents
[c] Excel Spreadsheet, PivotTable, or Charts
[d] Word documents and PowerPoint presentations

8. A web site cannot have:
[a] multiple goals.
[b] multiple structures.
[c] incomplete web pages.
[d] navigational hyperlinks.

9. If you do not select a theme when creating a new web with a wizard:
[a] you cannot publish the web to a server.
[b] you must use the "under construction" symbol on each page.
[c] FrontPage applies a default theme.
[d] you cannot apply a different theme later.

10. You organize the contents on a web page in:
[a] a wizard.
[b] a template.
[c] tables.
[d] Navigation view.

Circle **T** if the statement is true or **F** if the statement is false.

T   F   1. Businesses of every kind use web sites to advertise and sell products and services.

T   F   2. One way to achieve balance in a web site structure is to limit the number levels of linked pages.

T   F   3. A "Top of Page" navigational hyperlink prevents viewers from having to scroll to the top of a page.

T   F   4. Using a company logo on each page at a web site can help viewers identify the pages.

chapter two

T F   5. Potential viewers must live in the same country where the web site is published.

T F   6. A well-designed web page should include contact information, a copyright notice, and the date each page was modified.

T F   7. A theme is a design scheme that contains coordinated graphics, colors, and fonts.

T F   8. Navigation bars are sets of text or button hyperlinks to other pages in the web.

T F   9. You cannot change the page title in the page Properties dialog box.

T F   10. You cannot create hyperlinks to Microsoft Office documents in a web page.

Glossary

Use online <u>H</u>elp to look up the following words in the FrontPage glossary. Then, using your word processing program, create a document listing each word and its glossary definition. Save and print the document.

1. current web

2. current page

3. discussion group

4. editor

5. e-mail

6. file

7. file type

8. navigation bar

9. page title

10. page template

11. path

12. publish

13. web name

14. web structure

15. wizard

Skills Review

Exercise 1

1. Use the Personal Web template to create a new web named My_Personal.

2. Display the Folder List and verify the saved pages.

3. Open the *index.htm* file in the Normal tab in Page view.

4. View the *index.htm* in the HTML tab and the Preview tab then return to the Normal tab.

5. View each of the remaining pages in the Normal, HTML, and Preview tabs.

6. Add a new page using the Guest Book page template.

7. Save the page as *guestbook.htm* in the My_Personal.

8. Use the shortcut menu method to view the Properties for each page.

9. Change the *guestbook.htm* title to Guest Book on its Properties page.

10. Print preview and print each of the pages.

11. Close the web.

Exercise 2

1. Use the Project Web template to create a new web named My_Project.

2. Display the Folder List and view the *index.htm* page in the Normal tab in Page view.

3. Review each of the other pages in the web in the Normal tab.

4. Print preview and print each of the pages.

5. Close the web.

Exercise 3

1. Create a new web using the Discussion Web Wizard and name it My_Discussion.

2. Include the Table of Contents, Search Form, Threaded Replies, and Confirmation Page pages.

3. Use "Movie Reviews" as the descriptive title.

4. Name the discussion articles folder _reviews.

5. Select the Subject, Category, Comments set of input fields.

6. Select the default option for a nonprotected web.

7. Sort the list of posted articles in Newest to oldest order.

8. Set the Table of Contents page to be the home page.

9. Select the Subject, Size, Date, and Score option for the search form to match.

10. Choose the Citrus Punch theme, and then finish the web.

11. Add a new page in Page view using the New Page button on the Standard toolbar.

12. Change the page title to Movie List and save the page as *movielist.htm* in the Save As dialog box.

13. Print preview and print each page.

14. Close the web.

Exercise 4

1. Create a new web using the Customer Support Web template and name it My_ Support.

2. View the web in Navigation view.

3. Change the orientation to Portrait.

4. Preview and print the tree structure.

5. Change the orientation back to Landscape.

6. Preview and print the tree structure.

7. Preview each page in the Preview tab in Page view.

8. Close the web.

Exercise 5

1. Create a new web using the Empty Web template and name it My_New_Web.

2. Display the Folder List and create a new page using the New Page button on the Standard toolbar.

3. Change the page title to Home Page and save it as *index.htm* in the Save As dialog box.

4. Create a second new page using the shortcut method in the Folder List and the Two-column Body page template.

5. Change the page title to Advances in Technology and save the page as *advances.htm* in the Save As dialog box.

6. Add a third page using the Frequently Asked Questions page template.

7. Save the page as *faq.htm* with the title Frequently Asked Questions.

8. Add a fourth page using the Narrow Left-aligned Body page template.

9. Use the mouse to select the sample text in the narrow column to the left of the picture and then press the DELETE key to delete the text.

10. Insert the Word document, *Web_Design*, located in the Chapter_2 folder on the Data Disk, into the table.

11. Save the page as *webdesign.htm* with the title Web Design.

12. Save the picture file.

13. Move the picture file to the images folder.

14. Print preview and print each page.

15. Close the web and save pages if asked.

Exercise 6

1. Using the Web command on the New Page button drop-down list, create a new web named My_Business based on the One Page Web template.

2. View the *index.htm* page in the Normal tab.

3. Add a new page in Page view using the Confirmation Form page template.

4. Save the page as *confirmation.htm* with the title Confirmation Page.

5. Add a new page in Page view using the Narrow Right-aligned Body page template.

6. Save the page as *page2.htm* with the title Our Company.

7. Save the embedded graphic file when asked.

8. Print preview and print the pages.

9. Close the web.

Exercise 7

1. Open the My_Project you created in Exercise 2. If you have not yet created the web, do so now.

2. View the *index.htm* page in Hyperlinks view.

3. View the *members.htm* page in Hyperlinks view.

4. View the web in Reports View and answer the following questions on a sheet of paper:

a. How many files are in the web?

b. How many each internal, external, and broken hyperlinks are there?

c. How many graphic files (.gif) are there and what are their names?

5. Close the web.

Exercise 8

1. Create a new web named My_Corporate using the Corporate Presence wizard.

2. Include the <u>W</u>hat's New, <u>T</u>able of Contents, and <u>S</u>earch Form pages in addition to the home page.

3. Include the <u>I</u>ntroduction, <u>M</u>ission Statement, Company Pr<u>o</u>file, and Con<u>t</u>act Information topics on the home page.

4. Include the Press <u>R</u>eleases and <u>A</u>rticles and Reviews topics on the What's New page.

5. Keep the Table of Contents page automatically updated and use bullets for top-level pages.

6. Include the company logo and page title at the top of each page and the navigational links, e-mail address, copyright notice, and modification data at the bottom of each page.

7. Add the "under construction" symbol to each page.

8. Insert the following company information:

   Company name: A. B. Vickers Company
   One word version: Vickers
   Street address: 1100 DeFoe Avenue, Colorado Springs, CO 80911-1100
   Phone number: 719-555-1333
   Fax number: 719-555-1233
   Webmaster: webmaster@vickers.com
   General info: information@vickers.com

9. Apply the Blends theme and finish the web.

10. Print preview and print the pages in the web.

11. Close the web.

Case Projects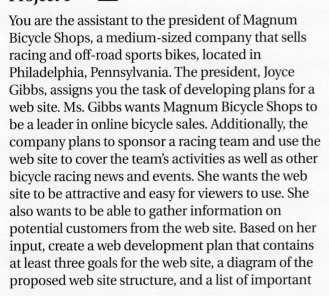

Project 1

You are the assistant to the president of Magnum Bicycle Shops, a medium-sized company that sells racing and off-road sports bikes, located in Philadelphia, Pennsylvania. The president, Joyce Gibbs, assigns you the task of developing plans for a web site. Ms. Gibbs wants Magnum Bicycle Shops to be a leader in online bicycle sales. Additionally, the company plans to sponsor a racing team and use the web site to cover the team's activities as well as other bicycle racing news and events. She wants the web site to be attractive and easy for viewers to use. She also wants to be able to gather information on potential customers from the web site. Based on her input, create a web development plan that contains at least three goals for the web site, a diagram of the proposed web site structure, and a list of important design elements. Use your word processing program to create the plan text. Save and print a copy of the plan document. Following your plan, use FrontPage wizards and templates to create a sample web for Magnum Bicycle Shops. Print the web pages.

Project 2

Sarah Whaley, the owner of Sarah's PartyWorld, overheard you discussing navigational hyperlinks and navigation bars and asks you to send her a memo describing what they are and how you plan to use them in the new web site. Research navigational hyperlinks and navigation bars in online <u>H</u>elp. Then, using your word processing program, create a memo to Sarah that describes these features and how you plan to use them.

chapter two

Project 3

Tony Daversa, the executive vice president of Daversa Importers, Inc., which is located in Trenton, New Jersey, and specializes in olive oil imports, hires you to create a web site. The company wants to establish a presence on the Web and develop a corporate image. His secretary suggests you create the web site "from scratch" in the Microsoft Word word processing program; however, you think it is more efficient to create it in FrontPage using the wizards and templates. You are meeting with Tony tomorrow to discuss the matter. Using your word processing program, create a list of reasons why it could be more efficient to use FrontPage wizards and templates to create the web than Microsoft Word. Save and print the list.

Project 4

You want to use the Web to research topics on how to develop and create a web site. Connect to the Internet, launch your web browser, and load the home page for a search engine. Search for web sites containing information on how to develop and create a web site. Print at least five web pages.

Project 5

Your friend, Marcy Davenport, calls to ask for your help. She is planning to use FrontPage to create a personal web site and wants to know which wizards or templates she should consider using to both create the web site and add additional pages. You agree to help. First, consider what kind of information Marcy might want to include at her web site. Then, review the web and page wizards and templates. Finally, use your word processing program to create a list of potential pages for her web. Recommend the wizards or templates she should use to create the pages and explain the basis for your recommendations. Save and print the document.

Project 6

Joe Novotny, the president of the West Highlands College alumni organization, needs help adding a page to the alumni web site that keeps track of viewers at the site. He knows the web is a

FrontPage web but doesn't know how to add a page. Mr. Novotny asks you update the web site with the new page. You are meeting with him on Wednesday to discuss how you will do it. Using your word processing program, create a list of meeting notes that describe exactly how you will add a page to the existing web using a FrontPage template. Identify the template you plan to use, and create and print a sample page based on the template.

Project 7

In addition to creating a new web site for Daversa Importers, Inc., Tony asks you to list ways to get the web site noticed after it is published. Connect to the Internet, launch your web browser, and use a search engine or directory to look for web sites that provide assistance in submitting web sites to various search engines and directories. Print at least five web pages.

Project 8

Greenfield Insurance Services is a large regional life, accident, and health insurance broker in Salem, Oregon. Cliff Greenfield, the president, is thinking about creating a web site for the company. However, he is not sure how having a web site would benefit the company. He asks you to review web sites published by similar companies, and then prepare a report recommending whether or not Greenfield Insurance Services should have a web site. Connect to the Internet, load your web browser, and use a search engine or directory to locate web sites for companies similar to Greenfield Insurance Services. Print all the pages of at least three web sites. Using your word processing program, write a memo to Mr. Greenfield describing the results of your research and making a recommendation about the proposed company web site. Save and print the memo. Create a sample web site to accompany your recommendation using FrontPage wizards and templates. Print all the web pages.

Formatting Web Pages

Chapter Overview

Y ou can make any web site look more attractive by using a design scheme, called a theme, which includes coordinated font styles, colors, and graphics. You can use one of the many preset themes or you can create a custom theme. In this chapter, you apply a preset theme to an individual page. Then you customize a preset theme and apply it to the entire web. You also create and modify tables and use them to organize text on a web page. Then you key and format the text. Finally, you use the Find and Replace commands to replace words on an individual page and on all pages in the web.

LEARNING OBJECTIVES

► Apply a theme to an entire web
► Create tables on a web page
► Key and format text on a web page
► Use global Find and Replace across a web site

Case profile

Before you meet with the other members of the web site development committee to review the sample Sarah's PartyWorld web site, you want to format the web pages by changing the theme. You also need to add the appropriate text to the home page. Bob calls to ask you to replace any references to electronic mail or mail with the text "e-mail." You need to make the appropriate corrections on each page.

chapter three

3.a Applying a Theme to an Entire Web

A FrontPage **theme** is a coordinated grouping of font styles and a color scheme that includes a background picture, graphics, navigation bars, and buttons. A theme provides an efficient way to add a polished and professional appearance to a web. Sarah, the owner of Sarah's PartyWorld, wants the overall color scheme of the new web site to be bright and cheerful. You think the default theme applied to the sample web in the wizard process does not satisfy Sarah's request; therefore, you decide to apply a more appropriate theme.

notes In this chapter, you open the Sample_Web you created in the previous chapter and modify it. In the following chapters you continue to build the web by opening the Sample_Web again and adding more modifications. If desired, you can copy the Sample_Web to a new folder before you begin each chapter. By doing this you maintain a copy of the Sample_Web as it looked before you began the current chapter modifications.

To open the Sample_Web you created in Chapter 2:

Step 1	*Start*	FrontPage 2000
Step 2	*Click*	the Open button list arrow 🗁▾ on the Standard toolbar
Step 3	*Click*	Open Web
Step 4	*Switch*	to the disk drive and folder where you store your webs
Step 5	*Click*	Sample_Web
Step 6	*Click*	Open
Step 7	*Switch*	to Page view, if necessary
Step 8	*Display*	the Folder List, if necessary
Step 9	*Open*	the *index.htm* page in the Normal tab in Page View, if necessary
Step 10	*Hide*	the Folder List

Your screen should look similar to Figure 3-1.

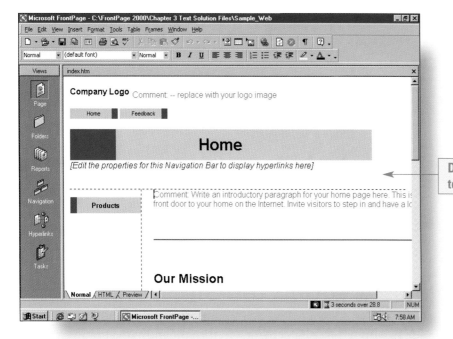

FIGURE 3-1
Sample_Web

Default theme applied to home page

Applying a New Theme to an Individual Web Page

You can apply a FrontPage theme to an individual page, several selected pages, or to the entire web. First, you want to preview several themes. Then, you apply a new theme to the home page.

To view the FrontPage themes:

| Step 1 | **Right-click** | the *index.htm* page in the workspace |
| Step 2 | **Click** | Theme |

The Themes dialog box opens. Your dialog box should look similar to Figure 3-2.

notes

The default theme applied to your Sample_Web in the wizard process and the themes listed in the Themes dialog box on your screen may vary from the illustrations in this book, depending on the themes installed with FrontPage and the last theme applied.

C

MENU TIP

You can apply a FrontPage theme by clicking the Theme command on the Format menu.

chapter
three

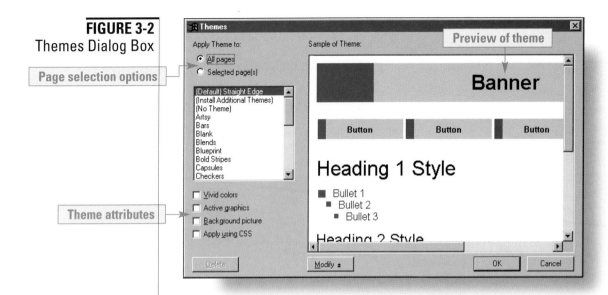

FIGURE 3-2
Themes Dialog Box

Page selection options

Theme attributes

Changing Theme Attributes

You can change the appearance of a theme by using the Vivid colors option to brighten the color scheme. To turn on animated graphics for banners, bullets, buttons, and other graphics, click the Active graphics option. You can add a background picture by clicking the Background picture option. A **style** is a set of formatting attributes—such as sizing, spacing, and color—that are saved together, assigned a name, and then applied to a web page element all at once. A **style sheet** is a collection of styles you can apply to an entire page. **CSS** is the abbreviation for cascading style sheets, which are multiple style sheets that apply to the same page. The Apply using CSS option enables FrontPage to create a style sheet and save it in the web.

notes If the themes used in these activities are not installed on your system, you should, with your instructor's permission, either install the additional themes from the FrontPage CD-ROM or apply a different theme.

To review a theme:

Step 1	*Click*	Network Blitz in the theme list
Step 2	*Observe*	the theme sample
Step 3	*Click*	the Vivid colors check box to insert a check mark
Step 4	*Click*	the Active graphics check box to insert a check mark

QUICK TIP

You can change the background for a page without applying a theme. Display the page in Page view, and then click the Background command on the Format menu to open the Background tab in the Page Properties dialog box. Then, select the background image or colors you want to apply.

If you have already applied a theme, you must first remove it with the (No Theme) option in the Themes dialog box and then change the page background.

Step 5	*Click*	the <u>B</u>ackground picture check box to insert a check mark
Step 6	*Observe*	the changes to the sample theme
Step 7	*Click*	the <u>B</u>ackground picture check box to remove the check mark

Your dialog box should look similar to Figure 3-3.

FIGURE 3-3
Modified Network
Blitz Theme

You want to see how the *index.htm* page looks with this theme applied.

| Step 8 | *Click* | the Sele<u>c</u>ted page(s) option button |
| Step 9 | *Click* | OK |

Your screen should look similar to Figure 3-4.

notes For the remainder of this text, it is assumed you use the Folder List when you need to open a page in the Normal tab in Page view. No detailed steps to display and hide the Folder List will be provided. When you are asked to close a page, it is assumed you will use the Close button in the workspace. No detail steps will be provided.

QUICK TIP

After you apply a theme to a blank web page, you can insert the missing navigation bars, page banners, horizontal lines, and other elements with commands on the <u>I</u>nsert menu.

chapter
three

FIGURE 3-4
Home Page with Modified
Network Blitz Theme

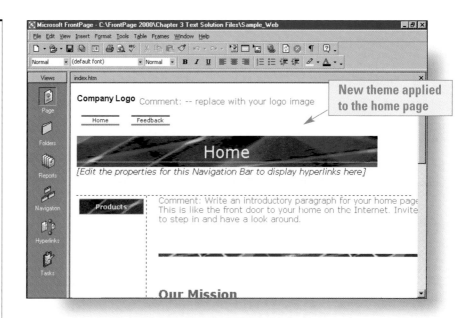

QUICK TIP

To apply a theme to multiple pages but not the whole web, switch to Folders view and select the multiple pages using the SHIFT + Click or CTRL + Click technique. Then open the Themes dialog box and apply the desired theme using the Selected page(s) option.

CAUTION TIP

The default page selection option in the Themes dialog box is All pages. Each time you open the dialog box, this option is selected. Be careful to select the Selected page(s) option button before applying a theme to individual or selected pages, or you could accidentally apply the theme to the entire web.

When you apply a theme to the open page, the page no longer uses the web's default theme settings. Any changes you apply to the entire web with the All pages option will *not* affect this page; they will affect those pages still formatted with the default theme.

None of the other pages in the web have the new theme. To verify the theme is applied only to the *index.htm* page:

Step 1	*Display*	the Folder List
Step 2	*Open*	the *products.htm* page in the Normal tab in Page view
Step 3	*Observe*	that the original theme is still applied
Step 4	*Click*	the Close button ⊠ in the workspace
Step 5	*Click*	No, if asked whether you want to save changes to the page
Step 6	*Hide*	the Folder List

After viewing the changes to the *index.htm* page, you decide to try a different theme. You can close the *index.htm* without saving it to return the page to its original theme. You can also open the Themes dialog box and remove the theme completely by applying the (No Theme) option or you can reapply the original theme. To close the *index.htm* web page without saving the theme change:

Step 1	*Close*	the *index.htm* page
Step 2	*Click*	No
Step 3	*Open*	the *index.htm* page in the Normal tab in Page view
Step 4	*Observe*	the original theme formatting

You continue to experiment with themes. To review a different theme:

Step 1	*Open*	the Themes dialog box
Step 2	*Click*	Blends in the theme list
Step 3	*Click*	the <u>V</u>ivid colors, Active <u>g</u>raphics, and <u>B</u>ackground picture check boxes to insert check marks, if necessary
Step 4	*Scroll*	the theme preview to view the changes to each of the theme elements

The color scheme in this theme is brighter and more cheerful. However, you still want to change some of the theme elements. You can do this by modifying the elements and then saving the theme as a custom theme.

Creating and Applying a Custom Theme

You can change the colors, replace the graphics, and change the text styles used in a theme. If you change a preset theme, you must save your changes as a new theme. You cannot replace the formatting in the preset theme.

To view the theme modification options:

Step 1	*Click*	<u>M</u>odify to view the color, graphics, and text option buttons

Your Themes dialog box should look similar to Figure 3-5.

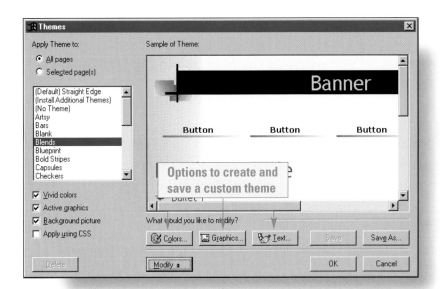

FIGURE 3-5
Themes Dialog Box

When you apply <u>V</u>ivid colors to the Blends theme, the heading text is blue, the body text is dark gray, and the hyperlinks are brown. You want all heading text to be red, the body text to be blue, and the hyperlink color to be red. To change the heading text, body text, and hyperlink colors:

| Step 1 | *Click* | C<u>o</u>lors 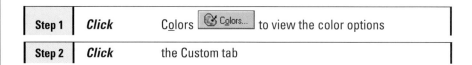 to view the color options |
| Step 2 | *Click* | the Custom tab |

The Custom tab in your Modify Theme dialog box should look similar to Figure 3-6. You can change the color of individual elements with options on the Custom tab.

FIGURE 3-6
Modify Theme Dialog Box

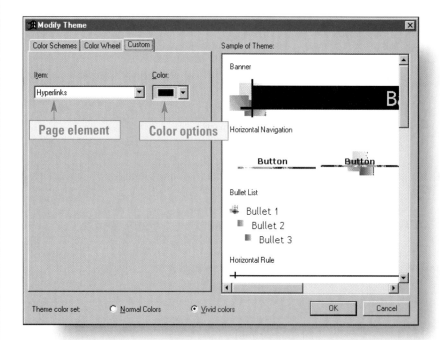

Step 3	*Click*	the I<u>t</u>em: list arrow
Step 4	*Click*	Heading 1 in the list
Step 5	*Click*	the <u>C</u>olor: list arrow
Step 6	*Click*	the Red tile in the color grid
Step 7	*Observe*	the changed Heading 1 Style in the theme preview
Step 8	*Continue*	by changing the color of the Heading 2 through Heading 6 styles to red
Step 9	*Select*	Body in the I<u>t</u>em: list
Step 10	*Select*	the Blue tile in the <u>C</u>olor: grid

Step 11	*Select*	Hyperlinks in the Item: list
Step 12	*Select*	the Red tile in the Color: grid
Step 13	*Click*	OK

Next, you want to replace the third-level blue bullet graphic with a gold bullet graphic. To view the graphics options in the Themes dialog box:

Step 1	*Click*	Graphics 

Your Modify Theme dialog box should look similar to Figure 3-7.

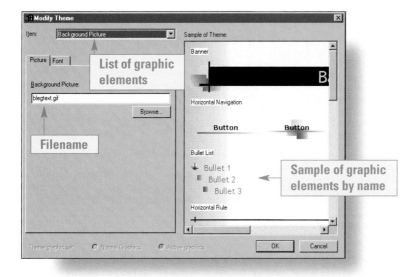

FIGURE 3-7
Modify Theme Dialog Box

You select the graphic element in this dialog box and then replace it. If the graphic image has text associated with it, you can change the text font also. To replace the third-level graphic bullet:

Step 2	*Select*	Bullet List in the Item: list

The Picture tab now contains the names of the three bullet graphic files. To find a new graphic file you can browse the current web or your file system.

Step 3	*Click*	the third Browse button

chapter three

The Select Picture dialog box that opens should look similar to Figure 3-8.

FIGURE 3-8
Select Picture Dialog Box

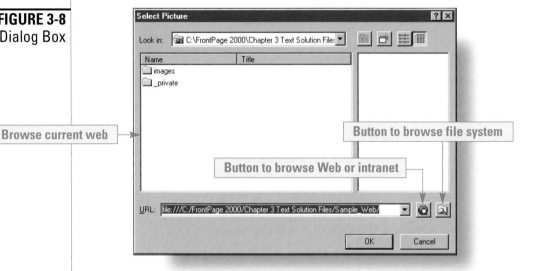

The gold bullet file is on the Data Disk, so you want to browse your file system to locate it.

Step 4	*Click*	the Select a file on your computer folder button 
Step 5	*Switch*	to the Chapter_3 folder on the Data Disk
Step 6	*Double-click*	*Bd10266_.gif*
Step 7	*Observe*	that the *Bd10266.gif* filename is now in the List Bullet <u>3</u> text box and the sample theme shows the gold third-level bullet
Step 8	*Click*	OK

Before you apply the theme to the web, you need to save the theme with a new name. To save the theme:

| Step 1 | *Click* | Sav<u>e</u> As |

The Save Theme dialog box opens.

| Step 2 | *Key* | Sarah's Theme in the <u>E</u>nter new theme title: text box |
| Step 3 | *Click* | OK |

Next, you apply the new custom theme to the web. To apply the custom Sarah's Theme to the entire web:

Step 1	*Click*	Sarah's Theme in the theme list, if necessary
Step 2	*Verify*	the All pages option button is selected
Step 3	*Click*	OK
Step 4	*Verify*	that the theme is applied to all the pages in the web
Step 5	*View*	the *index.htm* in the Normal tab in Page view

Now that you have created and applied a custom theme to the web, you are ready to begin modifying the individual pages to include the appropriate text. To organize the text on the pages, you place the text in tables.

3.b Creating Tables on a Web Page

A **table** is a grid of columns and rows used to organize information. The intersection of a column and row is called a **cell**. You place text and graphics in the table cells. Tables are also used on a web page to position text or text and graphics horizontally (side by side) rather than vertically. Creating and editing tables on a web page is similar to creating and editing tables in a word processing program, such as Microsoft Word. You can either insert a table or you can draw it.

Sometimes it is helpful to view hidden page elements, such as line breaks, paragraph marks, and bookmarks, when you are inserting tables and text. You can view the hidden page elements with the Show All button on the Standard toolbar.

You want to modify the home page by adding an introductory paragraph welcoming viewers to the Sarah's PartyWorld web site. You can place the welcome text on the page by keying it in a table.

To view the hidden page elements and create a table with one column and one row:

| Step 1 | *Click* | the Show All button on the Standard toolbar to view the paragraph marks |

QUICK TIP

You can delete a custom theme by selecting it in the theme list and clicking the Delete button.

C

MENU TIP

You can create a table by pointing to the Insert command on the Table menu and then clicking Table or by clicking the Draw Table command on the Table menu.

CAUTION TIP

When you create a new table, the table width is determined by options in the Table Properties dialog box. These options may show the width of the last table you created.

chapter
three

Your screen should look similar to Figure 3-9.

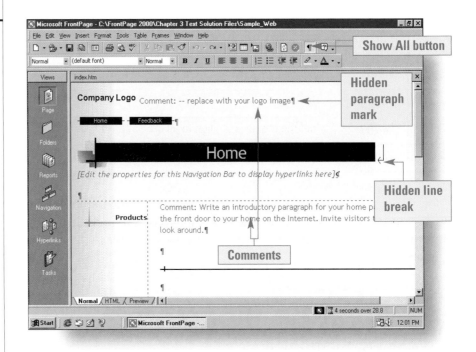

Step 2	*Click*	at the paragraph mark below the comment in the Products section to position the insertion point
Step 3	*Click*	the Insert Table button ▦ on the Standard toolbar
Step 4	*Click*	the first cell on the grid (1 by 1 Table)

A one-cell table with borders appears. The border color is based on the table border color in the custom theme. The **insertion point**, or keying position, is in the table cell. Your screen should look similar to Figure 3-10.

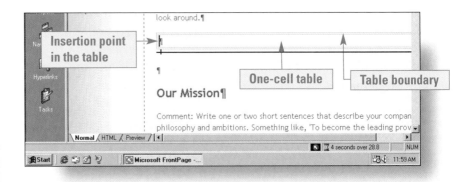

You can change the table size, alignment, and border properties in the Table Properties dialog box. To view the table properties:

| Step 1 | Right-click | the table |
| Step 2 | Click | Table Properties |

The Table Properties dialog box that opens should look similar to Figure 3-11.

FIGURE 3-11
Table Properties
Dialog Box

MENU TIP

You can view the table properties by pointing to the Properties command on the Table menu and clicking Table.

QUICK TIP

You can review the different options in a dialog box by clicking its Help button, and then clicking the option with the help pointer to display the help ScreenTip. Press the ESC key or click the mouse button to close the help ScreenTip. Note that the help pointer is also called the What's This? pointer.

Because this is a complex dialog box with many options, you want to review each option with the help pointer.

Step 3	Click	the Help button in the dialog box
Step 4	Click	the Alignment: option
Step 5	Review	the ScreenTip
Step 6	Press	the ESC key to close the ScreenTip
Step 7	Continue	to review the other dialog box options

Resizing Tables

The standard table doesn't exactly fit the web page design plan. You want to center the table, resize it to half its 100% size, and remove the border. You can do this in the Table Properties dialog box.

C

chapter
three

MENU TIP

You can view the table properties by right-clicking a table and clicking the Table Properties command.

To change the table properties:

Step 1	*Click*	the Alignment: list arrow
Step 2	*Click*	Center
Step 3	*Key*	50 in the Specify width: text box
Step 4	*Verify*	that the In percent option button is selected
Step 5	*Click*	the down spin arrow on the Borders Size: text box to set the border size to zero (0)
Step 6	*Click*	OK

The table is centered, resized, and the border is removed. Your screen should look similar to Figure 3-12.

FIGURE 3-12
Modified Table

MOUSE TIP

You can create a table by clicking the Insert Table button on the Standard toolbar or the Draw Table button on the Tables toolbar. You can also use the other buttons on the Tables toolbar to insert rows or columns, align text in cells, distribute rows or columns evenly in a drawn table, add fill color to a table, and automatically size the table cells to fit their contents.

If you do not need a table, you can delete it by selecting the table and then pressing the DELETE key. To delete the modified table:

Step 1	*Verify*	that the insertion point is in the table
Step 2	*Click*	Table
Step 3	*Point to*	Select
Step 4	*Click*	Table
Step 5	*Observe*	the selected table
Step 6	*Press*	the DELETE key to delete the selected table
Step 7	*Press*	the ENTER key to insert a new paragraph mark

Instead of inserting a table grid, you can use the mouse to draw a table.

Drawing or Adding Table Rows or Columns

When you need more flexibility in the arrangement of columns and rows, try drawing a table using the Draw Table tool. The Draw Table tool enables you to use the mouse to create the exact table you want. You can turn on the Draw Table tool from the T<u>a</u>ble menu or from a button on the Tables toolbar.

To view the Tables toolbar and draw a table:

Step 1	*Display*	the Tables toolbar using the shortcut menu
Step 2	*Click*	the Draw Table button ✐ on the Tables toolbar
Step 3	*Observe*	that the mouse pointer becomes a drawing pointer
Step 4	*Position*	the drawing pointer at the left margin below the introduction comment text and following paragraph mark
Step 5	*Drag*	down approximately 1 inch and to the right approximately 5 inches to draw the table
Step 6	*Release*	the mouse button to view the completed one-cell table

You can also use the drawing pointer to insert columns and rows into a table. To draw column and row boundaries:

Step 1	*Position*	the drawing pointer at the top of the table approximately 1 ½ inches from the left table boundary

Your screen should look similar to Figure 3-13.

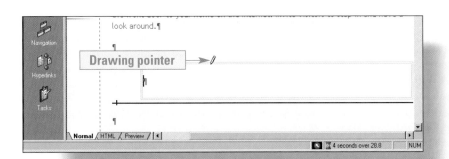

Step 2	*Drag*	down from the top table boundary to the bottom table boundary to draw a column boundary
Step 3	*Position*	the drawing pointer in the middle of the left table boundary

MENU TIP

You can add columns and rows in a table by first moving the insertion point into the column or row, pointing to the <u>I</u>nsert command on the T<u>a</u>ble menu, and then clicking Rows or Colum<u>n</u>s. In the Insert Rows or Columns dialog box, specify the number and location of rows or columns to be added. You can also right-click a cell and click Insert Row or Insert Column.

MOUSE TIP

You can resize a table by dragging the right boundary with the mouse pointer.

You can drag a row or column boundary with the mouse pointer to change the cell height or width.

FIGURE 3-13
Drawing Pointer and Table

| Step 4 | *Drag* | to the right across both columns to draw a row boundary |
| Step 5 | *Observe* | the table now has two columns and two rows |

You can also resize cells in a dialog box or with the mouse pointer.

Resizing Cells

You can resize cells by specifying cell height and width—either in pixels or in a percentage of the original size—in the Cell Properties dialog box.

To resize the cells in the first row:

| Step 1 | *Right-click* | the first cell in the first row |
| Step 2 | *Click* | Cell Properties |

The Cell Properties dialog box opens. You want to change the cell width to 100 pixels and the height to 50 pixels.

Step 3	*Key*	100 in the Specify width: text box
Step 4	*Verify*	the In pixels option button is selected
Step 5	*Key*	50 in the Specify height: text box
Step 6	*Verify*	the In pixels option button is selected
Step 7	*Click*	OK
Step 8	*Observe*	the new width and height of the cells in the first row

Erasing or Deleting Table Rows or Columns

When you want to remove a row or column, you can select the row or column and then use a command on a shortcut menu or the Table menu to delete it. You can also use the Delete Cells button on the Tables toolbar.

To delete the first row:

| Step 1 | *Click* | the Draw Table button 🖉 on the Tables toolbar to turn off the drawing tool, if necessary |
| Step 2 | *Move* | the mouse pointer to the left boundary of the first row until the pointer changes to a small, right-facing black arrow |

Step 3	*Click*	to select the first row
Step 4	*Right-click*	the selected row
Step 5	*Click*	Delete Cells
Step 6	*Delete*	the remaining row
Step 7	*Close*	the Tables toolbar

Now that you can create, edit, and delete a table, you are ready to add tables containing text to the home page.

3.c Keying and Formatting Text on a Web Page

So far, each of the pages in the web contains the standard text inserted during the wizard process, rather than the text appropriate for Sarah's PartyWorld. You want to key the appropriate text and delete the unneeded text and preset comments inserted during the wizard process. You begin with the home page.

To delete the comment, create a table, and key the welcome text:

Step 1	*Click*	the comment to select it
Step 2	*Press*	the DELETE key
Step 3	*Verify*	that the insertion point is on the first line
Step 4	*Create*	a one-cell, left-aligned table with no border and size it to 75 percent of its original size
Step 5	*Key*	Welcome to Sarah's PartyWorld! We have everything you need to make any party a success!

The text should be larger, darker, and centered in the table. You also want to change the font. To format the text:

Step 1	*Select*	the text inside the table
Step 2	*Click*	the Center button on the Formatting toolbar to center the text inside the cell
Step 3	*Click*	the Font Size button list arrow Normal ▾ on the Formatting toolbar

C

chapter
three

QUICK TIP

To draw the external table boundaries, you can drag the drawing pointer down and then to the right or you can drag the drawing pointer diagonally from the left to right.

You can convert selected text to a table or vice versa with the Con**v**ert command on the **T**able menu.

Step 4	*Click*	6 (24 pt)
Step 5	*Click*	the Bold button **B** on the Formatting toolbar
Step 6	*Click*	the Font button list arrow (default font) ▾ on the Formatting toolbar
Step 7	*Click*	Comic Sans MS
Step 8	*Deselect*	the text
Step 9	*Switch*	to the Preview tab to review the text and then return to the Normal tab

Below the welcome text, you want to include the mission for Sarah's PartyWorld. To add the mission statement text:

Step 1	*Delete*	the mission statement comment
Step 2	*Create*	a one-cell, left-aligned table with no border at the insertion point and size it to 75 percent of its original size
Step 3	*Key*	Our mission, at Sarah's PartyWorld, is to be the premier online retailer of party planning materials and services.

Using the Format Painter to Apply Formats

The Format Painter button on the Standard toolbar copies formats from text to text. To use the Format Painter, first position the mouse pointer within the text containing the formatting you want to duplicate. Then, click the Format Painter button. The mouse pointer changes to an I-beam with a paintbrush icon. Drag the I-beam pointer across unformatted text to "paint" the formats.

The Format Painter makes it simple to copy the welcome text format to the mission statement. To format the mission statement text:

MENU TIP

You can change the font, font size, font color, and other character formatting by clicking the **F**ont command on the F**o**rmat menu or shortcut menu. You can change text alignment by clicking the **P**aragraph command on the F**o**rmat menu or shortcut menu.

Step 1	*Click*	in the welcome text to position the insertion point
Step 2	*Click*	the Format Painter button 🖌 on the Standard toolbar
Step 3	*Observe*	the change to the mouse pointer
Step 4	*Drag*	the I-beam across the mission statement text inside the second table
Step 5	*Observe*	that the mission statement text formatting is now the same as the welcome text
Step 6	*Change*	the font size of the mission statement text to 4 (14 pt)

There are extra blank lines on the page that you want to remove in order to move the text closer together. You also want to remove some unnecessary text. To delete the blank lines and unnecessary text:

Step 1	*Click*	at the paragraph mark on the blank line below the welcome text
Step 2	*Press*	the DELETE key
Step 3	*Delete*	the blank lines above the text "Our Mission," below the mission statement, and above the "Contact Information" text
Step 4	*Delete*	the Contact Information comment and the resulting blank line
Step 5	*Delete*	the FAX text in the Contact Information
Step 6	*Delete*	the Sales: and Customer Support: lines in the Electronic mail section

Checking Spelling on a Page or across a Web Site

It is a good idea to check the spelling on every page before you publish a web to a server. By default, FrontPage checks for spelling or keying errors as you key text. When you key a word incorrectly, FrontPage adds a wavy red line below the word. You can correct the word by right-clicking it, then clicking a replacement word from the shortcut menu or opening the Spelling dialog box.

You can check the spelling on an entire page by clicking the Spelling button on the Standard toolbar or the Spelling command on the Tools menu. When FrontPage finds a misspelled word, the Spelling dialog box opens, with options for replacing the misspelled word or ignoring the word.

To check the spelling on all or multiple pages in a web, first switch to Folders view. If you want to check the spelling on selected pages (but not all the pages in the web), first select the pages using the SHIFT + Click or CTRL + Click technique. Then click the Spelling button or the Spelling command. The Spelling dialog box opens and you can select either the Selected Page(s) option or the Entire web option. When you click the Start button, the spelling check begins. The Spelling dialog box expands to list all the pages containing misspelled words. To edit the page, double-click it in the list to view the page in the Normal tab. Then make the appropriate corrections and follow the dialog box instructions to go to the next page.

MENU TIP

You can turn off the automatic spelling checker in the Page Options dialog box, which you open with the Page Options command on the Tools menu.

chapter
three

3.d Using Global Find and Replace across a Web Site

You can search for and replace text on the current page or on all pages in the web using the Replace command on the Edit menu. In addition, you can set options that enable you to search for matching case, where the upper- and lowercase characters must agree in the search text and found text. You can also search for whole words rather than a group of characters contained in a word. You need to replace the text "Electronic mail" on the home page and the word "mail" on all pages with "e-mail."

To search for the text "electronic mail" and replace it with "E-mail" on the current page:

Step 1	Press	the CTRL + HOME keys to move the insertion point to the top of the page
Step 2	Click	Edit
Step 3	Click	Replace

The Replace dialog box that opens should look similar to Figure 3-14.

FIGURE 3-14
Replace Dialog Box

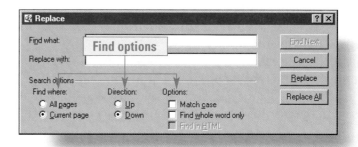

Step 4	Key	electronic mail in the Find what: text box
Step 5	Key	E-mail in the Replace with: text box
Step 6	Verify	the Current page option is selected
Step 7	Click	Find Next

The Electronic mail text is selected.

Step 8	Click	Replace
Step 9	Click	OK to confirm that FrontPage has finished the search

Next, you want to replace all occurrences of "mail" with "e-mail." To set the search options for the text "mail:"

Step 1	*Key*	mail in the Find what: text box
Step 2	*Key*	e-mail in the Replace with: text box
Step 3	*Click*	the All pages option button
Step 4	*Click*	Find in Web

The Replace dialog box expands to list all the pages on which the text "mail" appears. Your dialog box should look similar to Figure 3-15.

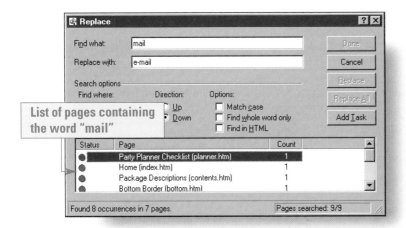

FIGURE 3-15
Expanded Replace
Dialog Box

You can add a task to replace the word at a later time by selecting the page in the list and clicking the Add Task button in the dialog box. You can double-click a file in the list to return to Page view and replace the text now.

When you created the Sample_Web using a wizard, the webmaster contact information was placed in a separate page named *bottom.htm*. The contents of the *bottom.htm* page appear in a **shared border**, a page region that is reserved for content you want to appear consistently throughout the web. When you change the content of a shared border, all the pages that share the border are changed. You learn more about shared borders in a later chapter. The text "mail" that you want to replace is in this shared border. To replace the text "mail" in the *bottom.htm* page in the shared border:

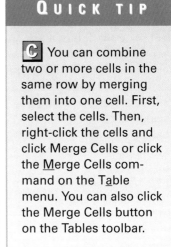

QUICK TIP

You can combine two or more cells in the same row by merging them into one cell. First, select the cells. Then, right-click the cells and click Merge Cells or click the Merge Cells command on the Table menu. You can also click the Merge Cells button on the Tables toolbar.

Step 1	*Double-click*	the Bottom Border (bottom.htm) file in the list
Step 2	*Observe*	that the page opens in the Normal tab and the text "mail" is selected
Step 3	*Click*	Replace

chapter
three

QUICK TIP

C If your web is stored on a server running FrontPage Server Extensions, FrontPage automatically creates a text index based on the words in your web pages. You can create a search form to let viewers search this index using specific words or phrases. For more information on search forms, see online Help.

MENU TIP

C A **page banner** is a section at the top of a web page that contains text and graphics. You can insert a page banner on any page. If a theme is applied to the web, the page banner graphic is coordinated as part of the theme. To insert a page banner, click the Page Banner command on the Insert menu.

The Continue with next document? dialog box opens. You do not want to change any other page.

Step 4	*Click*	Cancel
Step 5	*Observe*	the edited notation in the list for the Bottom Border page
Step 6	*Click*	Cancel to close the Replace dialog box
Step 7	*Save & Close*	the *bottom.htm* page
Step 8	*Review*	each page to verify the change

Before you close the web, you want to replace the text in the page banner. You can change the text in the banner page properties or in the file properties.

To change the banner page properties for the home page:

Step 1	*View*	the *index.htm* page in the Normal tab in Page view, if necessary
Step 2	*Right-click*	the page banner
Step 3	*Click*	Page Banner Properties
Step 4	*Key*	Sarah's PartyWorld in the Page banner text box
Step 5	*Click*	OK
Step 6	*Observe*	the new page banner text
Step 7	*Change*	the page banner text on the *feedback.htm* page to "Contest"
Step 8	*Change*	the page banner text on the *products.htm* page to "Party Packages"
Step 9	*Change*	the page banner text on the *prod01.htm* page to "Holiday Parties"
Step 10	*Click*	the Show All button ¶ on the Standard toolbar to turn off the view of hidden page elements
Step 11	*Close*	the web and save the pages when asked

Sarah's PartyWorld sample web looks more attractive with the modified theme and information organized in tables. Next, you'll add various graphic elements to enhance the web.

Summary

- ► Web page design schemes, called themes, contain coordinated font styles, colors, and graphics.

- ► You can apply a preset theme and modify it with vivid colors, animated graphics, and a background picture.

- ► You can change the colors, graphics, and fonts in preset themes and then save the theme as a new custom theme.

- ► Preset and custom themes can be applied to individual pages and to all the pages in a web.

- ► A table is a grid of rows and columns. The intersection of a row and column is called a cell.

- ► Tables are used on web pages to organize information and to position text or text and graphics side by side.

- ► You can insert a table grid with evenly spaced rows and columns or draw a table and place the row and column boundaries anywhere in the table.

- ► Entire tables and table cells can be resized with options in the Properties dialog box or with the mouse pointer.

- ► You can add or delete rows and columns in a table.

- ► After you key text in a table, you can select it and then format it with buttons on the Formatting toolbar or in the Font and Paragraph dialog boxes.

- ► You can search for and replace text either on the current page or across the web.

chapter three

Commands Review

Action	Menu Bar	Shortcut Menu	Toolbar/Mouse	Keyboard
Apply a theme	Format, Theme	Right-click the page and click Theme		ALT + O, T
Create a table	Table, Insert, Table Table, Draw Table			ALT + A, I, T ALT + A, B SHIFT + CTRL + ALT + T
Insert rows and columns	Table, Insert, Rows or Columns	Right-click selected row and click Insert Row Right-click selected column and click Insert Column		ALT + A, I, N
View table properties	Table, Properties, Table	Right-click the table, click Table Properties		ALT + A, R, T
View cell properties	Table, Properties, Cell	Right-click the table, click Cell Properties		ALT + A, R, C
Key text in a cell			Click the cell to position the insertion point	TAB SHIFT + TAB
Insert a comment	Insert, Comment			ALT + I, C
Format text	Format, Font or Paragraph	Right-click the text and click Font or Paragraph	Various buttons on the Formatting toolbar	ALT + O, F or P various shortcut keys ALT + ENTER
Copy formatting				CTRL + SHIFT + C (copy) CTRL + SHIFT + V (paste)
Remove font formatting	Format, Remove Formatting			ALT + O, R CTRL + Z
Check spelling on a page or entire web	Tools, Spelling			ALT + T, S F7
Find and Replace	Edit, Find or Replace			ALT + E, F or E CTRL + F CTRL + H
Change page banner text		Right-click the page banner, click Page Banner Properties		

Concepts Review

Circle the correct answer.

1. Which of the following is *not* an option for modifying a preset theme?
 [a] Vivid colors
 [b] Background picture
 [c] Title color
 [d] Active graphics

2. You can resize table cells by:
 [a] percentage or size.
 [b] pixels or percentage.
 [c] pixels or border.
 [d] percentage or alignment.

3. A comment is:
 [a] a coordinated color scheme.
 [b] text added to a page to provide information.
 [c] a text editing tool.
 [d] a model document.

4. A style is:
 [a] a set of formats saved and applied by name.
 [b] a special web page.
 [c] text added to a page to provide information.
 [d] a background picture.

5. To apply a theme to multiple pages (but not the entire web), switch to:
[a] Navigation view.
[b] Page view.
[c] Folders view.
[d] Hyperlinks view.

6. The intersection of a column and row in a table is called a:
[a] wizard.
[b] theme.
[c] comment.
[d] cell.

7. A pixel is:
[a] a color scheme.
[b] the basic unit of programmable color on a computer screen.
[c] a style.
[d] a theme.

8. A table is used on a web page to:
[a] change the color scheme.
[b] replace text.
[c] organize text and graphics.
[d] insert a background picture.

9. A style sheet is a:
[a] background picture.
[b] tool for organizing text on a page.
[c] special theme.
[d] collection of styles you can apply to an entire page.

10. Applying a theme to a web page adds:
[a] a lot of extra work.
[b] sample text.
[c] a polished and professional appearance.
[d] comments.

Circle **T** if the statement is true or **F** if the statement is false.

T   F   1. After applying a theme to a page, you cannot change to a different theme.

T   F   2. You can search for and replace text on all pages in a web.

T   F   3. You can modify a preset theme by applying more vivid colors.

T   F   4. You can check spelling on an individual page or on all pages in the web.

T   F   5. A grid of columns and rows is called a theme.

T   F   6. A pixel is the basic unit of color on a computer screen.

T   F   7. Tables can be inserted or drawn on a web page.

T   F   8. You can resize a table with the mouse pointer.

T   F   9. You can use the mouse pointer to change cell height and width.

T   F   10. You cannot create a custom theme and must use only the preset themes.

Glossary

Use online <u>H</u>elp to look up the following words in the FrontPage glossary. Then, using your word processing program, create a document listing and defining each word. Save and print the document.

1. cell padding

2. cell spacing

3. live web

4. Normal text

5. shared borders

6. table

7. theme

chapter three

Skills Review

Exercise 1

1. Open the Acme_Plumbing web located in the Chapter_3 folder on the Data Disk.

2. Open the *index.htm* file in the Normal tab in Page view.

3. Apply the Blueprint theme with vivid colors and active graphics to the home page.

4. Insert a picture page banner at the top of the page using the Page Banner command on the Insert menu. Replace the text "Home Page" with "Acme Plumbing."

5. Press the ENTER key twice to insert two blank lines below the banner.

6. Create a one-cell table at the second blank line.

7. Change the table properties to center the table and increase the border size to 2.

8. Key the following text in the table cell:

   Acme Plumbing is the largest plumbing wholesaler in the southeast. Our distribution centers are strategically located to provide you with quick delivery of your plumbing needs.

9. Select the text in the table and format it as blue, 5 (18 pt), bold, and centered, using buttons on the Formatting toolbar.

10. Click at the left margin below the table and press the ENTER key.

11. Display the Tables toolbar.

12. Draw a table with one row and two columns. The first column should be approximately 1 ½ inches wide. The second column should be approximately 3 ½ inches wide.

13. Key the text "Mission Statement" on two lines (insert a line break between the words using the SHIFT + ENTER keys) in the first column. Center-align the text horizontally with the Center button on the Formatting toolbar. Center-align the text vertically with the Center Vertically button on the Tables toolbar.

14. Key the following text in the second column:
    Our mission is to be the leading distributor of plumbing materials in the southeast.

15. Format the "Mission Statement" text as red, 4 (14 pt), and bold.

16. Use the Format Painter button to copy the formatting from the welcome text to the mission statement text.

17. Check the spelling on the page.

18. Preview, print preview, and print the *index.htm* page.

19. Save the page and close the web.

Exercise 2

1. Open the Beverly_Jones web located in the Chapter_3 folder on the Data Disk.

2. Open the Themes dialog box and select the Citrus Punch theme with vivid colors, active graphics, and a background picture.

3. Create a custom theme named Beverly's Theme, using the modified Citrus Punch theme with green body text.

4. Apply the Beverly's Theme custom theme to the entire web.

5. Preview, print preview, and print all the pages in the web.

6. Close the web and save pages if asked.

7. Delete the Beverly's Theme custom theme.

Exercise 3 [C]

1. Open the Chang_Services web located in the Chapter_3 folder on the Data Disk.

2. Apply the Postmodern theme with vivid colors and active graphics to the entire web.

3. The copyright date is in a shared bottom border. Search for the copyright date of 2001 and replace it with 2002. Then verify it is replaced on all pages.

4. Preview, print preview, and print the *index.htm* page.

5. Close the web and save pages if asked.

Exercise 4 [C]

1. Open the Ellis_Training web located in the Chapter_3 folder on the Data Disk.

2. Move the *earth.jpg* picture file to the images folder.

3. Create a custom theme based on the Artsy theme with vivid colors, active graphics, and an olive background color. Save the theme as Ellis Custom Theme and apply it to the entire web.

4. Review all the pages.

5. Delete the comment and blank line from the top of the *faq.htm* page and save the page.

6. Insert a page banner on the *index.htm* page. Replace the banner text "Home Page" with "Ellis Training & Consulting."

7. Draw a large table below the banner that is approximately 2 inches in height and extends to the end of the banner.

8. Insert the *Ellis_Training.doc* document located in the Chapter_3 folder on the Data Disk into the table.

9. Align the text at the top of the table using the Align Top button on the Tables toolbar.

10. Resize the table row height by dragging the bottom boundary upward with the mouse pointer to the last line of inserted text.

11. Format the text as 5 (18 pt), bold, and centered in the table.

12. Save and close the page.

13. Open the *webdesign.htm* page in the Normal tab in Page view.

14. Select the text "Your Heading Goes Here" and replace it with "Ellis Web Design Services."

15. Delete the blank row below the table heading row.

16. Check the spelling on the page.

17. Save and close the page.

18. Preview, print preview, and print all the pages.

19. Close the web and save pages if asked.

20. Close the Tables toolbar.

21. Delete the Ellis Custom Theme.

chapter three

Exercise 5

1. Open the Rameriz_International web located in the Chapter_3 folder on the Data Disk.

2. View the *index.htm* page in the Normal tab in Page view.

3. Change the page banner text to "Fieldstone Power Plant Project."

4. Replace the text "Project" with the text "Fieldstone Power Plant Project" on all the web pages. Match the case and find whole words only.

5. Change the theme for all pages to Geared Up Factory with vivid colors, active graphics, and a background picture.

6. Review the pages.

7. Check the spelling on the entire web.

8. Preview, print preview, and print the *index.htm* page.

9. Close the web and save pages when asked.

Exercise 6

1. Create a new web named Hamilton using the Empty Web template.

2. Add a blank page to the web using the New Page button on the Standard toolbar.

3. Save the new page as *index.htm* with the title "Hamilton Industrial Cleaning."

4. Create a custom theme named Hamilton Theme based on the Industrial theme with vivid colors and active graphics. Customize the theme to have blue body text and white background. Replace the first level bullet with the *bd14565_.gif* bullet file located in the Chapter_3 folder on the Data Disk. Apply the Hamilton Theme to the web.

5. Insert a page banner at the top of the *index.htm* page.

6. Insert a one-cell table below the banner. Center the table, size it to 75 percent of its original size, and remove the border.

7. Insert the text "Dirty Work Is Our Business!" in the table.

8. Change the text font style to Arial Rounded MT Bold or a different font of your choice, size the text to 6 (24 pt), and center it in the cell.

9. Check the spelling on the page.

10. Save, preview, print preview, and print the page.

11. Close the web.

12. Delete the Hamilton Theme.

Exercise 7

1. Create a new web named Chocolate using the Corporate Presence wizard.

2. Include an introduction, mission statement, company profile, and contact information.

3. Include one additional products page with product image, pricing information, and an information request form.

4. Include all the options on the feedback form.

5. Include the company logo, page title, and links to main web pages at the top of the page. Include the webmaster e-mail address, copyright notice, and modification date at the bottom of the page.

6. The name of the company is "Chocolate Velvet." The one-word version of the name is "Velvet." The company address is: 1100 Wood Pond Drive, Bradenton, FL, 34202-1100.

7. The phone number is: 850-555-1234. The fax number is: 850-555-1235. The webmasters e-mail address is webmaster@chocolatevelvet.com. The general information e-mail address is info@chocolatevelvet.com.

8. Apply the Sandstone theme with vivid colors, active graphics, and a background picture.

9. View the *index.htm* page and change the page banner text to "Chocolate Velvet."

10. View the *products.htm* page and change the page banner properties to "Hand-Dipped Chocolates."

11. View the *prod01.htm* page and change the page banner properties to "Truffles."

12. Switch to the index.htm page, delete the introduction comment, and create a one-cell table to contain the introduction. Format the table attractively on the page.

13. Insert a two-line introductory paragraph in the table about the Chocolate Velvet company, which makes hand-dipped chocolate candies. Format the text attractively in the table.

14. Check the spelling on the entire web.

15. Preview, print preview, and print all the pages.

16. Close the web and save pages if asked.

Exercise 8

1. Create a new web named Secretarial using the One Page Web template.

2. Apply the Poetic theme with vivid colors, active graphics, and background picture.

3. View the *index.htm* page in the Normal tab in Page view.

4. Insert a page banner with the text "Applebee Secretarial Services."

5. Draw a two-column table below the banner. The first column is approximately 1 ½ inches wide and the second column extends to the end of the banner.

6. Insert the text "Our Services" on two lines (insert a line break between the words using the SHIFT + ENTER keys) in the first cell. Format the text with the Century Gothic font, 5 (18 pt) font size, and center it vertically and horizontally in the cell.

7. Close the web and save pages if asked.

Case Projects

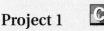

Project 1

Florists by Design is a large floral shop in San Jose, California, that specializes in providing flowers and other home or office decorations for special events and holidays. Jose Spinoza, the manager of Florists by Design, hires you to create a web site. Using a word processing program, create a plan for the web site. Then create the web site using FrontPage wizards or templates. Include at least three pages in addition to the home page. Include company contact information on the home page. Include webmaster contact information, a copyright notice, and modification date on each page. Create a custom theme based on one of the preset themes and apply it to the entire web. Create a table containing formatted text on the home page. Add appropriate text with formatting to the remaining pages. Use tables to organize the text if the wizard or template does not already provide tables. Print the web pages. Save and print the plan.

chapter three

Project 2

Tony Daversa, of Daversa Importers, Inc., agrees with your idea to use FrontPage wizards and templates to create the Daversa Importers web site. He asks you to create a sample web site for his review and final approval. Using a word processing program, create a plan for the Daversa Importers web site. Use appropriate FrontPage templates and wizards to create the web; include at least four pages in addition to the home page. Include company contact information on the home page. Include webmaster contact information, a copyright notice, and modification date on each page. Create a custom theme based on a preset theme and apply it to all the pages in the web. Use tables to organize text and include welcome text and a mission statement on the home page. Add appropriate text to the remaining pages. Use the Replace command to replace the copyright date with next year's date on all pages in the web. Print the web pages. Save and print the plan.

Project 3

LaTasha Cooper is the owner of a company that has three fast food restaurants in the Atlanta, Georgia, area. She wants to use a web site to promote her restaurants and to take delivery orders by e-mail. You are preparing a proposal to develop and create the web site for LaTasha's company. Before you begin the proposal, you want to research web sites for similar businesses. Connect to the Internet, load your web browser, and use a search engine or directory to find web sites for companies similar to LaTasha's company. Print all the pages for at least three web sites. Using a word processing program, create a document containing an analysis of the design of each web site, including both design strengths and design weaknesses. Save and print the document.

Project 4

As part of the Cooper proposal (see Project 3), you want to include a sample web site. Create the sample web site using FrontPage wizards and templates. Include at least three pages in addition

to the home page. Include company contact information on the home page. Include webmaster contact information, a copyright notice, and modification date on each page. Apply one of the preset themes to the entire web site. Create a table containing formatted text on the home page. Add appropriate text with formatting to the remaining pages. Use tables to organize the text if the wizard or template does not already provide the tables. Print the web pages.

Project 5

Laverne Washington, executive assistant to the human resources manager at Waltham Engineering Company, stops by your desk and asks for your help. The manager wants Laverne to change the color scheme but keep the overall theme of the departmental web page. Although she updates the web page text when necessary, she doesn't know how to modify the color scheme in the theme applied to the page. First, research how to create, save, and apply custom themes in online help. Using a word processing program, write down the instructions for selecting, modifying, and applying a preset theme. Then add the instructions for creating a custom theme based on a preset theme. Save and print the document.

Project 6

Joe Chen, the training manager for Anderson Technical Services, calls you. He needs you to give a fifteen-minute presentation on how create and edit tables in web pages to ten new employees. Using a word processing program, create an outline of your presentation. Save and print the document. With your instructor's approval, use the outline to describe the process to your classmates.

Project 7

You want to find some new web bullet, banner, and navigation graphics to use on your web pages. Your friend, Mark Rifkin, suggests you look for free web graphics on the Web. Connect to the Internet, load your web browser, and using a search engine or directory locate web pages offering free web graphics. With your instructor's permission, download two new bullet files, four new navigation button files, and three new banner files. Using a word processing program, create a document containing a list of the new graphic files, the web page from which they were downloaded, and the location on your hard drive or network where the files are stored. Save and print the document.

Project 8

David Wilson is the new assistant to the manager of the Red Ball Oil Company. The company has changed its name to Red Ball, Inc. The manager asks David to correct the company name on all the pages in the company web site. David has never done this and asks for your help. Using a word processing program, write down the steps to find and replace the company name across all pages in the web. Use online Help, if necessary to review the process. Save and print the document.

Enhancing a Web Page

Chapter Overview

Special effects and graphics help enhance and enliven a web. Bulleted and numbered lists itemize information. Page transitions provide special animation effects that viewers see when they enter or exit a web or browse from page to page at the web. You can also apply animation effects to page elements, such as text, buttons, and pictures. Horizontal divider lines, hit counters, scrolling marquees, and animations add excitement and movement to web pages. Shared borders make editing elements across pages easy. In this chapter, you create a bulleted list, apply page transition animation, and then add, format, and animate web page text. You also edit the contents of a shared border.

LEARNING OBJECTIVES

- ▶ Add and edit web page elements
- ▶ Add animation to web page elements
- ▶ Format page transitions
- ▶ Preview a web in a web browser
- ▶ Edit content within shared borders for an entire web

Case profile

Now that the home page for Sarah's PartyWorld contains appropriate text, you are ready to add text to the catalog page. You also want to show the other committee members how bulleted or numbered lists, page transition animation, page element animation, a hit counter, a horizontal divider line, and a scrolling marquee add interest to web pages.

chapter four

4.a Adding and Editing Web Page Elements

Various page elements can help make your web more appealing. You can apply graphic bullets or numbers to itemize lists of information. You can insert horizontal divider lines to separate sections of text, and include a hit counter to maintain a running total of viewers who have visited a web page. You can also insert a scrolling marquee of text to catch the viewers' eye when they load the page.

You want to edit the Sample_Web catalog page by adding page elements. To insert the product overview text on the catalog page:

Step 1	*Open*	the Sample_Web you modified in Chapter 3
Step 2	*Open*	the *products.htm* page in the Normal tab in Page view
Step 3	*Click*	the Show All button ¶ on the Standard toolbar
Step 4	*Delete*	the product overview comment
Step 5	*Click*	at the first blank line to position the insertion point, if necessary
Step 6	*Key*	We have prepackaged party supplies and decorations for every occasion. Each party package contains invitations, table decorations, room decorations, party favors, and ideas for games.
Step 7	*Select*	the text
Step 8	*Format*	the selected text with Comic Sans MS font, 4 (14 pt) font size, and center it

Your screen should look similar to Figure 4-1.

notes

For the remainder of this text, you can turn on the Show All button on the Standard toolbar to view the hidden page elements, as needed. No instructions to do so are provided.

chapter
four

FIGURE 4-1
Catalog Page

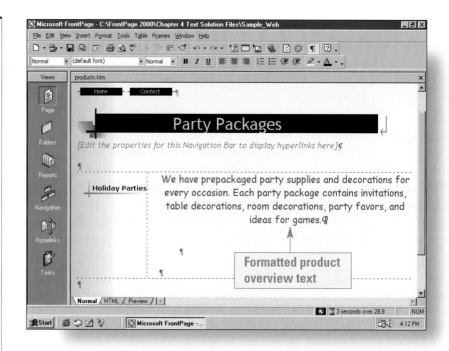

Adding and Formatting Multi-level Bulleted or Numbered Lists

A **bulleted list** is a list of items where a graphic image precedes each item. A **numbered list** is a list of items where a sequential number precedes each item. You want to create a bulleted list on the *products.htm* page (catalog page) in the Sample_Web to itemize the major party theme categories. To do this, you first create a simple bulleted list. Then, you expand the list by adding an additional level of detail.

Creating a Simple Bulleted List

Now you are ready to create a simple bulleted list, which includes only one level of bullets. To create a simple bulleted list:

Step 1	*Select*	the Name of product 1 and description of product 1 text
Step 2	*Delete*	the selected text
Step 3	*Click*	the Bullets button on the Formatting toolbar
Step 4	*Observe*	that the default first-level bullet graphic is inserted to the left of the insertion point

Your screen should look similar to Figure 4-2.

MENU TIP

You can create both bulleted and numbered lists with the Bullets and Numbering command on the Format menu. The options in the Bullets and Numbering dialog box enable you to apply plain bullets, graphic bullets, or numbers.

MOUSE TIP

You can create a numbered list by clicking the Numbering button on the Formatting toolbar.

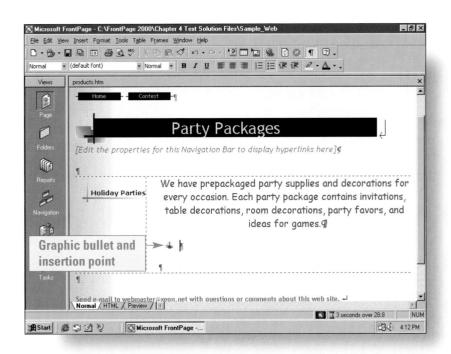

FIGURE 4-2
Inserted First-Level Bullet

QUICK TIP

You can change a numbered list to bullets or vice versa by selecting the list and clicking the Numbering or Bullets button on the Formatting toolbar. You can also key all the items in the list, select the items, and then click the Numbering or Bullets button to add numbers or bullets to each item all at once.

When you press the ENTER key after you key the first bullet text, the insertion point moves to the next line and inserts another bullet graphic. To key the bullet text:

Step 1	*Key*	Birthday Parties
Step 2	*Press*	the ENTER key
Step 3	*Observe*	that another bullet graphic is inserted
Step 4	*Key*	Baby Showers
Step 5	*Press*	the ENTER key
Step 6	*Continue*	by adding the following bullets: Bridal Showers Holiday Parties Special Event Parties

You decide that the Holiday Parties bullet should appear above the Birthday Parties bullet. Rather than rekey the bullet, you can move it. To move the Holiday Parties bullet:

| Step 1 | *Select* | the Holiday Parties bullet *and the following paragraph mark* |
| Step 2 | *Drag* | the bullet text up and to the left of the Birthday Parties bullet text |

MOUSE TIP

You can use the mouse pointer to select the text in a bulleted or numbered list. If you move the mouse pointer to the left of the first bullet, it becomes a selection pointer—a white, right-facing arrow. When the mouse pointer is a selection pointer, click the mouse button to select a single bulleted item or drag to select multiple items.

chapter
four

QUICK TIP

To remove bullets or numbers from a list, first select the list. Then, click the Bullets or Numbering button on the Formatting toolbar to turn off the bullets or numbers.

You can format text in a bulleted list just as you would any other text. To select and format all the bullet text:

Step 1	**Move**	the mouse pointer to the left of the first bulleted item
Step 2	**Drag**	down until all the bulleted items are selected
Step 3	**Format**	the bullet text with the Comic Sans MS font and 4 (14 pt) font size
Step 4	**Deselect**	the text

Your screen should look similar to Figure 4-3.

FIGURE 4-3
Formatted Simple
Bulleted List

You can also create a list with multiple nested levels.

Creating a Multi-Level List

A **multi-level list** consists of bulleted or numbered lists arranged in order of importance (highest to lowest) similar to a text outline. Each lower-level item is indented from the left. You want to add another list below the Special Event Parties bullet, with two examples of special event party themes. To create the multi-level list:

MENU TIP

To modify the bullets or numbers in a bulleted or numbered list, right-click the list and click List Properties to open the List Properties dialog box.

Step 1	**Click**	at the end of the Special Event Parties bulleted item (before the paragraph mark)
Step 2	**Press**	the ENTER key to create a new bulleted item
Step 3	**Click**	the Increase Indent button on the Formatting toolbar *twice* to create a nested bulleted item
Step 4	**Observe**	that the bullet graphic is the one specified for second-level bullets in the customized Sarah's Theme

Step 5	*Key*	Retirement
Step 6	*Press*	the ENTER key
Step 7	*Observe*	the new nested bulleted item
Step 8	*Key*	Graduation
Step 9	*Press*	the ENTER key

The list is finished. When you pressed the ENTER key, you automatically created a new bullet. You can press the BACKSPACE key to end the list and reposition the insertion point.

Step 10	*Press*	the BACKSPACE key *three* times to remove any bullets and place the insertion point at the left below the multi-level bulleted list

To distinctly separate the nested list from the contact information at the bottom of the page, you insert a horizontal divider line.

Inserting Horizontal Lines

Horizontal lines are used in web pages to separate text or add an attractive effect to the page. After you insert a horizontal line, you can modify its properties for width, height, color, and alignment by right-clicking the line and clicking Horizontal Line Properties. If the page already has a theme applied, FrontPage inserts the horizontal line as a graphic that matches the theme.

To insert a horizontal line below the multi-level list:

Step 1	*Click*	at the second blank line below the multi-level list to position the insertion point
Step 2	*Click*	Insert
Step 3	*Click*	Horizontal Line
Step 4	*Observe*	the horizontal line
Step 5	*Save & Close*	the catalog page

In the last committee meeting, Sarah asked how she and other viewers could know how many total viewers had visited the Sarah's PartyWorld home page. You add a hit counter on the home page to calculate the number of visitors.

chapter
four

Adding a Hit Counter to a Web Page

A **hit counter** calculates and displays the number of times a page has been visited. To satisfy Sarah's request, you decide to add a hit counter to the home page.

To add a hit counter between the mission statement and the contact information on the home page:

Step 1	*Open*	the *index.htm* page in the Normal tab in Page view
Step 2	*Click*	in front of the Contact Information heading to position the insertion point
Step 3	*Press*	the ENTER key to create a blank line
Step 4	*Click*	at the new blank line to position the insertion point
Step 5	*Key*	You are visitor number
Step 6	*Press*	the SPACEBAR
Step 7	*Select*	the text and following paragraph mark
Step 8	*Format*	the text with Comic Sans MS font, 4 (14 pt) font size, and blue color
Step 9	*Click*	in front of the paragraph mark to position the insertion point
Step 10	*Click*	the Insert Component button 🖼 on the Standard toolbar
Step 11	*Click*	Hit Counter

The Hit Counter Properties dialog box that opens should look similar to Figure 4-4.

FIGURE 4-4
Hit Counter Properties
Dialog Box

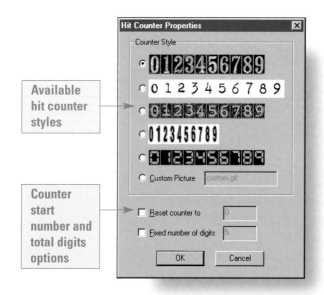

Available hit counter styles

Counter start number and total digits options

You can select the hit counter style, set the beginning number to zero or another number, and specify the number of digits in this dialog box.

Step 12	*Click*	the second option button
Step 13	*Click*	OK

Your screen should look similar to Figure 4-5.

You are visitor number [Hit Counter]¶

Contact Information¶

Telephone¶

Hit counter placeholder

FIGURE 4-5
Home Page with Hit Counter

The placeholder [Hit Counter] is inserted after the text. You cannot see the actual counter component until the page is published to a web server running FrontPage server extensions.

Step 14	*Save*	the page

You decide to use a marquee to remind viewers to submit contest entries.

Adding and Editing Scrolling Marquee Text

You can add a scrolling text message to a web page with a **marquee**, a text container, and then customize the marquee to set movement options and specify the number of times the text effect repeats in the marquee. You can also format the text and background in a marquee.

To insert a scrolling marquee above the hit counter on the *index.htm* page:

Step 1	*Insert*	a blank line above the hit counter line on the *index.htm* page
Step 2	*Click*	the Insert Component button on the Standard toolbar
Step 3	*Click*	<u>M</u>arquee

> **QUICK TIP**
>
> You can use the Date and <u>T</u>ime command on the <u>I</u>nsert menu to insert the modification date. You can insert symbols, such as the copyright symbol, using the <u>S</u>ymbol command on the <u>I</u>nsert menu.

chapter
four

The Marquee Properties dialog box that opens should look similar to Figure 4-6.

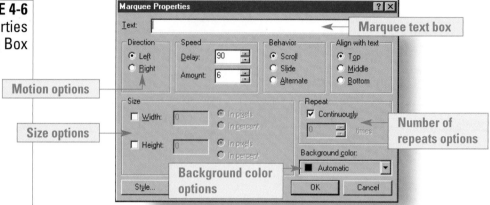

notes For the remainder of this book, it is assumed that when you open a new dialog box, you use the dialog box Help button to review unfamiliar options. The instructions will provide no steps to do this.

You key the text, set the marquee direction, speed, motion (behavior), and alignment options in this dialog box. You can also specify how many times to repeat the effect, size the marquee, and set a background color in this dialog box. You want the text to scroll from left to right. You also want the effect to appear continuously and the marquee to be half of its original width. Finally, you want to change the background color to black to match the page banner and navigation buttons. To key the text and set the options:

Step 1	*Key*	Don't forget to enter our contest for a chance to win a holiday party theme package!
Step 2	*Click*	the Left option button, if necessary
Step 3	*Verify*	that Delay is 90 milliseconds and the Amount is 6 pixels
Step 4	*Click*	the Scroll option button, if necessary
Step 5	*Click*	the Top option button, if necessary
Step 6	*Click*	the Width check box to insert a check mark
Step 7	*Key*	50 in the Width text box

Step 8	*Click*	the In percent option button
Step 9	*Click*	the Background color: list arrow
Step 10	*Click*	the black tile in the first row of the color grid
Step 11	*Click*	OK

Your screen should look similar to Figure 4-7.

FIGURE 4-7
Home Page with Marquee

You must preview the page to see the marquee animation.

Step 12	*View*	the page in the Preview tab and then return to the Normal tab

Next, you want to center the marquee on the page and change text font size to 3 (12 pt) and the color to light gold. You can format the marquee text with buttons on the Formatting toolbar just like other web page text. To format the marquee text and center the marquee:

Step 1	*Click*	the marquee to select it
Step 2	*Change*	the font size to 3 (12 pt)
Step 3	*Change*	the text color to light gold using the Font Color button on the Formatting toolbar (use the More Colors option to select the light gold font color with the Value: Hex={FF,CC,00} from the color wheel)
Step 4	*Center*	the marquee
Step 5	*Deselect*	the marquee

MENU TIP

You can format the text in a marquee by selecting the marquee and then opening the Font dialog box with the Font command on the Format menu or shortcut menu.

chapter
four

Your screen should look similar to Figure 4-8.

FIGURE 4-8
Formatted and Centered
Marquee

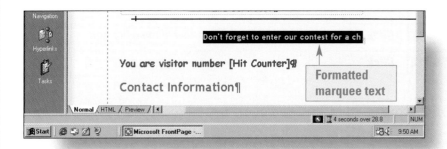

| Step 6 | *Preview* | the *index.htm* page and then return to the Normal tab |
| Step 7 | *Save & Close* | the page |

At lunch this afternoon, Bob mentioned that he read a brief article about adding animation effects to web pages and would like to see some examples of animation in the sample web site.

4.b Adding Animation to Web Page Elements

Dynamic HTML (DHTML) is an extension of the HTML language that enables you to add animation to text and objects on a web page. For example, text can fly into the page when the page loads, or the appearance of text can change when the mouse pointer moves over the text.

A good way to determine which kind of animation is appropriate is by experimenting with different effects. First, you can apply the animation effect. Then, you preview the page to see what the animation looks like in a web browser. To demonstrate DHTML effects in the Sample_Web, you apply animation to the introductory text on the *products.htm* page. To apply DHTML animation effects:

Step 1	*Open*	the *products.htm* page in the Normal tab in Page view
Step 2	*Select*	the introductory paragraph above the bulleted list
Step 3	*Click*	Format
Step 4	*Click*	Dynamic HTML Effects

The DHTML Effects toolbar opens, enabling you to apply DHTML effects. First, you select the event on which the effect will occur: when the viewer clicks or double-clicks the mouse button, moves the mouse over the text or object, or loads the page. Next, you apply the effect. Finally, you choose any effect settings that are applicable. The effect and setting options available on the DHTML toolbar vary, depending on the selected page element and event type.

To apply a DHTML effect that allows text to fly onto the page when the page loads:

Step 1	*Click*	the On button list arrow < Choose an event > ▾ on the DHTML Effects toolbar
Step 2	*Click*	Page load
Step 3	*Click*	the Apply button list arrow < Choose an effect > ▾ on the DHTML Effects toolbar
Step 4	*Click*	Fly in
Step 5	*Click*	the Effect button < Choose Settings > ▾ on the DHTML Effects toolbar
Step 6	*Click*	From right

Your DHTML Effects toolbar should look similar to Figure 4-9.

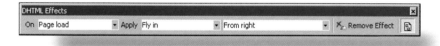

Step 7	***Deselect***	the text
Step 8	***Observe***	that the text is highlighted in light blue, indicating DHTML effects are applied
Step 9	***Move***	the mouse pointer (I-beam) to the highlighted text to display a ScreenTip indicating the type of DHTML effect applied—Dynamic Effect: Fly in From right
Step 10	***View***	the page in the Preview tab to see the animation and then return to the Normal tab

Before you can try out other DHTML effects, you need to remove this one. To remove the effect:

| Step 1 | *Click* | in the highlighted text |

FIGURE 4-9
DHTML Effects Toolbar

MOUSE **TIP**

To turn on or off the highlighting of DHTML effects in the Normal tab, click the Highlight Dynamic HTML Effects button on the DHTML Effects toolbar.

| Step 2 | *Click* | the Remove Effect button 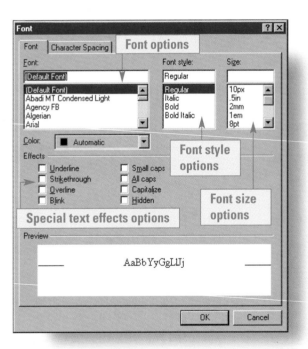 on the DHTML Effects toolbar |

Next, you try a different animation effect. To apply formatting to the introductory text on a mouse-over action:

Step 1	*Select*	the text
Step 2	*Click*	Mouse over in the On button list on the DHTML Effects toolbar
Step 3	*Click*	Formatting in the Apply button list on the DHTML Effects toolbar
Step 4	*Click*	Choose Font in the Effects button list on the DHTML Effects toolbar

The Font tab in the Font dialog box opens. Your dialog box should look similar to Figure 4-10.

FIGURE 4-10
Font Dialog Box

Step 5	*Click*	Bold in the Font style: list
Step 6	*Click*	The Red tile in the Color: grid
Step 7	*Click*	OK

| Step 8 | *View* | the page in the Preview tab and move the mouse pointer over the text to see the animation; then return to the Normal tab |

You can apply multiple effects to some page elements, such as text. In addition to the font formatting, you want to add a double border to the text on the mouse-over action. To add a double border:

| Step 1 | *Click* | Choose Border in the Effect button list on the DHTML Effects toolbar |

The Borders tab in the Borders and Shading dialog box opens. Your dialog box should look similar to Figure 4-11.

FIGURE 4-11
Borders and Shading
Dialog Box

MOUSE TIP

You can copy animation from one page element to another using the Format Painter button on the Standard toolbar.

Step 2	*Click*	Box in the Setting: group
Step 3	*Click*	double in the Style: list
Step 4	*Click*	the Blue tile in the Color: grid
Step 5	*Click*	OK
Step 6	*Review*	the animations in the Preview tab and return to the Normal tab
Step 7	*Deselect*	the text
Step 8	*Save & Close*	the *products.htm* page
Step 9	*Close*	the DHTML Effects toolbar

chapter
four

Page transitions are another type of animation you can add to a web page or site.

4.c Formatting Page Transitions

Page transitions are special animation effects added to a web. Viewers see these when entering or leaving the web site. You can also add page transition effects to individual web pages. Viewers see these transition effects as they browse the site, moving from page to page. You want to add transition effects to the home page as viewers enter or leave the page.

To add transition effects to the *index.htm* page:

Step 1	*Open*	the *index.htm* page in the Normal tab in Page view
Step 2	*Click*	Format
Step 3	*Click*	Page Transition

The Page Transitions dialog box that opens should look similar to Figure 4-12.

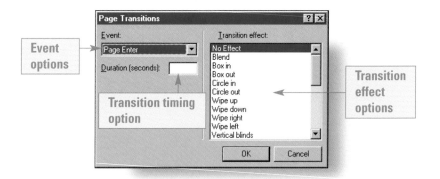

You select the transition event, effect, and duration in this dialog box.

Step 4	*Click*	the Event: list arrow
Step 5	*Click*	Page Enter, if necessary
Step 6	*Key*	3 in the Duration (seconds): text box
Step 7	*Click*	Vertical blinds in the Transition effect: list

Step 8	*Click*	OK
Step 9	*Open*	the Page Transitions dialog box
Step 10	*Click*	Page Exit in the Event: list
Step 11	*Key*	3 in the Duration (seconds): text box
Step 12	*Click*	Vertical blinds in the Transition effect: list
Step 13	*Click*	OK
Step 14	*Save*	the *index.htm* page

You can test the page transition animation in the Preview tab. To review the page transitions:

Step 1	*View*	the *index.htm* page in the Preview tab
Step 2	*Click*	the Party Packages hyperlink
Step 3	*Observe*	the animation as the *products.htm* page loads
Step 4	*Click*	the Home navigation button at the top of the page
Step 5	*Observe*	the animation as the *index.htm* page loads
Step 6	*Switch*	to the Normal tab

Now you want to see how your changes look when the web pages are viewed in a web browser.

4.d Previewing a Web in a Web Browser

One way to see how a web page looks is to view it in the Preview tab in Page view. However, this doesn't always show you exactly how page transitions or web elements appear on the page when viewed in a web browser. To get a more accurate preview, you can launch your web browser and load the current page with a button on the Standard toolbar.

To preview the *index.htm* page in a web browser:

Step 1	*Click*	the Preview in Browser button on the Standard toolbar

> **CAUTION TIP**
>
> For best results when previewing page transitions, you should open your web browser and then open the *index.htm* as a local file. The page transitions appear as you move to and from the *index.htm* page.

chapter
four

Step 2	*Observe*	that the page banner is not centered on the page
Step 3	*Point to*	the Party Packages hyperlink to view the animated hyperlink
Step 4	*Click*	the Party Packages hyperlink
Step 5	*Observe*	the page transition animation as the Party Packages page loads
Step 6	*Observe*	the position of the page banner
Step 7	*Point to*	the introduction text to observe the DHTML effects
Step 8	*Click*	the Home navigational hyperlink button above the page banner
Step 9	*Observe*	the page transition animation as the home page reloads
Step 10	*Close*	the web browser

To enhance the appearance of the pages that contain navigation buttons and a page banner, you want to center them horizontally on the page.

4.e Editing Content within Shared Borders for an Entire Web

A **shared border** is an area at the top, bottom, left, or right edge of a web page that is common to multiple pages in a web. The Corporate Presence wizard you used to create the Sample_Web included navigation bars and a page banner in the top shared border on all pages. If you edit an element, such as the page banner on one page, the editing occurs on all the pages that share the border.

You can select web page elements, such as page banners, navigation buttons, and horizontal lines, and then position them with the alignment buttons on the Formatting toolbar.

To center the page banner on the *index.htm* page:

| Step 1 | *Click* | the page banner to select it |
| Step 2 | *Click* | the Center button ▦ on the Formatting toolbar |

Step 3	*Click*	the Home and Contest navigation buttons above the page banner to select them (both are selected with one click)
Step 4	*Click*	the Center button ▤ on the Formatting toolbar
Step 5	*Click*	the Preview in Browser button 🔍 on the Standard toolbar
Step 6	*Click*	Yes to save the page
Step 7	*Click*	OK to close the confirmation dialog box
Step 8	*Observe*	the realigned navigation buttons and page banner
Step 9	*Click*	the Party Packages hyperlink
Step 10	*Observe*	the realigned navigation buttons and page banner
Step 11	*Close*	the web browser
Step 12	*Close*	the web and save pages if asked

The animation and other effects you added to the Sample_Web will help capture viewers' attention. Your next step is to add images and sound to pages in the web.

chapter
four

Summary

- ► Bulleted and numbered lists are used in web pages to itemize information.

- ► You can create, or quickly switch between, bulleted and numbered lists by selecting the list text and clicking the appropriate button on the Formatting toolbar.

- ► You can also create multi-level bulleted or numbered lists to nest itemized information.

- ► Horizontal lines are used in a web page to separate text or add an attractive element.

- ► A hit counter calculates and displays the number of times a page has been visited.

- ► Scrolling text used in a web page to catch a viewer's eye can be added in a marquee.

- ► Dynamic HTML (DHTML) is an extension of the HTML language; it enables you to add animation effects to web page elements.

- ► Page transitions are special animation effects that viewers see when they enter or exit a web site or browse from page to page at a web site.

- ► To get a more accurate preview of a web page, you can preview it in your web browser instead of the Preview tab in Page view.

- ► Shared borders permit easy editing of common page elements.

Commands Review

Action	Menu Bar	Shortcut Menu	Toolbar/Mouse	Keyboard
Create a bulleted or numbered list	Format, Bullets and Numbering			ALT + O, N
Create a nested, multi-level list				
Insert a horizontal line	Insert, Horizontal Line			ALT + I, L
Insert a hit counter	Insert, Component, Hit Counter			ALT + I, O, C
Insert a marquee	Insert, Component, Marquee			ALT + I, O, M
Format text in a marquee	Format, Font	Right-click the marquee, click Font	Various buttons on the Formatting toolbar	ALT + O, F
Apply DHTML animation effects	Format, Dynamic HTML Effects			ALT + O, E
Apply page transition effects	Format, Page Transition			ALT + O, A
Preview a page in a web browser	File, Preview in Browser			ALT+ F, B CTRL + SHIFT + B

Concepts Review

Circle the correct answer.

1. You can use horizontal lines to:
[a] itemize information.
[b] add movement to a page when the viewer enters the web site.
[c] create text that scrolls across the page.
[d] separate text on a web page.

2. A hit counter:
[a] adds animation to a web page element.
[b] adds movement to page when the viewer exits the web site.
[c] calculates and displays the number of viewers for a web page.
[d] enables you to preview page transitions.

3. You can use a marquee to:
[a] add moving text to a web page.
[b] add DHTML effects to text on web page.
[c] separate text.
[d] view page transitions.

4. You preview a web page in a browser:
[a] to more clearly see the page transitions and placement of elements on a page.
[b] because it takes less time.
[c] to see page transitions that cannot be viewed in the Preview tab.
[d] to see DHTML animation that cannot be viewed in the Preview tab.

5. You can quickly format the text in a marquee with buttons on the:
[a] DHTML Effects toolbar.
[b] Standard toolbar.
[c] Formatting toolbar.
[d] Report toolbar.

6. DHTML is the abbreviation for:
[a] Dynamic HTML.
[b] Dynamic HyperMedia Markup Language.
[c] Diversified HyperText Markup Language.
[d] Diversified HTML.

7. Which of the following is not one of the three steps in applying DHTML effects:
[a] select the event.
[b] save the page.
[c] apply the effect.
[d] choose effect settings.

8. You can copy animation effects from one page element to another using the:
[a] Copy Effects button.
[b] Insert Component button.
[c] Format Painter button.
[d] Page Transition button.

9. To finish a bulleted or numbered list, you can press the:
[a] SHIFT key.
[b] ALT key.
[c] BACKSPACE key.
[d] SPACEBAR.

10. Special animation effects that viewers see when they enter or exit a web site or browse pages at a web site are called:
[a] DHTML effects.
[b] page transition effects.
[c] formatting effects.
[d] programming effects.

Circle **T** if the statement is true or **F** if the statement is false.

T   F   1. You can use graphic bullets but not numbers to itemize information on a web page.

T   F   2. To remove bullets or numbers from a list, you must use the Bullets and Numbering command on the Format menu.

T   F   3. Dynamic HTML is an extension of the HyperText Markup Language.

chapter four

T F   4. You can add page transitions to only the home page.

T F   5. You can apply only one DHTML effect to a web page element.

T F   6. Page banners and navigation bars that appear on all pages in the web are often placed in shared borders.

T F   7. Once you create a bulleted list, you cannot convert it to a numbered list.

T F   8. The only way to preview your web pages is in the Preview tab in Page view.

T F   9. You cannot see a hit counter component unless the web page is published to a server.

T F   10. You can create only single-level bulleted or numbered lists.

Glossary

Use online <u>H</u>elp to look up the following words in the FrontPage glossary. Then, using your word processing program, create a document listing each word and its definition. Save and print the document.

1. Dynamic HTML

2. Hit Counter component

3. page banner

4. Marquee component

Skills Review

Exercise 1

1. Open the Anderson web located in the Chapter_4 folder on the Data Disk.

2. Open the *index.htm* file in the Normal tab in Page view.

3. Select the introduction text.

4. Apply the DHTML effect: on page load, apply the spiral effect.

5. Preview the page to observe the effect.

6. Remove the DHTML effect.

7. Apply the DHTML effect: on click, apply the fly-out effect, apply the left effect.

8. Preview the page and click the text to test the effect.

9. Remove the DHTML effect.

10. Apply the DHTML effect: on double-click, apply a dark green border.

11. Preview the page and double-click the text to test the effect.

12. Remove the DHTML effect.

13. Apply the DHTML effect: on mouse over, apply the All Caps formatting effect.

14. Preview the page and move the mouse pointer over the text to test the effect.

15. Save the page and close the web.

16. Close the DHTML Effects toolbar.

Exercise 2

1. Open the Roberta_Maxwell web located in the Chapter_4 folder on the Data Disk.

2. Open the *favorite.htm* page in the Normal tab in Page view.

3. Select the list of web sites and add bullets to the list.

4. Save the page.

5. Open the *index.htm* page in the Normal tab in Page view.

6. Insert a blank line between the introductory paragraph and the contact information.

7. Insert a horizontal line at the new blank line.

8. Save the page.

9. Preview, print preview, and print the pages in the web.

10. Close the web.

Exercise 3

1. Open the Secretarial4 web located in the Chapter_4 folder on the Data Disk.

2. Open the *index.htm* page in the Normal tab in Page view.

3. Create a bulleted list in the second column of the table using the following text:

Letter and memo composition
Form letters and envelopes
Telephone answering services
Fax, e-mail, and mailbox services

4. Display the Tables toolbar and center the bulleted list vertically in the table.

5. Insert a blank line above the contact information.

6. Insert a horizontal line at the blank line.

7. Select the text "Contact me for our special volume rates!"

8. Open the Marquee properties dialog box and observe that the selected text already is in the <u>T</u>ext: text box.

9. Set the text to scroll continuously to the right and change the background color to silver.

10. Format the text with the Strong effect in the Font dialog box.

11. Preview, print preview, and print the page.

12. Save the page and close the web.

Exercise 4

1. Open the Rivers web located in the Chapter_4 folder on the Data Disk.

2. Open the *index.htm* page in the Normal tab in Page view.

3. Click at the first blank line.

4. Turn on bullets and key "Microsoft Office 2000."

chapter four

5. Create a multi-level bulleted list with the following items as second level-bullets below Microsoft Office 2000:

Word 2000
Excel 2000
PowerPoint 2000
Access 2000
FrontPage 2000

6. Select the first-level bullet and change the font size to 5 (18 pt).

7. Select all the second-level bullets and change the font size to 4 (14 pt) and the font color to brown.

8. Delete any blank lines following the bulleted list so that there is only one blank line between the list and the horizontal line.

9. Select the Software Applications text following the introductory text.

10. Apply the DHTML effect: on mouse over, apply a double, brown border.

11. Preview the DHTML effect.

12. Save the page.

13. Print preview and print the page.

14. Close the web.

15. Close the DHTML toolbar.

Exercise 5

1. Open the Rameriz4 web located in the Chapter_4 folder on the Data Disk.

2. Open the *index.htm* page in the Normal tab in Page view.

3. Add bullets to the detail items under each Date 1, 2, and 3 headings.

4. Open the *members.htm* page in the Normal tab in Page view.

5. Create a numbered list using the items beginning with "Alastname" and ending with "Zfirstname."

6. Open the *schedule.htm* page in the Normal tab in Page view.

7. Add a first-level bullet to the "This Week" and "Next Week" headings.

8. Add second-level bullets to the detail lines below each week heading.

9. Save all the edited pages.

10. Preview the web in your web browser.

11. Close the web and save pages when asked.

Exercise 6

1. Open the Hamilton4 web located in the Chapter_4 folder on the Data Disk.

2. Open the *index.htm* page in the Normal tab in Page view.

3. Create a borderless, centered, one-cell table below the text "We clean:".

4. Create a bulleted list inside the table using the following text:

windows, inside and out
carpets
furniture

5. Format the bulleted list text with the 4 (14 pt) font size.

6. Insert a horizontal line below the bulleted list table.

7. Center the text "You are visitor number," below the horizontal line.

8. Format the text with the 4 (14 pt) font size, if necessary.

9. Insert a hit counter using the fourth style after the "You are visitor number" text.

10. Center the following contact information below the hit counter. Use the SHIFT + ENTER keys between each line to insert a line break instead of a paragraph mark. Use the Symbol command on the Insert menu to insert the copyright symbol. Use the Date and Time command on the Insert menu to insert the date this page was last edited.

Hamilton Industrial Cleaning
9800 Streeter Avenue
Muncie, IN 47304-9800
Phone 219-555-7654 Fax 219-555-7655
hamilton@industrialcleaning.com
© 2001 Hamilton Industrial Cleaning
Last Updated (today's date)

11. Select the contact information text and format it with the 2 (10 pt) font size and bold.

12. Save the page and preview it in your web browser.

13. Check the spelling on the page.

14. Print preview and print the page.

15. Close the web.

Exercise 7

1. Open the Chocolate4 web located in the Chapter_4 folder on the Data Disk.

2. Open the *index.htm* page in the Normal tab in Page view.

3. Center the navigation buttons and the page banner.

4. Click in the introductory text table and use the Convert command on the Table menu to convert the table to text.

5. Left-align the introductory text.

6. Delete the mission statement comment and key the following text:

Our mission is to provide our customers with high-quality, unusual chocolate specialty items, including individually wrapped candies, boxed candies, cakes, pies, and specially-molded chocolate novelties.

7. Delete the company profile section, including the following horizontal line.

8. Select the introductory text and apply the DHTML effect: on page load, apply the wave effect.

9. Preview the animation effect.

10. Print preview and print the *index.htm* page.

11. Close the web and save pages if asked.

Exercise 8

1. Open the Nguyen_Software web located in the Chapter_4 folder on the Data Disk.

2. Open the *index.htm* page in the Normal tab in Page view.

chapter four

3. Apply the following page transition: on page entry, random dissolve in one second; on page exit, random dissolve in one second.

4. Save the page.

5. Preview the *index.htm* page in your web browser. Test the page transition by using the hyperlinks to load different pages in the web and then return to the home page.

6. Close the web browser.

7. Close the web and save pages if asked.

Case Projects

Project 1

Play City is a chain of childcare facilities with a home office in Los Angeles, California. Play City has childcare facilities located in malls in a number of major U.S. cities. These facilities specialize in providing childcare for mall employees or workers in nearby buildings. Jennifer Davis, the general manager of Play City, hires you to create a web site. Using a word processing program, create a plan for the web site. Then create the web site using FrontPage wizards or templates. Include at least three pages in addition to the home page. Include company contact information on the home page. Include webmaster contact information, a copyright notice, and modification date on each page. Create a custom theme based on one of the preset themes and apply it to the entire web site. Add appropriate text with formatting to the remaining pages. Use tables and bulleted or numbered lists as necessary to organize the text. Add DHTML effects to text on the home page. Insert a hit counter on the home page. Add page transitions to all the pages. Preview the web pages in your browser and make any necessary adjustments to the alignment of elements on the pages. Print the web pages. Save and print the plan.

Project 2

Mark Eng, of Eng Landscaping Partners located in Chicago, Illinois, hires you to create a web site for his company. Using a word-processing program, create a plan for the Eng Landscaping Partners web site. Use appropriate FrontPage templates and wizards to create the web site and include at least four pages in addition to the home page. Include company contact information on the home page. Include webmaster contact information, a copyright notice, and modification date on each page. Create a custom theme based on a preset theme and apply it to all the pages in the web. Use tables and bulleted and numbered lists to organize text on the pages. Key appropriate text in the pages. Insert a scrolling text marquee on the home page. Insert or remove horizontal lines as appropriate. Add DHTML effects to text on the home page. Print the web pages. Save and print the plan.

Project 3

Based on your proposal, LaTasha Cooper, owner of Cooper Enterprises in Atlanta, Georgia, hires you to create a web site for her company. Use appropriate FrontPage templates and wizards to create the web site and include at least five pages in addition to the home page. Include company contact information on the home page. Include webmaster contact information, a copyright notice, and modification date on each page. Create a custom theme based on a preset theme and apply it to all the pages in the web. Use tables and bulleted and numbered lists to organize text on the pages. Key appropriate text in the pages. Insert a scrolling text marquee and a hit counter on the home page. Insert or remove horizontal lines as appropriate. Add DHTML effects to text on the home page. Add page transitions on site entry and exit. Print the web pages.

Project 4

Beatrice Wang is the president of the nonprofit group Children Are Our Future. The organization provides speakers and training for educators in how to work with children who have special educational needs. You volunteer to help Ms. Wang create a web site for the organization. Connect to the Internet, launch your web browser, and search for examples of other web sites for nonprofit organizations. Print at least five web pages.

Using a word processing program, create a plan for the Children Are Our Future web site. Use appropriate FrontPage templates and wizards to create the web site and include at least three pages in addition to the home page. Include the organization contact information on the home page. Include webmaster contact information, a copyright notice, and modification date on each page. Create a custom theme based on a preset theme and apply it to all the pages in the web. Use tables and bulleted and numbered lists to organize text on the pages. Key appropriate text in the pages. Insert a scrolling text marquee and a hit counter on the home page. Insert or remove horizontal lines as appropriate. Add DHTML effects to text on the home page. Print the web pages. Save and print the plan.

Project 5

You meet Chamique Evans, executive assistant to the president of your company, for lunch. She mentions that the president wants to add more excitement to the company web site. She asks you what features can be added to the web site to make it more interesting to viewers. You agree to think about the problem and get back to her. Using a word processing program, write Chamique a memo explaining how itemizing with bullets and numbers, marquees, hit counters, horizontal lines, and animation can be used to enhance the web. Describe each feature and include the instructions for applying it. Save and print the memo.

Project 6

Joe Chen, the training manager for Anderson Technical Services, was so pleased with your seminar on creating and editing tables that he asks

you to prepare a demonstration on applying DHTML effects and page transitions to a group of managers who want to see some examples of animation they can use in their individual department web pages. Using a word processing program, create an outline of your presentation. Save and print the document. With your instructor's approval, use the outline to describe the process to your classmates.

Project 7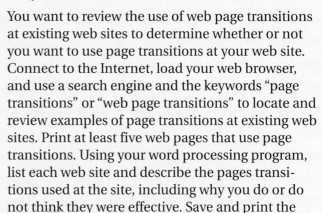

You want to review the use of web page transitions at existing web sites to determine whether or not you want to use page transitions at your web site. Connect to the Internet, load your web browser, and use a search engine and the keywords "page transitions" or "web page transitions" to locate and review examples of page transitions at existing web sites. Print at least five web pages that use page transitions. Using your word processing program, list each web site and describe the pages transitions used at the site, including why you do or do not think they were effective. Save and print the document.

Project 8

Moira Kennedy, a new employee in your department, has been assigned the task of updating a web. She notices that when she makes her modifications on one page, all the other pages in the web are automatically changed. She asks you for an explanation. Using online <u>H</u>elp, review all the topics on shared borders. Then, using a word processing program, write Moira a memo describing shared borders and explaining how to edit their content. Save and print the memo.

Adding Multimedia to Web Pages

Chapter Overview

The World Wide Web is a multimedia environment, which means that web pages can include text, spoken audio, music, images, animation, and video. Some web sites use multimedia to identify, or "brand," a web site or to express thoughts and ideas. Images, such as photos and drawings, help illustrate the ideas or products on a page. Sound and video enhance the web site message by adding music and movement. In this chapter, you insert and edit various images, such as a company logo, and then explore adding sound and video to web pages.

Case profile

Sarah Whaley and Bob Avila were pleased with the sample Sarah's PartyWorld web you presented at the last committee meeting, and they approved it. Before the next meeting you want to add the company logo to all pages and insert images and text on the individual party theme page to illustrate and describe the available theme packages. You also consider adding sound and video to the web.

chapter five

5.a Adding or Importing Images

You can insert two kinds of images on a web page: clip art and photos. **Clip art**, electronic illustrations, and photos are available in a variety of file formats, but the most common formats inserted in a web page are **GIF** (Graphics Interchange Format) or **JPEG** (Joint Photographic Experts Group) format. GIF and JPEG files compress an image, reducing the file size and enabling a web page to load faster.

You want to insert the new company logo on all the pages in the sample Sarah's PartyWorld web. You have the logo GIF file on disk. Because the Corporate Presence Wizard you used to create the Sample_Web inserted shared borders, you can insert the logo in a shared border on the home page, which then automatically inserts the logo on the other pages in the web. To insert the company logo on the home page:

> **MENU TIP**
>
> You can insert images by pointing to the Picture command on the Insert menu and clicking Clip Art, From File, or Video.

Step 1	**Open**	the Sample_Web you modified in Chapter 4
Step 2	**Open**	the *index.htm* page in the Normal tab in Page view
Step 3	**Delete**	the logo comment at the top of the page
Step 4	**Delete**	the Company Logo text object at the top of the page
Step 5	**Click**	the Insert Picture From File button on the Standard toolbar

The Picture dialog box that opens should look similar to Figure 5-1.

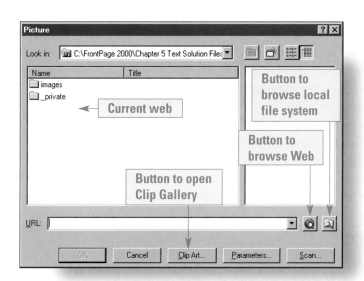

FIGURE 5-1
Picture Dialog Box

You can insert a picture from the current web, another web page, or your file system in this dialog box. The logo image is stored on your file system.

Step 6	*Click*	the File button 🔍 to open the Select File dialog box
Step 7	*Switch*	to the Chapter_5 folder on the Data Disk
Step 8	*Select*	the *sarahslogo.gif* file
Step 9	*Click*	OK
Step 10	*Observe*	the new logo graphic inserted in the page

You can format the logo image by repositioning it on the page, changing its orientation, and sizing it. To select and center the logo:

Step 1	*Click*	the logo to select it
Step 2	*Click*	the Center button 🢒 on the Formatting toolbar
Step 3	*Deselect*	the logo

Your screen should look similar to Figure 5-2.

FIGURE 5-2
New Company Logo
Centered on Home Page

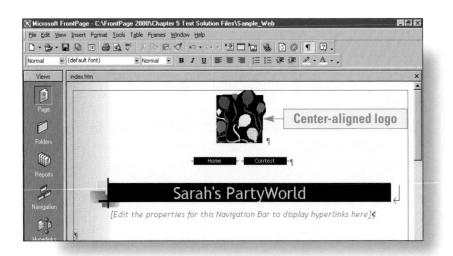

Step 4	*Save*	the *index.htm* page

The Save Embedded Files dialog box that opens should look similar to Figure 5-3.

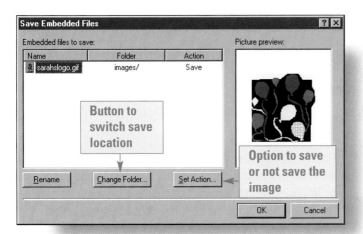

FIGURE 5-3
Save Embedded Files
Dialog Box

When you insert an image that is not already stored in the current web, FrontPage prompts you to save the image. It is a good idea to save a copy of the image file in the current web so that it is always available, in case the original file is moved or deleted from its original location. You want to save it in the images folder of the current web.

| Step 5 | *Click* | Change Folder |

The Change Folder dialog box that opens should look similar to Figure 5-4.

You specify the images folder in this dialog box.

| Step 6 | *Click* | the images folder |
| Step 7 | *Click* | OK in each dialog box |

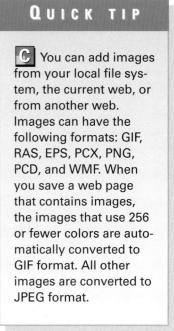

QUICK TIP

C You can add images from your local file system, the current web, or from another web. Images can have the following formats: GIF, RAS, EPS, PCX, PNG, PCD, and WMF. When you save a web page that contains images, the images that use 256 or fewer colors are automatically converted to GIF format. All other images are converted to JPEG format.

FIGURE 5-4
Change Folder Dialog Box

Step 8	*Preview*	the *index.htm* page
Step 9	*Preview*	the remaining pages and observe that the logo image is automatically inserted on all the pages
Step 10	*View*	the *index.htm* page in the Normal tab in Page view

notes

For the remainder of this book, you should preview any modifications you make to a web page in the Preview tab or in your web browser. The instructions will not include preview steps, unless required to complete the activity.

After previewing the home page, you decide that the company logo should appear in the bottom shared border above the webmaster contact and copyright information.

Using the Clipboard

You can **copy** (or duplicate) a web page element, such as text or an image, and then **paste** (or insert) it at a new location on the same web page or a different web page. You can also move text or an image to a new location by **cutting** (removing) it from the current location and pasting it at the new location. Any web page element you cut or copy is stored temporarily on the **Clipboard**, a reserved place in your computer's memory that stores one item at a time. When you cut or copy a second element, that item replaces the contents of the Clipboard.

You want to move the company logo to the shared border at the bottom of the page. To cut and paste the logo:

Step 1	*Right-click*	the logo image
Step 2	*Click*	Cut
Step 3	*Scroll*	to view the shared border at the bottom of the page
Step 4	*Right-click*	at the blank line above the webmaster contact information
Step 5	*Click*	Paste
Step 6	*Center*	the logo image

You also want to center the information below the logo image.

Step 7	*Click*	in the webmaster contact information below the logo image
Step 8	*Center*	the text
Step 9	*Save*	the page

MENU TIP

In Page view, you can cut or copy and paste web elements with the Cut, Copy, and Paste commands on the Edit menu or shortcut menu. In Folders view or the Folder List, these commands enable you to move or duplicate files or folders. In Navigation view, these commands enable you to rearrange or expand the web site's structure.

Your screen should look similar to Figure 5-5.

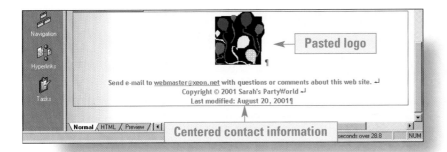

FIGURE 5-5
Company Logo Pasted at
Bottom of Home Page

Now you are ready to add appropriate text and images for each of the available Holiday Party theme packages on the individual product page.

Positioning Text and Graphics on a Web Page

To add some fun to a web page, you can insert **animated clip art** (sometimes called an **animated GIF** or **motion clip**), which is an illustration that includes movement. You decide to use motion clips on the individual holiday party theme page.

Centering an Image or Text within a Table Cell

You can use multi-column tables to organize the motion clips and appropriate text side by side. To create a table and insert motion clips with text:

Step 1	*Open*	the *prod01.htm* page in the Normal tab in Page view
Step 2	*Select*	the text beginning "This paragraph contains" and delete it
Step 3	*Create*	a two-column table at the insertion point
Step 4	*Edit*	the table to remove the border and center it
Step 5	*Size*	the first column to be approximately 1 inch wide and the second column to be approximately 2 ½ inches wide, using the mouse pointer
Step 6	*Click*	in the first cell to position the insertion point, if necessary
Step 7	*Click*	the Insert Picture From File button [image] on the Standard toolbar
Step 8	*Open*	the Chapter_5 folder on the Data Disk
Step 9	*Double-click*	New_Year's_Eve
Step 10	*Press*	the TAB key to move the insertion point to the second column

M O U S E   T I P

In Page view, you can cut or copy and paste web elements with the Cut, Copy, and Paste buttons on the Standard toolbar. In Folders view or the Folder List, these commands enable you to move or duplicate files or folders. In Navigation view, these commands enable you to rearrange or expand the web site's structure.

chapter
five

| Step 11 | *Key* | New Year's Eve Party |
| Step 12 | *Format* | the text as bold, 5 (18 pt) font size, and centered in the cell |

You want to add descriptive text in a second row that spans the width of the entire table. To add text in a second row:

Step 1	*Add*	a second row by moving the insertion point to the last cell in the table and pressing the TAB key
Step 2	*Merge*	the cells in the second row by selecting the row and clicking the Merge cells command on the Tables menu
Step 3	*Key*	Our New Year's Eve Party package helps you ring in the new year in style on December 31st!
Step 4	*Format*	the text in the second row as 4 (14 pt), bold, and centered
Step 5	*Delete*	the Key Benefits heading and following bulleted list
Step 6	*Save*	the page and save the New_Year's_Eve file in the images folder in the current web
Step 7	*Preview*	the page and observe the animation

You follow the same procedure to add the information for the remaining holiday party packages. First, you create the two-column table. Then, you insert the appropriate image from the Chapter_5 folder on the Data Disk, and key and format the package name. Finally, you create a second row, merge the cells, and then key and format the descriptive text of your choice. Include the calendar day in your descriptive text whenever possible. Each holiday should appear in a separate table; insert a blank line between each table.

| Step 8 | *Continue* | by creating tables and adding the appropriate images and formatted text for:
Valentine's_Day
St._Patrick's_Day
Easter
Memorial_Day
Independence_Day
Labor_Day
Halloween
Christmas
Hanukkah
Kwanzaa |
| Step 9 | *Save* | the page |

After adding the images and text to the holiday party page, you want to look at ways to further modify the company logo.

5.b Editing Images

There are many ways to change the appearance of an image or picture by using buttons on the Pictures toolbar. When you select an image, the Pictures toolbar usually appears at the bottom of the window above the status bar. If it does not appear, you can display it with the toolbar shortcut menu.

Coloring Images

You can edit an image by modifying its color. **Contrast** is the degree of difference between the lightest and darkest areas of an image. **Brightness** is the measure of the total amount of light in the image colors. **Wash out** decreases a picture's contrast and increases its brightness. You can also convert images from color to black and white. You can remove areas of an image that you don't want by **cropping** the image. You can also crop an image to change its proportions. Buttons for all these functions are included on the Pictures toolbar.

To display the Pictures toolbar:

Step 1	*Scroll*	to view the logo image
Step 2	*Click*	the logo image to select it
Step 3	*Observe*	the Pictures toolbar above the status bar

Your screen should look similar to Figure 5-6.

QUICK TIP

C If you want to label an image, you can insert text on it. First, select the image and then click the Text button on the Pictures toolbar. If the picture is a format other than GIF, FrontPage prompts you to save it in GIF format, the only format that supports text on an image. Then, key the text in a text box on the image. Use the mouse to move and size the text box. To format the text, click the text box to select it, select the text with the mouse, and format it as desired.

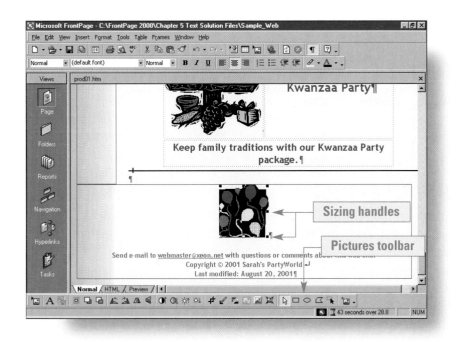

FIGURE 5-6
Selected Logo on Holiday Party Page

chapter
five

You want to experiment with different changes to the logo.

Rotating Images

Rotating an image changes its angle on the page. You can rotate an image in 90-degree increments to the left (counterclockwise) or right (clockwise). Any changes you make to an image are not effective until you save the image. Therefore, before you save the page and the image, you can use the Restore button on the Pictures toolbar to return an image to its last saved appearance.

To rotate the logo to the left 180 degrees and then restore it:

Step 1	*Verify*	the logo image is selected
Step 2	*Click*	the Rotate Left button 🔄 on the Pictures toolbar
Step 3	*Observe*	the logo's new angle

Your screen should look similar to Figure 5-7.

FIGURE 5-7
Rotated Logo on Holiday
Party Page

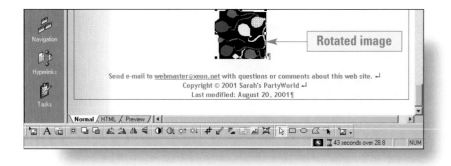

Step 4	*Click*	the Rotate Left button 🔄 on the Pictures toolbar
Step 5	*Observe*	the logo's new angle
Step 6	*Click*	the Restore button 🖼 on the Pictures toolbar

Flipping Images

Images can be **flipped**, or reversed, both vertically and horizontally. You may want to flip an image to emphasize a different aspect of the image. To flip the logo image and restore it:

Step 1	*Click*	the Flip Horizontal button 🔀 on the Pictures toolbar
Step 2	*Observe*	that the image is reversed left to right

Step 3	*Click*	the Restore button on the Pictures toolbar
Step 4	*Click*	the Flip Vertical button on the Pictures toolbar
Step 5	*Observe*	that the image is reversed top to bottom
Step 6	*Restore*	the image

Beveling Images

To add a border with a raised, three-dimensional appearance, you can **bevel** the image. One reason you might want to bevel an image is to use the image as a button-style hyperlink.

To add a beveled border to the logo:

Step 1	*Click*	the Bevel button  on the Pictures toolbar
Step 2	*Observe*	the three-dimensional border on the bottom and right side of the image

A beveled border is not appropriate for the logo.

Step 3	*Restore*	the image

Resizing and Resampling Images

Web pages with images can take a long time to download. One way to speed up the download time for pages with images is to resize and resample the images. **Resizing** changes the dimensions of an image displayed in a web browser. However, resizing does not change the size of the original image file. Although you can make the on-screen image smaller, the download time remains unchanged until you resample the image. **Resampling** an image changes its pixel size to match the display size.

To resize and resample the logo image:

Step 1	*Move*	the mouse pointer to the lower-right corner sizing handle
Step 2	*Drag*	the sizing handle diagonally up until the image is approximately half its current size
Step 3	*Click*	the Resample button on the Pictures toolbar
Step 4	*Deselect*	the image
Step 5	*Save*	the page and the logo image

M O U S E   T I P

You can resize an image by changing its height and width in the Appearance tab of the image's Properties dialog box or by dragging its selection or sizing handles. If you drag a corner sizing handle, the image is sized proportionally.

chapter
five

| Step 6 | *Open* | the *products.htm* page in the Normal tab in Page view |
| Step 7 | *Scroll* | the page and observe the resized logo image |

Sarah wants to use the original logo, which is stored in the old Sarah's PartyWorld web, on one page in the new web.

5.c Adding or Importing Elements from a Web Site

You can add web page elements from other sites on the Web or a company intranet to your web pages. When you add an image from another site, you can either save the image to your web or save a reference to the image on the original web page on your own web site. However, if a referenced image is removed from the original web page, it is no longer available for your web page. When viewers download a page, they may see a placeholder where the image should appear.

You should also be very careful when copying text or images, sound, or video from other sources or other web pages to your own pages. Most music, video, and web page content is copyrighted. You *must* contact the organization and get permission before you use any material from another source or web site in your web pages.

notes

You will need to access the Chapter_1 folder on the Data Disk to complete this activity.

You want to use the original Sarah's PartyWorld logo, named *birthday.wmf* on the catalog page. To make room at the top of the *products.htm* page for the image:

Step 1	*Verify*	that the insertion point is at the beginning of the text at the top of the page
Step 2	*Press*	the ENTER key to create a new line above the text
Step 3	*Remove*	the DHTML effects from the new line
Step 4	*Display*	the Folder List, if necessary

You displayed the Folder List so you can see the imported image file. To import the original logo from the old web:

| Step 1 | *Click* | File |
| Step 2 | *Click* | Import |

The Import dialog box opens. You can import a file or folder or an entire web from this dialog box.

Step 3	*Click*	Add File
Step 4	*Switch*	to the Chapter_1 folder on the Data Disk
Step 5	*Open*	the images folder in the My_Webs folder
Step 6	*Double-click*	Birthday (.wmf)
Step 7	*Observe*	the *birthday.wmf* image is listed in the Import dialog box

Your Import dialog box should look similar to Figure 5-8.

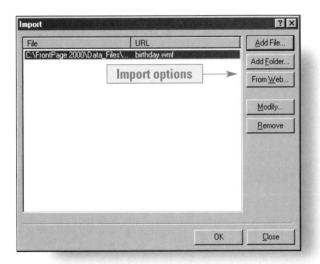

FIGURE 5-8
Import Dialog Box

| Step 8 | *Click* | OK |
| Step 9 | *Observe* | that the *birthday.wmf* file is now listed in the Folder List |

chapter
five

QUICK TIP

You can add a border to an image in the Appearance tab of the Picture Properties dialog box.

You want to copy the birthday image from the Folder List to the open web page and then store the logo in the images folder. You can do this using drag and drop. To place and format the birthday image:

Step 1	**Drag**	the *birthday.wmf* file to the blank line at the top of the web page
Step 2	**Drag**	the *birthday.wmf* file to the images folder
Step 3	**Close**	the Folder List
Step 4	**Resize**	the image approximately 20% larger by dragging the lower-right sizing handle down diagonally
Step 5	**Deselect**	the image
Step 6	**Save**	the page

Your screen should look similar to Figure 5-9.

FIGURE 5-9
Catalog Page with Imported and Enlarged Image

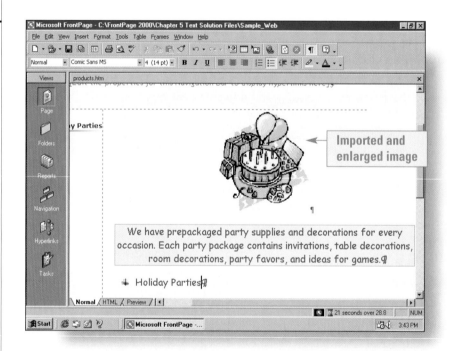

MENU TIP

You can set an option to display alternative text in place of an image if the image cannot be displayed in the viewer's browser. Some browsers may also display this alternative text as the image is downloading. To set the alternative text option, right-click the image and click Picture Properties. Then, click the General tab and key the alternative text in the Alternative representations Text: box.

Sarah calls to tell you that she just loaded a competitor's home page in her web browser and music played while she was viewing the page. She asks you to add background music to the new Sarah's PartyWorld home page.

5.d Adding Sound and Video Elements

Many web sites offer sound and video, in addition to informational text and images, to enhance the viewing experience. Sound files have a variety of formats. The smallest and most widely supported web page sound file format is MIDI. When you add background sound, you can have the sound **loop** (start over) and continue to play either the entire time the page is viewed or for a specified number of times and then stop.

You want to add a background sound to the home page that loops continuously while it is being viewed. To add the sound:

Step 1	*Open*	the *index.htm* page in the Normal tab in Page view
Step 2	*Right-click*	the page
Step 3	*Click*	Page Properties
Step 4	*Click*	the General tab, if necessary

The Page Properties dialog box that opens should look similar to Figure 5-10.

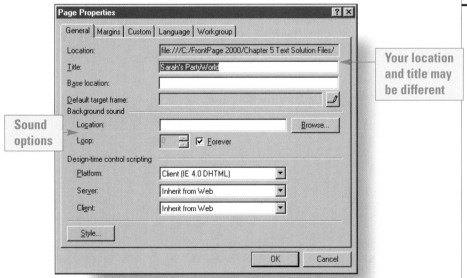

FIGURE 5-10
Page Properties Dialog Box

chapter
five

You can browse your local file system to select a sound file in this dialog box. The sound file you want is located on the Data Disk. To select the file:

Step 1	*Browse*	to open the Background Sound dialog box
Step 2	*Click*	the File button 🔍 to browse your file system
Step 3	*Switch*	to the Chapter_5 folder on the Data Disk
Step 4	*Double-click*	*jazzy.mid*
Step 5	*Click*	the Forever check box to insert a check mark, if necessary
Step 6	*Click*	OK
Step 7	*Save*	the page and save the sound file to the images folder
Step 8	*Preview*	the page to hear the sound
Step 9	*Close*	the web and save pages if asked

You can also add any kind of video clips that can be played by the Windows Media Player, a tool that plays audio, video, or animation files and that controls the settings for your multimedia computer devices. To add video, point to the Picture command on the Insert menu and click Video. If you have the Internet Explorer web browser installed, you can preview the video on the Preview tab in Page view.

The clip art images and background sound you added and edited really enhance the site. Next, you create internal and external hyperlinks in the sample web to help viewers navigate.

Summary

▶ You can insert two types of images on a web page: clip art and photos.

▶ The most commonly inserted image file types are GIF and JPEG.

▶ You can use the Clipboard to cut, copy, and paste web page elements.

▶ Images can be rotated, flipped, beveled, and resized.

▶ You can change an image's brightness, contrast, and colors to black and white.

▶ To decrease download time when a page has a large image, you can create a thumbnail image.

▶ You can insert clip art, photos, sound, and video clips from the Clip Gallery, from a location on your file system, or from another web page.

Commands Review

Action	Menu Bar	Shortcut Menu	Toolbar/Mouse	Keyboard
Insert images	Insert, Picture		◻	ALT + I, P
Duplicate or reposition an image in Page view using the Clipboard	Edit, Cut or Copy Edit, Paste	Right-click image and then click Cut or Copy Right-click the page and then click Paste	◻ ◻ ◻	ALT + E, T or C ALT + E, P CTRL + C CTRL + X CTRL + V
Rotate an image			◻ ◻	
Flip an image			◻ ◻	
Bevel an image			◻	
Resample an image			◻	
Restore an image			◻	
Create a thumbnail image			◻	
Import an image from a local file or a web page	File, Import			ALT + F, I
Display Page Properties		Right-click the page, then click Page Properties		

chapter five

Concepts Review

SCANS

Circle the correct answer.

1. Background sound on a web page:
[a] brands a web site.
[b] adds movement to a page when the viewer enters the web site.
[c] appears in a thumbnail.
[d] is stored in GIF format.

2. Images *cannot* be added from:
[a] your local file system.
[b] the Options dialog box.
[c] the current web.
[d] another web site.

3. Which of the following commands does *not* use the Clipboard:
[a] Copy.
[b] Paste.
[c] Cut.
[d] Replace.

4. Another term for a GIF image that contains animation is:
[a] media clip.
[b] active clip.
[c] motion clip.
[d] theme clip.

5. To remove an area of an image, you can:
[a] bevel it.
[b] crop it.
[c] rotate it.
[d] flip it.

6. To give a picture a raised, three-dimensional appearance, you can:
[a] resize it.
[b] change its contrast.
[c] change its brightness.
[d] bevel it.

7. Which of the following actions changes the actual size of an image file?
[a] resizing
[b] resampling
[c] rotating
[d] beveling

8. When you save a web page that contains images, any images that have fewer than 256 colors are automatically saved as:
[a] RAS files.
[b] TIFF files.
[c] JPEG files.
[d] GIF files.

9. The Clipboard is a:
[a] button on the Formatting toolbar.
[b] feature in the Pictures dialog box.
[c] tool to preview and insert clip art.
[d] reserved place in your computer's memory

10. Rotating an image gives it:
[a] increased brightness.
[b] a different angle.
[c] darker contrast.
[d] a black-and-white appearance.

Circle **T** if the statement is true or **F** if the statement is false.

T F 1. Contrast is the measure of the total amount of light in an image.

T F 2. When you insert an image that is not already in the current web, you are prompted to save the image.

T F 3. You can copy and paste text, but not images.

T F 4. GIF and JPEG files compress images, allowing for a smaller file size and faster downloading.

T   F   5. Brightness is the degree of difference between the lightest and darkest areas of an image.

T   F   6. You can flip images both horizontally and vertically.

T   F   7. Changes you make to an image are not final until you save the image.

T   F   8. You can place text on a GIF image but not a JPEG image.

T   F   9. Resizing an image changes its pixel size to match the display size.

T   F   10. It is not necessary to get permission from a webmaster before you import text or images from a web site into your own web.

Glossary

Use online <u>H</u>elp to look up the following words in the FrontPage glossary. Then, using your word processing program, create a document listing each word and its glossary definition. Save and print the document.

1. animated GIF

2. Aspect Ratio

3. Auto Thumbnail

4. background sound

5. bevel

6. embedded files

7. GIF

8. graphics file formats

9. interlaced GIF

10. JPEG

11. Microsoft Image Composer

12. PCX

13. PNG

14. progressive JPEG

15. RAS

16. TGA

17. TIFF

18. wash out

19. watermark

20. WMF

Skills Review

Exercise 1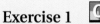

1. Open the Anderson5 web located in the Chapter_5 folder on the Data Disk.

2. Open the *index.htm* file in the Normal tab in Page view.

3. Insert a blank line above the contact information at the bottom of the page.

4. Insert a horizontal line at the blank line.

5. Insert the *building_supplies.wmf* file at the blank line above the contact information.

6. Resize the image proportionally until it is approximately 1¼ high by 1 inch wide.

7. Resample the image.

8. Save the page and save the image in the images folder.

chapter five

9. Preview, print preview, and print the page.

10. Close the web.

Exercise 2   [C]

1. Open the Roberta_Maxwell5 web located in the Chapter_5 folder on the Data Disk.

2. Open the *photo.htm* page in the Normal tab in Page view.

3. Select the first photo image and delete it.

4. Insert the *Sunset.jpg* photo image located in the Chapter_5 folder on the Data Disk.

5. Right-click the *Sunset.jpg* image and click Picture Properties. On the Appearance tab, set the Height in pixels to 300. Click the Keep Aspect ratio check box to insert a check mark, if necessary. Observe that the Width is automatically reset then click OK.

6. Replace the text "A great city:" with "My favorite beach:"

7. Delete the second photo image.

8. Insert the *Beach.jpg* photo image located in the Chapter_5 folder on the Data Disk.

9. Save the page and save both image files in the images folder.

10. Preview, print preview, and print the page.

11. Close the web.

Exercise 3   [C]

1. Open the Secretarial5 web located in the Chapter_5 folder on the Data Disk.

2. Open the *index.htm* page in the Normal tab in Page view.

3. Scroll to view the bottom of the page.

4. Click at the blank line above the contact information to position the insertion point.

5. Use the Picture command on the Insert menu to open the Clip Art Gallery dialog box.

6. Explore the clip art categories and insert an appropriate clip into the web page by right-clicking the clip and then clicking Insert on the pop-up menu.

7. Resize the clip as necessary and resample it.

8. Wash out the colors in the image.

9. Save the page and save the image in the images folder.

10. Preview, print preview, and print the page.

11. Close the web.

Exercise 4   [C]

1. Open the Rivers5 web located in the Chapter_5 folder on the Data Disk.

2. Open the *webdesign.htm* page in the Normal tab in Page view.

3. Delete the picture and the picture caption.

4. Insert the *Butterfly.gif* image located in the Chapter_5 folder on the Data Disk in the second column.

5. Resize the image approximately three times larger.

6. Save the page and save the image to the images folder.

7. Print the page.

8. Copy the image to the Clipboard.

9. Open the *index.htm* page in the Normal tab in Page view.

10. Insert a blank line above the welcome text.

11. Paste the image at the blank line.

12. Flip the image horizontally.

13. Restore the image on the *index.htm* page.

14. Save the page but do not resave the image. (*Hint:* Use the <u>S</u>et Action button in the Save Embedded Files dialog box to turn off the save option for the image.)

15. Preview, print preview, and print the page.

16. Close the web and do not save the image, if asked.

Exercise 5

1. Open the Rameriz5 web located in the Chapter_5 folder on the Data Disk.

2. Open the *index.htm* page in the Normal tab in Page view.

3. Add the *winter.mid* file located in the Chapter_5 folder on the Data Disk as background music to the home page. Let the music play continuously while the page is being viewed.

4. Open the Clip Gallery and locate an appropriate motion clip for the project logo.

5. Drag the image from the Clip Gallery into the *index.htm* page and position it immediately before the first word of the welcome paragraph.

6. Resize the image, as necessary, to fit attractively to the left of the introductory text.

7. Save the page and save the image and sound files in the images folder.

8. Preview, print preview, and print the page.

9. Close the web.

Exercise 6

1. Open the Hamilton5 web located in the Chapter_5 folder on the Data Disk.

2. Open the *index.htm* page in the Normal tab in Page view.

3. Insert the *Cleaning.gif* motion clip located in the Chapter_5 folder on the Data Disk above the hit counter.

4. Save the page and save the motion clip in the images folder.

chapter five

5. Preview the page in your web browser.

6. Print the page.

7. Close the web.

Exercise 7

1. Open the Chocolate5 web located in the Chapter_5 folder on the Data Disk.

2. Open the *products.htm* page in the Normal tab in Page view.

3. Delete the comment paragraph above the Name of Product text.

4. Create a one-cell table that is 75% of its original size with no boundary at the blank line.

5. Insert the *Chocolate_Strawberry.jpg* image located in the Chapter_5 folder on the Data Disk into the table and center the image in the table cell.

6. Open the Picture Properties dialog box and change the Width to 250 pixels. Maintain the aspect ratio.

7. Delete all text below the image and key the text "Hand-dipped chocolate strawberries."

8. Format the text as 4 (14 pt) and bold.

9. Insert a horizontal line below the text.

10. Create another table with the same properties below the horizontal line.

11. Insert the *Chocolate_Cake.jpg* image in the table.

12. Key "Chocolate cake specialties" and copy the text formatting with the Format Painter.

13. Save the page and save both image files in the images folder.

14. Preview, print preview, and print the page.

15. Close the web.

Exercise 8

1. Open the Nguyen5 web located in the Chapter_5 folder on the Data Disk.

2. Open the *index.htm* page in the Normal tab in Page view.

3. Import the *earth.jpg* image from the images folder in the Rivers5 web in the Chapter_5 folder on the Data Disk.

4. Drag the *earth.jpg* image from the Folder List to the blank line above the welcome text.

5. Center the image.

6. Rotate the image 180 degrees to the right.

7. Add the *Software.mid* background sound located in the Chapter_5 folder on the Data Disk to the home page.

8. Save the page and save the image and sound files in the images folder.

9. Preview, print preview, and print the page.

10. Close the web browser.

Case Projects

Project 1

Online Autos is a used-car business, located in Jackson, Mississippi, that displays online all the used automobiles available on the company's lots. Viewers can call or e-mail to set up an appointment to see and test-drive a car. Pat Mahoney, the general manager of Online Autos, hires you to create the web site. Using a word processing program, create a plan for the web site. Then create the web site using FrontPage wizards or templates. Include at least three pages in addition to the home page. Include company contact information on the home page. Include webmaster contact information, a copyright notice, and modification date on each page. Create a custom theme based on one of the preset themes and apply it to the entire web site. Add appropriate text with formatting to the remaining pages. Use tables and bulleted or numbered lists as necessary to organize the text. Add DHTML effects to text on the home page. Insert a hit counter on the home page. Add page transitions to all the pages. Insert and edit at least three images in the web. Preview the web pages in your browser and make any necessary adjustments to the alignment of elements on the pages. Print the web pages. Save and print the plan.

Project 2

Madeline Harris is the president of Harris Personnel, a temporary employment agency serving industrial clients. Ms. Harris hires you to create a web site for her company. Using a word processing program, create a plan for the Harris Personnel web site. Use appropriate FrontPage templates and wizards to create the web site and include at least three pages in addition to the home page. Include company contact information on the home page. Include webmaster contact information, a copyright notice, and modification date on each page. Create a custom theme based on a preset theme and apply it to all the pages in the web. Use tables and bulleted and numbered lists to organize text on the pages. Key appropriate text in the pages. Insert a scrolling text marquee on the home page. Insert or remove horizontal lines as appropriate.

Add DHTML effects to text on the home page. Use images to illustrate the kinds of industrial jobs Harris Personnel fills for their clients. Print the web pages. Save and print the plan.

Project 3

Roamona Pena is the assistant to the president of Bledsoe Security Systems, Inc. She calls you to update the web site you created for Bledsoe Security Systems last year. Roamona tells you that the president wants you to add a new page to the web site. The page should use graphic images and text to describe the company's services. Create an empty web for Bledsoe Security Systems, Inc. Then create a new page using a page template. Key appropriate text in the page and insert appropriate images from the Clip Gallery. Print the web page.

Project 4

You want to expand your collection of motion clips before you begin any new web page projects. Connect to the Internet and open the Clip Gallery. Use the Clips Online button to start your web browser and load the Microsoft Clip Gallery Live web page. With your instructor's permission, search for technology motion clips and download at least five clips. Create a one-page web, and insert the motion clips on the page. Print the page.

Project 5

You work for Pets-On-Holiday, a luxurious pet hotel in Dallas, Texas. The owner is so pleased with your suggestions for a company web site that she has authorized you to begin immediately. Using the Corporate Presence wizard, create a new web site for the company. Include at least two pages in addition to the home page. Apply a custom theme, add a hit counter and scrolling marquee, and use bulleted and numbered lists as appropriate. Add appropriate text, images, and sound to the home page. Print the home page.

chapter five

Project 6

You want to review the use of sound on web pages at existing web sites to determine whether or not you want to use sound at your web site. Connect to the Internet, load your web browser, and use a search engine and the keywords "web page sounds" or similar keywords to locate and review examples of pages using sound at existing web sites. Print at least five web pages that use sound. Using a word processing program, create a document listing each page and include your analysis of the effectiveness of the sound on each page. Save and print the document.

Project 7

Potter's Paradise, a craft store specializing in hand thrown and glazed pottery, is located in Altoona, Pennsylvania. Jim Bellows, the owner of Potter's Paradise, wants to begin selling pottery supplies online. He hires you to create the new store's web site. Using a word processing program, create a plan for the web site. Then create the web site using FrontPage wizards or templates. Include at least two pages in addition to the home page. Include company contact information on the home page. Include webmaster contact information, a copyright notice, and modification date on each page.

Create a custom theme based on one of the preset themes and apply it to the entire web site. Add appropriate text with formatting to the remaining pages. Use tables and bulleted or numbered lists as necessary to organize the text. Add DHTML effects to text on the home page. Insert a hit counter on the home page. Add page transitions to all the pages. Insert and edit at least three images in the web. Preview the web pages in your browser and make any necessary adjustments to the alignment of elements on the pages. Print the web pages. Save and print the plan.

Project 8

Martin Tamborello, the president of Computer Services, Inc., hires you to create a web site for the company. During your initial meeting with Mr. Tamborello, he indicates concern about adding graphic images to the company's web site. He doesn't want to annoy viewers by having the web pages take too long to download and asks how you plan to handle the problem. Using online Help, look up and review the topic "How graphics affect your web." Then, using a word processing program, write Mr. Tamborello a memo listing several ways to speed up the download process when web pages contain graphics. Save and print the memo.

Creating Hyperlinks

Chapter Overview

O ne key to the overwhelming success of the World Wide Web is the viewer's ability to move quickly from page to page within the same web site or to another web site using hyperlinks, which are text or images associated with another location. In this chapter, you create internal hyperlinks that enable viewers to move from one location to another within the same page and between pages at the same web site. You also create external hyperlinks that enable viewers to load pages from different web sites. Finally, you create a hyperlink that enables viewers to open a Word document at your web site.

LEARNING OBJECTIVES

- ▶ Use a bookmark and hyperlink on the same page
- ▶ Add hyperlinks to other pages in the web
- ▶ Work with navigation bars
- ▶ Adding hyperlinks to pages in different webs
- ▶ Open an Office document in a FrontPage web
- ▶ Verify hyperlinks

Case profile

The next step in creating Sarah's PartyWorld web is to add hyperlinks to help viewers navigate around the site, visit related web sites, and open a Word document with the party planner checklist. You decide to show Sarah and Bob a variety of hyperlinks, including text hyperlinks, graphic hyperlinks, and a clickable image map. You also add the remaining individual theme pages and the company information page and then edit the web site structure to modify the navigation bars.

chapter
six

6.a Using a Bookmark and Hyperlink on the Same Page

When web pages are long, it is helpful if the viewer can quickly get to the top of the page or another location in the page. Hyperlinks are a handy way to do this. To create a hyperlink to a destination on the same page, you first create a reference point, called a **bookmark** or **anchor,** at the destination. The bookmark can refer to a location in the page or to existing text, such as heading text. When you insert a location bookmark, a small flag appears at the location. When you insert a text bookmark, the text displays a dashed underline. After you create the bookmark, you assign a hyperlink to the bookmark destination using text or an image.

Creating a Bookmark

After viewing the sample web pages in your browser, you think it would be a good idea to insert a hyperlink at the bottom of each page that viewers can click to return to the top of that page.

To open the Sample_Web and create a bookmark using the word "Welcome":

Step 1	*Open*	the Sample_Web you modified in Chapter 5
Step 2	*Open*	the *index.htm* page in the Normal tab in Page view
Step 3	*Select*	the word "Welcome" at the top of the page
Step 4	*Click*	Insert
Step 5	*Click*	Bookmark

The Bookmark dialog box that opens should look similar to Figure 6-1. You give the bookmark a name in this dialog box. In this case, you want to use the selected word as the bookmark name.

QUICK TIP

If you use a bookmark to reference heading text on a long page, you can quickly go to a specific heading by opening the Bookmark dialog box, clicking the bookmark name in the list, and then clicking Goto. To delete a bookmark, open the Bookmark dialog box, click the bookmark name in the list, and click Clear.

To remove a location bookmark, you can also select the location bookmark flag in the page and press the DELETE key.

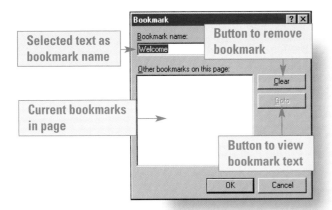

Selected text as bookmark name

Current bookmarks in page

Button to remove bookmark

Button to view bookmark text

FIGURE 6-1
Bookmark Dialog Box

MENU TIP

You can create a hyperlink by clicking the Hyperlink command on the Insert menu.

Step 6	*Click*	OK to name the bookmark "Welcome"
Step 7	*Deselect*	the word "Welcome"
Step 8	*Observe*	the dashed underline

Your screen should look similar to Figure 6-2.

Bookmark text

FIGURE 6-2
Home Page with Bookmark

MOUSE TIP

You can create a hyperlink by clicking the Hyperlink button on the Standard toolbar.

Now you are ready to insert text at the bottom of the page and create the hyperlink.

Creating a Hyperlink

A **hyperlink** is a connection from one location to another and can be either text or an image. In this situation, you use the text "Top of Page" for the hyperlink. To key the text and create the hyperlink:

Step 1	*Scroll*	to view the bottom of the page
Step 2	*Click*	at the end of the Last modified: date line
Step 3	*Press*	the ENTER key to create a new centered paragraph

chapter
six

Step 4	*Key*	Top of Page
Step 5	*Select*	the Top of Page text
Step 6	*Right-click*	the selected text
Step 7	*Click*	Hyperlink

The Create Hyperlink dialog box that opens should look similar to Figure 6-3.

FIGURE 6-3
Create Hyperlink Dialog Box

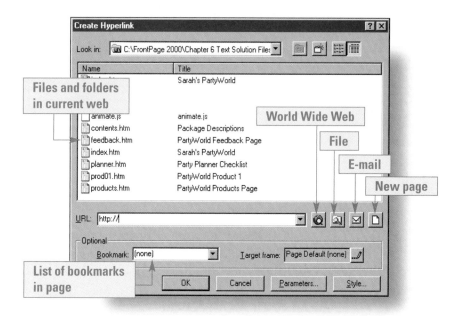

In this dialog box, you select a web page **URL**, the path to a page on your local file system, an e-mail address, a new web page, or a bookmark, to hyperlink to. You want to select the Welcome bookmark from the Bookmark list.

Step 8	*Click*	the Bookmark: list arrow
Step 9	*Click*	Welcome
Step 10	*Observe*	the #Welcome text in the URL: text box, indicating the path to the bookmark
Step 11	*Click*	OK
Step 12	*Deselect*	the hyperlink text
Step 13	*Observe*	that the text is now a different color and underlined, indicating a hyperlink

You can preview the page in the Preview tab or your browser to test the hyperlink. Testing a hyperlink while you edit the page is called **following the hyperlink**. You can also quickly follow a hyperlink in the Normal tab in Page view by holding down the CTRL key and clicking the hyperlink. To follow the Top of Page hyperlink:

Step 1	*Press & Hold*	the CTRL key
Step 2	*Move*	the mouse pointer to the Top of Page hyperlink
Step 3	*Observe*	the pointing hand pointer and ScreenTip
Step 4	*Click*	the Top of Page hyperlink
Step 5	*Release*	the CTRL key
Step 6	*Observe*	that you are viewing the top of the page at the word "Welcome"
Step 7	*Close*	and save the page

Editing a Hyperlink

Because the sample web was created with shared borders, the Top of Page hyperlink text is automatically inserted on all the other pages. However, the hyperlink does not work properly on the other pages because the bookmark reference is missing from the top of each page. You need to edit the hyperlink properties to correct the bookmark reference.

To create a bookmark and edit the hyperlink on the *contents.htm* page:

Step 1	*Open*	the *contents.htm* page in the Normal tab in Page view
Step 2	*Select*	the main heading and subheading text
Step 3	*Key*	Party Package Contents
Step 4	*Format*	the new text as 6 (24 pt) and bold
Step 5	*Select*	the word Party
Step 6	*Create*	a bookmark named Top using the Party text
Step 7	*Scroll*	to the bottom of the page to view the Top of Page text
Step 8	*Right-click*	the Top of Page hyperlink text
Step 9	*Click*	Hyperlink Properties
Step 10	*Select*	Top in the Bookmark: list, if necessary
Step 11	*Click*	OK
Step 12	*Follow*	the hyperlink to test it
Step 13	*Save & Close*	the page

chapter
six

| Step 14 | *Continue* | by inserting a bookmark named Top and testing the Top of Page hyperlink as indicated below, using the previous steps as your guide |

Page	Bookmark text
feedback.htm	Please
planner.htm	Party
prod01.htm	New

You can also use an image to create a bookmark. To create a bookmark using an image:

Step 1	*Open*	the *products.htm* page in the Normal tab in Page view
Step 2	*Select*	the *birthday.wmf* image
Step 3	*Create*	a bookmark named Top using the image
Step 4	*Edit*	the Top of Page hyperlink to go to the Top bookmark
Step 5	*Save*	the page

The Top of Page hyperlinks are completed. Next, you create hyperlinks to other pages in the web.

6.b Adding Hyperlinks to Other Pages in the Web

A **navigation bar** is a collection of buttons that contain hyperlinks to other pages in the web based on the web structure. Viewers can move from page to page in your web by clicking hyperlink buttons in the navigation bars and by clicking text or image hyperlinks in the body of the page. Hyperlinks that navigate a viewer within a web site are called **internal hyperlinks**. For example, on the catalog page, you created a bulleted list of the individual party theme pages. You can use the bulleted list text to create a hyperlinks to the individual theme pages.

To create internal hyperlinks on the *products.htm* page:

Step 1	*Verify*	that the *products.htm* page is open in the Normal tab in Page view
Step 2	*Select*	the Holiday Parties bullet text
Step 3	*Right-click*	the selected text
Step 4	*Click*	Hyperlink to open the Create Hyperlink dialog box

Step 5	*Click*	the *prod01.htm* page in the list
Step 6	*Click*	OK
Step 7	*Deselect*	the Holiday Parties text
Step 8	*Observe*	that the text is a different color and underlined, indicating a hyperlink

Your screen should look similar to Figure 6-4.

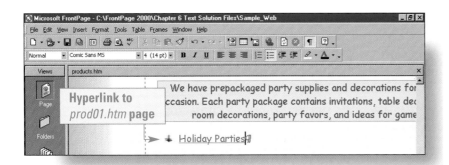

FIGURE 6-4
Catalog Page with
One Hyperlink

Step 9	*CTRL + Click*	the Holiday Parties bulleted list hyperlink to follow it
Step 10	*Save & Close*	the Holiday Parties theme page

You want to use the bulleted list text to create hyperlinks to the other individual theme pages. However, you have not yet created those pages.

Creating a Hyperlink to a New Page

You cannot create a hyperlink to a page that does not exist. However, you can create the page as you create the hyperlink. FrontPage creates the hyperlink and opens the new page for you to edit. You can edit the new page or create a task to remind you to finish the page later. The hyperlink is not valid until you save the page.

To create a hyperlink and a new page using the Birthday Parties bullet:

Step 1	*Select*	the Birthday Parties bullet text
Step 2	*Open*	the Create Hyperlink dialog box
Step 3	*Click*	the New Page button
Step 4	*Double-click*	the Normal Page icon in the New dialog box
Step 5	*Observe*	that the new page is formatted with the custom theme and shared bottom border

Step 6	*Save*	the page as *birthday.htm*, change the title to Birthday Parties, and close the page
Step 7	*Follow*	the Birthday Parties hyperlink
Step 8	*Close*	the Birthday Parties page
Step 9	*Continue*	by creating hyperlinks and new pages as indicated below, using the previous steps as your guide

Bullet	**Filename**	**Title**
Baby Showers	*baby.htm*	Baby Showers
Bridal Showers	*bridal.htm*	Bridal Showers
Special Event Parties	*specialevent.htm*	Special Events

After closing last new page and deselecting the hyperlink text, your screen should look similar to Figure 6-5.

FIGURE 6-5
Catalog Page with
Hyperlinks to Other Pages

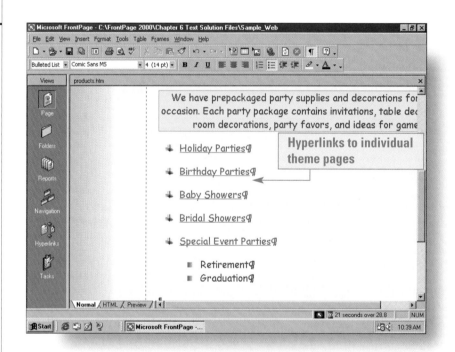

Another alternative is to create hyperlinks on an image.

Creating a Hotspot Clickable Image Map

A **hotspot** is an area on an image to which you assign a hyperlink. An image that contains hotspots is called an **image map**. You can draw objects—such as rectangles, circles, or polygons—and use them as hotspots on an image.

You want to use the *birthday.wmf* image as an image map with hotspots for each of the individual theme pages. To create the hotspots:

Step 1	*Verify*	that the *products.htm* page is open in the Normal tab in Page view
Step 2	*Select*	the *birthday.htm* image at the top of the page
Step 3	*Click*	the Circular Hotspot button ⬭ on the Pictures toolbar

The mouse pointer becomes a drawing pen pointer.

Step 4	*Move*	the drawing pointer to the birthday cake portion of the image

Your screen should look similar to Figure 6-6.

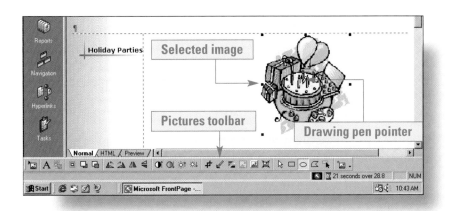

FIGURE 6-6
Selected Image on Catalog Page

QUICK TIP

You can also create text hotspots on a GIF image. A text hotspot is text that you place on an image and to which you assign a hyperlink. You create the text hotspot by using the Text button on the Pictures toolbar to create text box on the image, key the text, and then double-click the text box border to assign the hyperlink. For more information on text hotspots, see online <u>H</u>elp.

You drag the drawing pen pointer downward diagonally to draw a very small circle. When you drag the mouse pointer, the circle expands proportionally from the pointer. Do not draw a circle larger than the top of the cake.

Step 5	*Draw*	a small circle on the top of the cake

The Create Hyperlink dialog box opens.

Step 6	*Double-click*	*birthday.htm* in the file list
Step 7	*Point*	to the circular hotspot on the image
Step 8	*Observe*	the destination filename in the status bar

Your screen should look similar to Figure 6-7.

FIGURE 6-7
Catalog Page with
a Hotspot

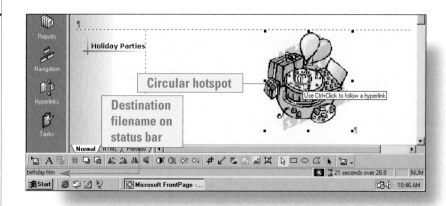

FIGURE 6-7
Catalog Page with
a Hotspot

Step 9	**Deselect**	the image
Step 10	**Follow**	the circular hotspot hyperlink
Step 11	**Close**	the *birthday.htm* page
Step 12	**Create**	a circular hotspot on the *birthday.htm* image in the location of your choice for Holiday Parties, Baby Showers, Bridal Showers, and Special Events Parties
Step 13	**Save & Close**	the page

You need to organize the web's structure in Navigation view and update the navigation bar hyperlink buttons.

6.c Working with Navigation Bars

You create the navigational structure for the Sample_Web by organizing the pages in Navigation view. This navigation structure determines which hyperlinks are placed on the navigation bars. A **navigation bar** is a set of text or button hyperlinks viewers use to browse the pages at a web site. The page titles become the labels for the navigation bar hyperlinks.

The committee structures the new Sarah's PartyWorld web site with the home page at the top level, and the party planner, catalog, package contents, and contest registration pages at the next level. The third level includes the individual theme pages and the company information page.

Adding Existing Pages in Navigation View Using Drag and Drop

You begin by adding the existing pages to the appropriate level. The simplest way to do this is by using drag and drop in Navigation view. To set the structure of the sample web:

Step 1	***Switch***	to Navigation view
Step 2	***Display***	the Folder List, if necessary
Step 3	***Display***	the Navigation toolbar, if necessary
Step 4	***Drag***	the *planner.htm* page from the Folder List and drop it to the left of the Party Package page in the workspace
Step 5	***Drag***	the *contents.htm* page from the Folder List and drop it to the right of the Party Packages page in the workspace
Step 6	***Drag***	the Contest page in the workspace and drop it to the right of the Package Descriptions page
Step 7	***Continue***	by dragging the *birthday.htm, baby.htm, bridal.htm,* and *specialevent.htm* pages from the Folder List and drop them to the right of the Holiday Parties page in the third level
Step 8	***Hide***	the Folder List

Your screen should look similar to Figure 6-8.

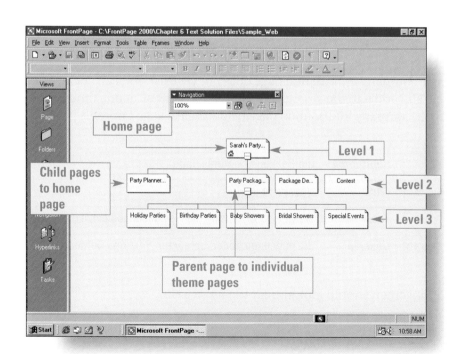

FIGURE 6-8
Existing Pages Organized in Navigation View

You can change a page title in Navigation view to assure that it has a meaningful name.

Renaming Pages in Navigation View

The titles you see on the pages in Navigation view are the text used in the navigation bar hyperlinks. If a title is too long, it may not fit the navigation bar buttons used in the web page theme. You may need to create briefer, but still meaningful, titles. To accommodate the button size in the custom theme you applied to the sample web, you want to change the Party Packages page title to "Catalog," the Package Description page title to "Package Contents," and the Party Planner Checklist page title to "Party Checklist." To rename the pages:

Step 1	*Right-click*	the Party Packages page in the workspace
Step 2	*Click*	Rename
Step 3	*Observe*	that the page name is selected
Step 4	*Key*	Catalog
Step 5	*Press*	the ENTER key
Step 6	*Rename*	the Package Descriptions page to Package Contents
Step 7	*Rename*	the Party Planner page to Party Checklist

The next page you need to add is the company information page.

Adding New Pages in Navigation View

The company information page does not yet exist. You can create a new page and add it to the structure in Navigation view all at one time. To create the company information page below the Package Contents page:

Step 1	*Right-click*	the Package Contents page
Step 2	*Click*	New Page
Step 3	*Zoom*	the view to 75%, using the Navigation toolbar, if necessary
Step 4	*Observe*	the new page added below the Package Contents page

Your screen should look similar to Figure 6-9.

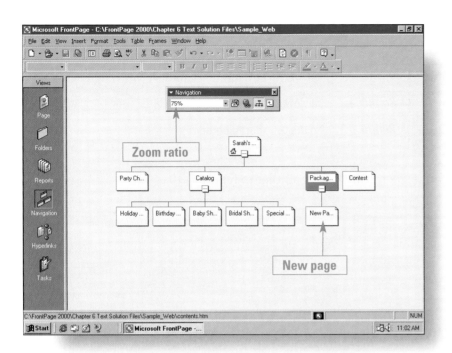

FIGURE 6-9
New Page Added in
Navigation View

MENU TIP

If you do not see a file-
name in the Folder List
you expect to see, click
View, Refresh or press
the F5 key to refresh the
view of files in the
Folder List.

QUICK TIP

You can delete a page
from the structure in
Navigation view by
selecting the page and
pressing the DELETE
key. You then select to
delete the page from
only the navigation bar
or from the web.

Step 5	*Rename*	the New Page page Company_Profile
Step 6	*Double-click*	the Company_Profile page to open it in Page view
Step 7	*Display*	the Folder List, if necessary
Step 8	*Observe*	that the *company_profile.htm* page is saved to the web
Step 9	*Close*	the page
Step 10	*Hide*	the Folder List

The sample web structure matches the basic structure proposed by
the committee during the planning process. You are ready to review
and edit the navigation bars for each page.

Selecting and Changing Levels of Navigational Buttons in a Navigation Bar

You can add a navigation bar to any page. Placing a navigation bar in
shared borders is a quick way to add or edit navigation bar hyperlinks
in one page and have the changes apply to all the pages sharing the
border. The custom theme you applied to the sample web includes top
and left navigation bars in shared borders. You want to view and edit
the navigation bars.

chapter
six

To view and edit the navigation bars on the home page:

Step 1	*Open*	the *index.htm* page in the Normal tab in Page view
Step 2	*Scroll*	to view the top and left shared borders and navigation bars
Step 3	*Return*	to the top shared border

Your screen should look similar to Figure 6-10.

FIGURE 6-10
Navigation Bars and
Shared Borders on the
Home Page

You want all the pages in the web to include navigational hyperlinks to the home page and to each of the second-level pages. For consistency, you want these hyperlinks to appear at the top of the pages. To do this for all pages, you first remove the navigation bar above the page banner and then edit the navigation bar below the page banner in the shared top border. To remove the first navigation bar and add the second-level pages:

| Step 1 | *Click* | the navigation bar containing the Home button above the page banner |
| Step 2 | *Press* | the DELETE key twice to delete the navigation bar and the blank line |

You want to edit the navigation bar below the page banner to include hyperlinks to the second-level pages.

| Step 3 | ***Double-click*** | the navigation bar bracketed text below the page banner |

The Navigation Bar Properties dialog box that opens on your screen should look similar to Figure 6-11.

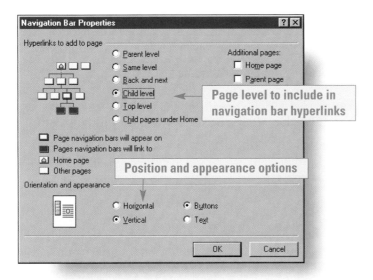

FIGURE 6-11
Navigation Bar Properties
Dialog Box

You can add hyperlinks between different page levels. A **parent page** is a page that has other pages directly below it in the web structure. A **child page** is a page that has another page directly above it in the web structure. The Parent level option adds hyperlinks to the page above the current page in the structure. The Child level option adds hyperlinks to the pages below the current page. The Child pages under Home option adds hyperlinks to the second-level pages.

Step 4	***Click***	the Child pages under Home option button
Step 5	***Click***	the Home page check box to insert a check mark, if necessary
Step 6	***Click***	OK
Step 7	***Deselect***	the navigation bar
Step 8	***Observe***	the new second-level page and home page hyperlinks in the navigation bar

The page now has duplicate navigation bars because the left navigation bar also contains hyperlinks to the second-level pages. To remove the navigation bar on the left side of the page, you turn off the left shared border for this page.

Turning On or Off Shared Borders

If you turn off shared borders, all the content in the shared border is lost. You cannot undo this action with the Undo button or command. To reverse this action, you must reapply the shared border and recreate its content.

To turn off the left shared border for the home page:

Step 1	*Right-click*	the page background
Step 2	*Click*	Shared Borders

The Shared Borders dialog box that opens should look similar to Figure 6-12.

FIGURE 6-12
Shared Borders Dialog Box

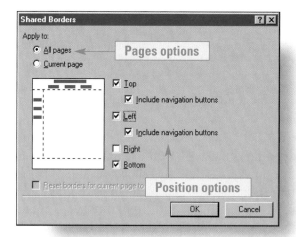

You can turn on or off shared borders for all pages or just the current page with options in this dialog box.

Step 3	*Click*	the Current page option button
Step 4	*Click*	the Left check box to remove the check mark
Step 5	*Click*	OK
Step 6	*Observe*	that the left shared border and navigation bar hyperlinks are removed

Because the left shared border is no longer taking up space on the page, you need to reorganize the tables and text on the page.

To reorganize the web page elements:

| Step 1 | *Center* | the two tables, the heading text, and hit counter line on the page |
| Step 2 | *Arrange* | the contact information on the page using Figure 6-13 as your guide |

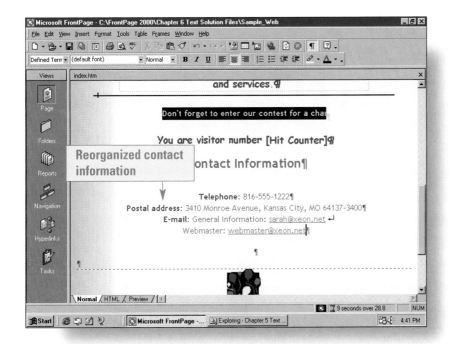

FIGURE 6-13
Rearranged Contact Information

> **QUICK TIP**
>
> Remember that you can use the Cut, Copy, and Paste commands or toolbar buttons to reorganize web page elements on the page.

| Step 3 | *Preview* | the page |
| Step 4 | *Save & Close* | the page |

> **MENU TIP**
>
> You can change text alignment, indentation, and line spacing with the Paragraph command on the Format menu.

You do not need the left navigation bar on the catalog page. To remove it, you remove the left shared border. Then you indent the bulleted list to make the text arrangement more attractive.

To edit the catalog page:

Step 1	*Open*	the *products.htm* page in the Normal tab in Page view
Step 2	*Observe*	that the navigation bar below the page banner contains hyperlinks to the second-level pages and the home page
Step 3	*Remove*	the left shared border on the current page
Step 4	*Select*	the bulleted lists

chapter
six

Step 5	**Click**	the Increase Indent button ⊞ on the Formatting tool-bar five times
Step 6	**Save & Close**	the page

You also need to revise the Party Checklist page by removing the left navigation bar and then reorganizing the page. To edit the Party Checklist page:

Step 1	**Open**	the *planner.htm* page
Step 2	**Observe**	the navigation bar
Step 3	**Remove**	the left shared border on the current page
Step 4	**Center**	the tables on the page
Step 5	**Save & Close**	the page

You also need to remove the left shared border from the Contest page. To edit the Contest page:

Step 1	**Open**	the *feedback.htm* page
Step 2	**Observe**	the navigation bar
Step 3	**Remove**	the left shared border on this page
Step 4	**Save & Close**	the page

Currently, viewers visiting the Holiday Parties page can hyperlink to only the home page or other second-level pages. You need to edit the left navigation bar so that viewers can also hyperlink to pages of the same level. To edit the left navigation bar on the Holiday Parties page:

Step 1	**Open**	the *prod01.htm* page
Step 2	**Delete**	the navigation bar above the page banner with the Home and Up buttons and the resulting blank line, if necessary
Step 3	**Double-click**	the left navigation bar
Step 4	**Click**	the Same level option button

QUICK TIP

To exclude a page auto-matically included in a navigation bar, switch to Navigation view, right-click the page, and click Included in Navigation Bars to clear the check mark. This excludes the current page *and all child pages under the excluded page*.

To display text hyper-links instead of buttons in navigation bars, select the text option in the Navigation Bar Properties dialog box.

Step 5	*Click*	OK
Step 6	*Observe*	the new left navigation bar hyperlinks
Step 7	*Save & Close*	the page
Step 8	*Verify*	that the top navigation bar for the *baby.htm*, *birthday.htm*, *bridal.htm*, and *specialevent.htm* pages contain second-level and home-page hyperlinks and the left navigation bar contains same-level hyperlinks

The contents page has a duplicate navigation bar. To fix this, you can remove the left shared border on this page. To edit the contents page:

Step 1	*Open*	the *contents.htm* page in the Normal tab in Page view
Step 2	*Remove*	the left shared border on this page

Adding a Navigation Bar to a Web Page

You can add a navigation bar to any page either in a shared border at the top, bottom, left, or right side of the page or as part of the page body. The company profile page is a child page to the contents page. You want viewers to be able to hyperlink to the company profile page from the contents page, so you insert a new row at the bottom of the table and then insert a navigation bar in the row.

To insert a row at the bottom of the table and add a navigation bar to the contents page:

Step 1	*Insert*	a new row at the bottom of the table
Step 2	*Merge*	the cells
Step 3	*Verify*	that the insertion point is in the new row
Step 4	*Click*	Insert
Step 5	*Click*	Navigation Bar
Step 6	*Click*	the Child level option button
Step 7	*Click*	OK
Step 8	*Center*	the one-button navigation bar in the cell

Your screen should look similar to Figure 6-14.

FIGURE 6-14
Contents Page with
Navigation Bar in Table Cell

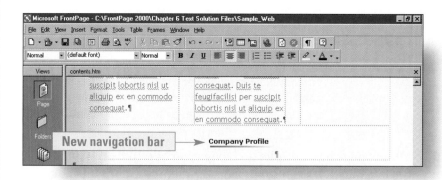

| Step 9 | *Save & Close* the page |

The last page you need to review is the company profile page. To review the *company_profile.htm* page navigation bars:

Step 1	*Open*	the *company_profile.htm* page
Step2	*Observe*	that viewers can hyperlink to the second-level pages and the home page
Step 3	*Remove*	the left shared border on this page
Step 4	*Save & Close* the page	

Currently, the only hyperlink to the company profile page is on the contents page. You also want viewers to be able to hyperlink to the company profile page from the home page. To add the hyperlink to the home page:

Step 1	*Open*	the *index.htm* in the Normal tab in Page view
Step 2	*Scroll*	to view the contact information near the bottom of the page
Step 3	*Click*	at the blank line below the webmaster e-mail reference
Step 4	*Key*	Company Profile
Step 5	*Create*	a hyperlink to the *company_profile.htm* page using the text Company Profile
Step 6	*Follow*	the hyperlink and close the company profile page
Step 7	*Save & Close* the home page	

QUICK TIP

Don't forget that you can view the hyperlinks in a web in Hyperlinks view, which provides a picture of the hyperlinks to and from and page in a web. You can also customize Hyperlinks view by right-clicking the Hyperlinks view background and selecting custom options on the shortcut menu.

The hyperlinks within the web are complete. Now you are ready to add external hyperlinks to complementary pages on the web.

6.d Adding Hyperlinks to Pages on the World Wide Web

External hyperlinks are those that link your web pages to other web sites stored on your local file system or on the Web. For example, you might want to include hyperlinks to well-known search tools, such as Yahoo! or AltaVista, on your web pages. You can add external hyperlinks to web page contents by selecting text or an image and inserting the web page URL as the hyperlink. You can also add external hyperlinks to a navigation bar.

The committee recommended that the new Sarah's PartyWorld web site include hyperlinks to other web sites that present party planning ideas or materials, such as entertainment agencies. You decide to add these hyperlinks to the contents page as part of the navigation bar included in the table.

notes The hyperlinks provided for the following activity are suggestions only and were valid hyperlinks at the time this book was published. You may browse the Web and select different hyperlinks to insert, if necessary.

To add external hyperlinks to a navigation bar on the contents page:

Step 1	*Switch*	to Navigation view
Step 2	*Right-click*	the Package Contents page
Step 3	*Click*	External Hyperlink to open the Select Hyperlink dialog box
Step 4	*Key*	http://partyfinders.net in the URL: text box
Step 5	*Click*	OK
Step 6	*Rename*	the page to Party Net

Your screen should look similar to Figure 6-15.

chapter
six

FIGURE 6-15
Navigation View

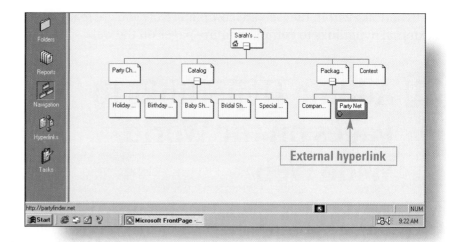

You use the same procedure to add other external hyperlinks. To add two more external hyperlinks:

Step 1	*Right-click*	the Package Contents Page
Step 2	*Click*	External Hyperlink
Step 3	*Key*	http://www.blissezine.com/ in the URL: text box
Step 4	*Click*	OK
Step 5	*Rename*	the page to Weddings
Step 6	*Add*	the http://barberusa.com/children.htm external hyper-link to the Package Contents page
Step 7	*Rename*	the page to Family Parties

The external hyperlinks are added to the navigation bar on the con-tents page. To view the Package Contents page in the Normal tab in Page view:

Step 1	*Double-click*	the Package Contents page in the Navigation view workspace
Step 2	*Scroll*	to view the navigation bar at the bottom of the table

Your screen should look similar to Figure 6-16.

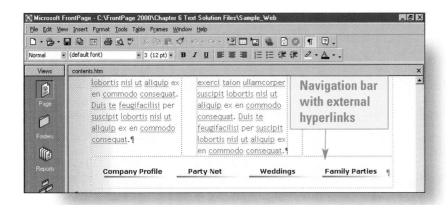

FIGURE 6-16
Contents Page with
External Hyperlinks

| Step 3 | *Close* | the page |

Sarah asks you to modify the Party Checklist page to remove the tables and text and add a hyperlink to the actual checklist Microsoft Word document.

6.e   Opening an Office Document in a FrontPage Web

In addition to creating hyperlinks to different locations on the same page, different pages in the same web, and different sites on the Web, you can create a hyperlink to a file, such as a Microsoft Office document. When a viewer clicks the hyperlink to a file, the document and its related application or viewer also open.

notes   It is assumed you are using Microsoft Internet Explorer for the activities in this section. If you are using a different browser, your results may vary from the illustrations in this section.

Sarah wants viewers to be able to open the *Party_Planner_and_Checklist* document and modify or print it using the Word application. First, you delete all the tables and text on the *planner.htm* page except the heading text. Then you add both an image hyperlink and a text hyperlink to the Word document. Next, you import the Word document into the web, shorten the filename, and then create the hyperlinks to it. To modify the Party Planner page:

Step 1	**Open**	the *planner.htm* page in the Normal tab in Page view
Step 2	**Select**	the text and three tables below the Party Planner and Checklist heading
Step 3	**Press**	the DELETE key
Step 4	**Format**	the Party Planner and Checklist heading as 6 (24 pt) and bold
Step 5	**Click**	at the end of the heading and press the ENTER key to create a new line
Step 6	**Insert**	the *checklist.gif* image located in the Chapter_6 folder on the Data Disk
Step 7	**Click**	at the blank line below the image
Step 8	**Key**	Use our free checklist to organize your next party!
Step 9	**Format**	the text as 5 (18 pt) and centered

To ensure that the *Party_Planner_and_Checklist* document is always available to viewers, you want to import it from the Chapter_2 folder on the Data Disk into the Sample_Web. One way to do this is to open Windows Explorer, copy the file to the Clipboard, close Windows Explorer, and then paste the file into the web using the Folder List or Folders view. To import the document using the copy and paste method:

Step 1	**Open**	Windows Explorer
Step 2	**Open**	the Chapter_2 folder on the Data Disk
Step 3	**Right-click**	the *Party_Planner_and_Checklist* filename
Step 4	**Click**	Copy
Step 5	**Close**	Windows Explorer
Step 6	**Maximize**	the FrontPage window, if necessary
Step 7	**Display**	the Folder List, if necessary
Step 8	**Right-click**	the root (main) folder for the Sample_Web
Step 9	**Click**	Paste
Step 10	**Observe**	that the Word document is imported into the web and appears in the Folder List
Step 11	**Rename**	the *Party_Planner_and_Checklist.doc* document *Checklist.doc*

To create the hyperlinks:

Step 1	**Select**	the *checklist.gif* image
Step 2	**Open**	the Create Hyperlink dialog box
Step 3	**Double-click**	the *Checklist.doc* file to create the link
Step 4	**Select**	the word checklist in the sentence below the graphic
Step 5	**Create**	a hyperlink to the *Checklist.doc* file
Step 6	**Save**	the page and save the *checklist.gif* file in the images folder

You should preview the page in your browser to test the hyperlinks. To test the hyperlinks:

Step 1	**Preview**	the page in your browser
Step 2	**Click**	the *checklist.gif* image
Step 3	**Observe**	that the actual *Checklist.doc* Word document opens in the browser
Step 4	**Observe**	that the browser menu bar and toolbar are modified to include the Word application editing tools

Your screen should look similar to Figure 6-17.

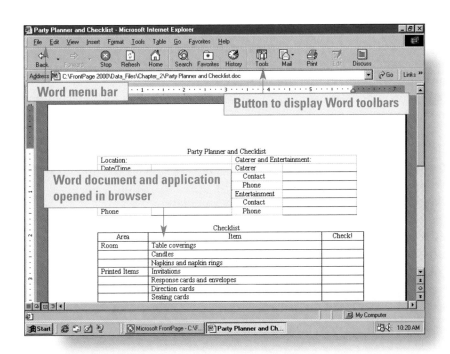

FIGURE 6-17
Word Document in Web Browser

Q U I C K   T I P

You can create an e-mail hyperlink, called a **mailto: link**, that opens the viewer's message composition window when clicked by keying an e-mail address and pressing the SPACEBAR. You can also create an e-mail hyperlink by clicking the E-mail button in the Create Hyperlink dialog box.

You can set a default hyperlink for an image. For example, you could assign a default hyperlink to your home page from a company logo image. You assign a default hyperlink to an image in the Picture Properties dialog box.

chapter
six

You can modify or print the document using Word features. The Tools button on the browser toolbar displays the Microsoft Word Standard and Formatting toolbars.

Step 5	*Click*	the Tools button on the Standard Buttons toolbar
Step 6	*Observe*	the Word toolbars below the Address bar
Step 7	*Click*	the Tools button on the Standard Buttons toolbar to hide the Word toolbars
Step 8	*Click*	the Back button ⇦ on the Standard Buttons toolbar to return to the web page
Step 9	*Test*	the checklist text hyperlink
Step 10	*Close*	the browser
Step 11	*Close*	the *planner.htm* page

Next, you verify that the hyperlinks in the sample web work properly.

C 6.f Verifying Hyperlinks

Broken hyperlinks, hyperlinks that lead nowhere or point to nonexistent pages, are extremely annoying to viewers. Broken hyperlinks occur when web pages or sites are deleted, moved, renamed, or assigned a different path or URL. Broken hyperlinks can occur if you key an incorrect URL when creating the hyperlink. A very important part of managing a web site is regularly verifying that the hyperlinks are valid. You can do this in Reports view.

You can check the number of broken hyperlinks in a web by switching to Reports view and then reviewing the Broken Hyperlinks row in the Site Summary report. To see a detail list of broken hyperlinks, double-click the Broken Hyperlinks row or use the Reporting toolbar to display the Broken Hyperlinks report. In this report, you can edit the hyperlink, edit the page containing the broken hyperlink, or add a task to remind you to edit the broken hyperlink later.

You want to verify the hyperlinks in the Sample_Web. You should always save all the pages before you verify hyperlinks to be certain the most current changes are saved. To verify the hyperlinks:

Step 1	*Save & Close*	any open pages
Step 2	*Switch*	to Reports view

Step 3	*Display*	the Reporting toolbar, if necessary

Step 4	*Click*	the Verify Hyperlinks button  on the Reporting toolbar

The Verify Hyperlinks dialog box that opens should look similar to Figure 6-18.

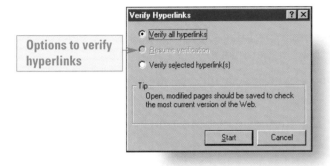

Options to verify hyperlinks

FIGURE 6-18
Verify Hyperlinks Dialog Box

Step 5	*Click*	the Verify all hyperlinks option button, if necessary

Step 6	*Click*	Start

If your web site contains many external hyperlinks, it may take several minutes to verify the links because FrontPage must connect to each external web site to verify the hyperlink. After the verification process, a list of broken hyperlinks appears. You can edit the hyperlink by selecting the hyperlink in the list and then clicking the Edit Hyperlinks button on the Reporting toolbar. This opens the Edit Hyperlink dialog box with options for editing the page that contains the hyperlink or the hyperlink URL.

Step 7	*Edit*	any broken hyperlinks in your web to correct them

Step 8	*Close*	the web

The hyperlinks you added to the Sarah's PartyWorld web are complete, enabling viewers to easily navigate the site and link to related web sites. Next, you complete the contents page.

Summary

▶ One key to the success of the Web is the viewer's ability to move quickly from page to page at the same site or to another site using hyperlinks.

▶ A bookmark or anchor is a reference point in a web page.

▶ A hyperlink is a connection from one location to another and can be either text or an image.

▶ Internal hyperlinks are hyperlinks to pages inside the current web. External hyperlinks are hyperlinks to pages outside the current web.

▶ You can test or follow hyperlinks while you are editing a web page in Page view.

▶ Viewers can use navigation bars to move from page to page inside a web site.

▶ You can create hyperlinks to a new page and the page itself at one time.

▶ An image map is a picture or image that contains hyperlinks called hotspots.

▶ You organize the navigational structure of a web and determine the hyperlinks that appear on the navigation bars in Navigation view.

▶ You can add both new pages and external hyperlinks to a page's navigation bars in Navigation view.

▶ You can create hyperlinks to Microsoft Office documents. When the viewer clicks the hyperlink, the Office document and Office application open in their browser.

▶ You should manage a web by regularly verifying the hyperlinks.

Commands Review

Action	Menu Bar	Shortcut Menu	Toolbar/Mouse	Keyboard
Insert a bookmark	Insert, Bookmark			ALT + I, K
Insert or edit a hyperlink	Insert, Hyperlink	Right-click selected text or image, click Hyperlink	🔗	ALT + I, H CTRL + K
Follow a hyperlink in the Normal tab in Page view		Right-click the hyperlink, click Follow Hyperlink		CTRL + Click the hyperlink
Insert or modify shared borders	Format, Shared Borders	Right-click a page, click Shared Borders		ALT + O, D
Insert or modify a navigation bar	Insert, Navigation Bar	Right-click navigation bar, click Navigation Bar Properties	Double-click the navigation bar	ALT + I, V
Include or exclude pages from navigation bar		Switch to Navigation view, right-click the page, click Include in Navigation Bars	🔲	
Indent selected text	Format, Paragraph	Right-click selected text and click Paragraph	📑 📑	ALT + O, P
Verify hyperlinks	Tools, Recalculate Hyperlinks		🔲	ALT + T, R

Concepts Review

Circle the correct answer.

1. An anchor is another name for a:
[a] template.
[b] bookmark.
[c] hyperlink.
[d] image map.

2. A hyperlink is a:
[a] file on your local hard drive.
[b] bookmark.
[c] connection from one location to another.
[d] page title.

3. A URL is:
[a] an image map.
[b] a bookmark.
[c] a child page.
[d] the path to a web page.

4. A bookmark is a:
[a] reference point in a page.
[b] hyperlink.
[c] parent page.
[d] navigation bar.

5. To follow a hyperlink when editing a page in Page view, you use:
[a] CTRL + Click.
[b] SHIFT + ENTER.
[c] ALT + Click.
[d] ALT + ENTER.

6. A hotspot is a(n):
[a] navigation bar.
[b] invisible hyperlink.
[c] followed hyperlink.
[d] bookmark.

7. A navigation bar is a(n):
[a] image that contains hotspots.
[b] child page.
[c] bookmark.
[d] set of hyperlinks to pages inside the web.

8. To add or modify a navigation bar for several pages at one time, you can place the navigation bar in:
[a] the Create Hyperlink dialog box.
[b] the Select Hyperlink area.
[c] shared borders.
[d] an image map.

9. To create a hyperlink to a new location on the same page, you must first create a reference point, which is called a(n):
[a] image map.
[b] hyperlink.
[c] URL.
[d] bookmark.

10. Broken hyperlinks are:
[a] untested hyperlinks.
[b] missing hyperlinks.
[c] deleted hyperlinks.
[d] hyperlinks that lead to nowhere.

Circle **T** if the statement is true or **F** if the statement is false.

T   F   1. Navigational hyperlinks are not useful to viewers of a web page.

T   F   2. When you modify a navigation bar in a shared border, only the current page is changed.

T   F   3. You can change the page title in Navigation view.

T   F   4. You can add new pages in only Page view.

T   F   5. A parent page is a page that has other pages directly below it in the web structure.

chapter six

T F 6. You can create a page and the hyperlink to it in one step.

T F 7. External hyperlinks cannot be added to navigation bars.

T F 8. Shared borders can be turned on or off for all the pages in the web.

T F 9. External hyperlinks link your web pages to each other.

T F 10. Broken hyperlinks can be edited in Reports view.

Glossary

Use online <u>H</u>elp to look up the following words in the FrontPage glossary. Then, using your word processing program, create a document listing each word and its glossary definition. Save and print the document.

1. absolute URL

2. active hyperlink

3. bookmark

4. broken hyperlink

5. default hyperlink

6. external hyperlink

7. FAQ

8. followed hyperlink

9. hotspot

10. hyperlink

11. hypertext

12. image map

13. internal hyperlink

14. parent page

Skills Review

Exercise 1

1. Open the Anderson6 web located in the Chapter_6 folder on the Data Disk.

2. Open the *index.htm* file in the Normal tab in Page view.

3. Change the theme to Bars with vivid colors, active graphics, and background picture for all pages.

4. Select the text "Anderson Building Supply" in the introductory paragraph and create a hyperlink to a new page using the Normal page template.

5. Save the new page as *companyinfor.htm* with the title Company Info.

6. Switch to Navigation view and drag the *companyinfo.htm* page from the Folder List to a position immediately below the home page.

7. View the *companyinfor.htm* page in the Normal tab in Page view.

8. Insert a navigation bar containing a home page hyperlink and center it on the page.

9. Insert a page banner below the navigation bar and center it.

10. Insert five blank lines following the page banner.

11. Open the *index.htm* page in the Normal tab in Page view.

12. Edit the navigation bar at the top of the page to include child-level pages. Center the Navigation Bar.

13. Create a shared bottom border for all pages.

14. Cut the contact information from the *index.htm* page and paste it into the shared border. Delete the comment in the shared border.

15. Preview and print the pages.

16. Close the web and save the pages.

Exercise 2

1. Open the Roberta_Maxwell6 web located in the Chapter_6 folder on the Data Disk.

2. Switch to Navigation view.

3. Add an external hyperlink to http://www.yahoo.com to the home page. Rename the page to Yahoo!

4. Add an external hyperlink to http://www.altavista.com to the home page. Rename the page to AltaVista.

5. Add an external hyperlink to http://www.hotbot.com to the home page. Rename the page to HotBot.

6. Open the *index.htm* page in the Normal tab in Page view.

7. Save all the pages.

8. Verify the hyperlinks.

9. Print the *index.htm* page.

10. Close the web.

Exercise 3

1. Open the Secretarial6 web located in the Chapter_6 folder on the Data Disk.

2. Open the *index.htm* page in the Normal tab in Page view.

3. Create hyperlinks to new pages from the bulleted list items as follows:

Bullet	Filename	Title
Letter and memo	*letters.htm*	Letters and Memos
Form letters	*forms.htm*	Mass Mailing
Telephone answering	*telephone.htm*	Answering Services
Fax, e-mail	*fax.htm*	Mail Services

4. Switch to Navigation view and drag the new pages below the home page to create second-level pages.

5. Insert a top shared border on all pages.

6. Insert a navigation bar in the shared border.

7. Edit the navigation bar to include hyperlinks to the child pages under the home page and the home page.

8. Open the *index.htm* page in the Normal tab in Page view.

9. Cut the page banner and paste it into the shared border below the navigation bar.

10. Center the navigation bar and page banner.

11. Print all the pages.

12. Close the web and save the pages.

Exercise 4

1. Open the Rivers6 web located in the Chapter_6 folder on the Data Disk.

2. Open the *index.htm* page in the Normal tab in Page view.

chapter six

3. Add a left shared border to all the pages.

4. Insert a navigation bar in the left shared border with hyperlinks to all the child pages under the home page and the home page.

5. Delete the navigation bar at the top of the page.

6. Open the *webdesign.htm* page in the Normal tab in Page view.

7. Select and delete the table.

8. Key the text "Web Design" at the top of the page.

9. Center the text and format it as 6 (24 pt) and bold.

10. Press the ENTER key to create a new line.

11. Display the Folder List, if necessary, and open the images folder.

12. Drag the *earth.jpg* image from the images folder in the Folder List to the blank line.

13. Size the image to approximately one third of its original size, and then deselect it.

14. Press the ENTER key to create a new line below the image.

15. Key the text "Read all about our web design strategies."

16. Import the *Web_Design.doc* Word document, located in the Chapter_2 folder on the Data Disk, into the web using the copy and paste method.

17. Select the *earth.jpg* image and create a hyperlink to the *Web_Design.doc* document.

18. Select the text "web design" in the last sentence and create a hyperlink to the *Web_Design.doc* document.

19. Preview the page in your browser and test the hyperlinks.

20. Print the *Web_Design.doc* using the Word toolbar inside your browser window and then close the browser.

21. Print the web pages.

22. Close the web and save the pages.

Exercise 5

1. Open the Rameriz6 web located in the Chapter_6 folder on the Data Disk.

2. Open the *index.htm* page, in the Normal tab in Page view.

3. Scroll to the bottom of the page, insert a blank line following the update date in the shared border.

4. Select the "Back to Top" text immediately above the bottom shared border and drag the selected text into the bottom shared border. Drop it at the new blank line.

5. Follow the Back to Top hyperlink on the *index.htm* page.

6. Save the page.

7. Open each of the following pages, delete the Back to Top text in the page body, and follow the new Back to Top hyperlink in the shared border.

archive.htm
members.htm
schedule.htm
search.htm

8. Preview and print the home page.

9. Close the web and save the pages.

Exercise 6

1. Open the Hamilton6 web located in the Chapter_6 folder on the Data Disk.

2. Open the *index.htm* page in the Normal tab in Page view.

3. Apply the Blueprint theme with vivid colors, active graphics, and background picture to all pages.

4. Add top and left shared borders and include navigation buttons in the left shared border for all pages.

5. Cut the page banner and paste it into the top shared border, replacing the comment.

6. Switch to Navigation view and add a new page titled Our Services.

7. Open the Our Services page in the Normal tab in Page view.

8. Edit the left navigation bar to include hyperlinks to the child pages under the home page and the home page.

9. Open the *index.htm* page in the Normal tab in Page view.

10. Click at the blank line above the text "Dirty Work Is Our Business!"

11. Insert a bookmark named "Top" at the blank line.

12. Key the text "Back to Top" at the bottom of the page below the update date.

13. Create a hyperlink to the Top bookmark using the "Back to Top" text.

14. Select the bookmark flag (drag the mouse pointer over the flag) and copy it to the Clipboard.

15. Open the *our_services.htm* page, and then paste the bookmark at the first paragraph mark and center it.

16. Open the *index.htm* page and copy the Back to Top hyperlink to the Clipboard.

17. Open the *our_services.htm* page and paste the hyperlink three lines below the bookmark.

18. Follow the Back to Top hyperlink. (*Hint:* Because the page is short, the page does not scroll but the bookmark flag becomes selected.)

19. Print the pages.

20. Close the web and save the pages.

Exercise 7

1. Open the Chocolate6 web located in the Chapter_6 folder on the Data Disk.

2. View the web in Navigation view.

3. Drag the Feedback page to the second level in the structure to the right of the Chocolates page.

4. Right-click the Truffles page and click Copy to copy the page to the Clipboard.

5. Right-click the Chocolates page and click Paste to create a duplicate Truffles page below the Chocolate page.

6. Change the title of the new page to "Pralines."

7. Use the Paste command to create a second copy of the Truffles page below the Chocolate page and change the page title to "Creams."

8. Use the Paste command to create a third copy of the Truffles page below the Chocolate page and change the page title to "Caramels."

9. Create a new second-level page and change the title to "Cookies."

10. Create a new second-level page and change the title to "Cakes."

11. Open the *index.htm* page in the Normal tab in Page view. Delete the company logo object and comment at the top of the page. Edit the navigation bar above the page banner to show hyperlinks to child pages under the home page and the home page. Remove the left shared border on the page.

12. Open the *products.htm* page and delete the navigation bar below the page banner. Remove the left shared border on the page. Delete all the body text, leaving only a one-cell table. (Do not delete the bottom shared border text.) Insert a vertical navigation bar with child-page hyperlinks in the table. Center the navigation bar.

13. Open the *prod01.htm* page and edit the left navigation bar to show hyperlinks to pages at the same level.

14. Open the *cakes.htm*, *cookies.htm*, and *feedback.htm* and remove the left shared border on each of the pages.

15. Print each page.

16. Close the web and save the pages.

Exercise 8

1. Open the Nguyen6 web located in the Chapter_6 folder on the Data Disk.

2. View the *index.htm* page in the Normal tab in Page view.

3. Create a hotspot on the *earth.jpg* image for the *whatsnew.htm*, *faq.htm*, *bugrep.htm*, *suggest.htm*, *download.htm*, *discuss.htm*, and *search.htm* pages.

4. Follow the hyperlinks from Page view.

5. Close the web and save the page.

Case Projects

Project 1

Gourmet Kitchens is a new online cooking and kitchenware supply located in Richmond, Virginia. Mark Steinman, the owner of Gourmet Kitchens, hires you to create a web site. Connect to the Internet, load your web browser, and search for online companies similar to Gourmet Kitchens. Print at least five web pages.Using a word processing program, create a plan for the Gourmet Kitchens web site. Include a critique of the web pages you reviewed, listing their strengths and weaknesses. Compare these web sites to your proposed Gourmet Kitchens web site.

Create the Gourmet Kitchens web site using FrontPage wizards or templates. Include at least five pages in addition to the home page. Include the appropriate company and webmaster contact information, copyright notice, and modification date on all the pages. Apply a custom theme. Add

appropriate text with formatting and images to the remaining pages. Use tables and bulleted or numbered lists as necessary to organize the text. Organize the pages in Navigation view and modify the navigation bar as necessary. Add external hyperlinks to three complementary sites on the Web to one of the pages and verify them. Preview the Gourmet Kitchens web pages in your browser and make any necessary adjustments to the alignment of elements on the pages. Print the web pages. Save and print the plan.

Project 2

Liz Montez is the president of Montez Wholesalers, a company that sells products, such as hair dryers, cutting tools, and shampoos, to hair salons. Ms. Montez hires you to create a web site for Montez Wholesalers. Using a word processing program, create a plan for the web site. Create a one-page web and then view the web in Navigation view. Add at least two second-level pages and three third-level pages in Navigation view. Add appropriate page titles. Apply a theme to the web. Add top and bottom shared borders on all pages. Add a left shared border to the third-level pages. In the bottom shared border, include company contact information, webmaster contact information, a copyright notice, and modification date. In the top shared border, include a page banner and a navigation bar. The navigation bar should include hyperlinks to child pages under the home page and the home-page hyperlinks. In the left shared border on the third-level pages, include a navigation bar with hyperlinks to pages at the same level. Insert text and use text, tables and bulleted and numbered lists and images as appropriate in the body of each page. Insert a scrolling text marquee on the home page. Insert or remove horizontal lines as appropriate. Print the web pages. Save and print the plan.

Project 3

Damon Yang is the owner of Yang Landscaping Services. He hires you to update the company web site, which has not had major modifications in three years. Mr. Yang tells you he wants to include hyperlinks to other complementary pages on the Web and he wants the web site to have a completely new look.

Connect to the Internet, load your web browser, and search for web sites that are appropriate to hyperlink to Yang Landscaping Services web pages. Print at least five web pages.

Using a word processing program, create a plan for the Yang Landscaping Services web site. Create the web site using FrontPage wizards or templates. Include at least three pages in addition to the home page. Include the appropriate company and webmaster contact information, copyright notice, and modification date on all the pages. Apply a custom theme. Add appropriate text with formatting and images to the remaining pages. Use tables and bulleted or numbered lists as necessary to organize the text. Organize the pages in Navigation view and modify the navigation bar as necessary. Add external hyperlinks to five complementary Web sites on one of the pages. Preview the Yang Landscaping Services web pages in your browser and make any

necessary adjustments to the alignment of elements on the pages. Print the web pages. Save and print the plan.

Project 4

You are the program committee chairperson of the local chapter of International Web Designers. At the next chapter luncheon, you plan to make a 15-minute presentation on using FrontPage navigation bars and shared borders. Using online Help, review working with navigation bars and shared borders. Then, using your word processing program, create an outline for the presentation. Explain how to turn on and off shared borders and how to create and edit navigation bars. Create a three-page web with a navigation bar and shared borders to use as an illustration. Print the outline and the web pages. With your instructor's permission, use the outline to demonstrate to your classmates how to work with navigation bars and shared borders.

Project 5

Bette Lindsey is the president of LadyFingers, a company that imports silver jewelry from the Middle East and then sells the jewelry at "jewelry parties" held in private homes. During a party, participants are encouraged to schedule additional jewelry parties. Ms. Lindsey wants her customers to be able to view some of the jewelry products and schedule jewelry parties online. She hires you to create a web site. Using a word processing program, create a plan for the LadyFingers web site. Create the web site using FrontPage wizards or templates. Include at least three pages in addition to the home page. Include the appropriate company and webmaster contact information, copyright notice, and modification date on all the pages. Apply a custom theme. Add appropriate text with formatting to the remaining pages. Use tables and bulleted or numbered lists as necessary to organize the text. Organize the pages in Navigation view and modify the navigation bar as necessary. Insert an appropriate image on the home page and use it to create an image map to the other pages. Insert sound, DHTML effects, scrolling text, motion clips, or other web page

chapter six

elements as appropriate to enhance the web. Preview the web pages in your browser and make any necessary adjustments to the alignment of elements on the pages. Print the web pages. Save and print the plan.

Project 6

You are the new web designer for Lindsey-Bates Travel, a travel agency located in New York City that specializes in custom tours of the British Isles. Your first task is to add some external hyperlinks to the existing web site. The hyperlinks should be to web sites of interest to potential customers who may be booking their custom tour through your company. Connect to the Internet, load your web browser, and use search tools to find at least five appropriate web sites. Print the web pages at each site.

Project 7

Thomas Rutkowsky is the owner of AutoGraph Hounds, a small company that collects and then resells celebrity autographs. He wants to advertise his business online and he hires you to create a web site for his company. Using a word processing program, create a plan for the AutoGraph Hounds web site. Create the web site using FrontPage wizards or templates. Include at least three pages in addition to the home page. Include the appropriate company and webmaster contact information, copyright notice, and modification date on all the pages. Apply a custom theme. Add appropriate text with formatting and images to the pages. Use tables and bulleted or numbered lists as necessary to organize the text. Organize the pages in Navigation view and modify the navigation bar as necessary. Insert sound, DHTML effects, scrolling text, motion clips, or other web page elements as appropriate to enhance the web. Preview the web pages in your browser and make any necessary adjustments to the alignment of elements on the pages. Print the web pages. Save and print the plan.

Project 8

You are the information technology manager for a food wholesaler in Detroit, Michigan. Your company has recently made Internet access available for all its employees. Several employees have indicated their confusion about the term URL. You decide to write an interoffice memo to all employees defining the term. Using online Help, research the term URL. Then, using a word processing program, create an interoffice memo to all employees, which defines the term URL and gives at least three examples. Save and print the memo.

Customizing Web Pages

Chapter Overview

FrontPage themes provide a fast way to apply an attractive and consistent color scheme to a web. You also can add background pictures and color to an individual page or to table cells on a page. You can use styles to quickly apply multiple text and paragraph formats to web page elements. Hover buttons add interest to web pages by adding animation or sound to a button-style hyperlink. In this chapter, you apply background color and a picture to a web page and background color to table cells. You add character and line spacing. Then you create and apply a style to text and insert a hover button.

Case profile

Before your next committee meeting presentation, the Sarah's PartyWorld web should include the completed contents page. To complete the contents page, you want to add background color and specially formatted text. Additionally, you want to create and apply custom text styles on the page, and add a hover button.

LEARNING OBJECTIVES

- Apply colors to web page elements
- Add a background image
- Enhance text
- Format special styles for fonts, paragraphs, and hyperlinks
- Add and edit a hover button
- View the estimated time to download a page

chapter
seven

7.a Applying Colors to Web Page Elements

Colors can help to distinguish and enhance individual web page elements—such as text, page backgrounds, table backgrounds, table borders, hyperlinks, and horizontal lines. For any page that does not use a theme, you can change the page background color, hyperlink colors, and default text color in that element's Properties dialog box. The color you select may be part of a color grid or you can mix a custom color.

You want to manually edit the contents page by changing the font colors and adding a background color or picture. To prepare the contents page for the new formatting, you open the page and create a new row at the bottom of the table. Next, you copy the logo and contact text from the bottom shared border to the new row. Then, you remove the theme and the top and bottom shared borders. Finally, you insert an appropriate navigation bar in the second row of the table.

To edit the *contents.htm* page:

Step 1	*Open*	the Sample_Web you modified in Chapter 6
Step 2	*Open*	the *contents.htm* page in the Normal tab in Page view
Step 3	*Insert*	a new row at the bottom of the table
Step 4	*Copy*	the text following the logo, including the Top of Page hyperlink, to the Clipboard
Step 5	*Paste*	the Clipboard contents into the new row
Step 6	*Insert*	the *sarahslogo.gif* image located in the images folder above the pasted text and verify that it is centered
Step 7	*Remove*	the top and bottom shared borders on the current page
Step 8	*Select*	the second row in the table
Step 9	*Merge*	the cells
Step 10	*Apply*	the (No Theme) option to the selected page
Step 11	*Insert*	a navigation bar with Child pages under Home and Home page hyperlinks in the second row of the table
Step 12	*Center*	the navigation bar in the cell

Your screen should look similar to Figure 7-1. Notice that the theme and shared borders are removed from the page.

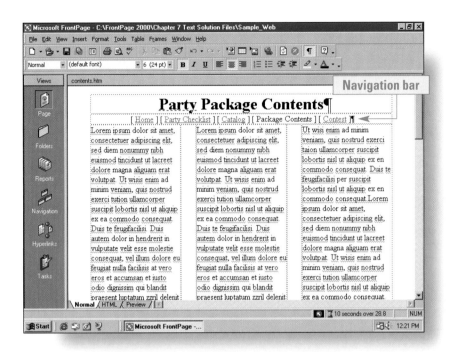

FIGURE 7-1
Contents Page with
Navigation Bar

QUICK TIP

Computer monitors display color by combining different amounts of the primary colors: red, blue, and green. These color combinations are identified by decimal values (base 10) between 0 and 255. For example, a 0 red value means no red appears in that color, whereas a 255 red value means the maximum amount of red appears in that color. The Value: text box in the More Colors dialog box displays the hexadecimal value (base 16) of the color selected on the grid. When you specify colors in a web page (in HTML), the red, green, and blue color values are converted from decimal values (base 10) to hexadecimal values (base 16). To create a custom color combination, click the Custom button in the More Colors dialog box. To pick any visible color on your screen, click the Select button. For more information on selecting and creating custom colors, see online Help.

Now that you have prepared the page, you are ready to format the individual page elements. You begin by adding a background color to the page.

Adding Background Color to a Page

If you are using a theme in a web, you can change the background color for an individual page or all pages in the web by modifying the theme and saving it as a custom theme. If you are not using a theme, you can set the background color for a page in the Page Properties dialog box.

To add a background color to the contents page:

Step 1	*Right-click*	the page background
Step 2	*Click*	Page Properties
Step 3	*Click*	the Background tab

The Page Properties dialog box on your screen should look similar to Figure 7-2. You can select a background color from the Background: color grid, select a color from a color wheel, or you can mix a custom color. You want to select a color from the color wheel.

FIGURE 7-2
Page Properties
Dialog Box

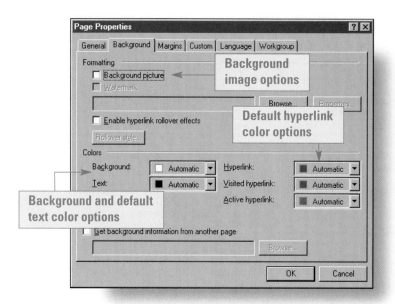

CAUTION TIP

A theme controls the
background color and
default text color used in
a web. The Background
tab does not appear in
the Page Properties dia-
log box for any page that
has a theme applied to it.

Step 4	*Click*	the Ba<u>c</u>kground: list arrow

Step 5	*Click*	<u>M</u>ore Colors

The More Colors dialog box opens. You want to select a very pale blue
for the background color.

Step 6	*Click*	the pale blue color on the color wheel (sixth row from the top and sixth color from the left)

Your More Colors dialog box should look similar to Figure 7-3.

FIGURE 7-3
More Colors Dialog Box

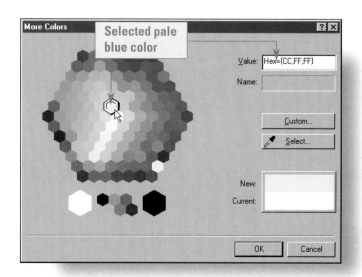

Step 7	*Click*	OK
Step 8	*Observe*	the pale blue color in the Colors Background: box
Step 9	*Click*	OK
Step 10	*Observe*	the new pale blue page background

Because the table has no background color, you can see the page background behind the table text. To make the text easier to read, you add a background color to the table.

Adding Background Color to an Entire Table or a Table Cell

A background color can enhance the look of a table or cell, and make it stand out from the page background. You open the Table Properties dialog box to add a background color to the entire table. If you want to add a background color to individual cells, first select the cells and then open the Cell Properties dialog box.

To add a white background color to the entire table:

Step 1	*Right-click*	the table
Step 2	*Click*	Table Properties
Step 3	*Click*	the Background Color: list arrow
Step 4	*Click*	the White tile in the first row on the color grid
Step 5	*Click*	OK
Step 6	*Observe*	the white background in the table

Next, you want to set the default font color for the page.

Setting Font Color

A theme uses a complementary default font color, which you can change by customizing the theme. You also can format specific text by selecting it and then choosing a color from the Font Color button on the Formatting toolbar or the Color grid in the Font dialog box. If you are not using a theme, you can set the default font for a page in the Page Properties dialog box.

To set the default font for the page to blue:

Step 1	*Open*	the Background tab in the Page Properties dialog box

MENU TIP

You can open the Table or Cell Properties dialog box by pointing to the Properties command on the Table menu and then clicking Table or Cell.

MOUSE TIP

You can set a background color for a table or selected cells with the Fill Color button on the Tables toolbar.

chapter
seven

Step 2	*Click*	the <u>T</u>ext: list arrow
Step 3	*Click*	the Blue tile in the second row of the color grid
Step 4	*Click*	OK
Step 5	*Observe*	that the text color is now blue

To draw attention to the hyperlinks in the navigation bars in the table, you want to change the color from blue to red.

Setting Hyperlink Color

There are three color choices for hyperlinks—the regular hyperlink color, the visited or followed hyperlink, and the active hyperlink. For the contents page, you want to change the hyperlink color to red, the visited hyperlink color to gold, and the active hyperlink to navy. To change the hyperlink colors:

QUICK TIP

You can change the alignment of cell contents in the Cell Properties dialog box. You can also mark cells as **Header cells**, which use boldface to emphasize their contents.

Step 1	*Open*	the Background tab in the Page Properties dialog box
Step 2	*Click*	the <u>H</u>yperlink: list arrow
Step 3	*Click*	the Red tile in the second row on the color grid
Step 4	*Click*	the <u>V</u>isited hyperlink: list arrow
Step 5	*Click*	<u>M</u>ore Colors
Step 6	*Click*	the gold color on the color wheel (third row from the bottom and fourth color from the left)
Step 7	*Click*	OK
Step 8	*Click*	the <u>A</u>ctive hyperlink: list arrow
Step 9	*Click*	the Navy tile in the first row on the color grid
Step 10	*Click*	OK
Step 11	*Observe*	the new hyperlink color in the navigation bar in the second row

A horizontal line is a good way to separate the table text from the navigation bar at the bottom of the table.

Setting Color for Graphic Elements

If you are not using a theme, you can manually set the color for graphic elements in a web, such as horizontal lines and marquees. You want to add and format a horizontal line above the navigation bar in the table. To insert and format a horizontal line:

Step 1	*Insert*	a new row above the navigation bar row at the bottom of the table
Step 2	*Insert*	a horizontal line in the row
Step 3	*Right-click*	the horizontal line
Step 4	*Click*	Horizontal Line Properties

The Horizontal Line Properties dialog box that opens should look similar to Figure 7-4.

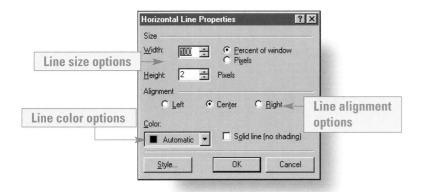

FIGURE 7-4
Horizontal Line Properties
Dialog Box

You can set the height, width, alignment, and color of the horizontal line in this dialog box.

Step 5	*Key*	75 in the Width: text box
Step 6	*Verify*	that the Percent of window option button is selected
Step 7	*Key*	5 in the Height: text box
Step 8	*Click*	the Blue tile in the Color: grid
Step 9	*Click*	OK
Step 10	*Deselect*	the horizontal line
Step 11	*Delete*	the blank line below the horizontal line in the cell

Your screen should look similar to Figure 7-5.

FIGURE 7-5
Contents Page with
Formatted Horizontal Line

After reviewing your changes, you decide to experiment with adding a background image instead of color to the page.

7.b Adding a Background Image

A background image is a good way to add a special pattern, design, or picture to a page. If you are using a theme, you can modify the background picture in the theme when you create a custom theme. If you are not using a theme, you can use pictures from another FrontPage web, another web site, your local file system, or the Clip Gallery as background pictures. When you add a background image to a page, all other page elements, such as text and images, appear on the top of the background picture. If you add the background picture as a **watermark**, the background picture does not scroll with the text as the viewer scrolls the page.

Adding a Background Image to a Web Page

You want to use an image with balloons, party hats, and party favors as the watermark-style background picture for the contents page. To add the background picture:

Step 1	*Open*	the Background tab in the Page Properties dialog box
Step 2	*Click*	the Background picture check box to insert a check mark
Step 3	*Click*	the Watermark check box to insert a check mark
Step 4	*Click*	Browse

Step 5	*Switch*	to the Chapter_7 folder on the Data Disk
Step 6	*Double-click*	the *Background.wmf* file
Step 7	*Click*	OK
Step 8	*Scroll*	the page to view the background picture behind the table

Adding a Background Image to an Entire Table or a Table Cell

You can also add a background image to a table or table cell. You want to visually separate the text columns by adding an image to the empty cell on either side of the center column.

To add the *Background.wmf* image to the cells:

Step 1	*Click*	the Show All button on the Standard toolbar, if necessary
Step 2	*Scroll*	the *contents.htm* page until you can see the paragraph marks in the two empty cells on either side of the center column
Step 3	*Click*	at the paragraph mark in the first empty cell

Your screen should look similar to Figure 7-6.

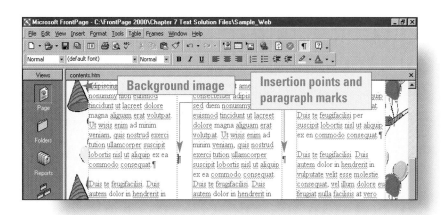

Step 4	*Right-click*	at the insertion point
Step 5	*Click*	Cell Properties

C

FIGURE 7-6
Contents Page with Background Image

The Cell Properties dialog box that opens should look similar to Figure 7-7.

FIGURE 7-7
Cell Properties Dialog Box

Alignment
and size
options

Border and
color options

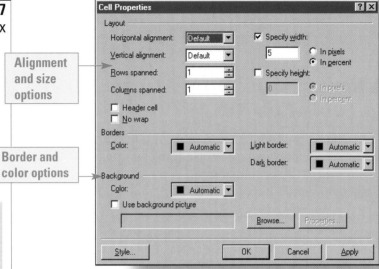

Step 6	*Click*	the Use background picture check box to insert a check mark
Step 7	*Click*	Browse
Step 8	*Switch*	to the Chapter_7 folder on the Data Disk
Step 9	*Double-click*	the *Background.wmf* file
Step 10	*Click*	OK
Step 11	*Observe*	the image in the cell
Step 12	*Insert*	the *Background.wmf* image into the empty cell to the right of the center column

You have modified the background and colors. Next, you insert the appropriate text and add text enhancements to the page.

7.c Enhancing Text Position

You can enhance text by adding, increasing, or decreasing space between the characters; by adding background space before or after a paragraph; and by adding borders and shading. When you created the contents page from a template, it included sample text to illustrate three columns of text. Now you need to delete the sample text and insert the appropriate text, which is available in three separate Word documents.

To insert the appropriate text in the three columns:

Step 1	*Delete*	the sample text in each of the three columns
Step 2	*Click*	in the first empty cell to position the insertion point
Step 3	*Insert*	the *Basic.doc* file located in the Chapter_7 folder on the Data Disk
Step 4	*Insert*	the *Special.doc* file located in the Chapter_7 folder on the Data Disk in the second *empty* cell (skip the cell that contains the background picture)
Step 5	*Insert*	the *Elite.doc* file located in the Chapter_7 folder on the Data Disk in the last *empty* cell
Step 6	*Center*	the text in each cell
Step 7	*Format*	all the table text with the Comic Sans MS font
Step 8	*Save*	the page and save the *Background.gif* file in the images folder

Increasing or Decreasing Space Between Characters

To add a special effect to text, you can enlarge or shrink the spacing between selected characters. You want to increase the character spacing in the Party Package Contents heading. To increase the spacing:

Step 1	*Select*	the Party Package Contents text in the top row of the table
Step 2	*Open*	the Font dialog box
Step 3	*Click*	the Character Spacing tab

The Font dialog box on your screen should look similar to Figure 7-8.

chapter
seven

FIGURE 7-8
Character Spacing Tab in
the Font Dialog Box

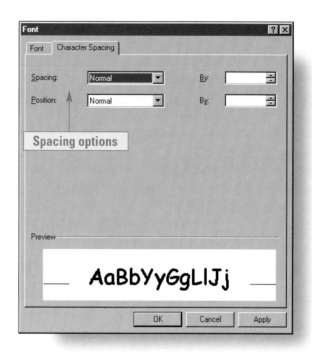

Step 4	*Click*	the Spacing: list arrow
Step 5	*Click*	Expanded
Step 6	*Key*	3 in the By: text box
Step 7	*Click*	OK
Step 8	*Deselect*	the text
Step 9	*Observe*	the additional space between the characters in the Party Package Contents text

Setting Line and Paragraph Spacing

Line spacing sets the amount of background space between lines within a paragraph. **Paragraph spacing** sets the amount of background space before and after a paragraph and between words within a paragraph. To emphasize the Party Package Contents paragraph, you want to increase the amount of background space before and after the paragraph.

To set the line spacing:

Step 1	*Select*	the Party Package Contents text
Step 2	*Right-click*	the text
Step 3	*Click*	Paragraph

The Paragraph dialog box that opens should look similar to Figure 7-9.

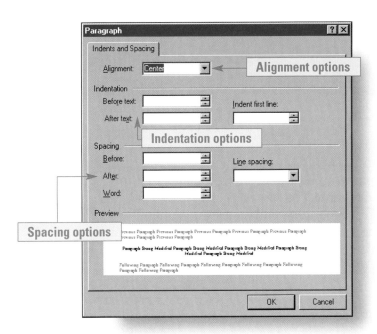

FIGURE 7-9
Paragraph Dialog Box

You can set alignment, indentation, and line spacing options in this dialog box. You want to add 6 points of space before and after the paragraph.

Step 4	*Key*	6 in the <u>B</u>efore: text box in the Spacing section
Step 5	*Key*	6 in the Aft<u>e</u>r: text box in the Spacing section
Step 6	*Click*	OK
Step 7	*Deselect*	the text
Step 8	*Observe*	the additional background space before and after the Party Package Contents paragraph

You want to make the table narrower and move it down one line so that more of the background image is visible. To size the table:

Step 1	*Change*	the width to 75% in the Table Properties dialog box
Step 2	*Click*	before the P in Party in the first row to position the insertion point
Step 3	*Press*	the ENTER key to create a new line above the table
Step 4	*Save*	the page

The contents page is almost complete. You want to modify the formatting for the Basic Package name text and then apply the formatting quickly to the other package names. You can do this by creating a style.

QUICK TIP

You can position or place elements, such as text and graphics, on a page to control their exact locations. When you want elements to be treated as a unit, you can combine positioning features to group the elements. For more information on positioning web page elements, see online <u>H</u>elp.

chapter
seven

C 7.d Formatting Special Styles for Fonts, Paragraphs, and Hyperlinks

A **style** is a group of formatting choices (such as font, font size, bold, center align, paragraph spacing, font color, etc.) that you save with a name. You can then select a web page element, such as text, paragraphs, pictures, hyperlinks, and tables, and apply all the formats at one time. A big advantage to using styles is that when you modify a style, all the elements formatted with that style are automatically updated with the new formatting.

Creating a Style

HTML provides standard styles that are listed in the Style button list box on the Formatting toolbar. When you create a custom style, the style is added to the list of available styles for that page, not for the entire web. To create a style that you can use on all pages in the web, you must use a style sheet. You want to create a style for package names, which includes font size, font style, special text effect, and spacing formats.

To create the style:

| Step 1 | *Click* | F̲ormat |
| Step 2 | *Click* | S̲tyle |

The Style dialog box that opens should look similar to Figure 7-10.

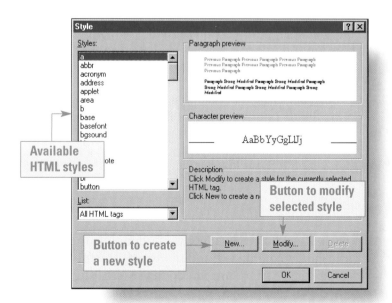

You can create, modify, or delete styles in this dialog box.

| Step 3 | *Click* | New |

The New Style dialog box that opens should look similar to Figure 7-11.

MOUSE TIP

You can apply styles from the Style button list on the Formatting toolbar.

FIGURE 7-11
New Style Dialog Box

QUICK TIP

You can open the Style dialog box and delete a user-defined style. When you delete a style from a page, the element formatted with the style reverts to its original formatting.

You name the style and specify the formatting attributes in this dialog box. You name the style "pkg" as an abbreviation for "package." Then you specify the Comic Sans MS font, Bold font style, 14 point font size, Small caps effect, and 6 points of background space before the text.

Step 4	*Key*	pkg in the Name (selector): text box
Step 5	*Click*	Format
Step 6	*Click*	Font in the drop-down list to open the Font dialog box
Step 7	*Click*	Comic Sans MS in the Font: list
Step 8	*Click*	Bold in the Font style: list
Step 9	*Click*	14pt in the Size: list
Step 10	*Click*	the Small caps check box to insert a check mark
Step 11	*Click*	OK to close the Font dialog box

Next you add the spacing format.

| Step 12 | *Click* | Format |

Step 13	*Click*	<u>P</u>aragraph
Step 14	*Key*	6 in the <u>B</u>efore: text box in the Spacing section
Step 15	*Click*	OK three times to close the Paragraph, New Style, and Style dialog boxes

After you create a style, you can apply it.

Applying a Style

Applying a style attaches the entire group of formatting options to a
page element. You apply a style by selecting the page element you want
to format, and then selecting the style from the Style button list on the
Formatting toolbar. To select the text and apply the style:

Step 1	*Select*	the Basic Package text in the first cell in the third row of the table
Step 2	*Click*	the Style button list arrow ⟦Heading 1 ▾⟧ on the Formatting toolbar
Step 3	*Scroll*	to the end of the Style list
Step 4	*Point to*	the .pkg style

Your screen should look similar to Figure 7-12.

FIGURE 7-12
Custom Style in Style List

Your custom style has been added to the default HTML styles in the
list with the name ".pkg."

Step 5	*Click*	the .pkg custom style in the list
Step 6	*Deselect*	the text

Step 7	*Observe*	the new formatting applied to the text
Step 8	*Select*	the Special Package text
Step 9	*Apply*	the .pkg style
Step 10	*Select*	the Elite Package text
Step 11	*Apply*	the .pkg style

After deselecting the text, your screen should look similar to Figure 7-13.

FIGURE 7-13
Reformatted Titles

After you review the formatting of the package names, you decide their font color should be red.

Modifying a Style

Modifying a style changes the existing style by adding a new formatting element or revising an existing one. When you modify a style, all the elements formatted with the style are updated automatically. You want to modify the .pkg style for a red color font. To modify the style:

Step 1	*Open*	the Style dialog box
Step 2	*Verify*	.pkg is selected in the Styles: list and User-defined styles is selected in the List: list
Step 3	*Click*	Modify

The Modify Style dialog box opens, and it contains the same options as the New Style dialog box. You change the font color in this dialog box.

chapter
seven

Step 4	*Click*	Format
Step 5	*Click*	Font
Step 6	*Click*	the Red tile in the second row of the Color: color grid
Step 7	*Click*	OK three times to close all the dialog boxes
Step 8	*Observe*	that the font color of the package titles is automatically changed to red
Step 9	*Save*	the page

Another way to add interesting animation to a page is to use a hover button.

7.e Adding and Editing a Hover Button

A **hover button** is a button that contains a hyperlink to another page or file. You can add special animation effects to a hover button so that when a viewer points to the button, the button color changes or the button appearance becomes three-dimensional. First you add a hover button, and then you experiment with different transitional effects.

Adding a Hover Button

A hover button is a FrontPage component like a marquee or hit counter. You want to insert a hyperlink to the home page at the bottom of the contents page table and you want to use a hover button component for the hyperlink.

To insert the hover button:

Step 1	*Scroll*	to view the bottom of the table
Step 2	*Click*	at the blank line below the Top of Page hyperlink and center the insertion point
Step 3	*Click*	the Insert Component button on the Standard toolbar
Step 4	*Click*	Hover Button

The Hover Button Properties dialog box that opens should look similar to Figure 7-14.

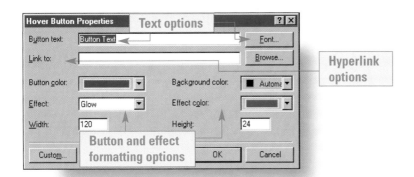

FIGURE 7-14
Hover Button Properties
Dialog Box

You can size the button, add text or a picture, add button background color or effect color, specify the animation effect, and specify the hyperlink in this dialog box. You want the button text to be "Home Page," the text font to be red Sans MS, the button color to be blue, and the effect color to be yellow. The first effect you want to try is the glow effect.

Step 5	Key	Home Page in the Button text: text box
Step 6	Click	Font
Step 7	Change	the font to MS Sans Serif, bold, 14 pt, and red in the Font dialog box
Step 8	Click	OK
Step 9	Click	in the Link to: text box
Step 10	Key	index.htm
Step 11	Click	the Blue tile in the Button color: color grid
Step 12	Click	Glow in the Effect: list, if necessary
Step 13	Click	the Yellow tile in the Effect color: color grid
Step 14	Click	OK
Step 15	Observe	the new blue hover button with a hyperlink to the home page

You must save the page before you can preview the hover button effect. To preview the hover button:

Step 1	Save	the page
Step 2	Preview	the page in the Preview tab
Step 3	Point to	the hover button to observe the glow effect

chapter
seven

Your screen should look similar to Figure 7-15.

FIGURE 7-15
Hover Button Preview

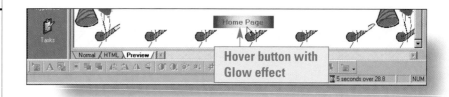

| Step 4 | *Switch* | to the Normal tab |

You decide to try a different effect.

Editing a Hover Button Transitional Effect

You can edit a hover button by opening the hover button Properties dialog box and changing the button size, color, or animation effect. You decide to make the hover button effect more dramatic by having the button color change completely when the viewer points to it. To change the animation effect:

Step 1	*Right-click*	the hover button
Step 2	*Click*	Hover Button Properties
Step 3	*Click*	Color fill in the <u>E</u>ffect: list box
Step 4	*Click*	OK
Step 5	*Save*	the page
Step 6	*Preview*	the page and test the hover button animation
Step 7	*Switch*	to the Normal tab

The contents page is complete. You are curious about how long it will take for a viewer to download the contents page.

7.f Viewing the Estimated Time to Download a Page

The more text, images, and other elements you add to a page, the longer the page takes to download in a viewer's web browser. Also, the slower a viewer's connection, the longer it takes to download the page. It is a good idea to monitor your pages to estimate the download time.

You can do this with the Slow Pages report in Reports view. You can also do this quickly for the current page using the status bar.

The status bar shows you the estimated time to download the current page based on the selected connection speed. When you point to the section of the status bar that includes an hourglass icon, the ScreenTip "Estimated Time to Download" appears. To view the estimated time to download for the contents page:

| Step 1 | *Point to* | the hourglass icon ⧖ in the right side of the status bar |
| Step 2 | *Observe* | the ScreenTip "Estimated Time to Download" |

To the right of the hourglass icon you see the estimated time of five seconds to download the contents page, based on a 28.8 modem connection. You can change the connection speed to see a revised estimated time to download. To change the connection speed in the estimate:

Step 1	*Right-click*	the Estimated Time to Download section on the status bar
Step 2	*Click*	56.6
Step 3	*Observe*	that the Estimated Time to Download changes to two seconds with a 56.6 modem
Step 4	*Right-click*	the Estimated Time to Download section on the status bar
Step 5	*Click*	28.8
Step 6	*Save*	the page
Step 7	*Close*	the web

The contents page is completed. The special background, table, and text formatting make the page fun and attractive. Next, you use frames to complete the company profile page.

MENU TIP

You can turn the status bar on or off in the General tab of the Options dialog box. To open the dialog box, click the Options command on the Tools menu.

chapter
seven

Summary

▶ When you are not using a theme to format pages in a web, you can manually format a page by adding background color or a background image, default font attributes such as font size and color, and hyperlink colors.

▶ You can add background color or image to an entire table or selected table cells.

▶ You can enhance text on a web page by adding shading, borders, or character and line spacing.

▶ To quickly format web page elements you can create a style containing multiple formats and then apply the style to individual elements.

▶ A hover button is a button-style hyperlink with animation effects.

▶ You can monitor the download time for your web pages with the Slow Pages report in Reports view or with the Estimated Time to Download section on the status bar.

Commands Review

Action	Menu Bar	Shortcut Menu	Toolbar/Mouse	Keyboard
Add page background color, page background image, or default hyperlink or font formatting	File, Page Properties	Right-click the page, click Page Properties		ALT + F, I
Add background color or image to a table or table cells	Table, Properties	Right-click the table, click Table Properties Right-click selected cells, click Cell Properties		ALT + A, R
Add shading to text	Format, Borders and Shading			ALT + O, B
Increase or decrease character spacing	Format, Font	Right-click text, click Font		ALT + O, F ALT + ENTER
Change paragraph or line spacing	Format, Paragraph	Right-click text, click Paragraph		ALT + O, P
Create or modify styles	Format, Style			ALT + O, S
Apply a style			Heading 1 ▾	CTRL + SHIFT + S
Insert a hover button	Insert, Component		⬛	ALT + I, O
View the properties for selected web page element	Format, Properties			ALT + O, I ALT + ENTER

Concepts Review

Circle the correct answer.

1. **A style is a:**
   [a] theme.
   [b] template.
   [c] group of formatting choices saved with a name.
   [d] image map.

2. **You can add a page background color or image with options in the:**
   [a] File Properties dialog box.
   [b] Page Properties dialog box.
   [c] Table Properties dialog box.
   [d] Web Properties.

3. **A watermark background picture:**
   [a] is an image map.
   [b] scrolls with the text.
   [c] has washed-out color.
   [d] does not scroll with the text.

4. **Which of the following tabs does not appear in the Page Properties dialog box when you apply a theme?**
   [a] Background
   [b] Margins
   [c] General
   [d] Custom

5. **You can add background color to an entire table in the:**
   [a] Page Properties dialog box.
   [b] Cell Properties dialog box.
   [c] Table Properties dialog box.
   [d] File Properties dialog box.

6. **A hover button contains a:**
   [a] picture of the home page.
   [b] hyperlink to another page or file.
   [c] style.
   [d] bookmark.

7. **Computer monitors show color on the screen by combining different amounts of the primary colors:**
   [a] yellow, orange, and red.
   [b] white, brown, and black.
   [c] red, blue, and green.
   [d] purple, orange, and green.

8. **If you want to share styles between pages, you must create:**
   [a] a style group.
   [b] an embedded style sheet
   [c] shared borders.
   [d] an external style sheet.

9. **You add background color to cells in the:**
   [a] File Properties dialog box.
   [b] Cell Properties dialog box.
   [c] Page Properties dialog box.
   [d] Table Properties dialog box.

10. **You can view the estimated time to download the current page on the:**
    [a] Standard toolbar.
    [b] Formatting toolbar.
    [c] status bar.
    [d] Views bar.

chapter seven

Circle **T** if the statement is true or **F** if the statement is false.

T   F   1. The more text, images, and other elements you add to a page, the faster the page downloads.

T   F   2. Adding text enhancements can make a web page more attractive and interesting.

T   F   3. You must use a theme to add a background image to a page.

T   F   4. You can add background color to an entire table, but not to selected cells.

T   F   5. You can apply the background picture, color, hyperlink colors, and text colors from one page to another.

T   F   6. You can add borders and shading to text.

T   F   7. You cannot change the amount of space between lines of text on a web page.

T   F   8. An external style sheet is a separate page in the web that contains custom styles.

T   F   9. You apply a style by selecting the web page element and then selecting the style from the Font list on the Formatting toolbar.

T   F   10. You can change the animation effect for a hover button.

Glossary

Use online <u>Help</u> to look up the following words in the FrontPage glossary. Then, using your word processing program, create a document listing each word and its glossary definition. Save and print the document.

1. Banner Ad Manager

2. category

3. embedded style sheet

4. Hover Button component

5. external style sheet

Skills Review

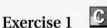

Exercise 1

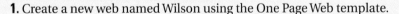

1. Create a new web named Wilson using the One Page Web template.

2. Open the *index.htm* file in the Normal tab in Page view.

3. Open the Page Properties dialog box and set the page background color to pale green (eighth color down, fifth color to the right with Hex={CC,FF,99}) and the default text color to Lime.

4. Insert and then center the banner image *bd10295_.gif* located in the Chapter_7 folder on the Data Disk.

5. Select the banner image and click the Text button on the Pictures toolbar to add a text box to the banner. Change the font size to 5 (18 pt), the font style to bold, and the font color to Lime. Then key "Home Page" in the text box on the banner.

6. Create a 1 by 1 Table below the banner 75% of its original size, centered, with a Lime border. Add a Navy background color to the table.

7. Key the following welcome message in the table:

   Welcome to Wilson Electronics. Check out our outstanding offers on portable organizers, computers, stereos, and TVs.

8. Format the table text with 6 (24 pt) font size and center it in the table. Add the DHTML effect: on mouse over, format the text with bold and the Small caps effect.

9. Create a new blank line below the table and insert a horizontal line. Format the line as 50% of the window width, 5 pixels high, center aligned, and Navy color.

10. Create a new blank line below the horizontal line.

11. At the new blank line insert a 2 by 4 Table with no border and add a Lime background color to the cells.

12. Select the first row of the new table, change the font color to Navy and the font size to 4 (14 pt). Then key and center the following text in the four cells:

Organizers
Computers
Stereos
TVs

13. Insert the button image *bd10311_.gif* located in the Chapter_7 folder on the Data Disk in the first cell in the second row.

14. Copy the button image to the Clipboard and then paste it into the remaining three cells. Center the buttons in the cells.

15. Save the page and save the images to the images folder.

16. Switch to Navigation view and add the following four pages as child pages under the home page:

Organizers
Computers
Stereos
TVs

17. Open the *organizers.htm* page. Copy the background information from the *index.htm* page to the *organizers.htm* page by doing the following: Open the Background tab in the Page Properties dialog box, click the Get background information from another page check box to insert a check mark, and then browse to select the *index.htm* page.

18. Copy the background information from the *index.htm* page to the other new pages.

19. Switch to the *index.htm* page and use the buttons in the second table to create hyperlinks to the appropriate pages. Then create a bookmark using the word "Welcome" in the first table.

20. Insert two blank lines below the second table on the *index.htm* page. Insert a centered hover button on the second blank line. Use the text "Back to Top" and then format the hover button with Navy text, a link to the Welcome bookmark, Glow effect, and Lime effect color.

21. Save the page and save the images in the images folder.

22. Preview the *index.htm* page to test the hyperlinks and DHTML effects, and then print preview and print it.

23. Close the web and save the pages.

Exercise 2   C

1. Create a new web named Citrus using the Empty Web template.

2. Add a new page in Page view.

3. Add the *bd14712_.gif* image located in the Chapter_7 folder on the Data Disk as a background image. Change the default hyperlink colors, using the color grid and color wheel as needed: Hyperlink to dark green, Visited hyperlink to Lime, and Active hyperlink to orange. Change the default font color to dark green.

4. Insert the *na00417_.gif* image located in the Chapter_7 folder on the Data Disk as a company logo in the upper-left corner of the page.

5. Size the picture to approximately 1 inch by 1 inch and resample it.

chapter seven

6. Create a new blank line below the logo image and center the insertion point. Then set the font to 7 (36 pt) bold and key "Citrus Valley, Inc."

7. Select the "Citrus Valley, Inc." text and expand the character spacing by three points.

8. Insert the *bd14689.gif* banner image located in the Chapter_7 folder on the Data Disk below the company name.

9. Size the picture to 50% of its original size and resample it.

10. Create a new blank line below the banner image and enter the following text:

    Welcome to Citrus Valley, the premier online retailer of citrus fruits and citrus fruit products.

11. Format the welcome text with the 6 (24pt) font.

12. Save the page as *index.htm* and save the three image files in the images folder.

13. Switch to Navigation view and add the following three new child pages below the home page:

    Oranges
    Lemons
    Limes

14. Create a centered 1 by 3 Table 75% of its original width below the welcome paragraph.

15. Insert the *fd01010_.wmf* image in the first cell; the *fd01006_.wmf* image in the second cell, and the *na01088_.wmf* image in the third cell. The image files are located in the Chapter_7 folder on the Data Disk. Size each image as you insert it to be approximately 1 inch high by 1½ inches wide with the mouse pointer. Center the images in the cells.

16. Create hyperlinks from each image to the appropriate page in the web.

17. Add a row to the bottom of the table and merge the cells. Add a white background color to the row. Insert a navigation bar with Child pages under Home hyperlinks in the new row. Center the hyperlinks.

18. Open the *lemons.htm* page. Copy the background information from the *index.htm* page to the *lemons.htm* page by doing the following: Open the Background tab in the Page Properties dialog box, click the Get background information from another page check box to insert a check mark, and browse to select the *index.htm* page. Save the page. Copy the background information from the *index.htm* page to the other new pages and save each page.

19. On the *lemons.htm* page, insert a hover button in the upper-left corner of the page. Format the hover button as follows: button text is "Home" in dark green font; hyperlink to *index.htm*; button color is orange; effect is Color fill; effect color is yellow. Save the page. Copy the hover button to the Clipboard. Paste the hover button in the *limes.htm* and *oranges.htm* pages and save the pages.

20. Preview the *index.htm* page and then test the hyperlinks to the child pages and test the hover button on each child page.

21. Print preview and print the pages.

22. Close the web and save pages and images if asked.

Exercise 3 C

1. Create a new web named Arts using the Personal Web template.

2. Open the *index.htm* page in the Normal tab in Page view.

3. Remove the theme from all pages.

4. Insert the *wb005311.gif* image as the background image and change the default Text color and Active hyperlink color to medium dark blue (Hex={66,00,FF}) on the *index.htm* page. Save the page and save the background image in the images folder.

5. Open the *favorite.htm* page. Copy the background information from the *index.htm* page to the *favorite.htm* page by doing the following: Open the Background tab in the Page Properties dialog box, click the <u>G</u>et background information from another page check box to insert a check mark, browse to select the *index.htm* page. Save the page. Copy the background information from the *index.htm* page to the other pages and save each page.

6. Switch to the *index.htm* page and remove the left shared border on all pages. Then edit the navigation bar in the top shared border to include hyperlinks to the C<u>h</u>ild pages under Home and the Ho<u>m</u>e page.

7. Switch to Navigation view and drag the *myfav3.htm* page to the right of the Favorites page.

8. Switch to the *index.htm* page in the Normal tab in Page view and replace the sample paragraph below the welcome heading with the following text:

I enjoy working with arts, crafts, and needlework of all kinds. The purpose of this web site is to share with you some of the interesting projects and online sources I've found.

9. Switch to the *interest.htm* page and delete the sample text above the horizontal line. Replace the sample bullet text with "Knit," "Crochet," and "Cross Stitch."

10. Switch to the *myfav3.htm* page and change the page banner text to "My Favorite Site." Delete the sample text and create a centered 1 by 1 Table 75% of its original size with a border color using the medium dark blue color of your choice.

11. Center the insertion point in the table and key "Stitchers' Paradise." Format the text as 7 (36 pt) bold. Create an external hyperlink using the "Stitchers' Paradise" text to http://www.stitchers-paradise.com/index.html.

12. Switch to the *favorite.htm* page and delete the sample text above the horizontal line.

13. Delete the *photo.htm* page from the web.

14. Preview, print preview, and print all the pages.

15. Close the web and save the pages.

Exercise 4

1. Create a new web named Penny using the One Page Web template.

2. Open the *index.htm* page in the Normal tab in Page view.

3. Insert the *bd00364_.gif* image located in the Chapter_7 folder on the Data Disk as a background image.

4. Create a style named "txt" that contains the following formatting: Arial Rounded MT Bold font, bold style, 24pt size, Navy color, Small caps effect, 12 points of space before and after, and center alignment.

5. Create a style named "bdy" that contains the following formatting: Arial font, 24pt size, Navy color, center alignment, and light purple (Hex={FF,CC,FF}) shading.

6. Press the ENTER key three times. On the last new line create a 1 by 1 Table, centered, 75% of its original width, with a Navy border. Add a light purple (Hex={FF,CC,FF}) background color to the table.

7. Key "Penny's Flower Power" in the table and apply the .txt style to the text.

8. Insert two new lines below the table and key the following on the second line:

Welcome to Penny's Flower Power, the fastest-growing silk flower shop on the web. We hope you enjoy shopping with us!

9. Apply the .bdy style to the welcome text.

10. Save the page and save the background image in the images folder.

11. Preview, print preview, and print the page.

12. Close the web.

Exercise 5

1. Open the Secretarial7 web located in the Chapter_7 folder on the Data Disk.

2. Open the *index.htm* page in the Normal tab in Page view.

3. Add a bookmark location named "Top" to the top of the page at the blank line below the top shared border.

4. Insert a new blank line at the bottom of the page and create a hover button hyperlink at the blank line to the Top bookmark formatted as follows: Top of Page button text; link to Top bookmark; button color Maroon; Glow effect; effect color Fuchsia.

5. Follow the Top of Page hover button hyperlink on the *index.htm* page.

6. Save the page.

7. Copy the bookmark location flag to the Clipboard and paste it at the top of the page (immediately below the top shared border) on the *fax.htm*, *forms.htm*, *letters.htm*, and *telephone.htm* pages.

8. Switch to the *index.htm* page and copy the hover button to the Clipboard. Paste it two lines below the location bookmark on the *fax.htm*, *forms.htm*, *letters.htm*, and *telephone.htm* pages. Save each page.

9. Preview the *index.htm* page to test the hover button.

10. Print preview and print all the pages.

11. Close the web.

Exercise 6

1. Create a new web named Pet_Grooming using the One Page Web template.

2. View the *index.htm* page in the Normal tab in Page view.

3. Set the page background color to Olive and the default font color and <u>H</u>yperlink color to light gold (Hex={FF,CC,00}). Set the <u>A</u>ctive hyperlink color to Olive.

4. Key the following text at the top of the page, inserting a line break (press the SHIFT + ENTER keys) after each line except the phone number. Press the ENTER key after the phone number.

Jose's Pet Grooming and Supplies
1100 Woodbury Road
Providence, RI 02905-1100
401-555-7888

5. Format the text with the Broadway font and 6 (24 pt) font size and center it.

6. Switch to Navigation view and add three new pages with the following names: Cats, Dogs, and Birds.

7. On the blank line below the phone number, insert a navigation bar with <u>C</u>hild pages under Ho<u>m</u>e page hyperlinks. Select the navigation bar and change the font size to 4 (14 pt), and center it.

8. Add a blank line below the navigation bar. Create a 1 by 1 Table centered with a gold 1 pt border. Insert the *bd08804_.wmf* image located in the Chapter_7 folder on the Data Disk as the table background.

9. Size the table by dragging the bottom table boundary down until the image pattern begins to repeat.

10. Insert a line below the table. Key the following text and then format the text with the 5 (18 pt) font and center it:

E-mail us at grooming@dogsandcats.com for our latest grooming price list and supplies catalog.

11. Create a bookmark location named "Top" at the top of the page. Center a Top of Page hover button with appropriate text, colors, and the effect of your choice below the e-mail text at the bottom of the page.

12. Save the page and the background image in the images folder.

13. Change the background color of the *cats.htm*, *birds.htm*, and *dogs.htm* pages to Olive. Add a hover button to the top of each page with a hyperlink to the home page. Format the hover button with appropriate colors and text. Save each page.

14. Preview the *index.htm* page and test the hyperlinks and hover button. Test the hover button on each of the remaining pages.

15. Print preview and print the pages.

16. Close the web.

Exercise 7

1. Create a new web named Markowitz using the Empty Web template.

2. Create a new page in Page view.

3. Create a 3 by 3 Table centered with no border. Merge the cells vertically in the first column. Merge the cells vertically in the third column. Add the Purple background color to the cell in the first column. Add the Navy background color to the third column.

4. Create a style named "txt" with the following formatting: Arial Narrow, Bold, 24pt Purple, centered, with 6 points of background space before and after the text.

5. Create a style named "txt2" with the following formatting: Arial Narrow, Bold, 18pt Purple, centered.

6. In the first blank cell in the middle column, key *Markowitz*. In the second blank cell in the middle column key *Consulting*. In the third blank cell in the middle column, key *Services*.

7. Select the three cells in the middle column and apply the .txt style to the text.

8. Create a new blank line. On the second line below the table, insert the Word document *mission.doc*. Apply the .txt2 style to the text.

9. Save the page as *index.htm* and change the title to Markowitz Consulting Services.

10. Preview, print preview, and print the page.

11. Close the web.

Exercise 8

1. Open the Rameriz7 web located in the Chapter_7 folder on the Data Disk.

2. Open the *index.htm* page in the Normal tab in Page view.

3. Replace the Back to Top hyperlink text in the bottom shared border with a hover button. Format the hover button appropriately to match the web's theme. Use the effect of your choice.

4. Save the page and preview the hover button.

5. Verify the hover button hyperlink works on all pages that share the bottom border.

6. View the estimated time to download the *index.htm*, *archive.htm*, *discuss.htm*, *members.htm*, *schedule.htm*, *search.htm*, and *status.htm* pages with a 14.4, 28.8, and 56.6 modem.

7. Print preview and print the *index.htm* page.

8. Close the web and save the pages.

chapter seven

Case Projects

Project 1

LaVernelle's Designer Dolls, owned by LaVernelle Washington, is a small company that specializes in creating custom collectible designer dolls. LaVernelle's Designer Dolls is located in Charleston, South Carolina. Ms. Washington wants to advertise and sell her dolls online and hires you to create a web site for her company. Before you begin, you want to see if there are similar companies doing business online. Connect to the Internet, load your web browser, and search for web sites that advertise and sell designer dolls.

Using a word processing program, create a plan for the LaVernelle's Designer Dolls web site. Include a critique of the web pages you reviewed, listing their strengths and weaknesses. Compare these web sites to the site you are proposing.

Create a sample web site with three pages, including the home page. Insert a background image and set the default text and hyperlink colors for the home page. Copy the background and default settings from the home page to the other two pages. Insert appropriately formatted text and appropriate page banner and button images from the Clip Gallery or other sources as provided by your instructor. Include the appropriate company and webmaster contact information, copyright notice, and modification date on all the pages. Use tables and bulleted and numbered lists as necessary to organize the text. Use background images or colors in the tables as appropriate. Turn on or off shared borders as appropriate. Organize the pages in Navigation view and insert appropriate navigation bars on all the pages. Use a hover button for the home page hyperlink on the child pages to the home page. Preview the web pages in your browser and make any necessary adjustments to the alignment of elements on the pages. Print the web pages. Save and print the plan.

Project 2

South Street Gourmet Coffee is a company that supplies gourmet coffee to restaurants around the country. Chris Chang, the president of South Street, wants to begin selling directly to consumers online. She hires you to create a web site for the company.

Using a word processing program, create a plan for the web site. Create a one-page web and then view the web in Navigation view. Add at least two second-level pages and three third-level pages in Navigation view. Add appropriate page titles. Apply a background image or color to all the pages. Add top and bottom shared borders on all pages. Add a left shared border to the third-level pages.

In the bottom shared border include company contact information, webmaster contact information, a copyright notice, and modification date. In the top shared border include a page banner image from the Clip Gallery (or other source provided by your instructor) and a navigation bar. The navigation bar should include hyperlinks to Child pages under the Home page and the Home page hyperlinks. In the left shared border on the third-level pages include a navigation bar with hyperlinks to pages at the same level.

Add text, tables and bulleted and numbered lists and images as appropriate in the body of each page. Add an appropriate background image or color to each page. View and write down the estimated time to download each page using a 28.8 modem, a 56.6 modem, and a T1 line. Print the web pages. Add the estimated time to download information to the plan, and then save and print the plan.

Project 3

Charlotte Johnson is the owner of WearAbleArt, a small company that hires disabled persons and teaches them to create custom clothing with hand-painted designs. Ms. Johnson reviewed several of her competitors' web sites and she thinks its time her company has a web site. She hires you to create one.

Using a word processing program, create a plan for the WearAbleArt web site. Create an empty web site and add three pages including the home page. Organize the pages in Navigation view. Apply a background image or color and set default text and hyperlink colors for the home page. Copy the background and default color settings to the other two pages. Insert tables, text, images, and FrontPage components as appropriate. Use styles as appropriate. View and write down the estimated time to download for each page using a 28.8 modem, a 56.6 modem, and a T1 line. Print the web pages. Add the estimated time to download information to the plan and then save and print the plan.

Project 4

You are the web author for your company, Angela's Homemade Pasta Sauce. Your supervisor read a brief article in a web design journal that mentioned using external style sheets and absolute positioning for web elements, and he is not familiar with either process. He asks you to research the topics and explain the processes to him. Using online <u>H</u>elp, research how to position web elements on the page and how to create and use external style sheets. Then, using a word processing program, write your supervisor a memo discussing how to use absolute-style positioning for web page elements and how to create and use external style sheets. Create a sample web with one page and use absolute positioning to position two images on the page. Create an external style sheet in the web. Print the web page and print the memo.

Project 5

Misty Manners is the president of Micron Books, a company that publishes adventure novels for teenagers and young adults. Ms. Manners wants to start advertising the company's book series online, and she hires you to create the company site.

Using a word processing program, create a plan for the Micron Books web site. Create the web site using the Empty Web template. Create the home page in Page view. Add two more pages in Navigation view. Apply a background color or image to the home page. Set the default font and hyperlink colors for the home page. Copy the background and default color settings to the two new pages. Include the appropriate company and webmaster contact information, copyright notice, and modification date on all the pages. Add appropriate text with formatting to the pages. Use tables and bulleted and numbered lists as necessary to organize the text. Insert sound, DHTML effects, scrolling text, motion clips, hover buttons, or other web page elements as appropriate to enhance the web. Preview the web pages in your browser and make any necessary adjustments to the alignment of elements on the pages. View and write down the estimated time to download each page using a 28.8 modem, a 56.6 modem, and a T1 line. Print the web pages. Add the estimated time to download information to the plan, and then save and print the plan.

Project 6

You are the new web designer for the Baby SuperStore, a company located in San Francisco, California, that specializes in selling baby products and supplies online. Your first assignment is to add three external hyperlinks to the existing web site. The hyperlinks should be to web sites of interest to potential customers who may be purchasing their baby supplies from Baby SuperStore. Connect to the Internet, load your web browser, and use search tools to find at least five appropriate web sites. Print the web pages at each site.

Project 7

Laura Linden is the president of The Exercise Club, a company that sells exercise videos, workout clothing, and exercise equipment. Laura wants to expand the company's business by selling directly to consumers online. She hires you to create a web site for The Exercise Club.

Using a word processing program, create a plan for The Exercise Club web site. Create a sample web site with three pages, including the home page. Insert a background image and set the default text and hyperlink colors for the home page. Copy the background and default settings from the home page to the other two pages. Insert appropriately formatted text and appropriate page banner and button images from the Clip Gallery or other sources as provided by your instructor. Include the appropriate company and webmaster contact information, copyright notice, and modification date on all the pages. Use tables and bulleted and numbered lists as necessary to organize the text. Use background images or colors in the tables as appropriate. Turn on or off shared borders as appropriate. Organize the pages in Navigation view and insert appropriate navigation bars on all the pages. Use a hover button for the home page hyperlink on the child pages to the home page. Preview the web pages in your browser and make any necessary adjustments to the alignment of elements on the pages. Print the web pages. Save and print the plan.

Project 8

You are the web designer for a small camping-equipment retailer in Boise, Idaho. Your company web site has several pages. The president calls you to ask if it is possible to add a table of contents to help viewers at the site. You have no experience creating one. Using online Help, research how to create a table of contents for a web. Then using your word processing program, write the president a memo describing how you can create a table of contents for the site. Open the multi-page web of your choice and create a table of contents page. Print the table of contents page.

Using Frames

Chapter Overview

FrontPage navigation bars and shared borders on web pages enable viewers to navigate quickly to different pages in a web and view the same information on different pages. Another alternative is to use frames to divide a viewer's screen into two or more areas that contain separate web pages. Frames enable viewers to change the content in one area of the screen without affecting other areas. In this chapter, you use a FrontPage template to create a page with two frames: one frame that contains a page with hyperlinks to other web pages, and a second frame to contain the linked page when the viewer clicks a hyperlink in the first frame.

LEARNING OBJECTIVES

▶ Use a template to create a new frames page
▶ Add target content within a frame
▶ Create a no-frames alternative

Case profile

During the last committee meeting, Sarah Whaley, the owner of Sarah's PartyWorld, commented that some of her competitors were using frames on their web pages. She asked to see an example of a frames page in the Sarah's PartyWorld web. You decide to add frames to the company profile page.

chapter eight

8.a Using a Template to Create a New Frames Page

You want viewers of the Sarah's PartyWorld company profile page to be able to view company background information and the company privacy policy for information gathered at the web site. You decide to experiment with frames pages on the company profile page to do this. A **frames page** is a web page that divides a browser window into different areas that can be scrolled or resized separately. A **frame** is the area of frames page that contains an individual page. A frames page, sometimes called a **frameset**, contains no visible content, but instead acts as a container that specifies which other pages to display and how the browser should display them.

For Sarah's PartyWorld web, you want to create a frames page with one frame that contains hyperlinks to the privacy policy page, the company background page, the contents page, and the home page. A **target frame** is the frame that displays the results of the hyperlink action. The company profile page should contain a target frame for the company background text or the privacy policy text when the viewer clicks those hyperlinks.

Creating a Frames Page

FrontPage comes with a variety of frames page templates. You want to create the new company profile page using one of them. First, you open the Sample_Web and delete the existing *company_profile.htm* page. To open the web and delete the page:

Step 1	**Open**	the Sample_Web you modified in Chapter 7
Step 2	**Display**	the Folder List, if necessary
Step 3	**Right-click**	the *company_profile.htm* page in the Folder List
Step 4	**Click**	<u>D</u>elete
Step 5	**Click**	<u>Y</u>es

Deleting the company profile page removes its hyperlink in the navigation bar on the contents page. Later in this chapter you modify the navigation bar on the contents page to again include the company profile page. At your request, Bob Avila created two new web pages: one named *initialpage.htm* that contains the background information text and one named *privacy.htm* that contains the privacy policy text.

CAUTION TIP

Remember that many viewers still use 14-inch monitors, which have limited viewing area. Crowding a page with frames makes it difficult for these viewers to see the web page content without excessive scrolling. Use frames sparingly for navigation, table of contents, or logo information and reserve most of the screen area for pages that contain information for the viewer.

He stored the pages and related image files in a folder on the Data Disk. You need to import this folder into the Sample_Web. To import the folder:

Step 1	*Click*	File
Step 2	*Click*	Import
Step 3	*Click*	Add Folder
Step 4	*Browse*	to open the Chapter_8 folder on the Data Disk
Step 5	*Click*	the Profile_Pages folder
Step 6	*Click*	OK twice to close Browse for Folder dialog box and the Import dialog box
Step 7	*Observe*	the new Profile_Pages folder in the Folder List
Step 8	*Close*	the Folder List

With the new pages available in the sample web, you are ready to create the new company profile frames page. To create a frames page using a Frames Page template:

Step 1	*Open*	the New (page) dialog box
Step 2	*Click*	the Frames Pages tab

The New dialog box on your screen should look similar to Figure 8-1.

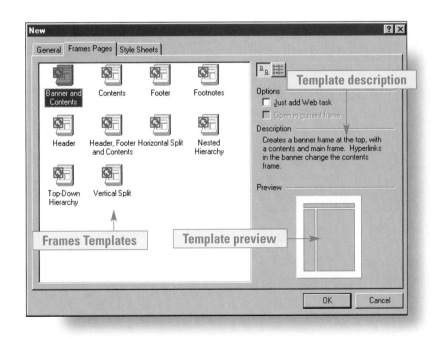

FIGURE 8-1
Frames Pages Tab in the New Dialog Box

chapter
eight

In this dialog box, you can select a template and then read a description and view a preview of the frames page that the selected template creates. Before you create the frames page, you want to review the templates.

| Step 3 | **Verify** | that the Banner and Contents template is selected |
| Step 4 | **Observe** | the Description and Preview areas of the dialog box |

The Banner and Contents template creates a frames page with three frames that contain separate pages: a banner frame, a contents frame, and a main frame. When a viewer clicks a hyperlink in the banner frame, the page in the contents frame changes.

| Step 5 | **Continue** | to review the remaining templates |

You decide to use the Header template to create the frames page.

| Step 6 | **Double-click** | the Header template |

A new page is created. Your screen should look similar to Figure 8-2.

FIGURE 8-2
New Frames Page

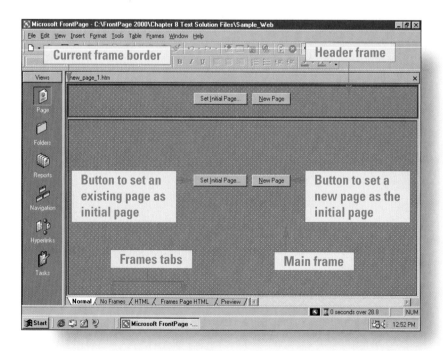

Now that you've created the frames page, you must specify the individual page that appears in each frame when a viewer downloads the company profile page.

Setting the Initial Page for a Frame

The **initial page**, the first page the viewer sees in each frame, can be an existing page or a new page you create. If you do not specify an initial page for each frame, the viewer's browser displays an empty frame when the page is downloaded. You want to create a new page as the initial page in the header frame and use the company background page as the initial page in the main frame.

To create a new page as the initial page in the header frame and an existing page as the initial page in the main frame:

| Step 1 | *Click* | New Page in the header frame |

Your screen should look similar to Figure 8-3.

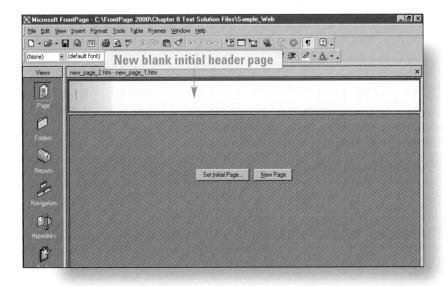

FIGURE 8-3
New Page in the Header Frame

Step 2	*Click*	Set Initial Page in the main frame
Step 3	*Double-click*	the Profile_Pages folder in the Create Hyperlink dialog box
Step 4	*Double-click*	initialpage.htm

Your screen should look similar to Figure 8-4.

chapter
eight

FIGURE 8-4
Initial Page in the
Main Frame

Existing initial page
in main frame

The initial pages are defined for both frames. Next, you add the content to the page in the header frame.

8.b Adding Target Content within a Frame

The page in the header frame on the company profile frames page should contain hyperlinks to the privacy policy page, the company background page, the contents page, and the home page. You want the privacy policy page and the company background page to open in the main frame. However, the contents and home pages should open in the whole screen instead of in a frame. You create the hyperlinks and identify the target or destination frame at the same time in the Create Hyperlink dialog box.

First, you create a table with the appropriate formatted text in the new page in the header frame. Then, you create the hyperlinks and set the target (destination) options for the hyperlinks. To create the content for the header page:

Step 1	*Click*	in the blank page in the header frame, if necessary, to make it the current page
Step 2	*Create*	a 1 by 4 Table, centered with no border, 100% size
Step 3	*Key*	Privacy Policy in the first cell
Step 4	*Format*	the text as Comic Sans MS, 3 (12 pt), bold, red, and centered
Step 5	*Key*	Company Profile in the second cell

Step 6	*Key*	Package Contents in the third cell
Step 7	*Key*	Home Page in the fourth cell
Step 8	*Copy*	the formatting from the first cell text to the other three cells using the Format Painter
Step 9	*Deselect*	the text

Your screen should look similar to Figure 8-5.

FIGURE 8-5
Page Content in the
Header Frame

Next, you create the hyperlinks and set the target frame for each hyperlink.

Editing Content within a Frame

By default, the hyperlinks you create in the page in the header frame point to pages that will appear in the main frame when the hyperlink is clicked. These hyperlinks **target** the main frame. Therefore, all you need to do is create the hyperlink for the privacy policy and company background pages, which automatically targets the main frame. To create the hyperlinks:

Step 1	*Select*	the Privacy Policy text in the page in the header frame
Step 2	*Create*	a hyperlink to the *privacy.htm* page in the Profile_Pages folder in the Sample_Web
Step 3	*Select*	the Company Profile text in the second cell
Step 4	*Create*	a hyperlink to the *initialpage.htm* in the Profile_Pages folder in the Sample_Web
Step 5	*Follow*	the Privacy Policy hyperlink in the Normal tab
Step 6	*Observe*	that the *privacy.htm* page opens in the main frame, replacing the *initialpage.htm*
Step 7	*Follow*	the Company Profile hyperlink in the Normal tab
Step 8	*Observe*	that the *initialpage.htm* opens in the main frame, replacing the *privacy.htm*

chapter
eight

Next, you create hyperlinks to the contents and home pages. For these, you need to change the target frame option. By default, the hyperlink target, or destination page, is set to open pages in the main frame. You want the contents and home pages to open in the whole screen, not the frame. You can change the target frame option when you create the hyperlink. To create the contents hyperlink and change the target frame option:

Step 1	*Select*	the Package Contents text
Step 2	*Open*	the Create Hyperlink dialog box
Step 3	*Select*	the *contents.htm* page in the Sample_Web folder in the Create Hyperlink dialog box file list

The Create Hyperlink dialog box on your screen should look similar to Figure 8-6.

FIGURE 8-6
Create Hyperlink
Dialog Box

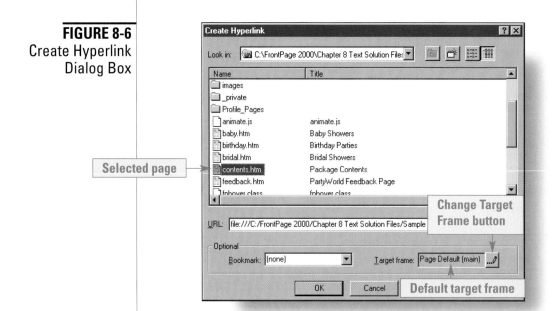

The Target frame: option allows you to change the target destination frame.

Step 4	*Click*	the Change Target Frame button 

The Target Frame dialog box that opens should look similar to Figure 8-7.

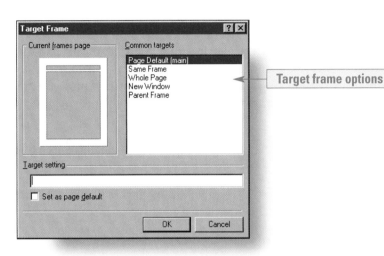

Target frame options

FIGURE 8-7
Target Frame Dialog Box

QUICK TIP

You can select the target frame by clicking the frame in the Current frames page picture in the Target Frame dialog box.

The common target options are predefined settings that are recognized by all browsers. You want to use the Whole Page setting.

Step 5	*Click*	Whole Page in the Common targets list
Step 6	*Click*	OK
Step 7	*Observe*	that Whole Page appears in the Target frame: text box
Step 8	*Click*	OK
Step 9	*Follow*	the Package Contents hyperlink in the Normal tab
Step 10	*Observe*	that the *contents.htm* page opens in the whole screen, not in the main frame of the frames page
Step 11	*Close*	the page

You use the same process to create the home page hyperlink. To create a hyperlink to the *index.htm* page so it opens in the whole screen:

Step 1	*Select*	the Home Page text
Step 2	*Create*	a hyperlink to the *index.htm* page with the target frame set to Whole Page
Step 3	*Follow*	the Home Page hyperlink in the Normal tab
Step 4	*Close*	the *index.htm* page

MENU TIP

You can change the target frame for an existing hyperlink by right-clicking the hyperlink and clicking Hyperlink Properties. Then click the Change Target Frame button to open the Target Frame dialog box and select a new target frame option.

---

chapter
eight

Controlling How a Browser Displays Frames

You can modify the frames page properties to control how a browser displays the frames. For example, you can turn on or off the borders that distinguish a frames area onscreen. You want to turn off the frame borders for the company profile page. To do this, you must make the entire frames page the active page, instead of just one of the frames.

To turn off the borders:

Step 1	**Press**	the F6 key until the entire frames page is selected
Step 2	**Observe**	the blue current frame indicator surrounding the work-space, which indicates that the entire frames page is selected or current
Step 3	**Click**	File
Step 4	**Click**	Properties
Step 5	**Click**	the Frames tab

The Frames tab in the Page Properties dialog box on your screen should look similar to Figure 8-8.

FIGURE 8-8
Frames Tab in the Page
Properties Dialog Box

Frame border and
spacing options

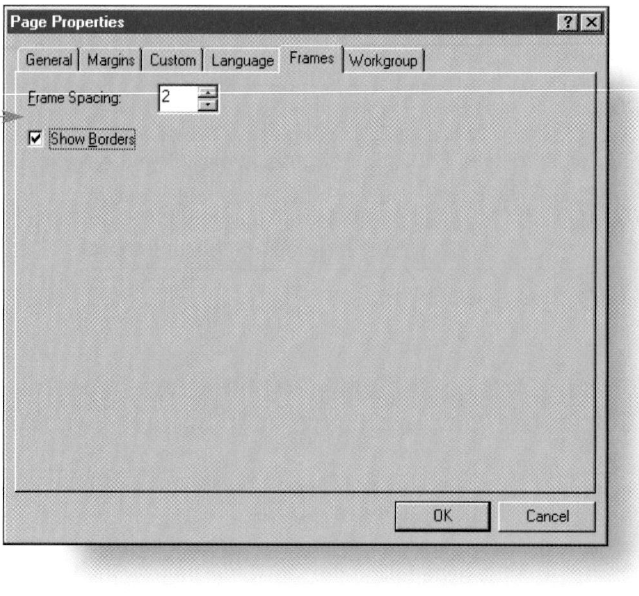

| Step 6 | **Click** | the Show Borders check box to remove the check mark |
| Step 7 | **Click** | OK |

| Step 8 | *Preview* | the page to observe that the border between frames is no longer visible |
| Step 9 | *Return* | to the Normal tab |

Before you continue you should save the frames pages.

Saving Frames Pages

You can save a new page created in a frame and you can save the frames page itself. If you want to save a new page created in a frame, use the commands on the Frames menu. If you want to save the entire frames page, use the commands on the File menu.

To save the page in the header frame:

Step 1	*Click*	the page in the header frame
Step 2	*Click*	Frames
Step 3	*Click*	Save Page As

The Save As dialog box that opens should look similar to Figure 8-9.

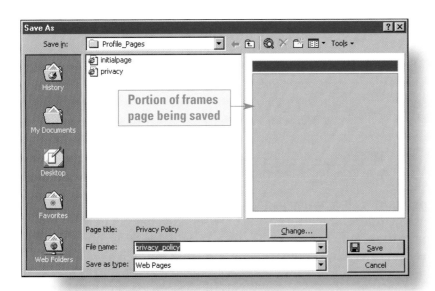

When saving a new page in a frame or an entire frames page, the Save As dialog box shows an illustration of what you are saving. The dark blue portion of the illustration indicates the part of the frames page being saved. In this case, you are saving the new page in the header frame.

FIGURE 8-9
Save As Dialog Box

chapter
eight

Step 4	*Key*	*header* in the File name: text box
Step 5	*Change*	the page title to Header Page
Step 6	*Switch*	to the Profile_Pages folder, if necessary
Step 7	*Click*	Save
Step 8	*Save*	the image files in the images folder, if asked

Next, you want to save the entire frames page. To save the frames page:

Step 1	*Click*	File
Step 2	*Click*	Save As
Step 3	*Observe*	the dark blue boundary surrounds the illustration of the frames page, indicating that you are saving the entire frames page
Step 4	*Key*	*company_profile* in the File name: text box
Step 5	*Change*	the page title to Company Profile
Step 6	*Switch*	to the Sample_Web folder, if necessary
Step 7	*Click*	Save

Because some older browsers may not be able to display frames, you decide to create a no-frames alternative for the company profile page.

8.c Creating a No-Frames Alternative

A **no-frames alternative page** is a web page that appears in the browser window for viewers using browsers that cannot display frames. When you create a frames page, FrontPage adds a default no-frames page, which contains the message that the web page uses frames and the viewer's browser doesn't support frames. This means that the viewer cannot view the page contents. In most cases, just providing this message is not sufficient. Instead, you should provide a true alternative page that includes the content from the frames page. You can do this by adding the content to the no-frames page. The no-frames page is available for editing on the No Frames tab in Page view.

To edit the no-frames page:

| Step 1 | *Click* | the No Frames tab |

Your screen should look similar to Figure 8-10.

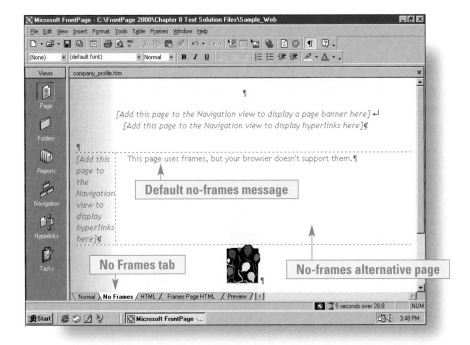

FIGURE 8-10
No Frames Tab in
Page View

You can edit this no-frames page to provide more meaningful information to viewers who cannot use frames. First, you delete the no-frames message and turn off the shared borders for the page. Next, you insert the company logo at the top of the page. Then, you copy the company background and privacy policy text from their respective pages in the Normal tab and paste the text into the no-frames page. Finally, you create a hyperlink to the home page at the bottom of the no-frames page.

Step 2	*Delete*	the no-frames message
Step 3	*Remove*	the shared borders from the current page
Step 4	*Insert*	and center the *sarahslogo.gif* file located in the images folder at the top of the page
Step 5	*Press*	the ENTER key
Step 6	*Copy*	the text from the *company_profile.htm* page in the Normal tab and paste it into the No Frames tab at the insertion point
Step 7	*View*	the *privacy.htm* page in the Normal tab

chapter
eight

| Step 8 | *Copy* | the text (except the Sarah's PartyWorld heading text) and paste it into the No Frames tab below the company background text |
| Step 9 | *Create* | a hyperlink to the *index.htm* page below the pasted text in the No Frames tab using the text Home |

After scrolling to the top of the page, your screen should look similar to Figure 8-11.

FIGURE 8-11
No-Frames Alternative
Page with New Content

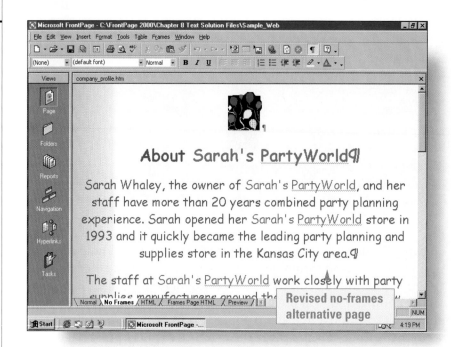

Step 10	*Return*	to the Normal tab
Step 11	*Close*	the *company_profile.htm* page and save changes if asked
Step 12	*Open*	the *index.htm* page and test the hyperlinks to the *company_profile.htm* page
Step 13	*Close*	the *company_profile.htm* page

When you deleted the original *company_profile.htm* page, you removed the page from the navigational structure and from the navigation bar on the contents page. You need to add the new *company_profile.htm* page to the navigational structure. To add the new *company_profile.htm* page to the navigational structure:

Step 1	*Switch*	to Navigation view
Step 2	*Display*	the Folder List
Step 3	*Drag*	the *company_profile.htm* page and drop it as a child page under the Package Contents page
Step 4	*Open*	the *contents.htm* page in the Normal tab in Page view
Step 5	*Follow*	the Company Profile hyperlink
Step 6	*Close*	the web and save pages if asked

The company profile page with frames is finished. Your next task is to complete the contest page.

chapter
eight

Summary

▶ A frames page is a page that divides a browser window into different areas that can be scrolled or resized individually.

▶ A frame is the area of a browser window that contains an individual page.

▶ A target frame is the frame that displays the results of a hyperlink action.

▶ The initial page is the first page the viewer sees in each frame when a frames page is loaded.

▶ You can control how a browser displays a frames page with options in the Frames or Page properties dialog box.

▶ You can edit the no-frames alternative page to remove the no-frames message and add actual page content.

Commands Review

Action	Menu Bar	Shortcut Menu	Toolbar/Mouse	Keyboard
Import a folder	File, Import			ALT + F, M
Display frame properties	Frames, Frame Properties File, Properties	Right-click the frame, click Frame Properties		ALT + R, P ALT + F, I
Display the Properties dialog box for a select page element				ALT + ENTER
Change the target frame option for a hyperlink	Insert, Hyperlink	Right-click the hyperlink, click Hyperlink Properties	Click in the frame in the Current frames page picture in the Target Frame dialog box	ALT + I, H CTRL + K
Save a new page in a frame	Frames, Save Page or Save Page As			ALT + R, S ALT + R, A
Make a frame the current frame			Click in the frame	F6 SHIFT + F6
Select the entire frames page			Click an internal frame boundary	F6 SHIFT + F6

Concepts Review

Circle the correct answer.

1. **A frame is:**
   [a] a page that divides a browser window into different areas.
   [b] a template.
   [c] the area of the browser window that contains an individual page.
   [d] a hyperlink.

2. **A frames page is a:**
   [a] target frame.
   [b] container.
   [c] hyperlink.
   [d] template.

3. **The initial page is:**
   [a] a template.
   [b] the first page the view sees in a frame.
   [c] a special style.
   [d] the target frame.

4. **You select the target frame option from the options list or frames page illustration for a hyperlink in the:**
   [a] Select File dialog box.
   [b] Create Hyperlink dialog box.
   [c] Target Frame dialog box.
   [d] Save As dialog box.

5. **A target frame is:**
   [a] a frames page.
   [b] the initial page.
   [c] the frame that displays the results of the hyperlink action.
   [d] a no-frames alternative.

6. **Which of the following is *not* a Frames Pages template?**
   [a] Banner and Contents
   [b] Header
   [c] Footer
   [d] Bottom-Up Hierarchy

7. **When a viewer clicks a hyperlink in one frame, a page opens in the:**
   [a] main frame.
   [b] target frame.
   [c] bottom frame.
   [d] top frame.

8. **Which of the following commands is *not* part of the Frames menu?**
   [a] Split Frame
   [b] Size Frame
   [c] Delete Frame
   [d] Frame Properties

9. **An alternative page that a viewer sees if his or her browser does not support frames is located on the:**
   [a] No Frames tab.
   [b] Normal tab.
   [c] Navigation tab.
   [d] Preview tab.

10. **You can modify frames page properties to:**
    [a] make the page look more attractive.
    [b] change the target frame.
    [c] control how a browser displays the page.
    [d] save the page.

chapter eight

Circle **T** if the statement is true or **F** if the statement is false.

T F 1. When saving a new page in a frame or the entire frames page, the Create Hyperlink dialog box is modified to illustrate exactly what is being saved.

T F 2. It is usually sufficient to display the no-frames message when a viewer's browser cannot display pages with frames.

T F 3. The initial page must be a new page.

T F 4. A page that divides a browser window into different areas that can be individually scrolled or resized is called a frames page.

T F 5. A frames page is just a container that identifies other pages a viewer can display and where those pages appear on the viewer's screen.

T F 6. Once you assign a target frame to a hyperlink, you cannot change it.

T F 7. You can resize a frame by dragging the frame boundary with the mouse pointer.

T F 8. All browsers can display frames pages.

T F 9. A frame is the area on a viewer's screen that contains a frames page.

T F 10. To view the Frames tab in the Page Properties dialog box, you must first click inside the frame.

Glossary

Use online <u>H</u>elp to look up the following words in the FrontPage glossary. Then, using your word processing program, create a document listing each word and its glossary definition. Save and print the document.

1. frame

2. frames page

3. Frames Page HTML tab

4. initial page

5. Include Page component

6. No Frames tab

7. target frame

Skills Review

Exercise 1

1. Open the Wilson8 web located in the Chapter_8 folder on the Data Disk.

2. Rename the *index.htm* page as *noframes.htm* from the Folder List and update the hyperlinks.

3. Create a new frames page using the Contents template.

4. Create a new page in the contents frame (left). Create a new page in the main frame.

5. Click in the contents frame (left) and get the background information from the *noframes.htm* page. Key and center the text "Check Out Our Products" on the first line. Format the text as 5 (18 pt), bold, and blue.

6. Press the ENTER key and then key the following text, pressing the ENTER key after each line:

Home

Computers

Organizers

Stereos

TVs

7. Create a hyperlink from each line of text to the appropriate page in the web. Use the *noframes.htm* page for the Home hyperlink.

8. Click in the main frame (right) and get the background information from the *noframes.htm* page. Press the ENTER key twice and create a 1 by 1 Table centered with a blue border 75% of its original size.

9. Key the following text in the table, and then format it as 6 (24 pt), bold, blue, and centered.

Welcome to Wilson Electronics, the world's fastest-growing online retailer of quality electronic products.

10. Save the new page in the contents frame (left) as *products.htm*. Save the new page in the main frame (right) as *welcome.htm*. Use the default titles. Save the entire frames page as *index.htm* with the title Wilson Electronics.

11. Display the no-frames alternative page. Select the no-frames message and replace it with the following text:

Your browser does not support frames. Click Home Page to view the Wilson Electronics home page without frames.

12. Select the text "Home Page" and create a hyperlink to the *noframes.htm* page.

13. Insert a hyperlink to the *welcome.htm* page in the contents frame (left) above the home page hyperlink.

14. Follow the hyperlinks in the contents frame (left).

15. Preview, print preview, and print the *welcome.htm* and *products.htm* pages.

16. Close the web and save the pages.

Exercise 2   C

1. Open the Citrus8 web located in the Chapter_8 folder on the Data Disk.

2. Rename the *index.htm* page as *framespage.htm* from the File List and update the hyperlinks.

3. Add a new frames page using the Banner and Content template.

4. Set the initial page for the main frame to *framespage.htm*.

5. Create a new page in the banner frame (top) and a new page in the contents frame (left). Get the background information for both new pages from the *framespage.htm* page.

6. Copy the first row of the table, which contains the images, in the main frame and paste it into the banner frame. Size the banner frame with the mouse pointer so you can see the entire table row. Center the table row and remove the border. View the hyperlink properties for each image in the table row in the banner frame to verify the hyperlink to the appropriate page and the contents frame as the target frame.

7. Insert the *na00417_.gif* logo image located in the images folder in the contents frame (left) and center it. Use the mouse pointer to size the frame to 1 ½ times as its current wide. Key the text "Citrus Valley, Inc." below the logo image.

8. Save the entire frames page as *index.htm* with the title Citrus Valley, Inc. Continue to save the two new pages: save the banner page as *banner.htm* with the title Products and save the contents page as *contents.htm* with the title Contents.

chapter eight

9. Edit the navigation bar in the *framespage.htm* page to show hyperlinks to child level pages and then save the page using the F<u>r</u>ames menu.

10. Press the F6 key until the entire frames page is the current page.

11. Preview the frames page in the browser and test the hyperlinks.

12. Print the *index.htm*, *banner.htm*, and *contents.htm* pages.

13. Close the web.

Exercise 3

1. Create an empty web named Marcy using the Empty Web template.

2. Create three blank pages and save them as *hobbies.htm* with the title Marcy's Hobbies, *book.htm* with the title Marcy's Books, and *movies.htm* with the title Marcy's Movies.

3. Create a new frames page using the Banner and Contents template.

4. Create a new page in each of the three frames.

5. Set the banner page (top) background color to Teal and the text color to White. Set the contents page (left) background color to Teal, the text color White, and the hyperlink color to White. Set the main page text color to Teal.

6. Key the text "Marcy's Home Page" in the banner page (top). Format the text as Arial Rounded MT Bold, 6 (24 pt) and centered. Save the banner page as *banner.htm* with the title Banner.

7. In the main frame page, insert, size, and center the *Marcy.wmf* image located in the Chapter_8 folder on the Data Disk. Save the main frame page as *marcy.htm* with the title Marcy. Save the images in the image folder.

8. Add the following text to the contents page (left):

Marcy

Movies

Books

Hobbies

9. Create hyperlinks to the appropriate pages using the text in the contents page (left). Save the page as *contents.htm* with the title Contents.

10. Save the entire frames page as *index.htm* with the title Marcy's Home Page.

11. Follow the hyperlinks in the contents page (left) in the Normal tab in Page view.

12. Print preview and print the *marcy.htm*, *banner.htm*, and *contents.htm* pages.

13. Close the web, saving pages as needed.

Exercise 4

1. Create an empty web named Native using the Empty Web template.

2. Create three blank pages and save them as *dolls.htm* with the title Dolls, *pottery.htm* with the title Pottery, and *jewelry.htm* with the title Silver Jewelry.

3. Create a new frames page using the Contents template.

4. Create a new page in each of the frames.

5. Add a background image as a watermark to the page in the contents frame (left) using the *an01505_.wmf* image file located in the Chapter_8 folder on the Data Disk. Change the text and hyperlink color to Purple. Key the following text separated by a blank line, and then format it as 5 (18 pt), bold, and centered. Select the text and use the Borders and Shading command on the Format menu to add yellow shading to each paragraph of text.

Dolls

Pottery

Jewelry

Home

6. Set the formatting for the page in the main frame. Change the background to light purple using the color wheel (Hex={CC,99,FF}), the text to Purple, and the hyperlinks to Red. Insert the *an01505_.wmf* image file located in the Chapter_8 folder on the Data Disk at the top of the page. Size the image to approximately ⅓ its original size with the mouse pointer and center it. Press the ENTER key. Key the following text below the image, pressing the SHIFT + ENTER keys to create a line break between the lines, and then center the text:

Native American Arts
2500 El Rialto Drive
Santa Fe, NM 60933-2500
505-555-9987
nar@newmexico.net

7. Save the entire frames page as *index.htm* with the title Native American Arts. Save the contents page as *contents.htm* with the title Contents. Save the page in the main frame as *noframes.htm* with the title Native American Arts. Save the images in the images folder.

8. Use the text in the contents frame page to create hyperlinks for the appropriate pages to open in the main frame. Use the *noframes.htm* page for the Home hyperlink. Save the *contents.htm* page.

9. Press the F6 key until the entire frames page is the current page and then preview the page in your browser. Test the hyperlinks and close the browser.

10. Print preview and print the *contents.htm* and *noframes.htm* pages.

11. Close the web.

Exercise 5

1. Create an empty web named Bookworm using the Empty Web template.

2. Create two blank pages and save them as *books.htm* with the title Books and *music.htm* with the title Music.

3. Create a new frames page using the Header template.

4. Create a new page in the header frame. Set the background color to Green, the hyperlink color to White, and the text color to White.

5. Import the *firstpage.htm* web page file located in the Chapter_8 folder on the Data Disk into the web. Insert the *firstpage.htm* page as the initial page in the main frame.

6. Insert the *bookworm.gif* image located in the Chapter_8 folder on the Data Disk within the table above the text in the page in the main frame.

chapter eight

7. Use the mouse pointer to resize the header frame, making it approximately twice as large as its current size. In the header frame page, create a 1 by 3 Table, centered, with a white border, and 75% of its original size. Insert images located in the Chapter_8 folder on the Data Disk in the table. In the first cell insert the *books.gif* image. In the second cell insert the *home.gif* image. In the third cell insert the *music.gif* image. Drag the frame border down until the entire table and all the images are visible, if necessary. Size the images to fit attractively in the table. Center the images in the cells.

8. Using the images in the header frame page table, create hyperlinks to the *books.htm*, *firstpage.htm* (home), and *music.htm* pages. You want the hyperlinks to target the main frame.

9. Save the entire frames page as *index.htm* with the title The Book Worm. Save the page in the header frame as *header.htm* with the title Header. Save the three header images in the images folder. Save the *firstpage.htm* page in the main frame and save the *bookworm.gif* image in the images folder.

10. Make the entire frames page the current page and preview it in your browser. Test the hyperlinks, then close the browser.

11. Create a hyperlink to the *firstpage.htm* page in the no-frames alternative page using the text of your choice.

12. Print preview and print the *firstpage.htm* and *header.htm* pages.

13. Close the web.

Exercise 6

1. Create a new web named Amy using the Empty Web template.

2. Create three new pages and save them as: *cards.htm* with the title Cards, *posters.htm* with the title Posters, and *autographs.htm* with the title Autographs.

3. Create a new frames page using the Nested Hierarchy template. Create a new page in the banner frame. Add the *dd00805_.wmf* image located in the Chapter_8 folder on the Data Disk as a background image to the page. Create a new page in the contents frame. Set the background color to Red, and the text and hyperlink colors to Lime.

4. Import the *amy.htm* page from the Chapter_8 folder on the Data Disk. Set the initial page in the main frame to the *amy.htm* page.

5. Insert three image files located in the Chapter_8 folder on the Data Disk in the empty table in the page in the main frame. In the first cell, insert *bd05640_.wmf* image and size it to approximately ½ inch by ½ inch. In the second cell, insert the *bd06880_.wmf* image and size it to approximately 1 inch wide by ½ inch long. In the third cell, insert the *en00498_wmf* image and size it to approximately 1 inch by 1 inch.

6. Create hyperlinks using the images in the main frame page table to the *cards.htm*, *autographs.htm*, and *posters.htm* pages. Set the target frame option for each hyperlink to Same Frame.

7. Click in the contents frame page and key "Check Out Our Terrific Collectibles!" Format the text with the Heading 2 style and center it. Then press the ENTER key.

8. Create hyperlinks to the *cards.htm*, *autographs.htm*, *posters.htm*, and *amy.htm* pages using the following text. Set the target frame to the main frame (right bottom frame) by clicking the right-bottom frame in the Current frames page picture in the Target Frame dialog box. The text "rbottom" appears in the Target setting text box when you click the correct frame.

   Trading Cards

   Celebrity Autographs

   Movie Posters

   Home

9. Save the entire frames page as *index.htm* with the title Amy's Collectibles. Save the banner page as *banner.htm* with the title Banner. Save the contents page as *contents.htm* with the title Contents. Save the *amy.htm* page in the main frame to update the changes. Save all images in the images folder when asked.

10. Follow the hyperlinks in the Normal tab in Page view.

11. Print preview and print the *contents.htm*, *banner.htm*, and *amy.htm*.

12. Close the web.

Exercise 7

1. Create a new web named Success using the Empty Web template.

2. Create two new pages. Set the background color to Purple and text color to Yellow for both pages. On the first page, key "Dressing for Success!" and then format the text as 7 (36 pt) and centered. Save the page as *dressing.htm* with the title Dressing for Success! On the second page, key "Positive Presentations!" and format the text as 7 (36 pt) and centered. Save the page as *presentations.htm* with the title Positive Presentations!

3. Import the *success.htm* page located in the Chapter_8 folder on the Data Disk into the web.

4. Create a frames page using the Contents template. Set the *success.htm* page as the initial page in the main frame. Add the background image *success.wmf* located in the Chapter_8 folder on the Data Disk to the page.

5. Create a new page in the contents frame. Set the default text color to Purple. Key "Attend a YourSuccess! seminar in your area today!" and then press the ENTER key.

6. Create hyperlinks to the *dressing.htm*, *presentations.htm*, and *success.htm* pages using the following text:

   Professional Attire

   Public Speaking

   Home

7. Save the entire frames page as *index.htm* with the title YourSuccess! Seminars. Save the contents page as *contents.htm* with the title Contents. Save the *success.htm* page in the mainframe to update the changes and save the *success.gif* image in the images folder.

8. Follow the hyperlinks in the Normal tab in Page view.

9. Print preview and print the *success.htm*, *contents.htm*, *dressing.htm*, and *presentations.htm* pages.

10. Close the web.

Exercise 8

1. Open the Penny8 web located in the Chapter_8 folder on the Data Disk.

2. Rename the *index.htm* page as *mainpage.htm* in the Folder List.

3. Add a new page and set the background color to light pink (Hex={FF,CC,FF}) and the text color to Navy. Save the page as *stems.htm* with the title Floral Stems. Add another new page with the same background color and text color. Save the page as *greenery.htm* with the title Greenery.

4. Create a new frames page using the Header frame template. Set the initial page in the main frame using *mainpage.htm*.

5. Create a new page in the header frame. Set the background color to light pink (Hex={FF,CC,FF}) and set the text and hyperlink colors to Navy. In the header frame page, create a 1 by 3 Table, centered with no border.

chapter eight

6. Key "Floral Stems" in the first cell, "Greenery" in the second cell, and "Home" in the third cell. Select the table row and format the text as 5 (18 pt), bold, and centered.

7. Use the text in the page in the header frame to create hyperlinks to the *stems.htm*, *greenery.htm*, and *mainpage.htm* pages. Target the default (main) frame.

8. Preview the entire frames page in the Preview tab and test the hyperlinks. Then return to the Normal tab.

9. Save the entire frames page as *index.htm* with the title Penny's Flower Power. Save the page in the header frame as *header.htm* with the title Header.

10. Print preview and print the *index.htm* and *header.htm* pages.

11. Close the web.

Case Projects

Project 1

Phil's Photo Shop, owned by Phil Templeton, is a full-service photo retail store in Wilmington, Delaware. Phil's Photo Shop is an authorized dealer for many top camera and photo supply companies. The company also buys and sells photographic and digital equipment from simple point-and-shoot cameras to professional medium-format equipment. Mr. Templeton hires you to create a web site for his company. Before you begin, you want to review some competitors' web sites. Connect to the Internet, launch your web browser, and use a search tool to find web pages for similar companies. Print at least three web pages.

Using a word processing program, create a plan for Phil's Photo Shop web site. Include a critique of the web pages you reviewed, listing their strengths and weaknesses. Compare these web sites to the site you are proposing.

Create a sample web site containing three pages. Then create a frames page as the home page using the Banner and Contents template. Create a new page in each frame. Insert a background image or color and set the default text and hyperlink colors for the page as desired. Insert text, images, and appropriate hyperlinks in the pages. Use FrontPage

components, such as hover buttons and scrolling text, as desired. Save the entire frames page and each individual new page. Select the entire frames page and preview it in your browser. Print the web pages. Save and print the plan.

Project 2

Aries Personal Shopper is a personal shopping service located in Bangor, Maine. Marge Swenson and Delores Pimlico are the co-owners. Ms. Pimlico invites you to submit a proposal to create a new online shopping service web site. Your proposal must contain a sample web with three pages.

Using a word processing program, create a plan for the Aries Personal Shopper web site. Then create a sample web site containing two pages. Create a frames page as the home page using the Header template. Create a new page in each frame. Insert a background image or color and set the default text and hyperlink colors for the pages as desired. Insert text, images, and appropriate hyperlinks in the pages. Use FrontPage components, such as hover buttons and scrolling text, as desired. Save the entire frames page and each individual new page. Select the entire frames page and preview it in your browser. Print the web pages. Save and print the plan.

Project 3

Tamika Cooper is the president of TeamClothes, a company that supplies women's sports teams with uniforms, athletic shoes, and sports-specific athletic accessories, such as knee guards and headbands. Ms. Cooper wants to create an online presence for the company and hires you to create the new company web site.

Using a word processing program, create a plan for the TeamClothes web site. Then create an empty web and add three pages. Create a frames page as the home page using the Contents template. Create two new pages in the content and main frames. Add background image or color and set default text and hyperlink colors both pages as desired. Create the appropriate hyperlinks to the three pages and the home page. Insert text, images, and FrontPage components as appropriate. Print the web pages. Save and print the plan.

Project 4

You are a member of the web site development committee for your company, Danish Furniture Imports. One of the other committee members does not want the company web pages to use frames because she thinks frames are confusing for a viewer. You are not certain whether the company web site should use frames so you decide to check out web sites that include them. Connect to the Internet, launch your web browser, and then locate and review at least ten pages that use frames. Print the pages. Using a word processing program, create a memo to the committee describing the good and bad points of the ten sample web sites that use frames. Save and print the memo. With your instructor's permission, use the memo to discuss the pros and cons of using frames with two classmates.

Project 5

Roberto Ramos is the president of EduWare, Inc., a computer software company that creates educational software for preschool children. EduWare has been selling its products to schools, but Mr. Ramos now wants to sell EduWare products directly to consumers online. He hires you to create a web site.

Using a word processing program, create a plan for the EduWare, Inc. web site. Then create an empty web and add three pages. Create a frames page as the home page using the Contents template. Create two new pages in the content and main frames. Add background image or color and set default text and hyperlink colors both pages as desired. Create the appropriate hyperlinks to the three pages and the home page. Insert text, images, and FrontPage components as desired. Print the web pages. Save and print the plan.

Project 6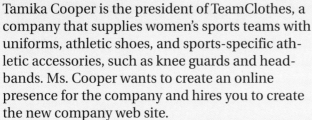

You are the new web designer for Access TV, a public access television channel in San Mateo, California. Your first assignment is to create a new web site. Before you begin, you want to check out other nonprofit organizations' web sites. Connect to the Internet, launch your web browser, and search for web sites for nonprofit organizations. Print at least three web pages.

Using a word processing program, create a plan for the Access TV web site. Then create an empty Web site and add three pages. Create a frames page as the home page using the Banner and Contents template. Create three new pages in the banner, content, and main frames. Add a background image or color and set the default text and hyperlink colors for both pages as desired. Create the appropriate hyperlinks to the three pages and the home page. Insert text, images, and FrontPage components as desired. Print the web pages. Save and print the plan.

chapter eight

Project 7

Devon Swoopes is the owner of Swoopes Auto Repair Directory, a new company that plans to provide an online directory of certified automotive repair shops around the country. Mr. Swoopes hires you to create the company's new web site.

Using a word processing program, create a plan for the Swoopes Auto Repair Directory web site. Then create an empty web and add three pages. Create a frames page as the home page using the frame page of your choice. Insert new pages in the frames. Add background image or color and set default text and hyperlink colors both pages as desired. Create the appropriate hyperlinks to the three pages and the home page. Insert text, images, and FrontPage components as desired. Print the web pages. Save and print the plan.

Project 8

You are the web designer for an automobile retailer in Houston, Texas. Your company web site has several pages that use frames and you want to find a quick way to include the same company information on each page. An associate mentions the Include Page component may be a simple way to do this. You decide to find out how to use it. Using online Help, research how to use the Include Page component. Then create a three-page web using frames and the Include Page component to insert the same company information on each page. Print the web pages.

Using Forms

Chapter Overview

P aper forms are used every day to gather information. For example, you may be asked to complete a form—a list of questions to which you provide answers—to open an account at a department store or apply for membership in an organization. Web page forms are just like paper forms. They enable viewers to answer questions and then send data to a web site. In this chapter, you create a form using a template, create a custom form, set form properties and data entry rules, and create a custom form confirmation page.

LEARNING OBJECTIVES

- ▶ Create a form using a template or wizard
- ▶ Save form results to a file
- ▶ Create a custom form
- ▶ Set form field properties and validation
- ▶ Send form results in an e-mail message
- ▶ Create a confirmation page
- ▶ Complete the individual party theme pages

Case profile

At the last committee meeting, Sarah and Bob approved the modifications to the package contents and company profile pages. After some discussion, the committee decided you should create a separate guest book page to solicit feedback from viewers. The committee also wants you to add order form and order confirmation pages so viewers can place orders for the party theme packages. Finally, Sarah asked you to complete the remaining individual party theme pages.

chapter
nine

9.a Creating a Form Using a Template or Wizard

A web page **form** is an arrangement of text boxes, check boxes, option buttons, and drop-down lists you can use to collect information from viewers at your web site. Web page forms enable a web site to be interactive. Viewers fill out web page forms by clicking option buttons, clicking check boxes, and keying text in text boxes. Web page forms have many uses. For example, viewers can order products and services, or they can provide feedback by keying and submitting text in a guest book page. Forms may also be used to require viewers to log on to a web site with a user name and password. One way to create web page form quickly is to use a form template or the Form Page Wizard.

Creating a Form with a Template

A **guest book** page is used to collect comments and other information from viewers. You want to create the new guest book page quickly so you decide to use the FrontPage Guest Book form template. When you use the Guest Book form template, FrontPage automatically creates another page, called a **guest book log**, which stores the viewers' responses as they submit them. The guest book log is included at the bottom of the guest book page below the form. This enables viewers to see other comments as well as their own.

To create a guest book page using the Guest Book form template:

Step 1	*Open*	the Sample_Web you modified in Chapter 8
Step 2	*Open*	the General tab in the New (page) dialog box
Step 3	*Double-click*	the Guest Book template icon
Step 4	*Save*	the page as *guestbook.htm* with the title Guest Book

You can view both new pages—*guestbook.htm* and *guestlog.htm*—by displaying the Folder List and refreshing the view of the files in the web.

Step 5	*Display*	the Folder List, if necessary
Step 6	*Click*	View
Step 7	*Click*	Refresh
Step 8	*Observe*	the *guestbook.htm* and *guestlog.htm* files in the Folder List

After you create the guest book page, you position it in the web structure in Navigation view to modify the appropriate navigation bar. To add the *guestbook.htm* to the second-level pages:

Step 1	*Switch*	to Navigation view
Step 2	*Drag*	the *guestbook.htm* below the home page
Step 3	*View*	the *guestbook.htm* page in the Normal tab in Page view
Step 4	*Hide*	the Folder List
Step 5	*Observe*	that the updated navigation bar in the top shared border includes a Guest Book hyperlink
Step 6	*Remove*	the left shared border on the current page
Step 7	*Scroll*	to view the form

After scrolling, the form on your screen should look similar to Figure 9-1.

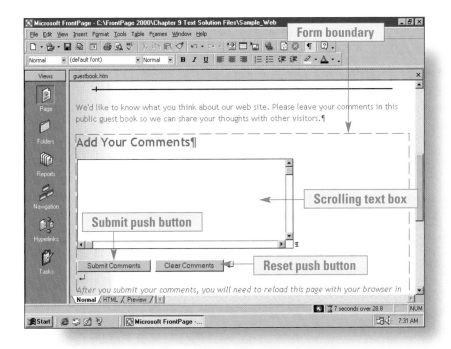

FIGURE 9-1
New Form

The guest book form consists of a scrolling text box and two push buttons. A **scrolling text box** is a text box that accepts multiple lines of keyed text. One of the buttons is a **Submit push button**, a button viewers click to send the information they entered in the form. The other button is a **Reset push button**, a button viewers click to clear the contents of the form, in this case the scrolling text box.

You edit the *guestbook.htm* page to delete the comment, the horizontal line below the comment, and any blank lines above the text that begins "We'd like to know." Then you format the text and position the form elements. To edit the page:

Step 1	***Delete***	the comment directly below the top shared border
Step 2	***Delete***	the blank line
Step 3	***Delete***	the horizontal divider line
Step 4	***Format***	the paragraph beginning "We'd like to know" as 5 (18 pt) and centered
Step 5	***Center***	the Add Your Comments text
Step 6	***Click***	the scrolling text box to select it
Step 7	***Center***	the scrolling text box
Step 8	***Click***	the Clear Comments push button to select it
Step 9	***Center***	the push button
Step 10	***Observe***	that both push buttons and the text following them also are centered because the buttons and text are separated by a line break
Step 11	***Observe***	the Form Results Inserted Here text below the form

The Guest Book template added the Include Page component below the form. This component automatically inserts the *guestlog.htm* page below the form. When viewers reload the *guestbook.htm* page in their browser, they can see their comments added to the guest log page. To view the Include Page component properties:

Step 1	***Right-click***	the Form Results Inserted Here text
Step 2	***Click***	Include Page Properties
Step 3	***Observe***	the *gueslog.htm* filename in the Page to include: text box

Your Include Page Properties dialog box should look similar to Figure 9-2.

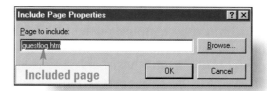

Step 4	*Click*	OK

Step 5	*Delete*	the sample contact information beginning "Author Information Goes Here" directly above the bottom shared border

Step 6	*Save*	the page

You want to review how the information viewers submit on the guest book page is saved at the Sarah's PartyWorld web.

9.b Saving Form Results to a File

Form results, the information submitted by viewers, can be saved in a variety of ways. FrontPage provides **form handlers,** options that take the form results and save them to a text or HTML file, or send them to an e-mail address, or send them to an **electronic database,** a file containing information that can be organized in specific ways.

By default, the Guest Book template saves the form results to the *guestlog.htm* file. You can view and change form results save options in the Form Properties dialog box. To view the Form Properties dialog box:

Step 1	*Right-click*	the form

Step 2	*Click*	Form Properties

Your Form Properties dialog box should look similar to Figure 9-3.

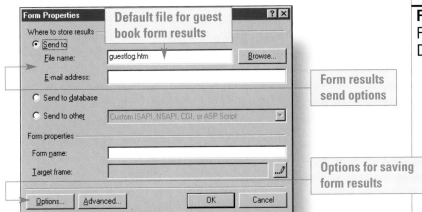

QUICK TIP

You can also create custom instructions, called **scripts**, to be used as form handlers. For more information on creating form handler scripts, see online <u>H</u>elp.

FIGURE 9-3
Form Properties
Dialog Box

chapter
nine

The default filename *guestlog.htm* appears in the File name: text box. You can enter a different filename and path or browse to locate a different file. You want the form results sent to the *guestlog.htm* page for public viewing, so you make no changes. You set options that control how the form results are reported in the Options for Saving Results of Forms dialog box.

Step 3	*Click*	Options
Step 4	*Click*	the File Results tab, if necessary

The File Results tab in the Options for Saving Results of Forms dialog box that opens should look similar to Figure 9-4.

FIGURE 9-4
Options for Saving Results
of Forms Dialog Box

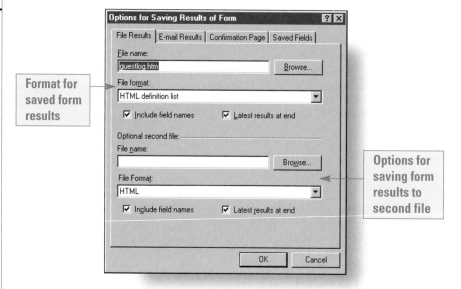

Format for
saved form
results

Options for
saving form
results to
second file

You can send the form results to an optional second file as well as to the original *guestlog.htm* file. In addition, you can set the format of the form results file. The File format: option for the guest log is the HTML definition list format. Each form element creates a **field** in which one piece of information or data is stored. For example, the scrolling text box form element creates a field named Comments that contains the comments data. A **definition list** presents a form field name with the field content indented below it. Because this presentation is appropriate for the guest log, you make no changes.

By default, field names are included in the guest log. You can choose to include or exclude the field names with the Include field names check box. By default, the latest form results are added to the bottom of the list. Thus, the page becomes increasingly longer as new comments are submitted. You want to include field names and add the latest form results to the bottom of the page, so you make no changes.

Step 5	*Click*	Cancel in each dialog box to close them without making changes
Step 6	*Preview*	the *guestbook.htm* page in your browser and click OK if reminded that certain components must be published to work properly
Step 7	*Click*	the Submit Comments button
Step 8	*Observe*	the web page message, which indicates that the form must be saved to a server running FrontPage server extensions
Step 9	*Close*	the browser
Step 10	*Close*	the page

Now that the guest book page is complete, you can create a custom order form.

9.c Creating a Custom Form

You can insert a form anywhere on a page except inside an existing form. When you insert a form, FrontPage inserts a rectangular box with a dashed-line border. Inside the box, you can insert text boxes, check boxes, option buttons, drop-down lists, and push buttons that viewers use to submit their order. By default, the Submit and Reset push buttons are added to a new form. You begin by creating a new page for the order form in the sample Sarah's PartyWorld web.

Creating a Custom Form on a New Page

You want to create a new order form page and place it on the same level as the individual theme package pages so that a hyperlink to the order form page is automatically added to the appropriate navigation bars. To create the new page:

Step 1	*Create*	a new page in Page view
Step 2	*Save*	the page as *orderform.htm* with the title Order Form
Step 3	*Switch*	to Navigation view

Step 4	*Display*	the Folder List, if necessary
Step 5	*Drag*	the *orderform.htm* file from the Folder List and drop it below the Catalog page to the right of the Special Events page
Step 6	*View*	the *orderform.htm* in the Normal tab in Page view
Step 7	*Scroll*	to view the navigation bar in the left shared border
Step 8	*Observe*	that the Order Form page hyperlink is added as the last item in the navigation bar

You are ready to insert the form and form elements.

Adding Form Elements

The first step in creating a custom form is to determine what kind of information you should collect. For the Sarah's PartyWorld order form, you need to collect the viewer's name, shipping address, e-mail address, telephone number, and credit card information. Viewers also must be able to enter the theme package name, the theme package contents option (Basic, Special, or Elite), and the quantity desired.

The second step is to insert the form on the page. To insert the form:

Step 1	*Verify*	that the insertion point is on the blank line immediately below the top shared border
Step 2	*Click*	Insert
Step 3	*Point to*	Form
Step 4	*Click*	Form

Your screen should look similar to Figure 9-5.

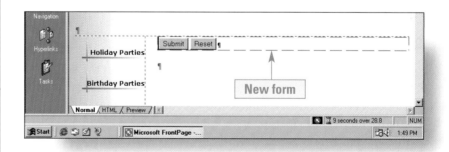

FIGURE 9-5
New Form on
orderform.htm

The third step is to insert the appropriate text and form elements, or fields, in the form. To create the form content:

Step 1	*Press*	the ENTER key to insert a blank line above the push buttons in the form
Step 2	*Move*	the insertion point to the blank line
Step 3	*Key*	Welcome to the Sarah's PartyWorld Order Form. Please fill out the form completely so that we may process your order promptly.
Step 4	*Format*	the text as Comic Sans MS, 4 (14 pt), and Red and center it
Step 5	*Press*	the ENTER key

You use tables in a form to organize the fields. You create one table for the viewer's name, address, and credit card information. To create and format the table:

Step 1	*Create*	a 12 by 2 Table with no border beginning at the left margin of the form below the form welcome text
Step 2	*Size*	the table to 100%, if necessary, and the first column in the table to approximately two inches wide, using the mouse pointer
Step 3	*Select*	the first column in the table
Step 4	*Click*	the Align Right button ▤ on the Formatting toolbar to automatically right-align the cell's contents as you key in the cell
Step 5	*Click*	the Bold button **B** on the Formatting toolbar to automatically bold the cell contents as you key in the cell
Step 6	*Change*	the font to Comic Sans MS
Step 7	*Deselect*	the column

One-line Text Boxes

A **one-line text box,** unlike the scrolling text box you used in the guest book form, collects a small amount of information, such as a name or e-mail address. You will insert several one-line text boxes in the order form to collect personal information. Later you set the data entry rules and form field properties for each of the text boxes. The text

associated with a form field is called a **label**. To insert the first label and one-line text box form field:

Step 1	*Click*	in the first cell in the table to position the insertion point
Step 2	*Key*	First Name:
Step 3	*Press*	the TAB key
Step 4	*Click*	Insert
Step 5	*Point to*	Form
Step 6	*Click*	One-Line Text Box

The one-line text box form field is inserted. Your screen should look similar to Figure 9-6.

FIGURE 9-6
Form with One Field

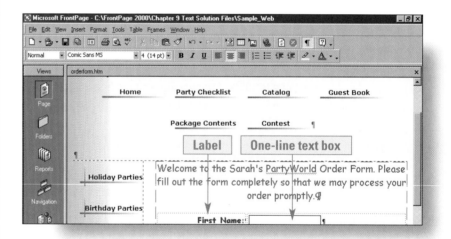

You use the same procedure to insert the remaining personal information fields. To add the labels and one-line text box form fields:

| Step 7 | *Press* | the TAB key |
| Step 8 | *Continue* | to add the remaining one-line text box form fields for:
Last Name:
E-mail Address:
Address:
City:
State or Province:
Postal Code:
Telephone: |

Your screen should look similar to Figure 9-7.

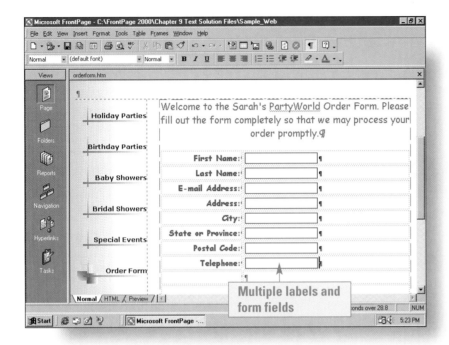

FIGURE 9-7
Partially Completed
Order Form

Drop-Down Menus

Drop-down lists, also called **drop-down menus,** provide a predefined list of choices from which viewers can select. You insert a drop-down menu for viewers to select a credit card type as they fill out the form. Later you set the data entry rules and form field properties for the drop-down menu, including the credit card type options. To insert a drop-down menu:

Step 1	*Move*	the insertion point to the next blank cell in the first column
Step 2	*Key*	Credit Card Type:
Step 3	*Press*	the TAB key
Step 4	*Click*	Insert
Step 5	*Point to*	Form
Step 6	*Click*	Drop-Down Menu

Your screen should look similar to Figure 9-8.

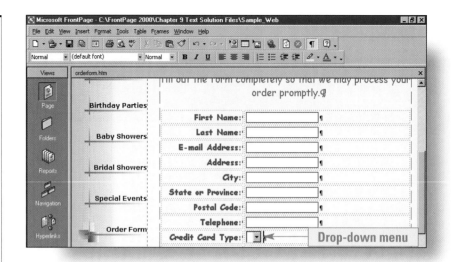

| Step 7 | *Continue* | by adding the following labels and one-line text box form fields: Credit Card Number: Expiration Month: Expiration Year: |
| Step 8 | *Widen* | the first column, if necessary, so that the labels fit on one line and do not wrap within the cell |

Radio Buttons

Option buttons are also called radio buttons. **Radio buttons** enable viewers to select one option from a group of options. In addition to the package name and quantity, viewers need to indicate which package contents they are purchasing: the Basic package, the Special package, or the Elite package. You use radio buttons in a new table to place this information on the order form.

notes   In this chapter, the term "radio button" is used when necessary to match the FrontPage application usage. The term "option button" is used in the steps when you are instructed to click an option button in a dialog box.

To create a new table:

Step 1	*Click*	to the left of the Submit button to position the insertion point
Step 2	*Press*	the ENTER key to create a blank line after the first table
Step 3	*Create*	a 2 by 3 Table with no border sized appropriately at the new blank line

| Step 4 | *Key* | the following heading text in the three cells in the first row: Package Name, Quantity, Package Option |
| Step 5 | *Format* | the heading text as Comic Sans MS, 4 (14 pt), bold, and centered |

You insert one-line text box form fields below the first two headings. To insert the Package Name and Quantity form fields:

Step 1	*Click*	in the empty cell below the Package Name heading
Step 2	*Insert*	a one-line text box
Step 3	*Center*	the text box in the cell
Step 4	*Move*	the insertion point to the empty cell below the Quantity heading
Step 5	*Insert*	a one-line text box
Step 6	*Center*	the text box in the cell

Next, you insert the radio button form fields for the three package option choices: Basic, Special, and Elite. You can also create a **clickable label** for each radio button, which allows viewers to click the label or the associated radio button to make a choice. To insert the Basic radio button field and create a clickable label:

Step 1	*Move*	the insertion point to the empty cell below the Package Option header
Step 2	*Display*	the Form submenu
Step 3	*Click*	Radio Button
Step 4	*Key*	Basic and press the SPACEBAR
Step 5	*Select*	the radio button and the Basic label (do not select the space following the word Basic)
Step 6	*Display*	the Form submenu
Step 7	*Click*	Label
Step 8	*Click*	at the paragraph mark to the right of the Basic label
Step 9	*Observe*	the dotted boundary around the Basic label, indicating that it is a clickable label
Step 10	*Insert*	a radio button
Step 11	*Key*	Special and press the SPACEBAR
Step 12	*Create*	a clickable label for the Special text and radio button

chapter
nine

Step 13	*Move*	the insertion point to the paragraph mark
Step 14	*Insert*	a radio button
Step 15	*Key*	Elite
Step 16	*Create*	a clickable label for the Elite text and radio button
Step 17	*Center*	the buttons and text in the cell

You need to add the shipping options to the form.

Check Boxes

Check boxes are used to turn options on or off, enabling viewers to select multiple options from a list. You want the viewer to choose the shipping method by clicking a check box. You can also create clickable labels for check boxes. You add this information in a new table. To create and format a new table:

Step 1	*Create*	a new blank line above the Submit and Reset buttons
Step 2	*Insert*	a 2 by 1 Table with no border sized appropriately at the new blank line
Step 3	*Key*	Shipping Method in the first row
Step 4	*Copy*	the formatting from the Package Name text to the Shipping Method text using the Format Painter

To enter the clickable labels and check boxes:

Step 1	*Key*	Next Day Air in the second row and press the SPACEBAR
Step 2	*Display*	the Form submenu
Step 3	*Click*	Check Box
Step 4	*Press*	the SPACEBAR
Step 5	*Create*	a clickable label for the Next Day Air text and check box
Step 6	*Continue*	to add clickable labels and check box fields in the same row for the remaining two methods: 2nd Day Ground Regular Ground
Step 7	*Center*	the clickable labels and check boxes in the row

Your screen should look similar to Figure 9-9.

CAUTION TIP

To create a clickable label, be sure to select only the label text; *do not include* any spaces after the text. A good way to select just the label text is to use keyboard shortcut method to select the label by pressing the SHIFT + RIGHT ARROW keys or the SHIFT + LEFT ARROW keys.

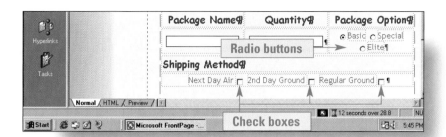

FIGURE 9-9
Form with Radio Buttons
and Check Boxes

| Step 8 | *Center* | the Shipping Method text |

Next, you need to set the form field properties and data entry rules for all the form fields.

9.d Setting Form Field Properties and Validation

Every form field has a name and value. The **name** is used internally to identify the form field and the **value** is the information contained in that field. FrontPage assigns a default name to each field, such as T1 for the first text box, T2 for the second text box, and so on. However, you can change the default names to make them more descriptive. You can set form field properties, such as the field's name and size, in the field's Properties dialog box.

To ensure that visitors complete the order form correctly, you can also set data entry rules, called **validation,** to specify how information must be entered in text boxes, drop-down menus, and radio buttons. For example, you can specify that only numbers and hyphens be entered in a text box form field for a credit card number or that only one item can be selected from a drop-down menu. When you submit the form, FrontPage verifies the data entry rules or validation. The viewer must correct any validation violations before the data can be submitted.

To set the validation and properties for the First Name field:

Step 1	*Scroll*	to view the First Name: one-line text box form field
Step 2	*Right-click*	the form field
Step 3	*Click*	Form Field Properties

The Text Box Properties dialog box that opens should look similar to Figure 9-10.

MENU TIP

You can open a form field's Properties dialog box by clicking the form field to select it and then clicking Prope<u>r</u>ties on the F<u>o</u>rmat menu. You can also right-click a form field and click Form Field Properties.

MOUSE TIP

You can double-click a form field to open its Properties dialog box.

chapter
nine

> **MOUSE TIP**
>
> You can also size a text box by dragging one of its sizing handles with the mouse pointer.

In the Name: text box, you can assign a name to the text box that FrontPage uses internally to identify the field. In the Initial value: text box, you can add default text to be displayed when the form page is first opened. You can indicate that the text box is used as a password field. Viewers can press the TAB key to move from field to field in a form. The default tab order is from top to bottom. You can change the tab order by specifying new tab order position. You can size the text box field based on the maximum number of characters it can contain.

You want to assign a more descriptive field name, set no default value, set a 20-character width, and accept the default tab order.

| Step 4 | *Key* | FirstName in the Name: text box |

The next step is to set the validation. To open the Text Box Validation dialog box and set the validation options:

| Step 1 | *Click* | Validate |

The Text Box Validation dialog box that opens should look similar to Figure 9-11.

You set the data-entry rules in this dialog box. For example, you can require that the data keyed in the field be a specific data type, such as text, have specific formatting, have a minimum or maximum length, and a specific value or range of values before the form can be success-fully submitted. You can also specify whether or not a field is required to contain data before the form can be submitted. You can add a dis-play name that becomes part of a validation warning message. For example, if the last name form field is required, you can add the dis-play name Last Name. Then, if a last name is not entered, the viewer sees the message: "Please enter a value for the **Last Name** field."

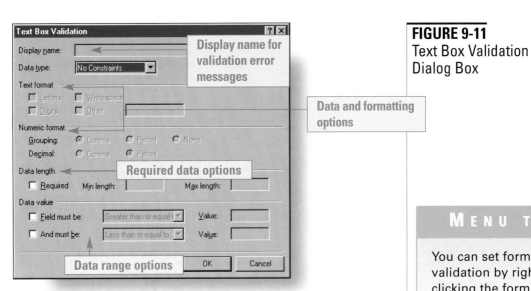

FIGURE 9-11
Text Box Validation
Dialog Box

MENU TIP

You can set form field validation by right-clicking the form field and clicking Form Field Validation.

For the order form, the First Name: field data is required and should contain no more than 20 characters of alphabetic text. You want to allow spaces, commas, or other characters.

Step 2	*Click*	the Data type: list arrow
Step 3	*Click*	Text
Step 4	*Click*	the Letters check box to insert a check mark (to accept alphabetic characters)
Step 5	*Click*	the Whitespace check box to insert a check mark (to accept spaces)
Step 6	*Click*	the Other check box to insert a check mark (to accept other characters that you specify)
Step 7	*Key*	a comma (,) and a period (.) and a hyphen (-) in the Other text box (to indicate which other characters are accepted)
Step 8	*Click*	the Required check box to insert a check mark (to require that the field be completed)
Step 9	*Key*	First Name in the Display name: text box
Step 10	*Key*	1 in the Min length: text box (to require at least one character)
Step 11	*Key*	20 in the Max length: text box (to allow no more than 20 characters)
Step 12	*Click*	OK in each dialog box to close them

chapter
nine

Step 13	*Continue*	to set the one-line text form field properties and validation as follows:

Label	Form Field Properties	Form Field Validation
Last Name	name=LastName width=25	1-25 required text characters; can contain letters, spaces, commas, hyphens, periods; display name=Last Name
E-mail Address	name=Email width=25	1-25 required no constraints characters; display name=E-mail Address
Address	name=Address width=25	1-25 required no constraints characters; display name=Address
City	name=City width=25	1-25 required text characters; can contain letters, spaces, hyphens, periods; display name=City
State or Province	Name=StateorProvince width=15	1-15 required text characters; can contain letters, spaces, commas, hyphens, periods; display name=State or Province
Postal Code	name=PostalCode width=15	1-15 required no constraints characters; display name=Postal Code
Telephone	name=Telephone width=20	1-20 required no constraints characters; display name=Telephone

Next, you set the properties and validation for the credit card type drop-down list. To set the drop-down list properties and validation:

Step 1	*Right-click*	the Credit Card Type: drop-down menu form field
Step 2	*Click*	Form Field Properties

The Drop-Down Menu Properties dialog box that opens should look similar to Figure 9-12.

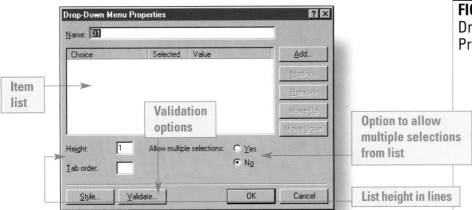

FIGURE 9-12
Drop-Down Menu
Properties Dialog Box

You enter the list of credit cards in this dialog box. You can also specify the height of the list based on the number of lines of visible text, which determines whether the list is a drop-down menu or scrollable text box. You can also specify whether or not viewers can make multiple choices from the list. Sarah's PartyWorld accepts the MasterCard, Visa, and American Express credit cards. Viewers can select only one from the list.

Step 3	*Key*	CreditCard in the Name: text box
Step 4	*Click*	Add

The Add Choice dialog box that opens should look similar to Figure 9-13.

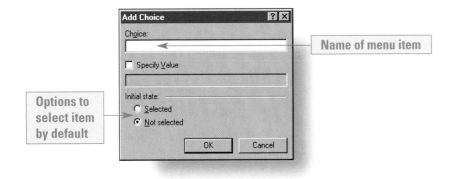

FIGURE 9-13
Add Choice Dialog Box

In this dialog box, you enter the name of the drop-down menu item and specify whether or not the item is the default selection.

chapter
nine

Step 5	*Key*	MasterCard in the Choice: text box
Step 6	*Click*	the Not Selected option button, if necessary
Step 7	*Click*	OK
Step 8	*Observe*	that the MasterCard item is added to the menu list
Step 9	*Add*	the Visa and American Express items to the list as not selected items
Step 10	*Key*	1 in the Height: text box, if necessary
Step 11	*Click*	the No option button, if necessary
Step 12	*Click*	OK
Step 13	*Continue*	to set the one-line text box form field properties and validation as follows:

Label	Form Field Properties	Form Field Validation
Credit Card Number	name=CardNumber width=25	1-25 required text characters; can contain digits, spaces, and hyphens; display name=Credit Card Number
Expiration Month	name=Month width=2	2 required number characters; data values=greater than or equal to 01 and less than or equal to 12; display name=Expiration Month
Expiration Year	name=Year width=2	2 required number characters; data values=greater than or equal to 00; display name=Expiration Year
Package Name	name=Package width=20	1-20 required no constraints characters display name=Package Name
Quantity	name=Qty width=3	1-3 required number characters; data value=greater than or equal to 1 and less than or equal to 999; display name=Quantity

QUICK TIP

You cannot test a drop-down menu until you preview the page in your browser or in the Preview tab.

Next, you set the properties and validation for the radio buttons. To set the radio button properties and validation:

Step 1	**Right-click**	the first radio button (Basic)
Step 2	**Click**	Form Field Properties

The Radio Button Properties dialog box that opens should look similar to Figure 9-14.

FIGURE 9-14
Radio Button Properties
Dialog Box

An individual radio button is part of a group of choices. Viewers can select only one radio button from the group. To internally identify both the group and each individual button, FrontPage sets a default name for the group to which the button belongs and a default value for each button. The group name for the Basic radio button is R1 and the default value is V1. Because only one radio button in a group can be selected, you can specify which button in a group is selected by default in this dialog box. You want the Basic radio button selected by default in this group. It is not necessary to change the default group name or value.

Step 3	**Click**	the Selected option button, if necessary
Step 4	**Click**	Validate

The Radio Button Validation dialog box that opens should look similar to Figure 9-15.

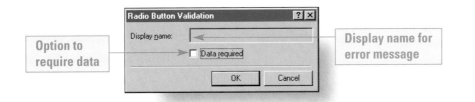

FIGURE 9-15
Radio Button Validation
Dialog Box

chapter
nine

You want to require the viewer select one of the buttons in the group.

Step 5	*Click*	the Data required check box to insert a check mark
Step 6	*Key*	Package Option in the Display name: text box
Step 7	*Click*	OK twice to close the dialog boxes
Step 8	*Size*	the first and second columns so that the radio buttons fit on one line and do not wrap within the cell, if necessary

Because the three radio buttons are part of a group, setting the field properties and validation for the first button automatically sets the field properties and validation for the remaining two buttons.

Finally, you set the properties for the check boxes. Because a check box is either turned on or off, there is no need to set validation. To set the properties:

Step 1	*Right-click*	the Next Day Air check box
Step 2	*Click*	Form Field Properties

The Check Box Properties dialog box that opens should look similar to Figure 9-16.

FIGURE 9-16
Check Box Properties
Dialog Box

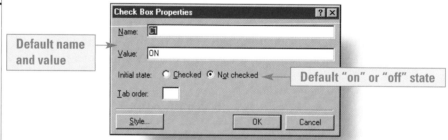

A check box is turned on when checked and turned off when not checked. The On text in the Value: text box is the value submitted when a viewer clicks the Next Day Air check box. You can specify initial on or off condition in this dialog box. You set a descriptive name and then accept the default on/off setting.

Step 3	*Key*	NextAir in the Name: text box
Step 4	*Click*	OK
Step 5	*Change*	the Name: property for the remaining two check boxes to "2ndGround" and "Regular," respectively

Before you preview the form, you want to edit the Submit and Reset push buttons. You want to use the text "Send" for the Submit push button label and the text "Clear" for the Reset push button label. To edit the push button form fields:

| Step 1 | *Right-click* | the Submit push button |
| Step 2 | *Click* | Form Field Properties |

The Push Button Properties dialog box that opens should look similar to Figure 9-17.

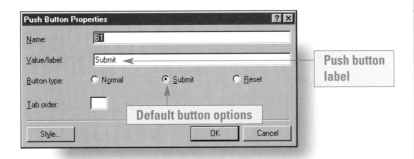

FIGURE 9-17
Push Button Properties
Dialog Box

You can change the label text and button type in this dialog box. Use the Normal button type to create a generic button to which you can assign special instructions or script.

Step 3	*Key*	Send in the Value/label: text box
Step 4	*Click*	OK
Step 5	*Change*	the Reset push button label to Clear
Step 6	*Center*	the buttons
Step 7	*Save*	the page
Step 8	*Preview*	the page in your browser and click OK if reminded that certain components must be published to work correctly
Step 9	*Close*	the browser

You can review the form page options and actually fill out the form. However, you cannot test the validation until the web is published to a server. If you click the Send button, your browser opens a page with a message reminding you that the form must be saved to a web server running FrontPage extensions to function properly.

QUICK TIP

You can set keyboard shortcut keys for a form field. Keyboard shortcut keys enable a viewer to move to a form field by pressing keys on the keyboard. For information on creating keyboard shortcut keys for a form field, see online Help.

To complete the form, you want to specify what information to collect from the form and how the information is transmitted.

9.e Sending Form Results in an E-mail Message

Recall that form results can be submitted in a variety of ways—saved to a text or HTML file, or sent to an e-mail address or database. To expedite orders, you want the order form data sent directly to the order department's e-mail address as well as to an HTML file. To set these save options:

Step 1	*Right-click*	the form
Step 2	*Click*	Form Properties
Step 3	*Key*	orders@xeon.net in the E-mail address: text box
Step 4	*Key*	Order Form in the Form name: text box
Step 5	*Click*	Options
Step 6	*Click*	the E-mail Results tab

The E-mail Results tab in the Options for Saving Results of Form dialog box on your screen should look similar to Figure 9-18.

FIGURE 9-18
E-mail Results Tab

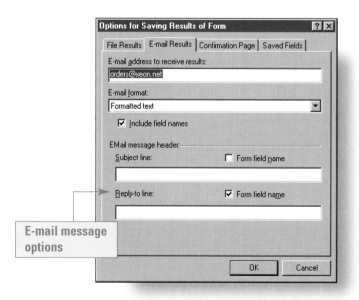

This tab includes options to specify the e-mail delivery address, the format of the e-mail text, and whether or not to include the form field names in the message. By default the text "Form Results" appears in the subject line of the message; you want to change the subject line text to "Order Form." The Form line (Reply to) in the message can contain text or, if you key in the form field name and click the Form field name check box, the contents of a form field. You want the Form line to contain the viewer's e-mail address. To set the E-mail results options:

Step 1	*Key*	Order Form in the Subject line: text box
Step 2	*Key*	Email in the Reply-to line: text box
Step 3	*Click*	the Form field name check box to insert a check mark, if necessary

You can specify the form field contents to save in the Saved Fields tab in the Options for Saving the Results of a Form dialog box. By default, all the form fields are saved. However you can delete fields or rearrange them by modifying the Form fields to save list in this dialog box. You can also save additional information such as the date and time the form was submitted or information about the viewer's computer and browser. You want to save the date and time of the form submission and the user name information, in addition to all of the form fields. To change the Saved Fields options:

Step 1	*Click*	the Saved Fields tab
Step 2	*Scroll*	the Form fields to save list to view the complete list of saved fields
Step 3	*Click*	the Date Format: list arrow
Step 4	*Click*	the third option in the list
Step 5	*Click*	the Time Format: list arrow
Step 6	*Click*	the second option
Step 7	*Click*	the Username check box to insert a check mark
Step 8	*Click*	OK in both dialog boxes to close them

If you are creating the Sample_Web as a disk-based web and FrontPage Server Extensions are not installed with the e-mail option, you get a reminder to install the option. If the message appears:

Step 9	*Click*	No to retain the save to e-mail options

chapter
nine

Step 10	***Save & Close*** the page

The final step in creating a form is to create a confirmation page.

9.f Creating a Confirmation Page

A **confirmation page** is a page that viewers see after they submit a form. It contains a "thank you" message as well as the contents of the form fields. The confirmation page provides viewers the opportunity to confirm the field data they entered and, if there is an error, resubmit a corrected form. FrontPage has a default confirmation page with a standard "thank you" message and the contents of all the saved fields. You can create your own confirmation page with a customized message and select the form field contents to display.

You want to add a custom confirmation page that thanks viewers for their order and includes certain fields. A quick way to do this is to modify the page created from the Confirmation Form template. To create a custom confirmation page:

Step 1	***Open***	the New (page) dialog box
Step 2	***Double-click***	the Confirmation Form template on the General tab
Step 3	***Remove***	the top and left shared borders on the current page

FrontPage **Confirmation Field components** consist of form field names enclosed in brackets, such as [Username]. You can edit the sample text, edit the existing Confirmation Field components, and insert additional Confirmation Field components as necessary. To delete the comment, edit the Confirmation Field component in the salutation, and edit the first text paragraph:

Step 1	***Delete***	the comment at the top of the page and the resulting blank line
Step 2	***Double-click***	the [Username] component

The Confirmation Field Properties dialog box that opens should look similar to Figure 9-19.

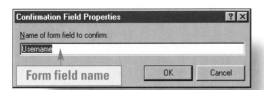

FIGURE 9-19
Confirmation Field
Properties Dialog Box

Step 3	*Key*	FirstName in the Name of form field to confirm: text box
Step 4	*Click*	OK
Step 5	*Select*	the first text paragraph and replace it with the following text *Thank you for your party theme package order. We will use the following information to contact you regarding your order, if necessary:*

You need to replace the sample form field names in the E-mail and Telephone components with the appropriate field name from the order form. You also want to delete the Fax component. To edit the three Confirmation Field components:

Step 1	*Double-click*	the [UserEmail] component
Step 2	*Key*	Email and click OK
Step 3	*Double-click*	the [UserTel] component
Step 4	*Key*	Telephone and click OK
Step 5	*Delete*	the Fax [UserFax] component and the resulting blank line

> **MENU TIP**
>
> You can insert a Confirmation Field component with the Component command on the Insert menu.

Next, you want to add another paragraph and the shipping information form fields. To add the text and form fields:

Step 1	*Key*	the following paragraph beginning at the left margin on a new line above the last paragraph *We will use the following information to ship your order:*
Step 2	*Press*	the ENTER key
Step 3	*Click*	the Increase Indent button 〔≣〕 on the Formatting toolbar
Step 4	*Key*	First Name: and press the SPACEBAR
Step 5	*Click*	the Insert Component button 〔🔲〕 on the Standard toolbar

chapter
nine

Step 6	*Click*	Confirmation Field
Step 7	*Key*	FirstName and click OK
Step 8	*Press*	the SHIFT + ENTER keys to insert a line break
Step 9	*Continue*	by adding the following Confirmation Field components:

Text	**Field Name**
Last Name:	LastName
Address:	Address
City:	City
State or Province:	StateorProvince
Postal Code:	PostalCode

Step 10	*Copy*	the formatting from the Telephone: label to the First Name: through Postal Code: labels using the Format Painter

Your screen should look similar to Figure 9-20.

FIGURE 9-20
Modified Text and
Confirmation Field
Components

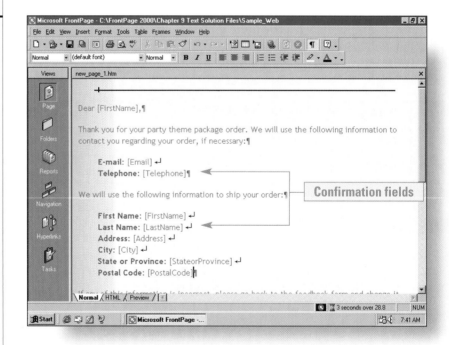

Step 11	*Replace*	the word "feedback" with the word "order" wherever it appears in the page
Step 12	*Replace*	the text "taking the time to help us be a better company." with "your order."
Step 13	*Replace*	the text "Customer Services" in the signature line with the text "Order Department"
Step 14	*Delete*	the Revised: (date) red text immediately above the bottom shared border

Step 15	*Save*	the page as *confirmation.htm* with the title Order Confirmation
Step 16	*Close*	the page

The final step in creating a custom confirmation page is assigning it to a form. To assign the *confirmation.htm* page to the *orderform.htm* page:

Step 1	*Open*	the *orderform.htm* page in the Normal tab in Page view
Step 2	*Open*	the Form Properties dialog box
Step 3	*Click*	Options and click the Confirmation Page tab

The Confirmation Page tab in the Options for Saving Results of Form dialog box that opens should look similar to Figure 9-21.

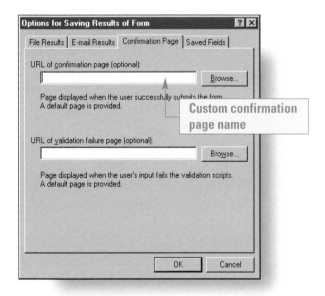

FIGURE 9-21
Confirmation Page Tab

You can key the path and filename to the custom confirmation page or you can browse to locate it.

Step 4	*Click*	Browse next to the first text box
Step 5	*Double-click*	the *confirmation.htm* filename in the Current Web dialog box
Step 6	*Click*	OK in both dialog boxes
Step 7	*Click*	No if asked to remove the e-mail recipient
Step 8	*Save & Close*	the page

Now that the guest book, order form, and confirmation pages are complete, you should finalize the remaining party theme pages.

9.g Completing the Individual Party Theme Pages

In addition to the holiday parties' theme page, the sample Sarah's PartyWorld web contains theme pages for birthday parties, baby showers, bridal showers, and special event parties. You need to complete those pages by adding images and text organized in tables in the same way you completed the holiday parties' theme page. All of the image files you need to complete the pages are stored in the Chapter_9 folder on the Data Disk.

Because you created the holiday parties theme page some time ago, you want to review the page. To review the page:

Step 1	*Open*	the *prod01.htm* page in the Normal tab in Page view
Step 2	*Scroll*	the page to review it
Step 3	*Close*	the page

The *baby.htm*, *bridal.htm*, *birthday.htm*, and *specialevent.htm* pages should contain motion clips and text for each individual package similar to the individual holiday packages on the *prod01.htm* page. To update the pages:

Step 1	*Open*	the *baby.htm* party theme page
Step 2	*Complete*	the page using the following appropriately sized, centered image and formatted package names organized in two-column tables. Add the formatted descriptive text of your choice below the images and package names; save the images in the images folder, if asked **Image** **Package Name** *j0076140.gif* It's A Girl! Baby Shower *ag00318_.gif* It's A Boy! Baby Shower *ag00320_.gif* It's A Baby! Baby Shower
Step 3	*Create*	a bookmark named Top using the first word of the package name
Step 4	*Follow*	the Top of Page hyperlink in the Normal tab
Step 5	*Save & Close*	the page

| Step 6 | *Complete* | the remaining pages using the following images and package names with descriptive text; don't forget to create the bookmark and test the Top of Page hyperlink on each page and then save the page when you are finished updating it |

Page	Image	Package Name
birthday.htm	*ag00352_.gif*	Magic Island Birthday Party
	ag00031_.gif	Baby's First Birthday Party
	ag00391_.gif	Happy Teddy Birthday Party
	ag00171_.gif	Celebration Birthday Party
bridal.htm	*ag00319_.gif*	Wedding Wonderland Shower
	j0076123.gif	Kitchen Helper Shower
	ag00002_.gif	Garden Party Shower
	ag00500_.gif	Just Married Shower
specialevent.htm	*ag00595_.gif*	Mystery Dinner Party
	ag00178_.gif	Beach Party
	j0095699.gif	Graduation Party
	j0076182.gif	Retirement Party

| Step 7 | *Close* | the web, saving pages as needed |

Now that the guest book, order form, confirmation, and party theme pages are complete, you are ready to finish the contest page and add a search form to the web.

Summary

▶ A web page form is an arrangement of text boxes, check boxes, option or radio buttons, and drop-down lists or menus used to collect information from viewers at a web site.

▶ A guest book page is used to collect comments or feedback from viewers.

▶ A scrolling text box contains multiple lines of text.

▶ A Submit push button sends form results to the web to be stored in a file, sent via e-mail, or stored in a database.

▶ A Reset push button clears the form contents.

▶ A field is a form element such as first name or address that can contain data input by viewers.

▶ A one-line text box is used to collect a small amount of information such as a name or e-mail address.

▶ The text associated with a field is called a label.

▶ Drop-down lists or menus provide viewers a list of choices.

▶ Viewers use radio or option buttons to select one option from a group of options.

▶ Check boxes are used to turn on or off an item, enabling viewers to select multiple items from a list of options.

▶ A confirmation page contains a "thank you" message and the contents of the completed form.

Commands Review

Action	Menu Bar	Shortcut Menu	Toolbar/Mouse	Keyboard
Insert a form element	Insert, Form			ALT + I, M
Open the Form Properties dialog box		Right-click the form, click Form Properties		
Open a form field's Properties dialog box	Select the form field and then Format, Properties	Right-click a form field, click Form Field Properties	Double-click a form field	ALT + O, I after form field is selected
Set form field validation	Select the form field and then Format, Properties, Options	Right-click a form field, click Form Field Properties; then click Options Right-click a form field, click Form Field Validation	Double-click a form field; then click Options	ALT + O, I, O
Set options for saving form results		Right-click the form, click Form Properties, then click Options		
Insert a Confirmation Field component	Insert, Component		🔲	ALT + I, O
Refresh the Folder List	View, Refresh			ALT + V, R F5

Concepts Review

Circle the correct answer.

1. A web page form is a(n):
[a] target frame.
[b] template.
[c] arrangement of text boxes, check boxes, drop-down menus, and radio buttons.
[d] hyperlink.

2. A guest book page is used to:
[a] submit product orders.
[b] collect feedback from viewers.
[c] add color to a page background.
[d] submit form results.

3. A Reset push button:
[a] submits form results.
[b] reformats a form.
[c] creates hyperlinks to the guest book page.
[d] clears a form.

4. You cannot save form results:
[a] to a file.
[b] in an e-mail message.
[c] to an electronic database.
[d] as a hyperlink.

5. When you use the Guest Book form template, FrontPage automatically creates a:
[a] frames page.
[b] guest log page.
[c] modified navigation bar.
[d] no-frames alternative page.

6. A one-line text box is used to:
[a] provide a list of options.
[b] contain multiple lines of text.
[c] collect a small amount of text.
[d] provide a yes or no choice.

7. The text associated with a form field is called a:
[a] label.
[b] frame.
[c] text box.
[d] radio button.

8. The form element that provides a yes or no choice is a:
[a] radio button.
[b] one-line text box.
[c] check box.
[d] drop-down menu.

9. Every form field has:
[a] a hyperlink.
[b] a name and value.
[c] validation.
[d] a confirmation field.

10. Data entry rules for form fields are called:
[a] forms.
[b] components.
[c] form results.
[d] validation.

chapter nine

Circle **T** if the statement is true or **F** if the statement is false.

T   F   1. Form results can only be saved to a file.

T   F   2. You can insert a form anywhere on a web page except inside an existing form.

T   F   3. The first step in creating a form is to determine what kind of information you want to collect.

T   F   4. E-commerce means only online shopping.

T   F   5. A scrolling text box is used to collect a small amount of information.

T   F   6. Radio buttons are used to select one option from a group of options.

T   F   7. You must create a custom confirmation page if you want the viewer to confirm their form data.

T   F   8. Confirmation Field components consist of field names enclosed in brackets.

T   F   9. Form handlers are options that save form results to a file, send results by e-mail, or store results in a database.

T   F   10. You must first insert a blank form on a page before you can insert a form element.

Glossary

Use online <u>H</u>elp to look up the following words in the FrontPage glossary. Then, using your word processing program, create a document listing each word and its glossary definition. Save and print the document.

1. Confirmation Field component

2. check box

3. data validation

4. drop-down menu field

5. form

6. form field

7. form handler

8. name-value pair

9. push button

10. radio button

11. Save Results form handler

Skills Review

Exercise 1

1. Open the Amy09 web located in the Chapter_9 folder on the Data Disk.

2. Create an order form page and save the order form as *orderform.htm* with the title Order Form.

3. Get the background colors and text colors from the *amy.htm* page.

4. Insert the following welcome text at the top of the page, apply the Heading 1 style, and center the text:

Welcome to the Amy's Collectibles order form page.

5. Insert a form on the line below the heading text.

6. Create a 15 by 2 Table, and insert the form fields with the following labels, field properties, and validation:

Label	Form Field and Form Field Properties	Form Field Validation
First Name	one-line text box name=FirstName, width=20	1-20 required text characters; can contain letters, spaces, commas, hyphens, periods; display name=Last Name
Last Name	one-line text box name=LastName, width=25	1-25 required text characters; can contain letters, spaces, commas, hyphens, periods; display name=Last Name
E-mail Address	one-line text box name=Email, width=25	1-25 required no constraints characters; display name=E-mail Address
Address	one-line text box name=Address, width=25	1-25 required no constraints characters; display name=Address
City	one-line text box name=City, width=25	1-25 required text characters; can contain letters, spaces, hyphens, periods; display name=City
State or Province	one-line text box name=StateorProvince, width=15	1-15 required text characters; can contain letters, spaces, commas, hyphens, periods; display name=State or Province
Postal Code	one-line text box name=PostalCode, width=15	1-15 required no constraints characters; display name=Postal Code
Telephone	one-line text box name=Telephone, width=20	1-20 required text characters; can contain spaces, digits, hyphens, and parentheses; display name=Telephone
Credit Card Type	Drop-down menu default properties	three credit card names: World Express, Vita, and Master Charge
Credit Card Number	one-line text box name=CardNumber, width=25	1-25 required text characters; can contain digits, spaces, and hyphens; display name=Credit Card Number
Expiration Month	one-line text box name=Month, width=2	2 required number characters; data values=greater than or equal to 01 and less than or equal to 12; display name=Expiration Month
Expiration Year	one-line text box name=Year, width=2	2 required number characters; data values=greater than or equal to 00; display name=Expiration Year
Item	one-line text box name=Item, width=20	1-20 required text characters; can contain letters, spaces, and hyphens; display name=Item
Quantity	one-line text box name=Qty, width=3	1-3 required number characters; data value=greater than or equal to 1 and less than or equal to 999; display name=Quantity
Shipping Method	two radio buttons	Rush and Regular (selected by default)
Submit push button	text=Send	
Reset push button	text=Clear	

7. Send the form results by e-mail to order@amys.com.

8. Create a hyperlink to the *index.htm* page at the bottom of the *orderform.htm* page.

9. Save the *orderform.htm* page to update it.

10. Create a hyperlink to the *orderform.htm* page in the *contents.htm* page in the left shared frame on the *index.htm* page using the text "Order Form."

11. Save the *contents.htm* page.

12. Preview the *index.htm* page in your browser.

13. Preview, print preview, and print the *orderform.htm* page and the *contents.htm* page.

14. Close the web and save the pages.

Exercise 2

1. Open the Bookworm09 web located in the Chapter_9 folder on the Data Disk.

2. Create a guest book page using a template.

3. Save the guest book page as *guestbook.htm* with the title Guest Book.

4. Refresh the Folder List to view the *guestlog.htm* file and then close the Folder List.

5. Get the page background color and text color for the *guestbook.htm* page from the *header.htm* page.

6. Delete the comment and extra blank line and format the welcome text with the 5 (18pt) font and center it.

7. Center the text and form elements in the form.

8. Delete the line beginning "Author" at the bottom of the page.

9. Delete the [OrganizationName] field in the copyright information at the bottom of the page and replace it with "The Book Worm."

10. Create a hyperlink to the *firstpage.htm* page at the bottom of the *guestbook.htm* page below the copyright information using the text "Home Page." Center the text.

11. Save the form results to the default file.

12. Save the *guestbook.htm* page to update it.

13. Create a hyperlink to the *guestbook.htm* page at the top of the *firstpage.htm* page in the main frame on the *index.htm* page. Use the text "Please sign our guest book." Format the text as 5 (18 pt) and center it.

14. Save the *firstpage.htm* page to update it.

15. Follow the hyperlinks in the Normal tab in Page view.

16. Preview and print the *firstpage.htm* and *guestbook.htm* pages.

17. Close the web.

Exercise 3

1. Open the Chocolate09 web located in the Chapter_9 folder on the Data Disk.

2. Open the *feedback.htm* page in the Normal tab in Page view.

3. Format the welcome text as 4 (14 pt), bold, and centered.

4. Delete the form comment and extra blank line.

5. Edit the form field properties and validation as follows:

Label	Form Field and Form Field Properties	Form Field Validation
Name	one-line text box width= 40	40 text characters; can contain letters, spaces, commas, hyphens, periods; display name= Name
Title	one-line text box width=20	20 text characters; can contain letters, spaces, commas, hyphens, periods; display name=Title
Company	one-line text box width=25	25 no constraints characters
Address	one-line text box width=40	40 no constraints characters
Telephone	one-line text box width=20	20 text characters; can contain digits, spaces, commas, hyphens, parentheses; display name=Telephone
E-mail	one-line text box width=25	25 no constraints characters

6. Delete the row that contains the Fax label and form field.

7. Save the form results to the default file and send them by e-mail using the address feedback@chocolatevelvet.com.

8. Save the *feedback.htm* page to update it.

9. Preview and print the *feedback.htm* page.

10. Close the web.

Exercise 4

1. Open the Rivers09 web in the Chapter_9 folder on the Data Disk.

2. Create a guest book page using a template.

3. Save the page as *guestbook.htm* with the title Guest Book.

4. Switch to Navigation view and drag the *guestbook.htm* page from the Folder List to the child level under the home page to the right of the Web Design page.

5. View the *guestbook.htm* page in the Normal tab in Page view.

6. Delete the comment and extra blank line and format the welcome text as 5 (18 pt).

7. Create a new blank line below the scrolling text box and then insert a 6 by 2 Table with no border. Size the first column approximately 2 inches wide with the mouse pointer. Format the first column with right alignment and bold.

8. Insert the following labels and form fields in the table:

Label	Form Field Properties	Form Field Validation
First Name	one-line text box name=FirstName, width= 20	20 text characters; can contain letters, spaces, commas, hyphens, periods; display name=First Name
Last Name	one-line text box name=LastName, width=20	20 text characters; can contain letters, spaces, commas, hyphens, periods; display name=Last Name
Company	one-line text box name=Company, width=25	25 no constraints characters
Address	one-line text box name=Address, width=40	40 no constraints characters
E-mail	one-line text box name=Email, width=25	25 no constraints characters
Subscribe to newsletter	check box	Yes (on by default), No clickable labels

9. Save the form results to the default file.

10. Save the page.

11. Preview and print the *guestbook.htm* page.

12. Close the web.

Exercise 5

1. Open the Markowitz09 web located in the Chapter_9 folder on the Data Disk.

2. Create a new page in Page view and save it as *brochure.htm* with the title Brochure.

chapter nine

3. Key the following welcome text to the top of the page, and then format it as 5 (18 pt), Purple, and centered:

Submit the following form to request a brochure listing our services and prices.

4. Insert a form on the line below the welcome text. Insert a 5 by 2 Table with no border inside the form above the Reset and Submit buttons. Size the first column to approximately 1 ½ inches wide with the mouse pointer. Format the first column as right-aligned, 4 (14 pt), bold, and Navy.

5. Insert the following fields and set the field properties and validation.

Label	Form Field and Form Field Properties	Form Field Validation
First Name	one-line text box name=FirstName, width= 20	20 text characters; can contain letters, spaces, commas, hyphens, periods; display name=First Name
Last Name	one-line text box name=LastName, width=20	20 text characters; can contain letters, spaces, commas, hyphens, periods; display name=Last Name
Company	one-line text box name=Company, width=25	25 no constraints characters
Address	one-line text box name=Address, width=40	40 no constraints characters
E-mail	one-line text box name=Email, width=25	25 no constraints characters

6. Center the Reset and Submit buttons below the table.

7. Change the Submit button text to "Order a Brochure." Change the Reset button text to "Clear the Form."

8. Create a centered hyperlink to the *index.htm* page below the form using the text "Home Page." Format the hyperlink text as 5 (18 pt).

9. Send the *brochure.htm* form by e-mail using the address brochure@markowitz.com.

10. Save the *brochure.htm* page to update it.

11. Switch to Navigation view and drag the *brochure.htm* page to the child level below the home page.

12. View the *index.htm* page in the Normal tab in Page view.

13. Insert a centered navigation bar on a line below the last paragraph of text.

14. Save the *index.htm* page.

15. Create a custom confirmation page using the Confirmation Form template.

16. Delete the comment and resulting blank line. Edit the [Username] field properties in the salutation to be FirstName. Replace the first paragraph with the text "Thank you for requesting our brochure. Please review the following information for accuracy." Delete the sample fields and insert the labels and Confirmation Fields based on the *brochure.htm* form. Delete the last sentence in the last paragraph.

17. Save the page as *confirmation.htm* with the title Confirmation.

18. Assign the *confirmation.htm* page to the *brochure.htm* form.

19. Preview, print preview, and print the *index.htm*, *brochure.htm*, and *confirmation.htm* pages.

20. Close the web.

Exercise 6

1. Open the Native09 web located in the Chapter_9 folder on the Data Disk.

2. Create a new page using the Contents frame template. Set the initial page in the contents (left) frame to be the *contents.htm* page. Create a new blank page in the main frame. Get the background information for the new page from the *noframes.htm* page.

3. Create a guest book form using the <u>F</u>orm command on the <u>I</u>nsert menu on the new page to collect the name, address, e-mail address, and comments about the web from viewers. Precede the form with the text:

We want to hear from you. Send us the following information to receive a free catalog.

4. Format the text as 5 (18 pt) and centered.

5. Insert a form and use a table to organize the following form field data. Format the labels as 4 (14 pt), right-aligned, and bold.

6. Send the form results to the default file.

Label	Form Field and Form Field Properties	Form Field Validation
Name	one-line text box name=Name, width=35	35 no constraints characters
Address	one-line text box name=Address, width=35	35 no constraints characters
E-mail	one-line text box name=Email, width=20	20 no constraints characters
Comments	scrolling text box name=Comments, width=35, lines=5	35 no constraints characters on 5 lines

7. Save the form page as *dataform.htm* with the title Data Form. Save the entire new page as *getdata.htm* with the title Free Catalog.

8. Add a hyperlink to the *dataform.htm* page with the default target frame to the top of the *contents.htm* page. Use the text "Free Catalog" and format the hyperlink text to match the other hyperlinks on the page.

9. Open the *index.htm* page in the Normal tab in Page view. Follow the Free Catalog hyperlink in the Normal tab.

10. Print preview and print the *dataform.htm* page.

11. Close the web.

Exercise 7

1. Open the Citrus09 web located in the Chapter_09 folder on the Data Disk.

2. Create a new guest book page using the Guest Book form template. Get the background information from the *framespage.htm* page.

3. Delete the comment and insert the *na00417_.gif* image located in the images folder in the upper-left corner of the page.

4. On a new line below the image, key the heading text "Citrus Valley, Inc.," format it with the Heading 1 style, and center it.

chapter nine

5. Delete the default horizontal line and replace it with the *bd14689_.gif* image located in the images folder. Center the image, and then use the mouse pointer to size the image proportionally as wide as the heading text above it.

6. Format the welcome text with the Heading 2 style and center it.

7. Center the form elements.

8. Edit the scrolling text box properties to be 40 characters wide with 6 lines.

9. Save the form results to the default file.

10. Delete the horizontal line below the form and the line beginning "Author."

11. Delete the author line, and then center the copyright information below the form and replace the [OrganizationName] sample field with the "Citrus Valley, Inc." text.

12. Save the page as *guestbook.htm* with the title Guest Book and close it.

13. Open the *index.htm* page in the Normal tab in Page view.

14. Create two hyperlinks in the *contents.htm* page in the left frame: a Guest Book hyperlink and a Home Page hyperlink. Target both hyperlinks to the default main frame.

15. Save the *contents.htm* page.

16. Preview the *index.htm* page in your browser, test the hyperlinks, and then close your browser.

17. Print preview and print the *contents.htm* and *guestbook.htm* pages.

18. Close the web.

Exercise 8

1. Open the Penny09 web located in the Chapter_9 folder on the Data Disk.

2. Open the *index.htm* page in the Normal tab in Page view.

3. Create a new paragraph below the last paragraph in the *mainpage.htm* page in the main frame. Key the following text:

   Click here to register for a free basket of spring flowers. Winners will be advised by e-mail.

4. Create a new page and get the background information from the *mainpage.htm* page.

5. Key the following text at the top of the page, format the text as 6 (24 pt) and centered, and then apply light pink shading (Hex={FF,CC,FF}) to the paragraph:

   Complete and submit this form for a chance to win a free basket of spring flowers. Winners will be advised by e-mail.

6. Insert a form on the line below the welcome text.

7. Insert a 3 by 2 Table at the top of the form. Set the table background color as light pink and remove the border. Size the first column to be approximately 1 ½ inches wide. Format the first column text as 4 (14 pt), bold, and right-aligned.

Label	Form Field and Form Field Properties	Form Field Validation
Name	one-line text box name=Name, width=35	35 no constraints characters
Address	one-line text box name=Address, width=35	35 no constraints characters
E-mail	one-line text box name=Email, width=20	20 no constraints characters

8. Center the Submit and Reset buttons and change their text to "Submit Registration Form" and "Clear Registration Form" respectively.

9. Key the text "Home Page" below the form and center it. Copy the formats from the first paragraph to the Home Page text. Use the Increase Indent button to indent the Home Page paragraph shading so that the shading does *not* extend from margin to margin. Create a hyperlink to the *index.htm* page using the Home Page text.

10. Send the form results by e-mail to penny@silkflowers.com.

11. Save the new page as *registration.htm* with the title Registration Form and close it.

12. Open the *index.htm* page in the Normal tab in Page view. Use the "register" text in the *mainpage.htm* page in the main frame to create a hyperlink to the *registration.htm*. Follow the hyperlinks in the Normal tab.

13. Print preview and print the *mainpage.htm* and *registration.htm* pages.

14. Close the web.

Case Projects

Project 1

Mark's Cards & Calendars is a gift shop located in Little Rock, Arkansas, that specializes in unique greeting cards, calendars, and custom stationery. Mark Sobieski owns Mark's Cards & Calendars, and he is considering hiring you to create a new web site for his company. He wants to sell his calendar, card, and stationery products online. He asks you to submit a proposal for the new site and to include samples of other web sites with similar business offerings.

Connect to the Internet, load your web browser, and locate several web sites selling products similar to Mark's Cards & Calendars. Print at least three web pages. Using a word processing program, create a plan for the new web site that includes a comparison of your proposed web site to the existing web sites.

Create a sample web site containing a home page, three products pages, an order form page, and a custom confirmation page. Save the form results to a file. Use text, color, images, hyperlinks, and FrontPage components as desired to create an attractive and serviceable web site. Print the web pages. Save and print the plan.

Project 2

Daniel Gee is the president of EnviroPure, a company that manufactures and sells water purification systems for businesses. EnviroPure recently developed three smaller water purification systems for home installation and he wants to sell these systems directly to consumers from a company web site. He hires you to create the web site.

Using a word processing program, create a plan for the new web site that includes a home page, three product pages, an order form, and a confirmation page. Save the form results to a file and send them via e-mail. Create a sample web based on your plan. Use text, color, images, hyperlinks, and FrontPage components as desired to create an attractive and serviceable web site. Print the web pages. Save and print the plan.

Project 3

The Trophy Case is a small company located in Montpelier, Vermont. The Trophy Case sells trophies, badges, and buttons for conventions, parties, and youth sports via a printed catalog. Henley Marcus, the owner of The Trophy Case, wants to stop using a printed catalog and instead sell the company products online. He hires you to create a new web site for his company.

Using a word processing program, create a plan for the new web site that includes a home page, three product pages, an order form, and a custom confirmation page. Save the form results to a file and send them via e-mail. Create a sample web based on your plan. Use text, color, images, hyperlinks, and FrontPage components as desired to create an attractive and serviceable web site. Print the web pages. Save and print the plan.

Project 4

You are the information technology manager for your company, Window on the World, which sells custom

chapter nine

window coverings to professional interior designers. The president of your company is considering a company web site where designers can review and order window covering products online, but she is not knowledgeable about e-commerce. She is also concerned that e-commerce is just a passing fad and is afraid to commit company resources to this new way to sell products. She asks you where she can get more information about e-commerce issues, especially information about what kinds of business are involved in e-commerce and what security issues are involved with selling online.

Connect to the Internet, start your browser, and then locate and review at least ten web sites that discuss general e-commerce issues, such as who is currently involved in e-commerce, security issues, technology issues, and future expectations. Print at least 10 web pages. Using a word processing program, create a memo to the president itemizing the ten web sites and the kind of information she can get from each one. With your instructor's permission, use the memo to discuss e-commerce issues with two classmates.

Project 5

CandleLight is a small company located in Racine, Wisconsin. CandleLight manufactures and sells handcrafted candles and other gift items by a printed catalog. Jennifer Standley, the owner of Candlelight, also wants to begin selling candles and gifts online. She hires you to create a new web site for her company.

Using a word processing program, create a plan for the new web site that includes a home page, four product pages, a guest book page, an order form page, and a confirmation page. Send the form results via e-mail. Create a sample web based on your plan. Use text, color, images, hyperlinks, and FrontPage components as desired to create an attractive and serviceable web site. Print the web pages. Save and print the plan.

Project 6

Ireland's Bounty is a company located in New York City that imports Irish crystal, jewelry, woolen sweaters and scarves. Megan O'Rourke, the owner of Ireland's Bounty, wants to begin selling the imported Irish products online and hires you to create a new web site for the company.

Using a word processing program, create a plan for the new web site that includes a home page, four product pages, a guest book, an order form page, and a confirmation page. Save the form results to a file and send them via e-mail. Create a sample web based on your plan. Use text, color, images, hyperlinks, and FrontPage components as desired to create an attractive and serviceable web site. Print the web pages. Save and print the plan.

Project 7

Henri Bouquet is a world-famous chef and the owner of a new company named Chef's Paradise. Chef's Paradise, located in Palm Beach, Florida, specializes in kitchen implements and other products used by professional chefs. Mr. Bouquet wants to sell these products online and hires you to create a new web site for the company.

Using a word processing program, create a plan for the new web site that includes a home page, five product pages, a guest book, an order form page, and a confirmation page. Save the form results to a file and send them via e-mail. Create a sample web based on your plan. Use text, color, images, hyperlinks, and FrontPage components as desired to create an attractive and serviceable web site. Print the web pages. Save and print the plan.

Project 8

Rosa Gonzales is the owner of In Old Santa Fe, a tour guide service. Her company provides day tours of Santa Fe and Taos, New Mexico areas, including tours to several Native American reservations. She wants to add a company web site from which travelers can book her tours in advance.

Using a word processing program, create a plan for the new web site that includes a home page, a tour page, a guest book, an order form page, and a custom confirmation page. Send the form results via e-mail. Create a sample web based on your plan. Use text, color, images, hyperlinks, and FrontPage components as desired to create an attractive and serviceable web site. Print the web pages. Save and print the plan.

Working with Search Forms and Databases

Chapter Overview

When a web site contains many pages of information, viewers find it helpful to be able to locate the information they want by searching the web site for specific words. They also find it useful to have access to data, such as pricing information, which is stored in electronic databases. In this chapter, you create a search form page using a template, save form results to a database, retrieve information from a database using the Database Results Wizard, and add a Microsoft Access Data Access Page to a web.

LEARNING OBJECTIVES

► Add a search form to a web page
► Save form results to a database
► Use the Database Results Wizard
► Incorporate a Data Access Page into a web

Case profile

Sarah wants viewers to be able to search the new Sarah's PartyWorld web site to quickly locate the party theme pages. She also wants to make party theme package prices available to the viewers. Finally, she wants the contest registration page data saved to a database so the information can be used later for sales and marketing. You create a search page, add the package price information to the web, and finalize the contest registration page.

chapter ten

10

10.a Adding a Search Form to a Web Page

If you publish a web to a server running the FrontPage server extensions, FrontPage creates a list of the text words in your web, called an **index**. Each time you save a page in the web, FrontPage updates the text index to include any new words, making the index cumulative. This cumulative index enables viewers to search the web site by keying a specific word or group of words, called **keywords**, into a text box on a special form called a **search form**. When viewers submit the keywords, FrontPage compares them with the words in the index and returns a list of hyperlinks to pages in the web that contain those keywords.

You can insert a search form on any page in your web. However, if you do this, you must also remember to include instructions on how to use the form. A quick way to create a search form is with the Search Page template, which provides both the form and instructions on how to use it.

Creating a Search Page with a Template

You begin by opening the sample Sarah's PartyWorld web and adding a new page using the Search Page template.

To create the search form page:

Step 1	*Open*	the Sample_Web you modified in Chapter 9
Step 2	*Open*	the General tab in the New (page) dialog box
Step 3	*Double-click*	the Search Page template icon
Step 4	*Save*	the page as *searchpage.htm* with the title Search
Step 5	*Switch*	to Navigation view
Step 6	*Drag*	the *searchpage.htm* from the Folder List and drop it at the child level below home page to the right of the guest book page
Step 7	*Open*	the *searchpage.htm* page in the Normal tab in Page view
Step 8	*Remove*	the left shared border for the current page
Step 9	*Delete*	the comment below the top navigation bar and the resulting blank line
Step 10	*Scroll*	to view the page below the navigation bar

Your screen should look similar to Figure 10-1.

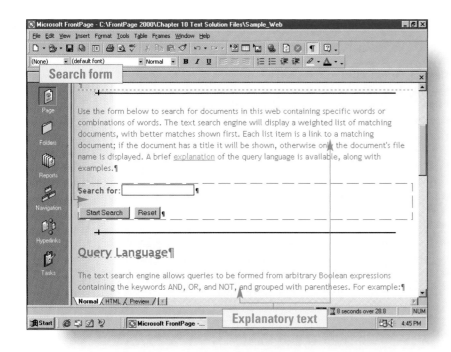

FIGURE 10-1
Search Form Page

M E N U   T I P

You can insert a search form by pointing to the Component command on the Insert menu and clicking Search Form.

M O U S E   T I P

You can insert a search form by clicking the Insert Component button on the Standard toolbar and then clicking Search Form.

You need to format the search page and edit the search form.

Formatting a Search Page

You want to format the explanatory text above the search form, remove any extraneous text and blank lines at the bottom of the page, create a bookmark named Top, and then follow the Back to Top and Top of Page hyperlinks. To edit the page:

Step 1	*Select*	the explanatory text immediately above the search form
Step 2	*Format*	the text as 4 (14 pt)
Step 3	*Scroll*	to the bottom of the page
Step 4	*Center*	the Back to Top hyperlink above the horizontal divider line
Step 5	*Delete*	the three lines of red text beginning "Author information" and the resulting blank line below the horizontal divider line
Step 6	*Create*	a bookmark named Top, using the first word in the explanatory paragraph at the top of the page
Step 7	*Follow*	the Back to Top and Top of Page hyperlinks to test them

Next, you want to widen the search form one-line text box and change the push button labels.

To edit the search form:

Step 1	*Right-click*	the search form
Step 2	*Click*	Search Form Properties
Step 3	*Click*	the Search Form Properties tab, if necessary

The Search Form Properties tab in the Search Form Properties dialog box on your screen should look similar to Figure 10-2.

FIGURE 10-2
Search Form Properties
Dialog Box

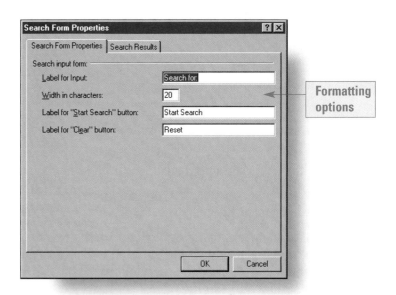

You want the text box to be 30 characters wide and the push button labels to be "Begin Search" and "Clear Keywords." To change the options:

Step 1	*Key*	30 in the Width in characters: text box
Step 2	*Key*	Begin Search in the Label for "Start Search" button: text box
Step 3	*Key*	Clear Keywords in the Label for "Clear" button: text box
Step 4	*Click*	OK
Step 5	*Save & Close*	the page

Next, you want to complete the contest page.

10.b Saving Form Results to a Database

MENU TIP

To create, modify, or remove a connection to a database, you can click the <u>W</u>eb Settings command on the <u>T</u>ools menu and then click the Database tab. Then you can use the Add button to specify the name and location of the database.

When you store data in a database, you can search the data to locate specific information or combine the data in a variety of ways. For example, you can use the data in a customer database to create form letters or mailing labels for all customers that reside in a specific city or state. You can create catalogs for selected products using data in a product database. Form results can be saved to an existing database. If the database does not yet exist, FrontPage can create it when you create the form.

Before you can save form results to an existing database, you must set up a connection between the database and the form. A **database connection** specifies the location, name, and type of database you are accessing. There are three types of connections: (1) to a database in your web, (2) to a database stored on a web server, and (3) to a large system database stored on a network database server. You can manually create the connections, or you can let FrontPage do it when you import a database into the web or when FrontPage creates a new database while creating a form.

Saving Form Results to a New Access Database

If the database does not yet exist, you can let FrontPage create a new Microsoft Access database in which to store form results. You want to store the contest page form results in a new Access database that the Sarah's PartyWorld staff can use later to create letters and other sales and marketing materials. When FrontPage creates a new database, it selects the new database as its database connection, names the database *Form.mdb*, and stores it in the fpdb folder in your web.

To modify the contest page:

Step 1	*Open*	the *feedback.htm* page in the Normal tab in Page view
Step 2	*Delete*	the welcome text and resulting blank line immediately above the form
Step 3	*Delete*	the comment, the Comments text, the scrolling text box, the Category text, the drop-down menu in the form, and resulting blank lines

chapter ten

QUICK TIP

If you are not familiar
with electronic data-
bases, search FrontPage
online Help for database
topics using the key-
word "database." The
topic "Working with
Databases" provides an
overview of database
basics.

If the database is
stored on a web or data-
base server, the server
administrator must set
up the database as a
data source. For more
information about con-
necting to a database on
a web or network server,
see online Help.

Step 4	*Replace*	the Contact Information text with the text: Register now for a chance to win the free party theme package of your choice! Winners are notified by e-mail.
Step 5	*Insert*	a line break between the sentences
Step 6	*Modify*	the existing form fields and add new table rows and form fields as needed to set up the following labels and form fields in order; size the left column in the table if necessary so that the labels do not wrap within the cell:

Label	Form Field and Form Field Properties	Form Field Validation
First Name	name=FirstName width=20	text characters, can contain letters, spaces, commas, hyphens, periods; display name=First Name
Last Name	name=LastName width=25	text characters; can contain letters, spaces, commas, hyphens, periods; display name=Last Name
E-mail Address	name=Email width=25	no constraints characters
Address	name=Address width=25	no constraints characters
City	name=City width=25	text characters; can contain letters, spaces, hyphens, periods; display name=City
State or Province	Name=StateorProvince width=15	text characters; can contain letters, spaces, commas, hyphens, periods; display name=State or Province
Postal Code	name=PostalCode width=15	no constraints characters
Telephone	name=Telephone width=20	no constraints characters
Package Name	name=Package width=20	no constraints characters

Step 7	*Format*	the label text as Comic Sans MS, bold, and no italic
Step 8	*Change*	the Submit Feedback button label to Submit Registration

Your screen should look similar to Figure 10-3.

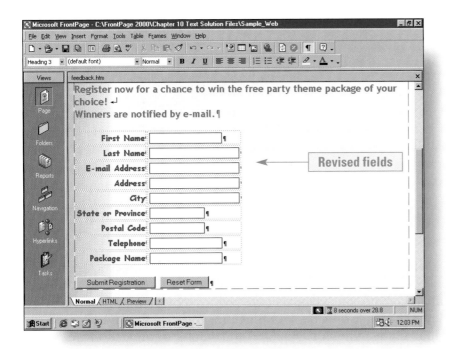

FIGURE 10-3
Contest Registration Form
with Revised Fields

To save the results to a new Microsoft Access database:

Step 1	*Open*	the Form Properties dialog box
Step 2	*Click*	the Send to database option button
Step 3	*Click*	Options
Step 4	*Click*	the Database Results tab, if necessary

The Database Results tab in the Options for Saving Results to Database dialog box on your screen should look similar to Figure 10-4. In this tab, you can specify an existing database or you can create a new database and select a custom confirmation form.

chapter
ten

FIGURE 10-4
Options for Saving Results
to Database Dialog Box

Options to create
a database
connection or
new database

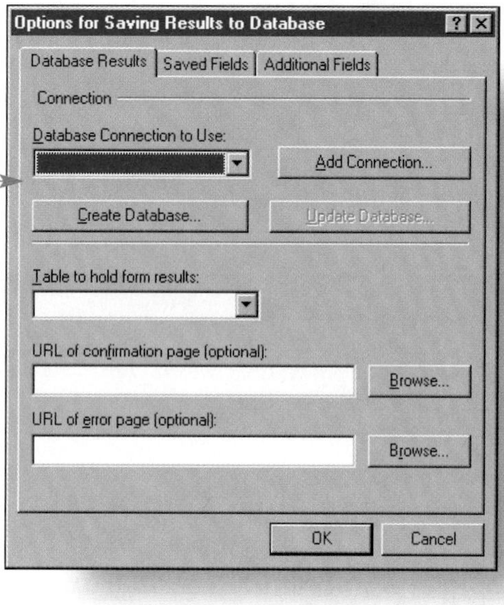

Step 5	**Click**	Create Database

Data in an Access database is stored in fields in an object called a
table. FrontPage automatically creates a database connection named
feedback, creates an Access database with a table named Results that
includes the same data fields in the form, and stores the database in
the fpdb folder. When the database and database connection are
successfully created, a confirmation dialog box appears.

Step 6	**Click**	OK to close the confirmation dialog box
Step 7	**Observe**	the feedback connection name in the Database Connection to Use: list box
Step 8	**Observe**	the Results table name in the Table to hold form results: list box

The form fields are **mapped**, or connected, to the data fields in the
new database. To view the field mapping:

Step 1	**Click**	the Saved Fields tab

The Saved Fields tab in the Options for Saving Results to Database
dialog box on your screen should look similar to Figure 10-5.
All the fields in the contest registration form are listed. For each listed
field, the database table column (or field) in which the form field data
are saved is also listed. For example, the Address form field data will be
saved in the Address column (or field) in the new database.

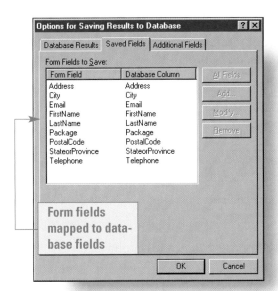

FIGURE 10-5
Saved Fields Tab

By default, additional information, such as browser type and user name, are also saved to the database. You can view these additional save options in the Additional Fields tab.

| Step 2 | *Click* | the Additional Fields tab |

The Additional Fields tab in the Options for Saving Results to Database dialog box on your screen should look similar to Figure 10-6.

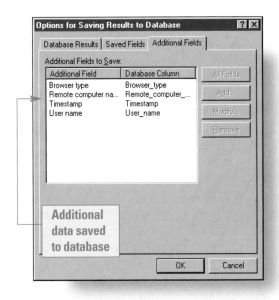

FIGURE 10-6
Additional Fields Tab

chapter
ten

| Step 3 | *Click* | OK twice to close the dialog boxes |

QUICK TIP

When you import an existing Access database into your web, FrontPage also creates the fpdb folder if it does not exist. This folder has permissions that prevent viewers from opening the folder contents in their web browser. To protect the privacy of the imported database, store it in the fpdb folder.

You can import a **Microsoft Excel database,** a range of cells on an Excel worksheet, into your web and then create a new connection to the Excel database file. For more information on importing an Excel database, see online <u>H</u>elp.

After you close the dialog boxes, a confirmation dialog box appears, indicating that you should resave or rename the contest page with an .asp file extension instead of the .htm file extension.

Step 4	*Click*	OK
Step 5	*Rename*	the file to *feedback.asp* in the Folder List
Step 6	*Click*	Yes twice to close the confirmation dialog box and update the hyperlinks
Step 7	*Save & Close*	the page

To view the new database folder and database:

Step 1	*Display*	the Folder List, if necessary
Step 2	*Open*	the fpdp folder
Step 3	*Observe*	the *feedback.mdb* database file
Step 4	*Close*	the fpdp folder and hide the Folder List

You want to provide viewers a way to check prices on the party theme packages.

10.c Using the Database Results Wizard

So that Sarah can easily modify the party theme package prices, she maintains the pricing data in an Access database. Sarah wants viewers to be able to check the package prices before they order, so you use the Database Results Wizard to add the pricing information from the database to the sample Sarah's PartyWorld web.

Importing an Existing Database

Before you can run the Database Results Wizard, you need to import the pricing database into the sample web. You can either open Windows Explorer, copy an existing database file, and paste it into your web in Folders view or import a database file using the <u>I</u>mport command on the <u>F</u>ile menu. With both methods, FrontPage prompts you to create the new database connection and to save the database file to the fpdp folder. You want to import the Access database that contains the prices into the web, but, in this instance, you want to store the file in the root folder instead of the fpdp folder.

To import the *PartyWorld_Price_List* database file:

Step 1	*Open*	Windows Explorer
Step 2	*Open*	the Chapter_10 folder on the Data Disk
Step 3	*Select*	the *PartyWorld_Price_List* database file
Step 4	*Copy*	the selected files to the Clipboard
Step 5	*Close*	Windows Explorer
Step 6	*Maximize*	the FrontPage window, if necessary
Step 7	*Switch*	to Folders view
Step 8	*Right-click*	the contents area
Step 9	*Click*	Paste

The Add Database Connection dialog box that opens should look similar to Figure 10-7.

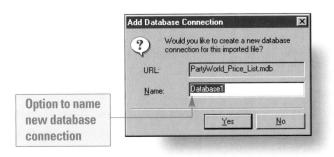

Option to name new database connection

Step 10	*Key*	Prices in the Name: text box
Step 11	*Click*	Yes
Step 12	*Click*	No to store the *PartyWorld_Price_List* database in the root folder in the web
Step 13	*Observe*	that the *PartyWorld_Price_List* database file is stored in the web

FIGURE 10-7
Add Database Connection Dialog Box

Incorporating Database Queries Using the Database Results Wizard

You are ready to add the database price list information to the catalog page. You want to add only the product name, the theme, and the prices for the Basic, Special, and Elite package contents. To do this, you can

chapter
ten

create a query that selects only those fields. A **query** is a question you create to interpret the data in a database. For example, you might create a query to determine how many customers Sarah's PartyWorld has in Arizona or which products have a price greater than $10. Query **results** provide the answer to the question. You use the Database Results Wizard to query a database.

You want viewers to be able to review the product name, party theme, and pricing data for all of the Sarah's PartyWorld products when they view the catalog page. To do this, you use the Database Results Wizard to create a region on the page that contains the data queried from the *PartyWorld_Price_List* database.

To add the pricing information to the *products.htm* page:

Step 1	*Open*	the *products.htm* page in the Normal tab in Page view
Step 2	*Move*	the insertion point to the blank line above the horizontal divider line at the bottom of the page
Step 3	*Click*	Insert
Step 4	*Point to*	Database
Step 5	*Click*	Results

The Database Results Wizard - Step 1 of 5 dialog box opens. You specify the database connection in this step.

| Step 6 | *Select* | Prices in the Use an existing database connection list |

Your dialog box should look similar to Figure 10-8.

FIGURE 10-8
Database Results
Wizard - Step 1 of 5
Dialog Box

Options to
select database
connection

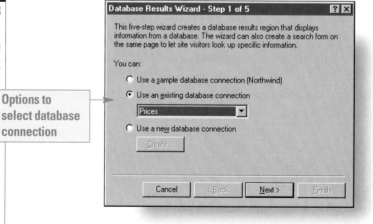

| Step 7 | *Click* | Next> |

The Database Results Wizard - Step 2 of 5 dialog box opens. In this step, you specify the name of the database table that contains the data. You also create the database query. To complete step 2:

Step 1	*Verify*	that Products is selected in the Record source: list
Step 2	*Click*	the Custom query option button
Step 3	*Click*	Edit

Structured Query Language (SQL) is a database query and programming language recognized by most modern databases. You can use SQL to query the *PartyWorld_Price_List* database to return the appropriate field data in a specific order. You do this by keying SQL keywords and database field names separated by commas in this dialog box.

| Step 4 | *Key* | the SQL statement using Figure 10-9 as your guide |

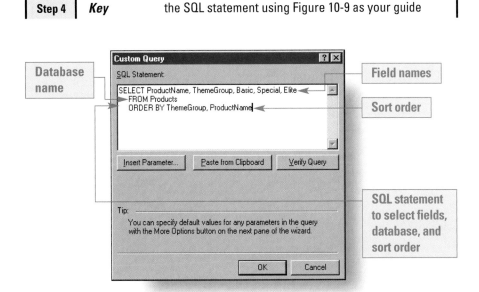

Database name

Field names

Sort order

SQL statement to select fields, database, and sort order

QUICK TIP

Indenting relevant lines of coding in an SQL statement makes the statement easier to read. You can indent lines in an SQL statement in the Custom Query Dialog Box by pressing the SPACEBAR.

If you are not familiar with writing SQL statements, but are familiar with the Access application, you can create a query in Access, have Access show you the SQL statement it generated, copy the SQL statement to the Clipboard, and then paste it into the SQL Statement: text box in the Custom Query dialog box when running the Database Results Wizard. For more information on creating Access queries and viewing SQL statements in Access, see Access online Help.

FIGURE 10-9
SQL Statement in the Custom Query Dialog Box

You can verify that the database field names and SQL statement syntax, or language rules, are correct against the previously selected database connection. When the syntax and field names are verified, a confirmation dialog box appears.

| Step 5 | *Click* | Verify Query |
| Step 6 | *Click* | OK twice to close the confirmation dialog box and the Custom Query dialog box |

chapter
ten

Your Database Results Wizard - Step 2 of 5 dialog box should look similar to Figure 10-10.

FIGURE 10-10
Database Results
Wizard - Step 2 of 5
Dialog Box

Option to select
database table

Option to create
custom query

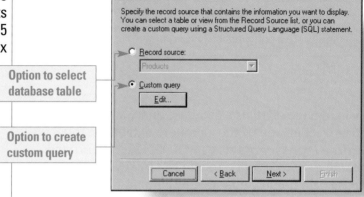

| Step 7 | *Click* | Next> |

In step 3, you verify the list of fields to include in the results. The field list contains only those fields you specified in the query. Your Database Results Wizard - Step 3 of 5 dialog box should look similar to Figure 10-11.

FIGURE 10-11
Database Results
Wizard - Step 3 of 5
Dialog Box

Field names
selected by
query

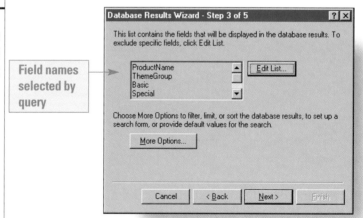

MOUSE TIP

If you have the Microsoft Access 2000 application loaded on your system, you can double-click the Access database filename in the Folder List to start the Access application. Then, double-click the table name to view the data in the table.

| Step 8 | *Click* | Next> |

In step 4, you specify how the database results appear in the page. You want the results to appear in a table with a border and header row. To set the database results:

Step 1	*Verify*	that Table - one record per row appears in the list
Step 2	*Click*	the Use table border, Expand table to width of page, and Include header row with column labels check boxes to insert check marks, if neccesary

Your Database Results Wizard - Step 4 of 5 dialog box should look similar to Figure 10-12.

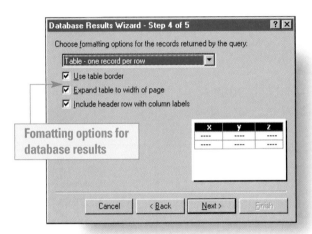

FIGURE 10-12
Database Results
Wizard - Step 4 of 5
Dialog Box

Step 3	*Click*	Next>

In step 5, you can set an option to display all the records at one time or display a small group of records with buttons viewers can use to move forward or backward through the database results. You want to display four records at a time. To set the display options:

Step 1	*Click*	the Split records into groups: option button, if necessary
Step 2	*Key*	4 in the records per group text box

Your Database Results Wizard - Step 5 of 5 dialog box should look similar to Figure 10-13.

chapter
ten

FIGURE 10-13
Database Results
Wizard - Step 5 of 5
Dialog Box

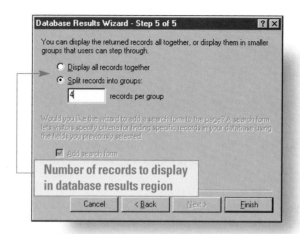

Step 3	*Click*	<u>F</u>inish

A confirmation dialog box opens to remind you to rename the page as an .asp file.

Step 4	*Click*	OK

The database results region appears in the page as a table. You cannot preview the database results until you publish your page to a web server. For now, you change the look of the table. To format the table:

Step 1	*Center*	the column headings in the first row and the field names in the third row
Step 2	*Center*	the table
Step 3	*Change*	the ProductName column heading to Product Name
Step 4	*Change*	the ThemeGroup column heading to Theme

The database results region on your screen should look similar to Figure 10-14.

Step 5	*Insert*	a $ in front of the <<field names>> for the Basic, Special, and Elite fields
Step 6	*Rename*	the page *products.asp* in the Folder List, confirming the filename extension change and updating the hyperlinks
Step 7	*Save & Close*	the page

MENU **TIP**

You can right-click the Database Results region and click Database Results Properties to open the Database Results Wizard.

MOUSE **TIP**

You can double-click the Database Results region to open the Database Results Wizard.

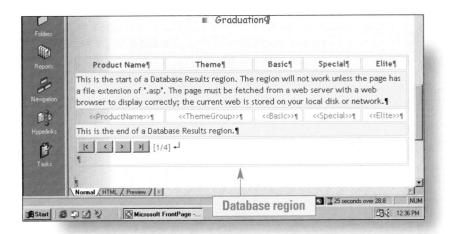

FIGURE 10-14
Database Results Region

Bob Avila gives you a copy of a professional journal article that discusses how to use the Microsoft Access 2000 Data Access Pages to make database information available to web page viewers.

10.d Incorporating a Data Access Page into a Web

A **Data Access Page** (DAP) is a web page used to view and work with data stored in an Access database or Microsoft SQL Server database. Data Access Pages are connected directly to an Access database; therefore, the database must be available to the viewer when they load the Data Access Page in their browser.

notes   If you do not have Access 2000 installed, you will be able to read but not do the hands-on activities for creating a Data Access Page. If you do have Access 2000 installed but are not familiar with the Access application, your instructor may provide additional explanations and instructions to complete the hands-on activities in this section.

You create a Data Access Page using an Access Wizard and save it in the Sample_Web folder. Then you open the Data Access Page and add text and theme formatting. Finally, you position the Data Access Page as a child page under the catalog page in Navigation view. To create the Data Access Page:

Step 1	*Verify*	that the Sample_Web is open
Step 2	*Display*	the Folder List

Step 3	**Double-click**	the *PartyWorld_Price_List.mdb* Access database filename in the Folder List to start Access and open the database
Step 4	**Click**	Pages in the Objects Bar to view the Data Access Page shortcuts, if necessary
Step 5	**Double-click**	the Create Data Access Page by using wizard shortcut

The first Page Wizard dialog box opens. You select the underlying table or query and the fields you want to include in the page in this step. To select the underlying table and add all the fields except the ProductID field:

Step 1	**Click**	the Tables/Queries drop-down list arrow
Step 2	**Click**	Table: Products, if necessary
Step 3	**Click**	the double-chevron button between the Available Fields: and Selected Fields: lists to add all the available fields
Step 4	**Click**	the ProductID field in the Selected Fields: list to select it
Step 5	**Click**	the left-pointing single-chevron button to remove the field and return it to the Available Fields: list
Step 6	**Observe**	that the Selected Fields: list now contains the ProductName, ThemeGroup, Basic, Special, and Elite fields
Step 7	**Click**	Next>

The second Page Wizard dialog box opens. You determine the grouping levels or arrangement in which you want the records to appear on the page. You want viewers to be able to view party theme package prices by first selecting the theme area, such as baby showers. To do this, you group the records by the ThemeGroup field. To group the records:

Step 1	**Double-click**	ThemeGroup in the field name list
Step 2	**Observe**	the blue group heading ThemeGroup in the preview section
Step 3	**Click**	Next>

The third Page Wizard dialog box opens. You can specify how you want the records sorted in this dialog box. You want the individual price records to be sorted in ascending order by the product name field. To specify the sort order:

| Step 1 | **Click** | the 1 drop-down list arrow |

| Step 2 | *Click* | ProductName |
| Step 3 | *Click* | <u>N</u>ext> |

The final Page Wizard dialog box opens. You give the Data Access Page a name and format it in this dialog box. To name and format the Data Access Page:

Step 1	*Key*	Prices in the What title do you want for your page? text box
Step 2	*Verify*	that the <u>M</u>odify the page's design. option button is selected
Step 3	*Click*	the Do you want to <u>a</u>pply a theme to your page? check box to insert a check mark
Step 4	*Click*	<u>F</u>inish

In a few seconds, the Data Access Page opens in Design view and then the Theme dialog box opens. To apply Sarah's Theme:

Step 1	*Click*	Sarah's Theme in the Choose a <u>T</u>heme: list
Step 2	*Click*	the Vivid <u>C</u>olors, Active <u>G</u>raphics, and <u>B</u>ackground Image check boxes to insert check marks, if necessary
Step 3	*Click*	OK
Step 4	*Observe*	the Sarah's Theme applied to the page

To add title text to the page:

Step 1	*Click*	the Click here and type title text area
Step 2	*Key*	Sarah's PartyWorld Price List
Step 3	*Press*	the ENTER key
Step 4	*Key*	Click the Back button in your browser window
Step 5	*Press*	the SHIFT + ENTER keys to insert a line break
Step 6	*Key*	to return to the previous page

chapter
ten

To open the header label properties dialog boxes and edit the header text:

Step 1	**Double-click**	the GroupofProducts: ThemeGroup label in the Header: Products ThemeGroup to open the object's properties dialog box
Step 2	**Click**	the Other tab
Step 3	**Key**	Theme in the InnerText text box
Step 4	**Close**	the dialog box
Step 5	**Observe**	the new label "Theme" in the Header: Products ThemeGroup
Step 6	**Double-click**	the ProductName label in the Header: Products
Step 7	**Click**	the Other tab, if necessary
Step 8	**Key**	Product Name in the InnerText text box
Step 9	**Close**	the dialog box

The Expand button object in the header is positioned slightly lower than the Theme label. You want the button to appear level with the label.

Step 10	**Click**	the Expand button 🔃 object in the header to select it
Step 11	**Drag**	the Expand button 🔃 object up until it is level with Theme label

Now you are ready to close Design view and save the page. To close and save the page:

Step 1	**Click**	the Close button ❌ on the Design view window
Step 2	**Click**	Yes to close the page
Step 3	**Switch**	to the location where the Sample_Web is stored
Step 4	**Save**	the page as *prices.htm* in the Sample_Web folder
Step 5	**Observe**	the shortcut named *prices* in the database
Step 6	**Close**	Access and the database

QUICK TIP

You can preview a Data Access Page in your browser by right-clicking the Data Access Page shortcut in the database window and clicking Web Page Preview.

| Step 7 | *Refresh* | the view of the Folder List to see the *prices.htm* page added to the web |

Next, you add the *prices.htm* Data Access Page to the child-level pages under the catalog page so that a hyperlink to the page appears on the navigation bar. To add the *prices.htm* page:

Step 1	*Switch*	to Navigation view
Step 2	*Drag*	the *prices.htm* Data Access Page to the child level under the catalog page and drop it the right of the order form page
Step 3	*Open*	the *baby.htm* page in the Normal tab in Page view
Step 4	*Scroll*	to view the *prices.htm* page hyperlink in the left navigation bar
Step 5	*View*	the *baby.htm* page in the Preview tab
Step 6	*Click*	the Prices hyperlink to preview the Data Access Page

The Data Access Page opens. It contains an area in which you view each record for a party theme group and a navigation toolbar. Your screen should look similar to Figure 10-15.

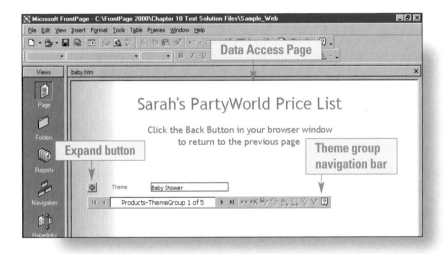

CAUTION TIP

If you follow the hyperlink to a Data Access Page in the Normal tab, the Data Access Page opens in the Access application.

FIGURE 10-15
Data Access Page

This Data Access Page enables you to view each party theme package name and prices. You decide to view the It's a Baby! baby shower theme package prices. To view the Baby Shower theme group:

| Step 1 | *Click* | the Expand button  to the left of the Theme text to expand the group |

chapter
ten

| Step 2 | *Observe* | the It's A Baby! baby shower theme package prices |

Your screen should look similar to Figure 10-16.

FIGURE 10-16
Expanded Baby Shower
Group

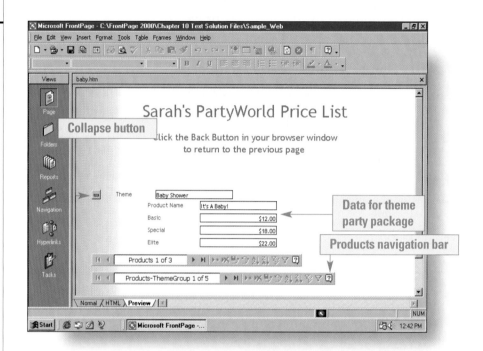

You can view the next record in the group by clicking the Next navigation button on the Products navigation toolbar. Click the Next button on the ThemeGroup navigation toolbar to view the next group.

Step 3	*Click*	the Next button ▶ on the Products navigation toolbar to view the It's A Boy! data
Step 4	*Click*	the Next button ▶ on the ThemeGroup navigation toolbar to view the Birthday Party group
Step 5	*Expand*	the Birthday Party group to view the Baby's First record
Step 6	*Click*	the Collapse button ▬ to collapse the Birthday Party group
Step 7	*Return*	to the Normal tab
Step 8	*Close*	the web

All the requested web pages in the sample Sarah's PartyWorld web are complete. You are ready to finalize the web and publish it.

Summary

▶ You can create a search page form to search a web site using a keyword index.

▶ You can save form results to an electronic database that is stored in the web, on a web server, or on a network server.

▶ A database connection specifies the location, name, and type of database being accessed from a web page.

▶ If a database does not exist, you can have FrontPage create it for you as you create a form.

▶ The Database Results Wizard is a tool you can use to add data stored in a database to a web page.

▶ You can import an existing database and other files by copying them from Windows Explorer and pasting them into a web in Folders view.

▶ A query is a question you create about data in a database. The query results are the answer to the question.

▶ A Data Access Page is a web page used to view and work with data stored in an Access database or Microsoft SQL Server database.

Commands Review

Action	Menu Bar	Shortcut Menu	Toolbar/Mouse	Keyboard
Update an index	Tools, Recalculate Hyperlinks			ALT + T, R
Warn when an index is out of date	Tools, Options			ALT + T, O
Create a search form page	Insert, Component, Search Form		🔲	ALT + I, O, S
Create, modify, or remove database connection	Tools, Web Settings			ALT + T, W
Start the Database Results Wizard	Insert, Database, Results	Right-click the Database Results region, click Database Results Properties	Double-click the Database Results region	ALT + I, D, R

chapter ten

Concepts Review

Circle the correct answer.

1. An index is a:
[a] hyperlink.
[b] list of text words in a web.
[c] database connection.
[d] form.

2. A Microsoft Excel database is a:
[a] special form.
[b] list of text words.
[c] range of cells in a worksheet.
[d] word processing application.

3. Connecting form fields to the corresponding database form fields is called:
[a] linking.
[b] formatting.
[c] inserting.
[d] mapping.

4. An .asp page is:
[a] not allowed in a FrontPage web.
[b] a standard HTML page containing server scripts.
[c] an electronic database.
[d] a map.

5. When you want to specify that data from a database be inserted in a data results region on a web page, you can create a:
[a] frame.
[b] navigation bar.
[c] query.
[d] report.

6. SQL is an abbreviation for:
[a] Structured Query Language.
[b] Simple Query Language.
[c] Structured Quality Language.
[d] Simple Quality Language.

7. A Data Access Page is:
[a] created in Microsoft Excel.
[b] used to view and work with an Access or SQL Server database.
[c] forbidden in a FrontPage web.
[d] created using an index.

8. Keywords:
[a] are a word or group of words used in a search process.
[b] are a special kind of FrontPage form.
[c] are used to create a database connection.
[d] must be mapped to database fields.

9. A database connection specifies the:
[a] date and time a web page is accessed.
[b] location, name, and type of database being accessed from a web page.
[c] range of cells in an Excel worksheet called a database.
[d] query results.

10. In order for an index to be created when a web site is published:
[a] the web server must be running FrontPage Server Extensions.
[b] the web site must include a search page.
[c] a database connection must be present.
[d] the form fields must be mapped.

Circle **T** if the statement is true or **F** if the statement is false.

T   F   1. The abbreviation for Active Server Page is SQL.

T   F   2. A search form checks for the most common English words such as "a" and "the."

T   F   3. You can create a search page only by using the Search Page template.

T   F   4. If you want viewers to be able to key more text in a search form text box, you must increase the width of the text box.

T   F   5. There are only two types of database connections: (1) to a database in the web and (2) to a network server.

T   F   6. The only databases you can access from a web page are Access databases.

T   F   7. Before you can use the Database Results Wizard, you must have access to an existing database.

T   F   8. A Data Access Page is a range of cells in an Excel worksheet.

T   F   9. Once you create a search page, you cannot alter it.

T   F   10. FrontPage can create a new Access database to store form results if a database does not already exist.

Glossary

Use online <u>H</u>elp to look up the following words in the FrontPage glossary. Then, using your word processing program, create a document listing each word and its glossary definition. Save and print the document.

1. Active Data Objects

2. Active Server Page or ASP

3. CGI

4. database

5. database results region

6. data connection

7. Database Results Wizard

8. FrontPage Server Extensions

9. Open Database Connectivity

10. relational database

11. Search Form component

12. Structured Query Language

Skills Review

SCANS

Exercise 1

1. Open the Amy10 web located in the Chapter_10 folder on the Data Disk.

2. Create a search form page using the Search Page template.

3. Get the background colors and text colors for the Search Form page from the *amy.htm* page.

4. Format the welcome text as 4 (14 pt) and center it.

5. Scroll to the bottom of the page and delete the sample Author information text line. Replace the [OrganizationName] field with "Amy's Collectibles." Then center both lines of text.

6. Insert a hyperlink to the *amy.htm* page below the two lines using the text "Home Page."

7. Save the page as *searchpage.htm* with the title Search Page and close it.

chapter ten

8. Open the *contents.htm* page and insert a hyperlink to the *searchpage.htm* page above the Home hyperlink using the text "Search." Change the font size for all the hyperlink text to 4 (14 pt), and then save and close the page.

9. Open the *index.htm* page in the Normal tab in Page view and preview the page in your browser. Test the hyperlinks and close the browser.

10. Print preview and print the *searchpage.htm* page.

11. Close the web.

Exercise 2

1. Open the Bookworm10 web located in the Chapter_10 folder on the Data Disk.

2. Open the *guestbook.htm* page in the Normal tab in Page view.

3. Open the Form Properties dialog box and send the form results to a database. Open the Options for Saving Results to Database dialog box and create a new Access database.

4. Edit the *guestbook.htm* page welcome text to "We'd like to know what you think about our web site. Please leave your comments in this guest book." Delete the text following the form. Delete the Include Page component immediately above the horizontal line below the form.

5. Rename the page *guestbook.asp* in the Folder List and update the hyperlinks.

6. Save the *guestbook.asp* page and close it.

7. Delete the *guestlog.htm* page in the Folder List.

8. Preview and print the *guestbook.asp* page.

9. Close the web.

Exercise 3

1. Open the Chocolate10 web located in the Chapter_10 folder on the Data Disk.

2. Create a search form page using the Search Page template.

3. Save the page as *searchpage.htm* with the title Search Page.

4. Switch to Navigation view and drag the *searchpage.htm* page from the Folder List to the child pages under home level to the left of the Chocolates page.

5. Open the *searchpage.htm* page in the Normal tab in Page view.

6. Remove the left shared border for the current page.

7. Delete the comment and the resulting blank line.

8. Delete the three lines of author information and copyright information immediately above the bottom shared border.

9. Save the page.

10. Print preview and print the page.

11. Close the web.

Exercise 4

1. Open the Rivers10 web located in the Chapter_10 folder on the Data Disk.

2. Import the *Rivers_Prices* database into the web and store it in the root folder. Create a database connection named Rates.

3. Switch to Navigation view and create a new page at the child level under the home page, then rename the page in the Folder List as *our_rates.htm*.

4. View the *our_rates.htm* page in the Normal tab in Page view.

5. Use the Data Results Wizard to insert the Services and Hourly data fields from the *Rivers_Prices* database into a database results region in the table format. Use the Rates database connection. Use the Services data source. Create a custom query to include only the Services and Hourly fields. Create a table that does *not* expand to fit the width of the page, but that has a border and column headings. Display all the records together.

6. Rename the *our_rates.htm* page as *our_rates.asp*.

7. Save the *our_rates.asp* page, and then preview and print it.

8. Close the web.

Exercise 5

1. Open the Markowitz10 web located in the Chapter_10 folder on the Data Disk.

2. Create a search page form using the Search Page template.

3. Delete the comment and the resulting blank line at the top of the page.

4. Format the page with the Purple background color, White text color, and lavender hyperlink color.

5. Delete the author information line at the bottom of the page and replace the [OrganizationName] sample field with "Markowitz Consulting Services."

6. Edit the search form properties to change the field label to "Keywords:", the Submit button label to "Begin Search," and the Reset button text to "Clear Keywords."

7. Save the page as *searchpage.htm* with the title Search.

8. Print preview, print, and then close the page.

9. Switch to Navigation view and add the Search page as a child level page under the home page. Place it to the left of the Brochure page.

10. Print preview and print the *index.htm* page.

11. Close the web.

Exercise 6

1. Open the Native10 web located in the Chapter_10 folder on the Data Disk.

2. Open the *dataform.htm* page in the Normal tab in Page view.

3. Open the Form Properties dialog box and send the results to a database. Open the Options for Saving Results to Database dialog box and create a new database.

4. Rename the file *dataform.asp* and save it.

5. Preview and print the *dataform.asp* page.

6. Verify the location and name of the new database using the Folder List.

7. Close the web.

Exercise 7

1. Open the Citrus10 web located in the Chapter_10 folder on the Data Disk.

2. Open the *contents.htm* page in the Normal tab in Page view.

3. Insert a search form, using the Insert Component button on the Standard toolbar. on a line below the Home Page hyperlink.

chapter ten

4. Open the Search Form Properties dialog box and change the field label to "Search:", the text box width to 15, the Submit button label to "Start," and the Reset button label to "Clear."

5. Print preview and print the page.

6. Save and close the page.

7. Open the *index.htm* page in the Normal tab in Page view.

8. Scroll the left frame to view the new search form.

9. Close the web.

Exercise 8   C

1. Open the Penny10 web located in the Chapter_10 folder on the Data Disk.

2. Open Windows Explorer, copy the *Pennys_Prices* database from the Chapter_10 folder to the Clipboard, and then close Windows Explorer.

3. Maximize the FrontPage window, switch to Folders view, and paste the file into the root folder (not the fpdp folder). Create a database connection named Prices.

4. Open the *Pennys_Prices* database from the Folder List, click Pages in the Objects Bar, and create a Data Access Page (DAP) using a wizard and the underlying Products table. Use the ProductName, UnitPrice, and ProductGroup fields. Group the records by ProductGroup. Sort the records by ProductName in ascending order. Add an appropriate title and background color formatting in Design view. Do not use a theme. Save the page as *Pennys_Prices* in the Penny10 root folder.

5. Open the *header.htm* page in the Normal tab in Page view.

6. Insert a new column at the end of the table.

7. Key "Prices" in the new cell.

8. Select the cells and change the font size to 4 (14 pt).

9. Create a hyperlink to the *Pennys_Prices* web page (Data Access Page) you just imported using the text "Prices."

10. Save the page.

11. Print preview, print, and close the page.

12. Open the *index.htm* page and preview it in the Preview tab.

13. Test the Prices hyperlink and expand and collapse the data groups in the Data Access Page.

14. Return to the Normal tab and close the web.

Case Projects

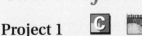

Project 1

Art for All is a new online art agency located in New York City that provides representation for a variety of painters, sculptors, and other artists who specialize in creating affordable art for homes. Beverly Branston owns Art for All, and she is considering hiring you to create a new web site for the company. She asks you to submit a proposal for a web site, which includes samples of other web sites that sell arts and crafts online.

Connect to the Internet, load your web browser, and locate several web sites that sell arts and crafts. Print at least five web pages. Using a word processing program, create a plan for the new Art for All web site, including a comparison of your proposed web site to the sampled web sites.

Create your proposed web site with at least a home page, three products pages, an order form page, a custom confirmation page, and a search page. Save the form results to a database and have FrontPage create the database for you. Use text, color, images, hyperlinks, and FrontPage components as desired to create an attractive and serviceable web site. Print the web pages. Save and print the plan.

Project 2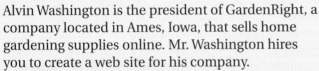

Alvin Washington is the president of GardenRight, a company located in Ames, Iowa, that sells home gardening supplies online. Mr. Washington hires you to create a web site for his company.

Using a word processing program, create a plan for the new web site that includes a home page, three product pages, an order form, a custom confirmation page, and a search form page. Create a sample web based on your plan. Save the form results to a database and have FrontPage create the database for you.

Use text, color, images, hyperlinks, and FrontPage components as desired to create an attractive and serviceable web site. Print the web pages. Save and print the plan.

Project 3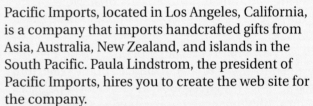

Rock Star Heaven is a small company located in Canton, Ohio. Rock Star Heaven sells rock-and-roll memorabilia from the 1950s and 1960s, including tour posters, autographed album covers, and hard-to-find records and tapes. Dennis Appleby, the owner of Rock Star Heaven, wants to begin selling his rock-and-roll memorabilia online. He hires you to create the web site for his company.

Using a word processing program, create a plan for the new web site that includes a home page, three product pages, an order form, a custom confirmation page, and a search page. Create a sample web based on your plan. Save the form results to a database and let FrontPage create the database for you. Use text, color, images, hyperlinks, and FrontPage components as desired to create an attractive and serviceable web site. Print the web pages. Save and print the plan.

Project 4

Pacific Imports, located in Los Angeles, California, is a company that imports handcrafted gifts from Asia, Australia, New Zealand, and islands in the South Pacific. Paula Lindstrom, the president of Pacific Imports, hires you to create the web site for the company.

Using a word processing program, create a plan for the new web site that includes a home page, three product pages, an order form, a custom confirmation page, and a search page. Create a sample web based on your plan. Save the form results to a database and let FrontPage create the database for you. Use text, color, images, hyperlinks, and FrontPage components as desired to create an attractive and serviceable web site. Print the web pages. Save and print the plan.

chapter ten

Project 5

Crystal Delights, located in Salt Lake City, Utah, sells minerals, rocks, and crystals to collectors. MaryBeth Bradley, the owner of Crystal Delights, wants to begin her collectibles online. She hires you to create a new web site for her company.

Using a word processing program, create a plan for the new web site that includes a home page, four product pages, a guest book page, an order form page, a confirmation page, and a search page. Create a sample web based on your plan. Save the guest book page results to a file and the order form page to a database. Let FrontPage create the database for you. Use text, color, images, hyperlinks, and FrontPage components as desired to create an attractive and serviceable web site. Print the web pages. Save and print the plan.

Project 6

Backpack Central is a camping equipment retailer in Missoula, Montana. Billy Bob Anderson, the manager of Backpack Central, wants to begin offering camping equipment to consumers online. He hires you to create the new company web site.

Using a word processing program, create a plan for the new web site that includes a home page, four product pages, a guest book, an order form page, a confirmation page, and a search page. Create a sample web based on your plan. Save the guest book form results to a file and the order form results to a database. Let FrontPage create the database for you. Use text, color, images, hyperlinks, and FrontPage components as desired to create an attractive and serviceable web site. Print the web pages. Save and print the plan.

Project 7

Manny's Martial Arts Supply, located in Boston, Massachusetts, sells martial arts equipment and supplies. Manny Lopez, the owner, asks you to submit a proposal for a new web site including samples of other web sites selling similar products.

Connect to the Internet, load your web browser, and locate several web sites selling martial arts supplies and equipment. Print at least three web pages. Using a word processing program, create a plan for the new Manny web's Martial Arts Supply web site.

Create a sample web site that includes a home page, three products pages, an order form page, a custom confirmation page, and a search page. Save the order form results to a database and have FrontPage create one for you. Use text, color, images, hyperlinks, and FrontPage components as desired to create an attractive and serviceable web site. Print the web pages. Save and print the plan.

Project 8

Ruby Vhu is the owner of Quality Skincare Products, a company that retails skincare and cosmetic products on a television cable-shopping channel. Ms. Vhu now also wants to sell the company's products to consumers online from a new company web site. She hires you to create the web site.

Using a word processing program, create a plan for the new web site that includes a home page, five product pages, a guest book, an order form page, a custom confirmation page, and a search page. Create a sample web based on your plan. Send the guest book form results to a file and the order form results to a database. Have FrontPage create the database for you. Use text, color, images, hyperlinks, and FrontPage components as desired to create an attractive and serviceable web site. Print the web pages. Save and print the plan.

Importing an Existing Web Site and Working with HTML

Chapter Overview

Importing existing web pages and folders into a new web with the Import Web Wizard is a quick way to create content for a new web. You can edit web pages using the HyperText Markup Language directly from Page view in the Normal tab or in the HTML tab. When two or more people are authorized to edit pages in the web, you can use source control to protect against two people trying to edit a file at the same time. In this chapter, you import existing web pages and folders into a new web, rename a web, edit pages using HTML, and review the source control feature.

Case profile

Sarah is buying a small catering company and asks you to create a separate web site for it after the Sarah's PartyWorld web is published. She wants you to use content similar to that in the sample Sarah's PartyWorld web so you decide to import the Sample_Web pages and folders into a new web that you can later modify for the catering company. Then, to finalize the Sarah's PartyWorld web, you rename the Sample_Web and make some final changes using HTML. Finally, you review how to protect the final web pages if both you and Bob are authorized to edit them.

chapter eleven

11.a Using the Import Web Wizard

The Import Web Wizard can import existing disk-based webs or server-based webs into a new web. **Disk-based webs** are web files and folders that are located on a hard drive or a network drive. **Server-based webs** are web files and folders that have been published to a web server.

Because Sarah wants you to use some of the content from the Sample_Web in the new catering company web, you decide to import the files and folders from the Sample_Web into a new web, which you can later modify for the catering company.

To import the Sample_Web files and folders into a new web:

Step 1	*Start*	FrontPage
Step 2	*Open*	the New (web) dialog box
Step 3	*Specify*	the location of the new web, using the web folder name Sample_Web2
Step 4	*Double-click*	the Import Web Wizard icon

The Import Web Wizard - Choose Source dialog box opens. You select the location of the existing web in this dialog box. The existing web can be a disk-based web located on your hard drive or a server-based web located. If the web is saved on your hard drive or network drive, the local path to the web is the location. The Sample_Web has not been published, so you can browse to locate it on a local drive.

Step 5	*Click*	the From a source <u>d</u>irectory of files on a local computer or network option button
Step 6	*Click*	<u>B</u>rowse
Step 7	*Switch*	to the disk drive and folder where the Sample_Web you modified in Chapter 10 is stored
Step 8	*Select*	the Sample_Web folder
Step 9	*Click*	OK
Step 10	*Click*	the Include <u>s</u>ubfolders check box to insert a check mark, if necessary

Your Import Web Wizard - Choose Source dialog box should look similar to Figure 11-1.

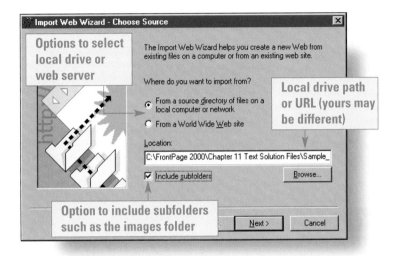

FIGURE 11-1
Import Web Wizard
Step 1 of 3

| Step 11 | *Click* | Next> |

The Import Web Wizard - Edit File List dialog box opens. By default the file list contains all the files in the web. You can select and exclude files or refresh the list of files, if necessary. You want to include all the files. Your Import Web Wizard - Edit File List dialog box should look similar to Figure 11-2.

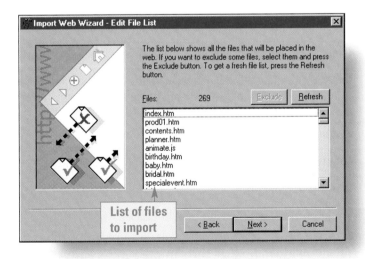

FIGURE 11-2
Import Web Wizard
Step 2 of 3

CAUTION TIP

Web page themes, shared borders, and the web navigational structure are *not* imported when you use the Import Web Wizard to create a new web content from an existing web.

| Step 12 | *Click* | Next> |

chapter
eleven

The Import Web Wizard - Finish dialog box that opens should look similar to Figure 11-3.

FIGURE 11-3
Import Web Wizard
Step 3 of 3

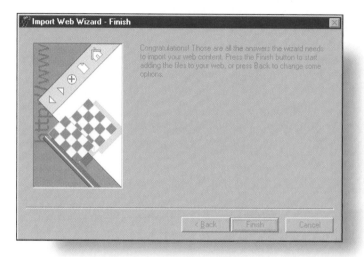

Step 13	*Click*	Finish

All the files and subfolders in the Sample_Web you modified in Chapter 10 are imported into Sample_Web2. The may take a few moments. To review the imported pages:

Step 1	*Open*	the *index.htm* page in the Normal tab in Page view
Step 2	*Observe*	that the navigation bar at the top of the page and the theme formatting are missing
Step 3	*Open*	the *baby.htm* page in the Normal tab in Page view
Step 4	*Observe*	that the navigation bar at the top of the page, the theme formatting, the shared borders, and the left navigation bar are missing
Step 5	*Switch*	to Navigation view
Step 6	*Observe*	that no navigational structure is set for the web
Step 7	*Close*	the web

Now that you imported the Sample_Web content into a new web for later use, you are ready to finalize the sample Sarah's PartyWorld web.

11.b Renaming a Web to Change the URL

When you rename a disk-based web, such as Sample_Web, the internal hyperlinks are automatically updated with the new name. When you rename a server-based web, the URL on the server is changed.

You want to rename the Sample_Web to PartyWorld now that the pages are approved. To rename the Sample_Web:

Step 1	*Open*	the Sample_Web you modified in Chapter 10
Step 2	*Click*	Tools
Step 3	*Click*	Web Settings
Step 4	*Click*	the General tab, if necessary

The General tab in the Web Settings dialog box on your screen should look similar to Figure 11-4.

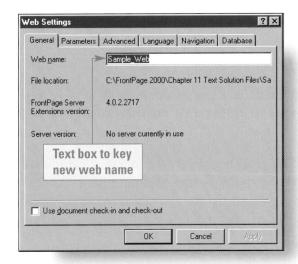

CAUTION TIP

If you rename a web after it is published, you must republish the entire web under the new name. Be aware that hyperlinks from other web sites to your old web won't work, so you must inform visitors to the old site of the new URL or path.

FIGURE 11-4
Web Settings Dialog Box

Step 5	*Key*	PartyWorld in the Web name: text box
Step 6	*Click*	OK
Step 7	*Close*	the web

chapter eleven

Renaming the web from the Web Settings dialog box does not rename the web folder. You want the folder name to also be PartyWorld. To change the web folder name:

Step 1	*Open*	Windows Explorer
Step 2	*Switch*	to the folder where the Sample_Web is stored
Step 3	*Right-click*	the Sample_Web folder name
Step 4	*Click*	Rename
Step 5	*Key*	PartyWorld to replace the highlighted name
Step 6	*Press*	the ENTER key
Step 7	*Close*	Windows Explorer
Step 8	*Maximize*	the FrontPage window, if necessary

You still have a couple of minor changes to make; you decide to make them in the HTML tab.

11.c Editing a Web Page Using HTML

If you are familiar with HyperText Markup Language, you can create and edit web pages by using HTML directly instead of allowing FrontPage to generate the HTML tags. To view the HTML tags and other elements created automatically by FrontPage, you can view a page in the HTML tab in Page view. Another way to view the HTML tags is to reveal them in the Normal tab.

Using Reveal Tags

When you are creating or editing a web page in the Normal tab in Page view, you can view the beginning and the end of all the HTML tags that indicate text, pictures, and other page elements you are inserting into the page. You do this by turning on the Reveal Tags feature.

To turn on the Reveal Tags feature:

Step 1	*Open*	the PartyWorld web you renamed in the previous section
Step 2	*Open*	the *index.htm* page in the Normal tab in Page view
Step 3	*Click*	View
Step 4	*Click*	Reveal Tags

The HTML tags appear. You can see the complete text of a tab including its **attributes**, the additional information required by the tag, such as formatting, by positioning the mouse pointer over a tag.

Step 5	*Scroll*	the page to review the HTML tags
Step 6	*Move*	the mouse pointer to the HTML font tag left of the word Welcome to view the ScreenTip with the tag's attributes

Your screen should look similar to Figure 11-5.

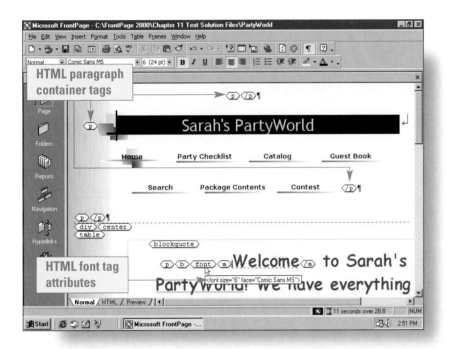

FIGURE 11-5
HTML Tags Viewed in the
Normal Tab

Step 7	*Close*	the page

You can insert HTML tags when editing a page in the Normal tab. When you insert HTML tags in this view, the syntax of the tag is not checked for accuracy. You want to insert a blank line at the top of the *contents.htm* page. The HTML tag for a blank line or new paragraph is <p>. To edit the HTML tags in the *contents.htm* page:

Step 1	*Open*	the *contents.htm* page in the Normal tab in Page view
Step 2	*Move*	the insertion point in front of the first HTML paragraph tag at the top of the page below the HTML body tag, if necessary

chapter
eleven

Step 3	*Click*	Insert
Step 4	*Point to*	Advanced
Step 5	*Click*	HTML

The HTML Markup dialog box that opens should look similar to Figure 11-6.

FIGURE 11-6
HTML Markup Dialog Box

Step 6	*Key*	<p>
Step 7	*Click*	OK
Step 8	*Observe*	the new blank line and HTML paragraph tags and the HTML Markup icon (the yellow icon with ?) inserted at the top of the page
Step 9	*Save & Close*	the page

You also want to edit HTML tag attributes for the font and table formatting. You can do this in the HTML tab.

Inserting and Modifying HTML Tags in Page View

You can use many of the standard editing tools in the HTML tab that you use when creating or editing a page in the Normal tab—including cut, copy, and paste, or find and replace. If you want to work directly with the HTML, you can insert HTML tags and text in the HTML tab. You also can use the various Properties dialog boxes when working in the HTML tab, in addition to directly editing the properties or attributes of an HTML tag. You want to review the home page HTML tag coding.

To review the home page in the HTML tab:

| Step 1 | *Open* | the *index.htm* page in the Normal tab in Page view |

QUICK TIP

To print the HTML tags, attributes, and values, switch to the HTML tab and print using the menu command or toolbar button.

| Step 2 | *Click* | the HTML tab |
| Step 3 | *Scroll* | the page to review the HTML tags, attributes, and values |

Sarah calls to ask you to make one final change to the format of the home page. She wants the welcome text to have a border around it. Because you are already reviewing the HTML tags for the page, you decide to make this change by editing the HTML tag that creates the table with the welcome text. To edit the HTML tag:

| Step 1 | *Scroll* | to position the HTML <body> tag at the top of the screen |
| Step 2 | *Click* | in the word "table" in the HTML tag <table border="0" width="75%" > on the third line below the HTML <body> tag to select the table tag |

Your screen should look similar to Figure 11-7.

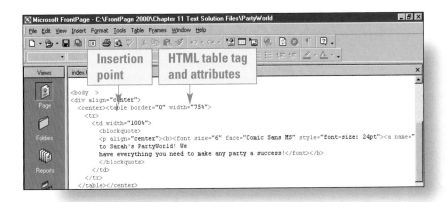

FIGURE 11-7
Home Page in the HTML Tab

Because you are familiar with setting table properties, you want to make your change in the Table Properties dialog box.

| Step 3 | *Right-click* | the word "table" |
| Step 4 | *Click* | Tag Properties |

The Table Properties dialog box opens.

Step 5	*Change*	the border size to 1
Step 6	*Click*	OK
Step 7	*Observe*	that the border= attribute is now "1"

MENU **TIP**

You can modify how FrontPage formats the HTML for a page viewed in the HTML tab by clicking the Page Options command on the Tools menu, clicking the HTML Source tab, and then changing the desired options. For more information on changing the HTML formatting options, see online Help.

QUICK **TIP**

Learning to create web pages by writing HTML code is beyond the scope of this book. If you are interested in learning to work directly with HTML, you can find many excellent HTML reference guides on the Web.

chapter
eleven

Step 8	*Switch*	to the Normal tab
Step 9	*Observe*	the new theme-formatted border around the welcome text
Step 10	*Point to*	the HTML </table> tag immediately below the table to view the HTML tag ScreenTip <table border="1" width="75%">
Step 11	*Click*	View
Step 12	*Click*	Reveal Tags to turn off the feature
Step 13	*Save & Close* the page	

You are planning to let Bob edit the Sarah's PartyWorld pages. To avoid errors and conflicts, you want to review the process that ensures only one person at a time can be editing a page.

11.d Checking Out and Checking In Web Pages

In some organizations, several people may be authorized to edit web pages. FrontPage provides a feature, called **source control,** that ensures only one person at a time is editing a web page. When source control is turned on, a web page can be **checked out,** which means that the page can be opened in Page view for editing. When you check out a page, a red check mark appears to the left of the filename in the Folder List. Other people see a padlock icon to the left of the filename. When the padlock icon appears next to a filename, others can open that page but they cannot edit it.

A page that is checked out for editing must be checked in after it is saved. **Checking in** a page makes the page available for editing by others. A page that is checked in has a small green dot to the left of the filename in the Folder List. To review the source control feature, you must first turn on the feature in the Web Settings dialog box. When you turn on or off the source control feature, the web hyperlinks are recalculated. To turn on the source control feature:

Step 1	*Verify*	that all the PartyWorld web pages are closed
Step 2	*Click*	Tools
Step 3	*Click*	Web Settings
Step 4	*Click*	the General tab, if necessary
Step 5	*Click*	the Use document check-in and check-out check box to insert a check mark

Step 6	*Click*	OK
Step 7	*Click*	Yes to close the confirmation dialog box and recalculate the web

It may take a moment or two for FrontPage to recalculate the hyperlinks.

Step 8	*Display*	the Folder List, if necessary

Your screen should look similar to Figure 11-8.

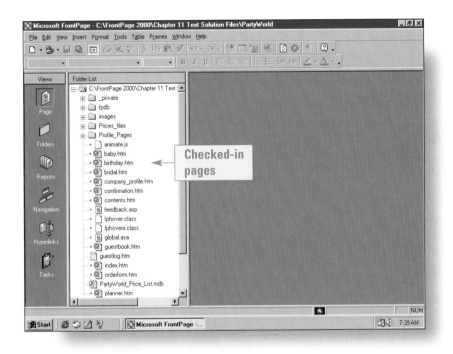

FIGURE 11-8
Folder List with Checked-in Files

MOUSE TIP

To check out a page for editing, right-click the filename and click Check Out. Then open the page as usual.

To undo a checkout, right-click the filename and click Undo Check Out. The page is checked in as though no changes had been made. When the page is published, FrontPage publishes the last *saved* version—not the last checked-in version.

To check out the *index.htm* page:

Step 1	*Double-click*	the *index.htm* page in the Folder List
Step 2	*Observe*	the confirmation dialog box, which indicates the page is under source control
Step 3	*Click*	Yes to check out the page and open it
Step 4	*Observe*	the red check mark to the left of the filename
Step 5	*Close*	the *index.htm* page without making any changes
Step 6	*Observe*	that the page is still checked out

chapter
eleven

To check in a page, you can use a shortcut menu.

Step 7	*Right-click*	the *index.htm* filename in the Folder List
Step 8	*Click*	Check In
Step 9	*Observe*	that the *index.htm* file is checked in and available for editing by others

This feature will work well if Sarah decides that both you and Bob should be able to edit the PartyWorld web. To turn off the source control feature:

Step 1	*Open*	the General tab in Web Settings dialog box
Step 2	*Click*	the Use document check-in and check-out check box to remove the check mark
Step 3	*Click*	OK
Step 4	*Click*	Yes to recalculate the web
Step 5	*Close*	the web

The PartyWorld web site is complete, and you are ready to publish and test it.

Summary

▶ When you want to quickly create content for a new web, you can import web pages from a disk-based web or from a server-based web.

▶ The theme, shared borders, and navigational structure are not imported when you use the Import Web Wizard to import an existing web into a new web.

▶ When you rename an existing web, you change the path or URL.

▶ You can edit a web page using HTML in either the Normal tab or the HTML tab.

▶ To see the HTML tags in the Normal tab, you must turn on the Reveal Tags feature.

▶ When the Reveal Tags feature is turned on, you can place the mouse pointer on an HTML tag to see the tag's attributes.

▶ You can open the various Properties dialog boxes in the HTML tab by first selecting the HTML tag and then using a shortcut menu to open the appropriate dialog box.

▶ To prevent more than one person from editing a web page at the same time, you can turn on the source control feature.

▶ When the source control feature is turned on, you must check a page out for editing, save your changes, and then check the page back in to make it available for others to edit.

Commands Review

Action	Menu Bar	Shortcut Menu	Toolbar/Mouse	Keyboard
Import an existing web into a new web	File, New, Web			ALT + F, N, W
Rename a web	Tools, Web Settings			ALT + T, W
Turn on or off Reveal Tags	View, Reveal Tags			ALT + V, A CTRL + /
Change HTML tab view options	Tools, Page Options			ALT + T, A
Open a Properties dialog box in the HTML tab		Click the tag, then right-click the tag and click Tag Properties		
Turn on or off source control	Tools, Web Settings			ALT + T, W
Check in or check out files when source control is turned on	Edit, Check In or Check Out	Right-click the filename, click Check In or Check Out	Double-click the filename, click Yes to check out the file and open it	ALT + E, I or CTRL + U ALT + E, K or CTRL + K
Undo a checkout	Edit, Undo Check Out	Right-click the filename, click Undo Check Out		ALT + E, H

chapter eleven

Concepts Review

Circle the correct answer.

1. **The Import Web Wizard is a quick way to:**
   [a] add a new theme to a web.
   [b] turn on source control.
   [c] add web content from an existing web to a new web.
   [d] turn on shared borders.

2. **Which of the following do you key as the location when importing a server-based web into a new web using the Import Web Wizard?**
   [a] the path to the new web on your hard drive
   [b] the path to the old web on your network drive
   [c] the server URL
   [d] the path to the new web on a floppy drive

3. **When you rename a disk-based web in the Web Settings dialog box, the internal hyperlinks:**
   [a] are automatically updated.
   [b] must be manually updated.
   [c] are removed.
   [d] are mapped.

4. **If you rename a web after it is published, you must:**
   [a] import the web into a new web.
   [b] save the web to a new location on your hard drive.
   [c] republish the web.
   [d] delete the web files.

5. **You can insert and modify HTML tags in the:**
   [a] Normal tab in Page view.
   [b] No Frames tab in Page view.
   [c] HTML tab in Page view.
   [d] Preview tab in Page view.

6. **HTML tag attributes are:**
   [a] additional information about the tag.
   [b] not visible in the HTML tab.
   [c] visible in the Normal tab without the Reveal Tags feature.
   [d] always added manually to a tag.

7. **The source control feature:**
   [a] allows you to import an existing web into a new web.
   [b] ensures that only one person at a time can edit a page.
   [c] is turned on in the Page Options dialog box.
   [d] is used to view and work with SQL Server databases.

8. **Checking in a page:**
   [a] allows you to edit a page under source control.
   [b] enables you to rename the web.
   [c] establishes a database connection.
   [d] makes the page available for others to edit.

9. **When others open a web and view the Folder List, which icon appears to the left of the filename of a checked out page?**
   [a] a green dot
   [b] a red check mark
   [c] a padlock
   [d] a blue question mark

10. **After you check out a file and edit and save it, you must:**
    [a] turn off source control.
    [b] import the page into the web.
    [c] check the page back in.
    [d] reset the navigation bars.

Circle **T** if the statement is true or **F** if the statement is false.

T   F   1. When you rename a server-based web, the URL on the server is changed.

T   F   2. You can use the SHIFT + PAGEUP and SHIFT + PAGEDOWN keys to quickly switch between tabs in Page view.

T   F   3. You cannot use standard editing tools—such as cut, copy, and paste or find and replace—when working in the HTML tab.

T   F   4. When you undo a checkout, all the changes you made to the page are automatically saved.

T   F   5. You can view HTML tags in the Normal tab with the Reveal Tabs feature.

T   F   6. You can print the HTML tags, attributes, and values by printing a web page from the HTML tab.

T   F   7. The Web is a poor source of additional information about working directly with HTML.

T   F   8. You must turn on the source control feature before you can check out and check in files.

T   F   9. When you import an existing web into a new web, the theme formatting, shared borders, and navigational structure of the existing web are also imported.

T   F   10. The only way to change an HTML attribute when working in the HTML tab is to open the appropriate Properties dialog box.

Glossary

Use online <u>H</u>elp to look up the following words in the FrontPage glossary. Then, using your word processing program, create a document listing each word and its glossary definition. Save and print the document.

1. HTML

2. HTML attribute

3. HTML character encoding

4. HTML tab

5. HTML tag

Skills Review

SCANS

Exercise 1   C

1. Open the Amy11 web located in the Chapter_11 folder on the Data Disk.

2. Turn on the source control feature.

3. Check out and open the *index.htm* page by double-clicking the filename in the Folder List. Click <u>Y</u>es to check out the *contents.htm, banner.htm,* and *amy.htm* pages.

4. Close the *index.htm* page.

5. Check back in each of the checked out pages using the shortcut menu.

6. Turn off the source control feature.

7. Close the web.

chapter eleven

Exercise 2

1. Import the Bookworm11 web located in the Chapter_11 folder on the Data Disk into a new web named Imported_Bookworm. Include subfolders and all the files.

2. Open the *index.htm* page in the Normal tab in Page view.

3. Change the *header.htm, music.htm,* and *books.htm* pages background color to Blue and save the pages.

4. Open the *firstpage.htm* page, change the table border color and table text to Blue, and then save the page.

5. Preview and print the *header.htm* and *firstpage.htm* pages.

6. Close the web.

Exercise 3

1. Open the Chocolate11 web located in the Chapter_11 folder on the Data Disk.

2. Open the *index.htm* page in the Normal tab in Page view.

3. Turn on the Reveal Tags feature.

4. Review the ScreenTip for the HTML heading tags that contain the Our Mission text.

5. Review the ScreenTip for the HTML paragraph tags that contain the mission statement text.

6. Center the Our Mission text and the mission statement text below it.

7. Review the ScreenTip for the HTML heading and paragraph tags to view the align="center" attribute added to the tags.

8. Center the Contact Information heading and following text and then review the HTML heading and paragraph tags to confirm the center attribute is added.

9. Turn off the Reveal Tags feature.

10. Save the page.

11. Print preview and print the page, then close it.

12. Close the web.

Exercise 4

1. Import the Rivers11 web in the Chapter_11 folder on the Data Disk into a new web with the name Imported_Rivers. Include subfolders and exclude the *global.asa, our_rates.asp,* and *Rivers_Prices.mdb* files.

2. Display the Folder List and rename the *index.htm* file to *default.htm*.

3. Switch to Navigation view and add the *faq.htm, guestbook.htm,* and *webdesign.htm* pages as child level pages under the home page.

4. Open the *default.htm* page in the Normal tab in Page view.

5. Turn on the top shared border for all pages.

6. Apply the theme of your choice.

7. Add a child level navigation bar to the *default.htm* page in the top shared border and delete any comments. Add a home level navigation bar to the remaining pages.

8. Save all the pages.

9. Preview, print preview, and print the pages.

10. Close the web.

Exercise 5

1. Open the Markowitz11 web located in the Chapter_11 folder on the Data Disk.

2. Turn on the source control feature.

3. Check out and open the *index.htm* page by double-clicking the filename in the Folder List.

4. Change the background color to Silver. Then, save the page, print it, and close it.

5. Check the page back in using the shortcut menu.

6. Turn off the source control feature.

7. Close the web.

Exercise 6

1. Open the Native11 web located in the Chapter_11 folder on the Data Disk.

2. Open the Web Settings dialog box and change the web name to Native_American.

3. Close the web.

4. Open Windows Explorer and rename the Native11 web folder to Native_American.

5. Close Windows Explorer.

Exercise 7

1. Open the Citrus11 web located in the Chapter_11 folder on the Data Disk.

2. Open the *framespage.htm* page in the Normal tab in Page view.

3. Turn on the Reveal Tags feature.

4. Verify the HTML font attributes for the welcome text using the mouse pointer.

5. Change the welcome text font to a script-style font of your choice and the 7 (36 pt) font size.

6. Verify the HTML font attributes for the welcome text using the mouse pointer.

7. Save the page.

8. Preview, print preview, and print the page.

9. Turn off the Reveal Tags feature.

10. Close the web.

Exercise 8

1. Open the Penny11 web located in the Chapter_11 folder on the Data Disk.

2. View the *mainpage.htm* in the HTML tab.

3. Move the insertion point to the HTML <body> tag near the top of the page.

4. Open the Page Properties dialog box using the shortcut menu. Remove the background picture, change the background color to light pink, and change the hyperlink color to Purple.

5. Switch back to the Normal tab using the keyboard and view the changes.

6. Save the page.

7. Preview, print preview, and print the page.

8. Close the web.

chapter eleven

Case Projects

Project 1

Blissful Valley Farm is a large herb farm in the Charlotte, North Carolina area that wholesales herb products. Madelyn Overton owns Blissful Valley Farm, and she is considering selling directly to consumers online. She asks you to submit a proposal for a new web site including sample web pages.

Create the proposed web site with a home page, three products pages, an order form page, a custom confirmation page, and a search page. Save the form results to a database and have FrontPage create one for you. Use text, color, images, hyperlinks, and FrontPage components as desired to create an attractive and serviceable web site. Turn on source control for the web. Print the web pages.

Project 2

Renee Hardison is the president of Kites, Inc., a company located in Bridgeport, Connecticut, that imports and sells unique and unusual kites. Ms. Hardison hires you to create a web site for her company.

Using a word processing program, create a plan for the new web site that includes a home page and three product pages. Create a sample web based on your plan. Use text, color, images, hyperlinks, and FrontPage components as desired to create an attractive and serviceable web site. Print the web pages. Save and print the plan.

Ms. Hardison approves the plan, but wants you to change the theme and make a few other changes. Import the sample web into a new web. Change the home page name, apply a new theme, and add appropriate shared borders and navigation bars. Add an order form, a custom confirmation page, and a search form page. Save the form results to a database and have FrontPage create the database for you. Print all the web pages.

Project 3

You are the manager of Home on the Range, a small company in Plano, Texas, that manufactures custom-designed ranch-style furniture. You want to know more about editing your web pages directly using HTML. Connect to the Internet, launch your web browser, and search for web sites that provide online classes about learning to create and edit web pages using HTML. Save and print at least four web pages.

Project 4

Adventure, Inc., is a tour company located in Miami, Florida, that specializes in providing wilderness adventure tours to South America. Ramona Mendez, the president of Adventure, Inc., hires you to create the web site for the company.

Using a word processing program, create a plan for the new web site that includes a home page, three product pages, guestbook page, and a search page. Create a sample web based on your plan. Use text, color, images, hyperlinks, and FrontPage components as desired to create an attractive and serviceable web site. Print the web pages. Save and print the plan.

After Ms. Mendez approves the plan and sample web site, rename the web site and the web site folder.

Project 5

David Anderson is the president of Nebraska Beef Specialties, a company located in Omaha, Nebraska, that is planning to sell frozen steaks and other beef products online. Mr. Anderson hires you to create the new company web site.

Using a word processing program, create a plan for the new web site that includes a home page, four product pages, a guest book page, an order form page, a confirmation page, and a search page. Create a sample web based on your plan. Save the guest book page results to a file and the order form page to a database. Let FrontPage create the database for you. Use text, color, images, hyperlinks, and FrontPage components as desired to create an attractive and serviceable web site. Turn on source control for the web. Print the web pages. Save and print the plan.

Project 6

The Magick Wand is a small company located in Denver, Colorado that sells crystals, fantasy art, and self-help books and tapes online. Denise Hamilton, the owner of The Magick Wand, hires you to update the company's old web site.

Using a word processing program, create a plan for the revamped The Magic Wand web site that includes a home page, three product pages, a guest book, an order form page, a confirmation page, and a search page. Create a sample web based on your plan. Save the guest book form results to a file and the order form results to a database. Let FrontPage create the database for you. Use text, color, images, hyperlinks, and FrontPage components as desired to create an attractive and serviceable web site. Print the web pages. Save and print the plan.

After Ms. Hamilton approves the plan, rename the web and the web folder.

Project 7

Fanny's Fantastic Frames, located in Philadelphia, Pennsylvania, sells art and photograph frames and framing supplies to discount stores around the country. Fanny Livingston, the president, asks you

to submit a proposal for a new web site that includes samples of other web sites that sell similar products.

Connect to the Internet, launch your web browser, and locate several web sites that sell martial arts supplies and equipment. Print at least three web pages. Using a word processing program, create a plan for the new Fanny's Fantastic Frames web site.

Create a sample web site that includes a home page, three products pages, an order form page, a custom confirmation page, and a search page. Save the order form results to a database and have FrontPage create the database for you. Use text, color, images, hyperlinks, and FrontPage components as desired to create an attractive and serviceable web site. Print the web pages. Turn on source control for the web. Save and print the plan.

Project 8

Liz Gee is the owner of Gee Investigative Services, a professional investigative agency that sells services to businesses. Ms. Gee wants to create an online corporate presence for her agency. She hires you to create the web site.

Using a word processing program, create a plan for the new web site that includes a home page, three services pages, a guest book, and a search page. Create a sample web based on your plan. Send the guest book form results to a file. Use text, color, images, hyperlinks, and FrontPage components as desired to create an attractive and serviceable web site. Print the web pages. Save and print the plan.

After you complete the new web site, import the web content into another new web for later use.

chapter eleven

Publishing and Testing a Web Site

Chapter Overview

The final step in creating a web is to publish it to a web server. This allows you to verify the look and functionality of all the pages in the web. Certain FrontPage components, such as the hit counter, cannot be tested until the web is published to a server with FrontPage Server Extensions. Also, publishing a web makes it available to others on a company intranet or the World Wide Web. In this chapter, you use the Microsoft Personal Web Server and FrontPage Server Extensions to publish and test a web.

LEARNING OBJECTIVES

- ► Publish a web
- ► Review a published web
- ► Set server permissions

Case profile

Sarah Whaley has approved the Sarah's PartyWorld web site additions and modifications. The web is complete. You are ready to publish the web to a server and test the web pages.

chapter twelve

12

12.a Publishing a Web

A web stored on your local system is a disk-based web. Its contents are not available to others on your network or to viewers on the Web. **Publishing** a web generally means to copy the files in your web to a web server, which creates a server-based web that others can access. A **web server** is a computer that is running web server software. Web server software is available for UNIX, Windows NT, Macintosh, and Windows 9x operating systems. You can also publish a backup copy of a web from a server to a folder on your local file system to ensure that all the necessary files are stored with the correct structure. Finally, you can publish a web from one server to another: for example, from a testing server to a final destination web server.

Before you make the PartyWorld web available to others, you must test it. Simply previewing your pages in the Preview tab or in your browser is not sufficient because you used several FrontPage components, such as the hit counter, that cannot be tested until the page is published to a web server running FrontPage Server Extensions. A good way to test a web before publishing it to its final destination is to install the Microsoft Personal Web Server software on your computer and configure it with the FrontPage Server Extensions. **FrontPage Server Extensions** work with web server software to provide support for special FrontPage features.

notes

This chapter covers installing Microsoft Personal Web Server and then testing and publishing webs. If you are not using Microsoft Personal Web Server, your instructor will provide alternate instructions for publishing and testing your webs.

In order to complete the hands-on activities in this section, you must have the Microsoft Personal Web Server 4.0 software, be connected to a network and have the TCP/IP networking protocol configured on your machine, and be running Windows 95 or 98. If you are installing an older version of Microsoft Personal Web Server, installing on a Windows NT workstation, or working on a computer that is not running the TCP/IP network protocol, your instructor may provide modified instructions.

CAUTION TIP

Microsoft Personal Web Server (PWS) is available on the Windows 98 CD-ROM and as a download from the Microsoft Web site. It runs on computers with Windows 98, Windows 95, or Windows NT Workstation installed. You must also have the TCP/IP networking protocol installed on your computer for PWS to work. For more information on configuring the TCP/IP protocol, see your network administrator or online Help for your operating system. PWS does not run on Windows NT server. Instead, you must install Microsoft Internet Information Server web server software on a Windows NT server.

chapter
twelve

Installing Microsoft Personal Web Server

The **Microsoft Personal Web Server**, also referred to as **PWS**, is designed to be the working web server only on a small intranet because it can handle up to 10 simultaneous connections. It is also a good choice for testing your webs because it is readily available from the Microsoft web site or the Windows 9x CD-ROM and is easy to install on your local computer. A web server, such as PWS, that you use for testing your web is also called a **staging web server**.

You want to install the PWS and test the new Sarah's PartyWorld web. To install PWS from the Windows 98SE CD-ROM:

Step 1	**Close**	all applications
Step 2	**Insert**	the Windows 98 or Windows 98SE CD-ROM in the CD-ROM drive
Step 3	**Display**	the Start menu
Step 4	**Click**	Run to open the Run dialog box
Step 5	**Browse**	to locate the \Setup\Add-ons\Pws\ folder
Step 6	**Double-click**	Setup.exe

The Run dialog box on your screen should look similar to Figure 12-1.

FIGURE 12-1
Run Dialog Box

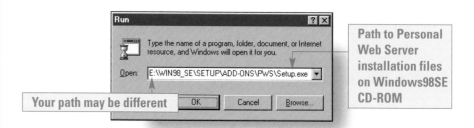

Step 7	**Click**	OK

In a few seconds, the Microsoft Personal Web Server Setup dialog box opens. Your dialog box should look similar to Figure 12-2.

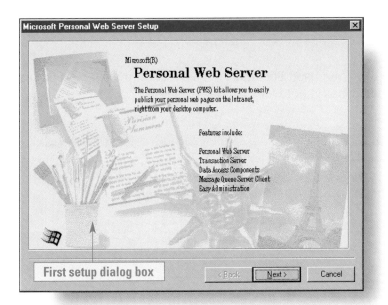

FIGURE 12-2
Microsoft Personal Web
Server Setup Dialog Box

Step 8	*Click*	<u>N</u>ext>

The second Microsoft Personal Web Server Setup dialog box opens.
Your dialog box should look similar to Figure 12-3.

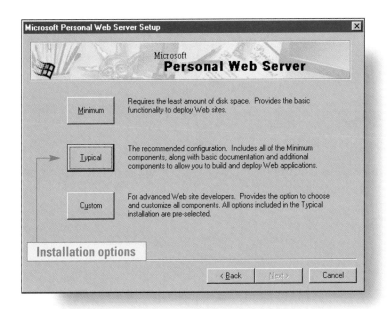

FIGURE 12-3
Second Setup Dialog Box

You select the type of installation you want in this dialog box. You
want to set up a typical installation.

chapter
twelve

Step 9	*Click*	<u>T</u>ypical

The third Microsoft Personal Web Server Setup dialog box opens. Your dialog box should look similar to Figure 12-4.

You specify the location and folder where your published webs are stored in this dialog box. By default, the default location and folder C:\Inetpub\wwwroot is selected in the <u>W</u>WW Service text box. You accept the default location.

Step 10	*Click*	<u>N</u>ext>

The fourth Microsoft Personal Web Server Setup dialog box opens, showing the installation progress. Your dialog box should look similar to Figure 12-5.

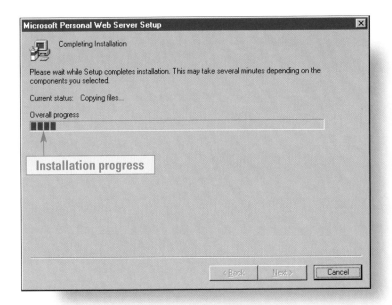

FIGURE 12-5
Fourth Setup Dialog Box

After the files are copied, the fifth Microsoft Personal Web Server Setup dialog box opens. You finish the setup in this dialog box.

Step 11	*Click*	Finish
Step 12	*Click*	<u>Y</u>es to restart your computer with the new PWS settings

The Personal Web Manager is used to access the Personal Web Server services. To view the Personal Web Manager:

Step 1	*Double-Click*	the Publish shortcut  on the desktop

The Personal Web Manager Main window opens and the Tip of the Day dialog box may open. You can go to PWS online <u>H</u>elp for more information about the tip, view another tip, or close the Tip of the Day dialog box.

Step 2	*Click*	<u>C</u>lose, if necessary, to close the Tip of the Day dialog box

The Personal Web Manager Main window that opens on your screen should look similar to Figure 12-6.

chapter
twelve

FIGURE 12-6
Personal Web Manager

If you are using PWS as an intranet server, you can stop and start the server to turn on or off the ability of others to access the web pages and you can view web site usage statistics. From this window you also can access tools to publish and maintain a home page, take a brief tour of PWS, and view the file structure of the root web. To stop the server:

Step 1	*Click*	Stop
Step 2	*Observe*	that the server is stopped and web address and home directory path are no longer visible
Step 3	*Observe*	that the Stop button becomes the Start button
Step 4	*Click*	Start
Step 5	*Observe*	that the server is now started and the web address and home directory path are now visible
Step 6	*Click*	the Close button ☒ on the PWS title bar to close it

In order for PWS to support all the FrontPage 2000 features, you must extend PWS capabilities by using FrontPage Server Extensions.

Working with FrontPage Server Extensions

When FrontPage Server Extensions are installed with your web server, your webs have full FrontPage functionality, including form handlers, hit counters, search forms, and other component features. Each time you publish a web, FrontPage compares the files on your computer with the files on the web server and updates the published pages that have changed, including changes to navigation bars, shared borders, and hyperlinks. If you are publishing to a web server with FrontPage Server Extensions installed, you can publish your pages using the HyperText Transfer Protocol, or HTTP, the same protocol used to download web pages in your browser.

FrontPage Server Extensions are available on the FrontPage 2000 CD-ROM and the Microsoft Office 2000 Premium CD-ROM and as part of the Office Server Extensions in the Microsoft Office 2000 Standard, Professional, and Premium packages; they support a variety of web servers. Installing the FrontPage Server Extensions copies the appropriate files to your hard drive and automatically updates PWS, if PWS is already installed. Once the server extensions are installed on your hard drive, you can access the Microsoft FrontPage Server Extensions Resource Kit documentation for more information on working with the FrontPage Server Extensions. This resource kit is installed in the C:\Program Files\Common Files\ Microsoft Shared\Web Server Extensions\40\serk\1033 folder.

notes If you installed PWS and are going to test your web on your local system, you can install the FrontPage Server Extensions on your hard drive using the Add/Remove Software feature in Control Panel and your FrontPage 2000 CD-ROM. The following activities assume you have installed the FrontPage Server Extensions.

If you install PWS *after* you install FrontPage Server Extensions, you must then configure the extensions. When you install the FrontPage Server Extensions, FrontPage also installs a server extensions administrative tool you can use to configure the extensions with PWS. To configure the extensions, if necessary:

Step 1	*Display*	the Start menu
Step 2	*Point to*	Programs
Step 3	*Point to*	Microsoft Office Tools
Step 4	*Click*	Server Extensions Administrator

The Microsoft Management Console, also known as MMC, opens along with the Tip of the Day dialog box.

| Step 5 | *Click* | Close to close the Tip of the Day dialog box |

You can expand the FrontPage Server Extensions folder in the left pane to view the PWS root web folder. Working in the console's left pane is like working in Windows Explorer.

| Step 6 | *Click* | the plus sign (+) to the left of the FrontPage Server Extensions folder to expand the folder |
| Step 7 | *Observe* | the PWS root web folder (the folder has your computer name) |

If PWS has never had FrontPage Server Extensions configured, complete the following steps. To configure PWS with FrontPage Server Extensions:

Step 1	*Right-click*	the PWS root web folder
Step 2	*Point to*	New
Step 3	*Click*	Web to open the Server Extensions Configuration Wizard
Step 4	*Follow*	the wizard steps to configure the mail server information and then finish the wizard process
Step 5	*Observe*	that the new folder in the console's right pane contains server extension files
Step 6	*Close*	the console window
Step 7	*Click*	Yes to save the console changes

If PWS has an earlier version of the FrontPage Server Extensions configured and you are updating to FrontPage 2000 extensions, complete the following steps. To configure PWS with updated FrontPage Server Extensions:

Step 1	*Right-click*	the root web folder
Step 2	*Point to*	Task
Step 3	*Click*	Upgrade Extensions
Step 4	*Close*	the console and save the changes

notes   The rest of this chapter assumes that you are publishing your web to PWS 4.0 on your hard drive with the FrontPage Server Extensions installed and configured with PWS. If you are publishing to any other web server, your instructor may modify the activities.

Publishing a Web to PWS

You are now ready to publish the renamed Sarah's PartyWorld web to PWS so you can test it. Before you publish your web, it is a good idea to check its spelling. To check the spelling of the web pages:

Step 1	*Open*	the PartyWorld web you renamed in Chapter 11
Step 2	*Switch*	to Folders view
Step 3	*Click*	the Spelling button [ABC✓] on the Standard toolbar
Step 4	*Click*	the Entire web option button in the Spelling dialog box, if necessary
Step 5	*Click*	Start
Step 6	*Correct*	any spelling errors on the listed pages (ignore the .asp pages and *prices.htm* page, which include database field names)
Step 7	*Close*	the Spelling dialog box

Now that you know your web has no spelling errors, you are ready to publish it. To publish the web:

Step 1	*Click*	File
Step 2	*Click*	Publish Web

The Publish Web dialog box that opens should look similar to Figure 12-7.

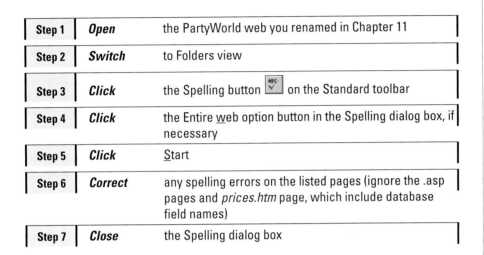

Web server URL; yours will be different

Online list of Web Presence Providers

Button to expand dialog box

FIGURE 12-7
Publish Web Dialog Box

Notice that the location or URL of PWS is listed in the Specify the location to publish your web to: text box. This is the same URL you see in the Personal Web Manager main window when the web server is started. You want to publish the PartyWorld web to a subweb on the web server. A **subweb** is a subdirectory of the root web.

chapter
twelve

Step 3	*Key*	the name of your web server followed by /PartyWorld in the Specify the location to publish your web to: text box
Step 4	*Click*	Options to expand the dialog box
Step 5	*Click*	the Publish all pages, overwriting any already on the destination option button

Except for the web server name, your expanded Publish Web dialog box should look similar to Figure 12-8.

FIGURE 12-8
Expanded Publish Web
Dialog Box

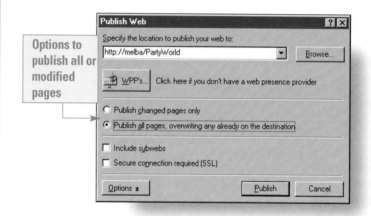

| Step 6 | *Click* | Publish |
| Step 7 | *Observe* | the process of publishing the web files in the Microsoft FrontPage dialog box |

QUICK TIP

You can also key the path to the server-based web, http://server name/subweb name, in the Folder name: text box in the Open Web dialog box to open the server-based web.

When the publishing process is completed, a confirmation dialog box appears. You can immediately open the web in your browser. However you must complete one additional step to make the database activities and .asp pages in your web function properly. You must open the new server-based PartyWorld web and turn on the option to allow the .asp files to function properly.

| Step 8 | *Click* | Done |
| Step 9 | *Close* | the web |

To open the server-based web and turn on the option to run programs:

| Step 1 | *Open* | the Open Web dialog box |
| Step 2 | *Look in* | the Web Folders |

Step 3	*Double-click*	the PartyWorld web folder name
Step 4	*Click*	Open
Step 5	*Display*	the Folder List, if necessary
Step 6	*Observe*	that the root web folder path and name for the server-based PartyWorld web is http://your machine name/PartyWorld
Step 7	*Observe*	that the home page *index.htm* is renamed to *default.htm*
Step 8	*Right-click*	the PartyWorld root web folder
Step 9	*Click*	Properties

The server-based web PartyWorld properties dialog box opens.

Step 10	*Click*	the Allow programs to be run check box to insert a check mark, if necessary
Step 11	*Verify*	that the Allow scripts to be run and Allow files to be browsed check boxes contain check marks
Step 12	*Click*	OK

You are ready to test your published web.

12.b Reviewing a Published Web

It is very important to review each page at your web site before making the web available to others on your company intranet or on the Web. You want to verify that the web pages have the correct appearance when opened and all graphic images load correctly. You should also check that hyperlinks to non-HTML documents and navigation bar hyperlinks work correctly. Additionally, you should verify that all FrontPage components, such as hit counters, scrolling marquees, form handlers, and form validation, are working correctly. When you find an error, you can edit the page to correct it and then republish the web, publishing only the page or pages that have changed.

QUICK TIP

If your web contains pages that you don't want to publish, you can exclude those pages options on the Publish Status report in Reports view. You can also exclude a file from being published in the Workgroup tab of the file's Properties dialog box.

If you added or deleted pages and/or external hyperlinks in your pages, it is a good idea to verify hyperlinks and recalculate hyperlinks. The Verify Hyperlinks button on the Reports toolbar checks external hyperlinks. The Recalculate Hyperlinks command on the Tools menu updates hyperlinks, navigation bars, as well as text indexes used for a Search form component.

chapter
twelve

Testing the Web Pages

To test the individual web pages, you view each page in your web browser. You can start with the home page and then follow the hyperlinks to the other pages in the web. To view the home page in your browser:

Step 1	*Open*	the *default.htm* page in the Normal tab in Page view
Step 2	*Preview*	the page in your web browser
Step 3	*Observe*	the hit counter

You can now see the hit counter in action. Each time the home page is loaded in a browser, the hit counter number increments. However, you notice that the hit counter is not positioned attractively in relation to the text on the same line. You want to edit the home page to place the hit counter on the line immediately below the text.

To edit the home page and then republish it:

Step 1	*Minimize*	the browser window
Step 2	*Insert*	a line break between the text "You are visitor number" and the [hit counter] component on the *default.htm* page
Step 3	*Save*	the page

You want to look at the page with the repositioned hit counter. To view the edited page:

Step 1	*Maximize*	the browser window
Step 2	*Click*	the Refresh button 🔄 on the Standard Buttons toolbar to reload the home page
Step 3	*Observe*	that the hit counter component result is now attractively positioned below the text

Next, you want to test the guest book, the update to the guest log, and default confirmation form. To test the guest book form and confirmation form:

Step 1	*Click*	the Guest Book hyperlink in the navigation bar at the top of the home page
Step 2	*Observe*	the DHTML transition effects when you exit the home page

Step 3	*Scroll*	to view the Add Your Comments scrolling text box, if necessary
Step 4	*Key*	Testing the Sarah's PartyWorld web site in the text box
Step 5	*Click*	the Submit Comments push button
Step 6	*Observe*	the default confirmation form page that opens in the browser

Your screen should look similar to Figure 12-9.

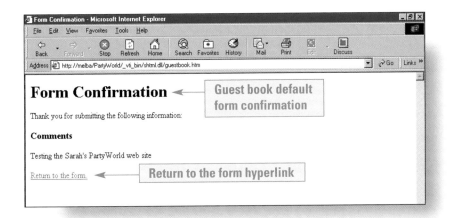

FIGURE 12-9
Default Guest Book Form Confirmation

Step 7	*Click*	the Return to the form hyperlink to view the guest book page
Step 8	*Scroll*	the page to view the Comments posted from the *guestlog.htm* page
Step 9	*Continue*	to test the remaining pages, making any necessary changes and saving the pages
Step 10	*Close*	the browser window when finished

Publishing a Backup Copy to the Local File System

When the testing is complete, you can publish the server-based web to a backup copy, disk-based web on your hard drive. You can also publish the tested server-based PartyWorld web to its final destination web server. If the final destination server has FrontPage Server Extensions installed, you can use the HTTP protocol to publish the web to the appropriate folder on the destination server. If not, use the FTP protocol to upload the web pages to the appropriate folder on the destination server.

To publish a backup copy of the tested web to your local file system:

| Step 1 | *Verify* | that the server-based PartyWorld web is open |

Step 2	*Click*	File
Step 3	*Click*	Publish Web
Step 4	*Key*	the local path and Backup folder name in the Specify location to publish your web to: text box or Browse to locate the folder indicated by your instructor
Step 5	*Click*	the Publish all pages, overwriting any that already on the destination option button, if necessary
Step 6	*Click*	Publish
Step 7	*Click*	Yes to publish the folder as a disk-based web folder
Step 8	*Click*	Continue to acknowledge that certain FrontPage components will not work in the disk-based web
Step 9	*Click*	Done

You can use Windows Explorer or open the backup disk-based web in FrontPage to verify it.

Publishing a web from One Server to Another

Now that the PartyWorld web is tested and backed up, you can publish it to its final web server destination.

notes If you are going to publish your server-based PartyWorld web to another web server, your instructor will provide the destination server URL, advise you whether or not to use HTTP or FTP, and indicate the subweb name (folder name) you should use.

To publish the tested web to its final destination:

Step 1	*Open*	the Publish Web dialog box
Step 2	*Key*	http://the server name/the subweb name or other path as specified by your instructor
Step 3	*Click*	Publish
Step 4	*Click*	Done when the publishing process is complete
Step 5	*Close*	the server-based web
Step 6	*Open*	your browser, key the URL to the PartyWorld web on the new server, and review the web

For more information about publishing webs using HTTP, FTP, or to your local file system, see online Help.

12.c Setting Server Permissions

In order to control who has access to your webs and who has permission to edit your web pages, FrontPage provides tools to set user, author, and administrator permissions. These permissions are set on the root web; any subwebs below the root automatically inherit the same permissions. You can set different permissions for each subweb, if desired.

FrontPage has three levels of permission: Browse, Author, and Administer. Users with the Browse permission have read-only access to the web. This means they can browse the web to read the pages but they cannot change the pages. Users with Author permission have read and write access. This means they can both browse the pages and make changes to them. The third level of permission is Administer. Users with this level of permission have full access. They can browse, edit, and change the user permissions for the web.

If your web server is a Windows NT server with IIS installed, the users and groups from which you choose when setting up permissions are created and maintained in Windows NT. You use the Windows NT accounts when setting your web permissions. Other web servers have similar user lists you can use in FrontPage or update on the server.

notes

If you are using PWS as your web server, you can read but not do the following activities.

To set user permissions for the web:

Step 1	*Open*	the PartyWorld web in FrontPage, if necessary
Step 2	*Click*	Tools
Step 3	*Point to*	Security
Step 4	*Click*	Permissions

The Permissions dialog box opens.

| Step 5 | *Click* | the Settings tab, if necessary |

Step 6	*Click*	the Use <u>s</u>ame permissions as parent web option button if the subweb uses the same permissions as the parent web *or* the Use <u>u</u>nique permissions for this web option button if the subweb has different permissions from the parent web
Step 7	*Click*	<u>A</u>pply

You can set permissions for individual users or for individual computers. The most common method is to set permissions for individual users. To select permissions for individual users:

Step 1	*Click*	the Users tab
Step 2	*Indicate*	whether or not everyone or only registered users can have browse access to the web by clicking the appropriate option button

Next, you add the appropriate user names. You can add one or more names. To add a new user:

Step 1	*Click*	A<u>d</u>d
Step 2	*Select*	the domain name or group from the Obtain list from: list box
Step 3	*Select*	or key a user name in the Names text box
Step 4	*Click*	<u>A</u>dd

Next, you set the type of permissions—Browse, Author, or Administer—for all the users you selected. The same permission is given to all users listed in the Add Names list box.

Step 5	*Select*	the type of access you want the user to have
Step 6	*Click*	OK
Step 7	*Continue*	to add, remove, or edit user permissions as necessary in the Permissions dialog box
Step 8	*Click*	OK when you finish, to close the dialog box
Step 9	*Close*	the web
Step 10	*Close*	FrontPage

The new Sarah's PartyWorld web is published and tested. Sarah is certain that the updated web will attract new customers. She thanks you for your help.

Summary

▶ You can make your disk-based webs available to others on a company intranet or the Web by publishing them to a web server.

▶ A web server is a computer that is running web server software.

▶ FrontPage Server Extensions work with web server software to provide support for special FrontPage features, such as the hit counter and form handlers.

▶ If you publish a disk-based web to a web server that does not have FrontPage Server Extensions installed, many FrontPage features will not work when viewers load the pages.

▶ Microsoft Personal Web Server (PWS) is designed to be the working web server on a small intranet and can be used to test your web pages before you publish them to the final destination server.

▶ Both Internet Service Providers (ISPs) and Web Presence Providers (WPPs) can provide web-hosting services.

▶ A subweb is a subdirectory of the root web.

▶ If you are using PWS, you cannot set user permissions for your web.

▶ If you are using a web server with user security, you can set three levels of user permissions for your web: Browse, Author, and Administer.

Commands Review

Action	Menu Bar	Shortcut Menu	Toolbar/Mouse	Keyboard
To publish a web to a server, from server to server, and from a server to a local drive	File, Publish Web			ALT + F, H
To set permissions for a web	Tools, Security, Permissions			ALT + T, Y, P

Concepts Review

Circle the correct answer.

1. Publishing a web generally means to:
[a] format the pages.
[b] add DHTML effects.
[c] install FrontPage Server Extensions.
[d] copy the web files to a web server so others can access the web.

2. Microsoft Personal Web Server is also called:
[a] MMC.
[b] PWS.
[c] URL.
[d] PSW.

3. WPP is an abbreviation for:
[a] a web server name.
[b] a web presence provider.
[c] a type of FrontPage Server Extensions.
[d] the Microsoft Management Console.

4. A subweb is:
[a] a tiny web.
[b] a subdirectory of the root web.
[c] another name for the root web.
[d] a database.

5. Which of the following is not a publishing activity?
[a] installing FrontPage Extensions
[b] uploading web files to an ISP using FTP
[c] copying web files to a server using HTTP
[d] copying web files and structure from a web server to the local file system

6. Which of the following is not a web server permission level?
[a] Browse
[b] Author
[c] Administer
[d] User

7. FrontPage Server Extensions work with a web server to:
[a] upload web pages.
[b] provide support for FrontPage special features.
[c] install PWS.
[d] set user permissions.

8. The Personal Web Manager is used to:
[a] install FrontPage Server Extensions.
[b] upload web files to an ISP.
[c] access PWS services.
[d] set user permissions.

9. You can convert a disk-based web to a server-based web by:
[a] publishing it.
[b] clicking the Convert button on the Standard toolbar.
[c] creating a style sheet.
[d] formatting it in the browser window.

10. Which of the following protocols can be used to publish a web?
[a] HTML
[b] MMC
[c] HTTP
[d] SQL

Circle **T** if the statement is true or **F** if the statement is false.

T   F   1. It is not necessary to test form results, files, and databases when testing a web.

T   F   2. A web server is a computer that is running web server software.

T   F   3. PWS is designed to be the web server on small intranets.

T   F   4. Once you start the PWS, you cannot turn it off.

T   F   5. If your web server does not have FrontPage Server Extensions installed, all FrontPage components still work properly.

T   F   6. If you install PWS after you install the FrontPage Server Extensions, you must manually configure the extensions in the Microsoft Management Console.

T   F   7. You cannot create a web or edit web pages directly on a web server.

T   F   8. An ISP and a WPP provide exactly the same services.

T   F   9. You can set user permissions for PWS.

T   F   10. You can run PWS on a Windows NT server.

Glossary

Use online <u>H</u>elp to look up the following words in the FrontPage glossary. Then, using your word processing program, create a document listing each word and its glossary definition. Save and print the document.

1. anonymous FTP

2. authentication

3. domain name

4. executable folders

5. firewall

6. FTP

7. HTTP

8. Internet Information Services

9. Internet Service Provider

10. intranet

11. IP address

12. Microsoft Management Console

13. multi-hosting

14. network location

15. parent web

16. password

17. proxy server

18. Secure Sockets Layer

19. staging web

20. subweb

21. TCP

22. UNIX

23. URL

24. virtual server

chapter twelve

The following Skills Review exercises assume you are using PWS. If you are not using PWS or if you do not have access to a web server, your instructor may modify the exercise steps.

Skills Review

Exercise 1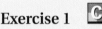

1. Open the Amy12 web located in the Chapter_12 folder on the Data Disk.

2. Complete the *cards.htm*, *posters.htm*, and *autographs.htm* web pages using the appropriate colors, text, images, hyperlinks, and FrontPage components of your choice.

3. Check the spelling of the web pages.

4. Publish the web to a web server as a subweb named Amy.

5. Preview the server-based web in your web browser and test all the hyperlinks, graphic images, non-HTML files, FrontPage components, form results, and formatting.

6. Make all necessary changes to the server-based web.

7. When the testing is complete, publish a backup copy of the edited web to your local file system in the location and folder specified by your instructor.

8. Set permissions for your web, if possible, to allow two classmates to be authors on the server-based web.

9. Print all the web pages.

10. Close the web.

Exercise 2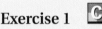

1. Open the Bookworm12 web located in the Chapter_12 folder on the Data Disk.

2. Complete the *books.htm* and *music.htm* web pages using the appropriate colors, text, images, hyperlinks, and FrontPage components of your choice.

3. Check the spelling of the web pages.

4. Publish the web to a web server as a subweb named Bookworm.

5. Preview the server-based web in your web browser and test all the hyperlinks, graphic images, non-HTML files, FrontPage components, form results, and formatting.

6. Make all necessary changes to the server-based web.

7. When the testing is complete, publish a backup copy of the edited web to your local file system in the location and folder specified by your instructor.

8. Set permissions for your web, if possible, to allow two classmates to be authors on the server-based web.

9. Print all the web pages.

10. Close the web.

Exercise 3

1. Open the Chocolate12 web located in the Chapter_12 folder on the Data Disk.

2. Complete the *cakes.htm*, *cookies.htm*, *prod01.htm*, *prod11.htm*, *prod12.htm*, and *prod13.htm* web pages using the appropriate colors, text, images, hyperlinks, and FrontPage components of your choice.

3. Check the spelling of the web pages.

4. Publish the web to a web server as a subweb named Chocolate.

5. Preview the server-based web in your web browser and test all the hyperlinks, graphic images, non-HTML files, FrontPage components, form results, and formatting.

6. Make all necessary changes to the disk-based web.

7. Republish the changed web pages.

8. Set permissions for your web, if possible, to allow all classmates to be browsers on the server-based web.

9. Print all the web pages.

10. Close the web.

Exercise 4

1. Open the Rivers12 web in the Chapter_12 folder on the Data Disk.

2. Complete the *faq.htm* web pages using the appropriate colors, text of your choice.

3. Check the spelling of the web pages.

4. Publish the web to a web server as a subweb named Rivers.

5. Preview the server-based web in your web browser and test all the hyperlinks, graphic images, non-HTML files, FrontPage components, form results, and formatting.

6. Make all necessary changes to the server-based web.

7. When the testing is complete, publish a backup copy of the edited web to your local file system in the location and folder specified by your instructor.

8. Set permissions for your web, if possible, to allow three classmates to be administrators on the server-based web.

9. Print all the web pages.

10. Close the web.

Exercise 5

1. Open the Markowitz12 web located in the Chapter_12 folder on the Data Disk.

2. Check the spelling of the web pages.

3. Publish the web to a web server as a subweb named Markowitz.

4. Preview the server-based web in your web browser and test all the hyperlinks, graphic images, non-HTML files, FrontPage components, form results, and formatting.

5. Make all necessary changes to the server-based web.

6. When the testing is complete, publish a backup copy of the edited web to your local file system in the location and folder specified by your instructor.

chapter twelve

7. Set permissions for your web, if possible, to allow all classmates to be browsers on the server-based web.

8. Print all the web pages.

9. Close the web.

Exercise 6   C

1. Open the Native12 web located in the Chapter_12 folder on the Data Disk.

2. Complete the *dolls.htm, jewelry.htm,* and *pottery.htm* web pages using the appropriate colors, text, images, navigation bars, shared borders, and FrontPage components of your choice.

3. Check the spelling of the web pages.

4. Publish the web to a web server as a subweb named Native.

5. Preview the server-based web in your web browser and test all the hyperlinks, graphic images, non-HTML files, FrontPage components, form results, and formatting.

6. Make all necessary changes to the disk-based web.

7. Republish the changed web pages.

8. Set permissions for your web, if possible, to allow all classmates to be browsers on the server-based web.

9. Print all the web pages.

10. Close the web.

Exercise 7   C

1. Open the Citrus12 web located in the Chapter_12 folder on the Data Disk.

2. Complete the *oranges.htm, limes.htm,* and *lemons.htm* web pages using the appropriate colors, text, images, navigation bars, shared borders, and FrontPage components of your choice.

3. Check the spelling of the web pages.

4. Publish the web to a web server as a subweb named Citrus.

5. Preview the server-based web in your web browser and test all the hyperlinks, graphic images, non-HTML files, FrontPage components, form results, and formatting.

6. Make all necessary changes to the server-based web.

7. Set permissions for your web, if possible, to allow all classmates to be browsers on the server-based web.

8. Print all the web pages.

9. Close the web.

Exercise 8   C

1. Open the Penny12 web located in the Chapter_12 folder on the Data Disk.

2. Complete the *stems.htm* and *greenery.htm* web pages using the appropriate colors, text, images, navigation bars, shared borders, and FrontPage components of your choice.

3. Check the spelling of the web pages.

4. Publish the web to a web server as a subweb named Penny.

5. Preview the server-based web in your web browser and test all the hyperlinks, graphic images, non-HTML files, FrontPage components, form results, and formatting.

6. Make all necessary changes to the server-based web.

7. Set permissions for your web, if possible, to allow all classmates to be browsers on the server-based web.

8. Print all the web pages.

9. Close the web.

notes These Case Projects assume you are using PWS. If you are not using PWS or do not have access to a web server, your instructor may modify the Case Project requirements.

Case Projects

Project 1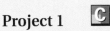

You are the IT manager for Barkersville Community College, located in Barkersville, Texas. The president of the college asks you to create a web site for the school. Create a web site for Barkersville Community College with at least five web pages. Use navigation bars, shared borders, graphic images, external hyperlinks, FrontPage components, and forms as appropriate to create an attractive and serviceable web site for the school. Save the form results to a file, to an e-mail address, and to a database and have FrontPage create a database. Publish the web site to PWS and test the web. Make all changes on the server-based web. Print the web pages. Create a backup web on the local file system when the testing is complete.

Project 2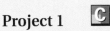

You are the newly hired web author for HealthAlert, part of the county hospital system in Memphis, Tennessee. The president of the hospital system hired you to create the new HealthAlert web site to provide viewers with health tips and information on health issues. Create a web site for HealthAlert with at least six web pages. Use navigation bars, shared borders, graphic images, external hyperlinks, FrontPage components, and forms as appropriate to create an attractive and serviceable web site. Save the form results to a file, to an e-mail address, and to a database created by FrontPage. Publish the web site to PWS and test the web. Make all changes on the server-based web. Print the web pages. Create a backup web on the local file system when the testing is complete.

Project 3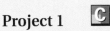

Mary McGuire, the owner of The Quilting Bee, a quilting supplies store in Raleigh, North Carolina, hires you to create a new web site for the company. Create a web site for The Quilting Bee with at least five web pages. Use navigation bars, shared borders, graphic images, external hyperlinks, FrontPage components, and forms as appropriate to create an attractive and serviceable web site for the company. Save the form results to a file, to an e-mail address, and to a database created by FrontPage. Publish the web site to PWS and test the web. Make all changes on the server-based web. Print the web pages. Create a backup web on the local file system when the testing is complete.

chapter twelve

Project 4

Nancy Nunez, the owner of Nunez Graphic Arts, hires you on a contract basis to create a sample web site. If she likes your work, she may hire you to be the manager of Nunez Graphic Arts new web authoring department. Create a web site for Nunez Graphic Arts with at least five web pages *directly on PWS*. Use navigation bars, shared borders, graphic images, external hyperlinks, FrontPage components, and forms as appropriate to create an attractive and serviceable web site for the company. Save the form results to a file, to an e-mail address, and to a database created by FrontPage. Test the web pages and print the final web pages. Create a backup web on the local file system when the testing is complete.

Project 5

The Otero County Historical Society in Alamogordo, New Mexico, hires you to create the Society's new web site. Connect to the Internet, launch your web browser, and search for other historical society web pages. Print at least three pages.

Create a web site for the Otero County Historical Society *directly on PWS* and include at least six web pages. Use navigation bars, shared borders, graphic images, external hyperlinks, FrontPage components, and forms as appropriate to create an attractive and serviceable web site for the society. Save the form results to a file, to an e-mail address, and to a database created by FrontPage. Make all changes on the server-based web. Print the web pages. Create a backup web on the local file system when the testing is complete.

Project 6

You work in the IT department for the City of Chicago, in Chicago, Illinois. Your supervisor assigns you the job of creating the new web site for the City Parks and Recreation Department. Create a web site for City of Chicago Parks and Recreation Department and include at least five web pages. Use navigation bars, shared borders, graphic images, external hyperlinks, FrontPage components, and forms as

appropriate to create an attractive and serviceable web site for the department. Save the form results to a file, to an e-mail address, and to a database created by FrontPage. Publish the web site to PWS and test the web. Make all changes on the disk-based web and republish pages as necessary. Print the web pages. Create a backup web on the local file system when the testing is complete.

Project 7

Lisa Rincon, the president of Rincon Systems, Inc., a company that sells time-management consulting services to business executives, hires you to create the Rincon Systems' new web site. Create a web site for Rincon Systems, Inc. with at least five web pages. Use navigation bars, shared borders, graphic images, external hyperlinks, FrontPage components, and forms as appropriate to create an attractive and serviceable web site for the company. Save the form results to a file, to an e-mail address, and to a database created by FrontPage. Publish the web site to PWS and test the web. Make all changes on the server-based web. Print the web pages. Create a backup web on the local file system when the testing is complete.

Project 8

Washington Real Estate is a real estate broker in Baltimore, Maryland. Tamika Washington, the president of Washington Real Estate, hires you to create a new web site for the company. Create a web site for Washington Real Estate with at least five web pages. Use navigation bars, shared borders, graphic images, external hyperlinks, FrontPage components, and forms as appropriate to create an attractive and serviceable web site for the company. Save the form results to a file, to an e-mail address, and to a database created by FrontPage. Publish the web site to PWS and test the web. Make all changes on the server-based web. Print the web pages. Create a backup web on the local file system when the testing is complete. Import the server-based web into a new web. Rename the server-based web.

Customizing FrontPage

Chapter Overview

Y ou can change the way you work in FrontPage by customizing the view and toolbars. You can float and dock toolbars, customize toolbars, and hide the Views bar. In this chapter, you work with the personalized menus and toolbars, float and dock toolbars, customize the menu bar, and hide and display the Views bar.

LEARNING OBJECTIVES

▶ Work with personalized menus and toolbars
▶ Display, hide, dock, and float toolbars
▶ Customize the menu bar and toolbars
▶ Hide and display the Views bar

Case profile

As you create web pages for Sarah's PartyWorld, you sometimes will want to add special commands to the menus and toolbars. Sarah Whaley, the owner of Sarah's PartyWorld, suggests that you review ways to customize the FrontPage menus and toolbars.

appendix

A.a Working with Personalized Menus and Toolbars

A **menu** is a list of commands you use to perform tasks in the FrontPage application. Some of the commands also have an associated image, or icon, which appears to the left of that command in the menu. Most menus are found on the menu bar, which is located below the title bar in the FrontPage application window. A **toolbar** contains a set of icons (the same icons you see on the menus) called "buttons" that you click with the mouse pointer to quickly execute a menu command.

notes The activities in this appendix assume that the personalized menus and toolbars are reset to their **default** (initial) settings. If your menus and toolbars are set at their default settings, open the Customize dialog box, click the Options tab, and turn on the personalized menu and toolbar features.

As you learn how to work with menus and toolbars, you are asked to select menu commands and toolbar buttons by clicking them with the mouse pointer. You will *not* learn how to use the menu command or toolbar button to perform a task in this appendix. Using menu commands and toolbar buttons to perform tasks is covered in chapters 1 through 12.

The first time you open the FrontPage application after you install it on your computer, the menus on the menu bar show only a basic set of commands and the Standard and Formatting toolbars contain only a basic set of buttons. These short versions of the menus and toolbars are called **personalized menus and toolbars**. As you work in the application, the commands and buttons you use most frequently are stored in the personalized settings. The first time you select a menu command or toolbar button that is not part of the basic set, that command or button is added to your personalized settings and appears on the menu or toolbar. If you do not use a command for a while, it is removed from your personalized settings and no longer appears on the menu or toolbar.

To view the personalized menus and toolbars in FrontPage:

Step 1	*Start*	FrontPage
Step 2	*Click*	Tools on the menu bar

| Step 3 | *Observe* | the short personalized menu, which contains only the basic commands |

The Tools menu you see on your screen should look similar to the open menu in Figure A-1.

FIGURE A-1
Personalized Tools Menu

If the command you want to use does not appear on the short personalized menu, you can expand the menu. To view all the commands, you can either pause for a few seconds until the menu automatically expands, click the expand arrows at the bottom of the menu, or double-click the menu name. To expand the Tools menu:

| Step 1 | *Pause* | until the menu expands automatically |

The expanded Tools menu on your screen should look similar to the open menu Figure A-2.

QUICK TIP

You can use keyboard shortcuts to perform tasks in the FrontPage application. Many of these keyboard shortcuts are shown on the menus, to the right of the menu command. You can also search FrontPage online Help for a list of keyboard shortcut keys.

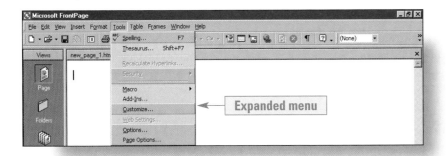

FIGURE A-2
Expanded Tools Menu

When you select a menu command, you move it from the expanded menu to the personalized menu. To add the Thesaurus command to the short personalized Tools menu:

| Step 1 | *Click* | Thesaurus |
| Step 2 | *Click* | Cancel in the Thesaurus dialog box to close the dialog box without making any changes |

appendix
A

Step 3	*Click*	<u>T</u>ools on the menu bar
Step 4	*Observe*	that the updated personalized <u>T</u>ools menu contains the Thesaurus command

The <u>T</u>ools menu on your screen should look similar to Figure A-3.

FIGURE A-3
Updated Personalized
<u>T</u>ools Menu

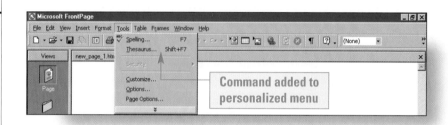

When you first open FrontPage, the Standard and Formatting tool-bars appear on one row below the title bar. In this position, you cannot see all their default buttons. If a toolbar button is not visible, you can reposition the Formatting toolbar by dragging it to the left or right. When the mouse pointer is positioned on a toolbar **move handle**, the gray vertical bar at the left edge of the toolbar, the mouse pointer changes from a white arrow pointer to a **move pointer**, a four-headed black arrow. You drag a move handle with the move pointer to resize the Formatting toolbar.

To reposition the Formatting toolbar:

Step 1	*Move*	the mouse pointer to the move handle on the Formatting toolbar
Step 2	*Observe*	that the mouse pointer becomes a move pointer
Step 3	*Drag*	the Formatting toolbar to the left until all the default Formatting toolbar buttons are visible
Step 4	*Observe*	that fewer buttons are visible on the Standard toolbar

The buttons that don't fit on the displayed area of a toolbar are collected in a More Buttons list. To view the remaining Standard tool-bar default buttons:

Step 1	*Click*	the More Buttons list arrow [»] on the Standard toolbar
Step 2	*Observe*	the default buttons that are not visible on the toolbar

The Standard toolbar More Buttons list on your screen should look similar to Figure A-4.

> **QUICK TIP**
>
> You can drag the Formatting toolbar below the Standard toolbar to view all the default buttons on both toolbars.

FIGURE A-4
More Buttons List

| Step 3 | *Press* | the ESC key to close the More Buttons list |

If you want to display one of the default buttons on a personalized toolbar, you can select it from the More Buttons list. To add the Format Painter button to the personalized Standard toolbar:

Step 1	*Click*	the More Buttons list arrow ⏸ on the Standard toolbar
Step 2	*Click*	the Format Painter button 🖌
Step 3	*Observe*	that the Format Painter button is added to the personalized Standard toolbar and the Format Painter is turned on

Your screen should look similar to Figure A-5.

FIGURE A-5
Updated Personalized
Standard Toolbar

If you want to view all the menu commands instead of a short personalized menu and all the default toolbar buttons on the Standard and Formatting toolbars, you can change options in the Customize dialog box. To open the Customize dialog box:

Step 1	*Click*	<u>T</u>ools
Step 2	*Click*	<u>C</u>ustomize
Step 3	*Click*	the <u>O</u>ptions tab, if necessary

The Customize dialog box on your screen should look similar to Figure A-6.

> **CAUTION TIP**
>
> When you update the personalized Standard or Formatting toolbar with a new button, a button that you have not used recently might move to the More Buttons list to make room for the new button.

appendix
A

FIGURE A-6
Options Tab in the
Customize Dialog Box

Personalized menu
and toolbar options

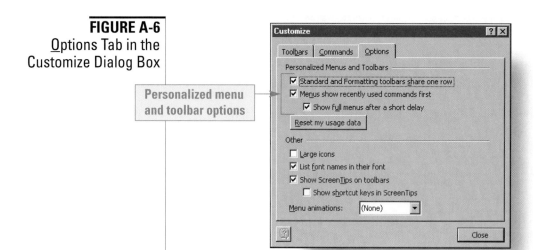

If you reposition the Formatting toolbar below the Standard toolbar, you can view all the default buttons on both toolbars. You do this by removing the check mark from the Standard and Formatting toolbars share one row check box. You can remove the check mark from the Menus show recently used commands first check box to view the entire set of menu commands for each menu instead of the short personalized menus. If you do not want the short personalized menus to expand automatically when you pause, you can remove the check mark from the Show full menus after a short delay check box. Then, to show the full menu you have to double-click the menu or click the expand arrows at the bottom of the menu.

To show all the Standard and Formatting toolbar buttons and menu commands:

Step 1	*Click*	the Standard and Formatting toolbars share one row check box to remove the check mark
Step 2	*Click*	the Menus show recently used commands first check box to remove the check mark
Step 3	*Click*	Close to close the dialog box
Step 4	*Observe*	the repositioned Standard and Formatting toolbars
Step 5	*Click*	Tools to view the entire set of Tools menu commands
Step 6	*Press*	the ESC key

You can return the menus and toolbars to their default settings in the Customize dialog box. To open the Customize dialog box and reset the default menus and toolbars:

Step 1	*Click*	Tools

Step 2	*Click*	Customize
Step 3	*Click*	the Options tab, if necessary
Step 4	*Click*	the Standard and Formatting toolbars share one row check box to insert a check mark
Step 5	*Click*	the Menus show recently used commands first check box to insert a check mark
Step 6	*Click*	Reset my usage data
Step 7	*Click*	Yes to confirm that you want to reset the menus and toolbars to their default settings
Step 8	*Close*	the Customize dialog box
Step 9	*Observe*	that the Tools menu and Standard toolbar are reset to their default settings

> **CAUTION TIP**
>
> Resetting the usage data to the initial settings does not change the location of toolbars and does not remove or add buttons to toolbars that you have customized in the Customize dialog box.

A.b Displaying, Hiding, Docking, and Floating Toolbars

The FrontPage application has additional toolbars that you can display when you need them. You can also hide toolbars when you are not using them. You can display or hide toolbars by pointing to the Toolbars command on the View menu and then clicking a toolbar name or by using a shortcut menu. A **shortcut menu** is a short list of frequently used menu commands. You open a shortcut menu by pointing to an item on the screen and clicking the right mouse button. This is called **right-clicking** the item. The commands on shortcut menus vary depending on where you right-click, so that you view only the most frequently used commands for a particular task. The shortcut menu provides an easy way to display or hide toolbars. To open the shortcut menu for FrontPage toolbars:

Step 1	*Right-click*	the menu bar, the Standard toolbar, or the Formatting toolbar
Step 2	*Observe*	the shortcut menu and the check marks next to the names of toolbars that are currently visible

Your screen should look similar to Figure A-7.

appendix
A

FIGURE A-7
Toolbars Shortcut Menu

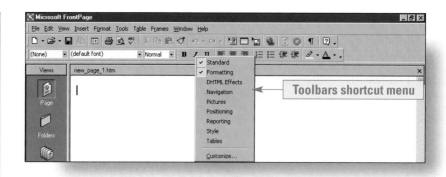

FIGURE A-7
Toolbars Shortcut Menu

| Step 3 | *Click* | DHTML Effects in the shortcut menu |
| Step 4 | *Observe* | that the DHTML Effects toolbar appears on your screen |

The DHTML Effects toolbar, unless a previous user repositioned it, is visible in its own window near the middle of your screen. When a toolbar is visible in its own window it is called a **floating toolbar**. You can move and size a floating toolbar with the mouse pointer just like you do any window. When a toolbar appears fixed at the screen boundaries, it is called a **docked toolbar**. The menu bar and Standard and Formatting toolbars are examples of docked toolbars because they are fixed below the title bar at the top of the screen. You can dock a floating toolbar by dragging its title bar with the mouse pointer to a docking position below the title bar or above the status bar. To dock the DHTML Effects toolbar below the Standard and Formatting toolbars:

| Step 1 | *Position* | the mouse pointer on the blue title bar in the DHTML Effects toolbar window |
| Step 2 | *Drag* | the toolbar window slowly up until it docks below the Standard and Formatting toolbars |

Similarly, you float a docked toolbar by dragging it away from its docked position toward the middle of the screen. To float the DHTML Effects toolbar:

| Step 1 | *Position* | the mouse pointer on the DHTML Effects toolbar move handle until it becomes a move pointer |
| Step 2 | *Drag* | the DHTML Effects toolbar down toward the middle of the screen until it appears in its own window |

When you are finished using a toolbar, you can hide it with a shortcut menu.

To hide the DHTML Effects toolbar:

Step 1	*Right-click*	the DHTML Effects toolbar
Step 2	*Click*	DHTML Effects to remove the check mark and hide the toolbar

A.c Customizing the Menu Bar and Toolbars

Recall that you can add a button to a personalized toolbar by clicking the More Buttons list arrow on the toolbar and selecting a button from the list of default buttons not currently visible. You can also add and delete buttons and commands on the menu bar or other toolbars with options in the Customize dialog box.

To open the Customize dialog box:

Step 1	*Right-click*	any toolbar (the menu bar, Standard toolbar, or Formatting toolbar)
Step 2	*Click*	Customize
Step 3	*Click*	the Commands tab, if necessary

The dialog box on your screen should look similar to Figure A-8.

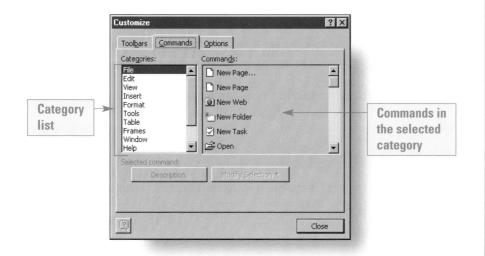

Category list

Commands in the selected category

> **MENU TIP**
>
> You can customize tool-bars by pointing to the Toolbars command on the View menu and clicking Customize.

> **QUICK TIP**
>
> Remember, the menu bar is also a toolbar. You customize the menu bar and other toolbars the same way.

FIGURE A-8
Commands Tab in the Customize Dialog Box

appendix
A

The <u>C</u>ommands tab in the Customize dialog box contains a list of category names and a list of commands available for the selected category. You can view a description of a command by selecting it and clicking the Descri<u>p</u>tion button. When you find the command you want to add, drag it from the dialog box to the menu bar or another visible toolbar. You decide to add a button on the menu bar to route the active presentation to other users on the network via e-mail. To customize the menu bar:

Step 1	*Verify*	that File is selected in the Cate<u>g</u>ories: list
Step 2	*Click*	Properties in the Comman<u>d</u>s: list (scroll the list to view this command)
Step 3	*Click*	Descri<u>p</u>tion to view the ScreenTip
Step 4	*Press*	the ESC key to close the ScreenTip
Step 5	*Drag*	the Properties command to the right of <u>H</u>elp on the menu bar
Step 6	*Click*	Close to close the dialog box and add the Properties command to the menu bar
Step 7	*Position*	the mouse pointer on the Properties command

Your screen should look similar to Figure A-9.

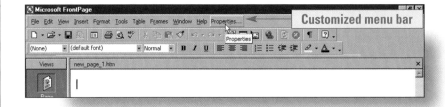

You can remove a command or button from a toolbar just as quickly. To remove the Properties command from the menu bar:

Step 1	*Open*	the Customize dialog box
Step 2	*Drag*	the Properties command from the menu bar into the dialog box
Step 3	*Close*	the dialog box

A.d Hiding and Displaying the Views Bar

If you want a larger view of the FrontPage workspace, you can hide the Views bar. With the Views bar hidden, you do not have access to the Folders, Reports, Navigation, Hyperlinks, and Tasks shortcuts you use to switch to those views. Instead, you switch views using commands on the <u>V</u>iew menu.

To hide the Views bar:

| Step 1 | *Click* | <u>V</u>iew |
| Step 2 | *Click* | <u>V</u>iews Bar to remove the check mark |

The Views bar is hidden. You want to switch to Navigation view.

| Step 3 | *Click* | <u>V</u>iew |

Your screen should look similar to Figure A-10.

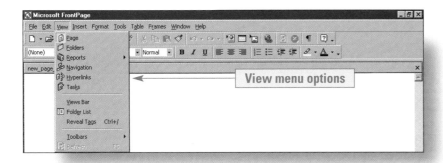

FIGURE A-10
<u>V</u>iew Menu

Step 4	*Click*	<u>N</u>avigation to switch to Navigation view
Step 5	*Click*	<u>V</u>iew
Step 6	*Click*	<u>P</u>age to switch back to Page view
Step 7	*Click*	<u>V</u>iew
Step 8	*Click*	<u>V</u>iews Bar to redisplay the Views bar
Step 9	*Close*	FrontPage

appendix
A

Summary

▶ Personalized menus and toolbars initially show only the basic set of commands and toolbar buttons and are updated to show frequently used commands and buttons as you work in FrontPage.

▶ You can reposition toolbars by dragging them to a new location in the FrontPage window.

▶ Docked toolbars are fastened in place below the title bar or above the status bar.

▶ Floating toolbars appear in their own window in the work area of the screen.

▶ You add or remove buttons and commands from toolbars, create custom toolbars, and set various menu and toolbar options in the Customize dialog box.

▶ To increase the size of your viewing area you can hide the Views bar and switch to different FrontPage views using the View menu.

Commands Review

Action	Menu Bar	Shortcut Menu	Toolbar/Mouse	Keyboard
Turn on or off personalized menus and toolbars	Tools, Customize	Right-click a toolbar, click Customize		ALT + T, C
	View, Toolbars, Customize			ALT + V, T, C
Hide or display the Views bar	View, Views Bar	Right-click the Views bar, click Hide Views Bar		ALT + V, V

Concepts Review

Circle the correct answer.

1. The personalized menus and toolbars have all the following features except:
  [a] Standard and Formatting toolbars share one row by default.
  [b] you can reset your usage data.
  [c] menus show recently used commands first.
  [d] you can view large icons.

2. Positioning a toolbar in its own window in the work area is called:
  [a] hiding the toolbar.
  [b] docking a toolbar.
  [c] floating a toolbar.
  [d] formatting a toolbar.

3. Which tab in the Customize dialog box contains a list of category names and a list of the commands for each category?
  [a] Toolbars
  [b] Options
  [c] Commands
  [d] General

4. Menu animation:
  [a] cannot be set in FrontPage.
  [b] is the movement the menu makes as it opens on your screen.
  [c] is set in the Options dialog box.
  [d] is set in the General dialog box.

5. A toolbar contains a:
  [a] list of commands.
  [b] set of icons.
  [c] move pointer.
  [d] display handle.

Circle **T** if the statement is true or **F** if the statement is false.

T   F   1. A shortcut menu is a short list of frequently used menu commands.

T   F   2. A docked toolbar appears fixed below the title bar or above the status bar.

T   F   3. A move pointer is a gray vertical bar at the left edge of a docked toolbar.

T   F   4. You cannot hide the Views bar.

T   F   5. Once you turn on the personalized menus and toolbars, you cannot turn them off.

Skills Review

Exercise 1

1. Open the FrontPage application.

2. Turn on all the personalized menu and toolbar options.

3. Add three buttons from the More buttons list to the Standard or Formatting toolbar.

4. Turn off all the personalized menu and toolbar options.

5. Close FrontPage.

Exercise 2

1. Open the FrontPage application.

2. Turn off the personalized menu and toolbar options, if necessary.

appendix A

3. Display the DHTML Effects toolbar with a shortcut menu.

4. Close the DHTML Effects toolbar with a shortcut menu.

5. Display the Positioning toolbar with the Toolbars command on the View menu.

6. Dock the Positioning toolbar below the Formatting toolbar.

7. Close the Positioning toolbar with the Close button on the toolbar title bar.

8. Turn on the personalized menu and toolbar options.

9. Close FrontPage.

Exercise 3

1. Open the FrontPage application.

2. Open the Customize dialog box from the Tools menu.

3. Add three new commands or buttons to the menu bar.

4. Close the Customize dialog box.

5. Open the Customize dialog box from the View menu.

6. Remove the three command or buttons you added to the menu bar.

7. Close the Customize dialog box.

8. Close FrontPage.

Exercise 4

1. Open the FrontPage application.

2. Hide the Views bar.

3. Switch to Hyperlinks view.

4. Switch to Page view.

5. Switch to Tasks view.

6. Display the Views bar.

7. Close FrontPage.

Exercise 5

1. Open the FrontPage application.

2. Open the Customize dialog box and view the Options tab.

3. Turn on show shortcut keys in ScreenTips.

4. Select the menu animation of your choice.

5. Close the Customize dialog box.

6. View your ScreenTip and menu animation changes by positioning the mouse pointer on toolbar buttons and by displaying several menus.

7. Open the Customize dialog box.

8. Turn off show shortcut keys in ScreenTips and menu animation.

9. Close the Customize dialog box.

10. Close FrontPage.

The Microsoft Office User Specialist Program

APPROVED COURSEWARE

What Is Certification?

The logos on the cover of this book indicate that the book is officially certified by Microsoft Corporation at the Core and Expert user skill levels for FrontPage 2000. This certification is part of the Microsoft Office User Specialist (MOUS) program that validates your skills as knowledgeable of Microsoft FrontPage 2000. The following grids outline the various Core and Expert skills and where they are covered in the book.

notes
Objectives are covered throughout the text and in multiple exercises and projects; these are representative examples.

FrontPage 2000 Core

Standardized Coding Number	Activity	Chapter Number	In-Chapter Activities	End-of-Chapter Exercises
FP2000.1	**Create a new Web site**			
FP2000.1.1	Save a FrontPage Web	1 2 3	FP 11, 23 FP 37 FP 46, 48	FP 28 EX2 FP 54 EX1 FP 86 EX7
FP2000.1.2	Create a Web site using a Web wizard	2	FP 36	FP 55, 57 EX3, 8; FP 57–58 CP1, 2, 5, 8
FP2000.1.3	Create a Web site using a Web template	2	FP 36	FP 54–56 EX1, 2, 4, 5, 6; FP 57–58 CP1, 2, 5, 6, 8
FP2000.2	**Open and edit an existing FrontPage-based Web site**			
FP2000.2.1	Open an existing FrontPage Web	1 3	FP 5 FP 60	FP 28–30 EX1–8 FP 84–86 EX1–5
FP2000.2.2	Modify and save changes to the Web site	1 3–11	FP 11 various	FP 28 EX2, 3 Sample_Web created in chapter 2 is modified and saved in chapters 3–11
FP2000.3	**Apply and edit a theme across the entire Web site**			
FP2000.3.1	Apply a theme to entire Web site	3	FP 60	FP 84–87 EX1, 3, 5, 7, 8; FP 88 CP4
FP2000.3.2	Apply a custom theme across entire Web site	3	FP 65	FP 84–86 EX2, 4, 6; FP 87–88 CP1, 2
FP2000.4	**Add a new Web page**			
FP2000.4.1	Create and preview a new Web page using a FrontPage page template or wizard	2	FP 47	FP 54 EX1, FP 57–58 CP1, 6
FP2000.4.2	Create a new page within Page view	2	FP 49	FP 55–56 EX5, 6

Standardized Coding Number	Activity	Chapter Number	In-Chapter Activities	End-of-Chapter Exercises
FP2000.5	**Open, view, and rename Web page**			
FP2000.5.l	View a Web document in Normal, HTML, and Preview view	1	FP 9	FP 28, 30 EX1, 8
FP2000.5.2	Open an Office document in a FrontPage Web	6	FP 161	FP 169 EX4
FP2000.5.3	Rename page title and change page URL	1 11 12	FP 18 Quick Tip FP 309 FP 329	FP 28 EX2, 3 FP 321 EX6 FP 344–346 EX1–8
FP2000.6	**Import text and images onto Web page**			
FP2000.6.1	Add or import images into a Web page (automatically converted to GIF/JPEG)	5	FP 117, 119 Quick Tip	FP 133–136 EX1–8; FP 137–138 CP1, 3, 4, 5
FP2000.6.2	Add or import text to a Web page (automatically converted to HTML)	2	FP 49	FP 55 EX5
FP2000.6.3	Add or import elements from a Web site to a FrontPage Web	5	FP 126	FP 136 EX8
FP2000.7	**Type and format text and paragraphs and create hyperlinks**			
FP2000.7.1	Type and format text/fonts on a Web page	3	FP 75	FP 84–87 EX1, 4, 6, 7, 8; FP 87–88 CP1, 2, 4
FP2000.7.2	Add multi-level bulleted or numbered lists to a Web page	4	FP 92, 94	FP 111–112 EX4, 5, 6
FP2000.7.3	Format bulleted or numbered lists	4	FP 94	FP 111–112 EX4, 5, 6
FP2000.7.4	Add hyperlinks pointing to: an existing page in the current site, the WWW, or a brand new page	6	FP 141, 144, 145, 159	FP 169–171 EX2, 3, 5, 6; FP 173 CP3
FP2000.7.5	Use the Format Painter to apply formats	3	FP 76	FP 84 EX1
FP2000.7.6	Use the Office Clipboard	5 6 7 10	FP 120 FP 176 FP 284–285	FP 134 EX4 FP 171 EX7 FP 202 EX5 FP 302 EX8
FP2000.8	**Edit images, apply image effects, create hotspots**			
FP2000.8.1	Rotate, flip, bevel, or resize images on a Web page	5	FP 124–125	FP 133–136 EX1–8
FP2000.8.2	Add text over image	5	FP 123 Quick Tip	
FP2000.8.3	Create a hotspot (clickable image)	6	FP 146	FP 172 EX8
FP2000.9	**Create and edit tables on a Web page**			
FP2000.9.1	Create tables on a Web page	3	FP 69	FP 84–86 EX1, 4, 6, 8; FP 87–88 CP1, 2, 4
FP2000.9.2	Erase or delete table rows or columns	3	FP 74	FP 84–86 EX1, 4, 6, 8; FP 87–88 CP1, 2, 4

Standardized Coding Number	Activity	Chapter Number	In-Chapter Activities	End-of-Chapter Exercises
FP2000.9.3	Draw or add table rows or columns	3	FP 73	FP 84–86 EX1, 4, 6, 8; FP 87–88 CP1, 2, 4
FP2000.9.4	Resize tables and cells	3	FP 71, 74	FP 84–86 EX1, 4, 6, 8; FP 87–88 CP1, 2, 4
FP2000.9.5	Select and merge table cells	3 5	FP 79 Quick Tip FP 122	
FP2000.10	**Insert dynamic, active clements and FrontPage components on a Web page**			
FP2000.10.1	Add a hit counter to Web page	4	FP 96	FP 112 EX6, FP 114–115 CP3, 4, 5
FP2000.10.2	Format page transition for Web page	4	FP 104	FP 110–113 EX1, 3, 7; FP 114–115 CP1–4, 6
FP2000.10.3	Add or edit scrolling marquee test on a Web page	4	FP 97	FP 111 EX3; FP 114 CP2, 3, 4
FP2000.10.4	Add a search form to Web page	3	FP 80 Quick Tip	
FP2000.11	**View and organize Web site documents**			
FP2000.11.1	View a Web site in Reports view, Hyperlinks view, or Folders view	1	FP 13	FP 28–29 EX2, 3, 5
FP2000.11.2	View your Web site structure and print it from Navigation view	1 2	FP 19, 21	FP 29 EX4 FP 55 EX4
FP2000.11.3	Move and organize files using drag and drop in Folders view and Navigation view	1	FP 17, 20	FP 28–29 EX2, 4
FP2000.12	**Manage a Web site (including all files, pages, and hyperlinks) and automatically keep contents up-to-date**			
FP2000.12.1	Check spelling on a page or across a Web site	3 12	FP 77 FP 333	FP 84–86 EX1, 4, 5, 6, 7 FP 344–346 EX1–8
FP2000.12.2	Change file name in Folders view and update its hyperlinks	1	FP 17	FP 28 EX2
FP2000.12.3	Verify hyperlinks	6	FP 164	FP 169 EX2; FP 172 CP1
FP2000.12.4	Use global Find and Replace across a Web site	3	FP 78	FP 85–86 EX3, 5
FP2000.13	**Manage tasks**			
FP2000.13.1	View task history	1	FP 22	FP 29 EX6
FP2000.13.2	View and sort tasks in Tasks view	1	FP 22	FP 29 EX6

FrontPage 2000 Expert

Standardized Coding Number	Activity	Chapter Number	In-Chapter Activities	End-of-Chapter Exercises
FP2000E.1	**Create a FrontPage Web using existing resources**			
FP2000E.1.1	Use Import Wizard to import an existing Web site from a file into FrontPage	11	FP 306	FP 320 EX2, 4; FP 322–323 CP2, 8
FP2000E.1.2	Use Import Wizard to import an existing Web site from a URL into FrontPage	11 12	FP 306 Quick Tip	FP 348 EX8
FP2000E.1.3	Modify HTML tags and verify results using Reveal Tags	11	FP 310, 312	FP 320–321 EX3, 7
FP2000E.1.4	Use buttons and drop-down menus to insert code directly in HTML view	11	FP 312	FP 321 EX8
FP2000E.2	**Apply and change themes for an entire Web site and individual Web pages**			
FP2000E.2.1	Select a new theme and apply to an individual Web page	3 7 10	FP 61 FP 176 FP 293	FP 84–87 EX1, 8; FP 87–88 CP1, 2
FP2000E.2.2	Change attributes (Vivid Colors, Active Graphics, Background Image) for a currently selected site-wide theme	3	FP 62	FP 84–87 EX2, 3, 7; FP 88 CP5
FP2000E.2.3	Change a custom theme and apply it to an individual Web page	3	FP 65	FP 86 EX6; FP 88 CP2
FP2000E.3	**Create and organize navigational structure for entire Web site**			
FP2000E.3.1	Rename new pages in Navigation view	6	FP 150	FP 171–172 EX6, 7
FP2000E.3.2	Add new pages to Navigation view	6	FP 150	FP 171–172 EX6, 7
FP2000E.3.3	Add existing pages to Navigation view	6	FP 149	FP 168–169 EX1, 3
FP2000E.3.4	Use drag and drop to organize/restructure pages in Navigation view	6	FP 149	FP 168–169 EX1, 3
FP2000E.4	**Modify the Web page layout**			
FP2000E.4.1	Position graphics on a page	5	FP 121	FP 134–136 EX2, 5, 7, 8; FP 137–138 CP1, 5, 7
FP2000E.4.2	Position text on a page	3 5 7	FP 75 FP 121 FP 184	FP 84–85 EX1, 4 FP 136 EX7; FP 137 CP2, FP 201–202 EX4, 6
FP2000E.5	**Add or edit shared borders across entire site and on individual Web pages**			
FP2000E.5.1	Turn off (deselect) site-wide shared borders for the current Web page	6 7 10	FP 154 FP 176	FP 173 CP4 FP 204–205 CP1, 7 FP 300 EX3
FP2000E.5.2	Edit content within shared borders for an entire Web site	4 6 7	FP 106	FP 168–170 EX1, 3, 5 FP 204 CP2
FP2000E.5.3	Edit content within shared borders for current Web page	6 7		FP 169–171 EX 3, 7 FP 203 EX8; FP 204 CP2

Standardized Coding Number	Activity	Chapter Number	In-Chapter Activities	End-of-Chapter Exercises
FP2000E.5.4	Turn on (set) alternate shared borders for the current Web page	6 7	FP 154	FP 168–171 EX1, 4, 6; FP 173 CP4 FP 204–205 CP1, 7
FP2000E.6	**Automatically add navigation bars and page banners to Web pages**			
FP2000E.6.1	Add navigation bar to the top of a Web page	6	FP 157	FP 168–171 EX1, 3, 4, 6; FP 172–174 CP1–5, 7
FP2000E.6.2	Add page banner to the top of a Web page	3 6	FP 80 Menu Tip	FP 85–86 EX4, 5, 6 FP 168–169 EX1, 3
FP2000E.6.3	Select/change levels of navigational buttons to include in navigation bar on Web page	6	FP 151	FP 169–171 EX4, 6; FP 172–174 CP1–5, 7
FP2000E.7	**Add background elements to Web page**			
FP2000E.7.1	Add a background image on a Web page	7	FP 182	FP 200–202 EX3, 4, 6; FP 204–205 CP1, 2, 3, 7
FP2000E.8	**Manipulate table contents on a Web page**			
FP2000E.8.1	Center image or text within a table cell	5 7	FP 121	FP 136 EX7 FP 199 EX2; FP 204 CP1
FP2000E.8.2	Add a custom background color or image to an entire table and to individual table cells	7	FP 179, 183	FP 198–202 EX1, 2, 7; FP 204 CP1
FP2000E.8.3	Add a table within a table	7	FP 183 Mouse Tip	
FP2000E.9	**Enhance or edit a Web page with custom text/hyperlink styles and formatting**			
FP2000E.9.1	View page Estimated Time to Download	7	FP 194	FP 203 EX8; FP 204–205 CP2, 3, 5
FP2000E.9.2	Resample/Restore image on Web page	5	FP 125	FP 133–134 EX1, 4
FP2000E.9.3	Format special styles for fonts, paragraphs, and hyperlinks	7	FP 180, 188	FP 201–203 EX4, 7; FP 204–205 CP3, 4
FP2000E.10	**Customize a Web page with dynamic, active elements and FrontPage components**			
FP2000E.10.1	Add hover button to a Web page	7	FP 192	FP 199–203 EX2, 8; FP 204–205 CP1, 7
FP2000E.10.2	Edit hover button transitional effect	7	FP 194	FP 199–203 EX2, 8; FP 204–205 CP1, 7
FP2000E.10.3	Change FrontPage component properties	4 7 10	FP 96, 97 FP 192 FP 278	FP 111–112 EX3, 6 FP 199 EX2 FP 301 EX5
FP2000E.10.4	Insert pre-built and Office Web components into a page	2	FP 49, 50 Caution Tip	
FP2000E.11	**Build a Web site for user input**			
FP2000E.11.1	Add text boxes, check boxes, radio buttons, drop-down pick lists, and push buttons	9	FP 240–247	FP 266–272 EX1, 3, 4, 5, 6, 8; FP 273 CP1–4

Standardized Coding Number	Activity	Chapter Number	In-Chapter Activities	End-of-Chapter Exercises
FP2000E.11.2	Save form to file	9	FP 237	FP 268–272 EX2, 3, 4, 6, 7; FP 273–274 CP1, 2, 3, 6, 7
FP2000E.11.3	Add search form to a Web page	10	FP 276	FP 299–301 EX1, 3, 5, 7; FP 303–304 CP1, 2, 4–8
FP2000E.11.4	Save form to e-mail	9	FP 256	FP 266–272 EX1, 5, 8; FP 273–274 CP2, 3, 5–8
FP2000E.11.5	Create a custom form on a Web page	9	FP 239	FP 266–272 EX1, 3, 4, 5, 6, 8; FP 273–274 CP1–8
FP2000E.12	*Integrate databases*			
FP2000E.12.1	Create a form that sends data to an Access database	10	FP 279	FP 300–301 EX2, 6; FP 303–304 CP1–8
FP2000E.12.2	Incorporate data access pages into a Web page	10	FP 291	FP 302 EX8
FP2000E.12.3	Incorporate database queries using the Database Results Wizard	10	FP 285	FP 300 EX4
FP2000E.13	*Use Collaboration features*			
FP2000E.13.1	Check in and check out FrontPage files	11	FP 314	FP 319–321 EX1, 5
FP2000E.13.2	Set rights to a FrontPage Web and subwebs	12	FP 339	FP 344–346 EX1–8
FP2000E.14	*Create and edit a Frames Web page*			
FP2000E.14.1	Edit size of existing frames in Frames page using drag and drop of border lines	8	FP 217 Mouse Tip	
FP2000E.14.2	Edit actual content within a frame on the Frames page	8	FP 213	FP 224–229 EX1–8; FP 230–232 CP1–3, 5–8
FP2000E.14.3	Create an entirely new frame on an existing Frames page by dragging and dropping existing Frames page outside border	8	FP 217 Mouse Tip	
FP2000E.14.4	Create a new Frames page from template or using Frames Wizard	8	FP 208	FP 224–229 EX1–8; FP 230–232 CP1–3, 5–8
FP2000E.14.5	Add target content within a frame	8	FP 212	FP 226–229 EX4, 6, 7
FP2000E.15	*Publish a Web site*			
FP2000E.15.1	Publish a Web from one server to another	12	FP 338	FP 347–348 CP1–8
FP2000E 15.2	Use FrontPage or Microsoft Personal Web Server as appropriate	12	FP 326	FP 344–346 EX1–8; FP 347–348 CP1–8
FP2000E 15.3	Set FrontPage/server permissions as appropriate	12	FP 339	FP 344–346 EX1–8

Index

A

.asp page, FP 289
Add Choice dialog box, FP 251
alignment options, FP 187
AltaVista, FP 159
alternative text, FP 128
anchor, FP 140, FP 166
animated clip art, FP 121
animation, FP 91, FP 97–99,
    FP 100–103, FP 108

B

background image, adding,
    FP 182–184
background, changing, FP 62
backup copy, publishing, FP 337–338
Banner and Contents template, FP 210
beveling, FP 125, FP 131
Bookmark dialog box, FP 140–141
bookmark, FP 140, FP 142, FP 166
    location flag for, FP 140
Borders and Shading dialog box,
    FP 103
borders, FP 186
    shared, FP 106–107
    turning on or off, FP 154–157
brightness, FP 123, FP 131
broken hyperlinks. *See* hyperlinks.
bulleted list, FP 91, FP 92, FP 108

C

cell contents, changing alignment of,
    FP 180
Cell Properties dialog box, FP 184
cell, FP 69, FP 81, FP 82
    combining, FP 79
    resizing, FP 74
    merging, FP 75
Change Folder dialog box, FP 119
character formatting, changing, FP 76
Check Box Properties dialog box,
    FP 254
check box, FP 246–247, FP 254, FP 264
check in, FP 314, FP 317
check out, FP 314, FP 317
child page, FP 149, FP 153
clickable image map, FP 146–148
clickable label, FP 245, FP 246
Clip Art Gallery, FP 122
clip art, FP 130, FP 131
Clipboard, using, FP 120–121, FP 131

collapsible list, FP 95
colors, applying to web page, FP 123,
    FP 131, FP 175–181
      adding to a cell or table, FP 179,
       FP 196
      background color, FP 177–179
      setting for hyperlink, FP 180
      settings for graphic elements,
       FP 180–182
comment, FP 70, FP 82
confirmation page, creating,
    FP 258–262, FP 264
Container tag, FP 9, FP 10
content, planning, FP 33–36
Contents area, FP 16
contrast, FP 123, FP 131
converting
    text to table, FP 76
    table to text, FP 76
Copy button, FP 121, FP 122, FP 126
Create Hyperlinks dialog box, FP 212,
    FP 214
cropping, FP 123
CSS, FP 62
custom form, creating, FP 239
Custom Query dialog box, FP 287
Customize dialog box, AP 12
Cut button, FP 120, FP 121

D

Data Access Page (DAP), FP 291–296
data entry, FP 247
database connection, FP 279, FP 297
database queries. *See* queries.
Database Results wizard, FP 284–291,
    FP 290, FP 297
database, FP 279–291, FP 297
    import an existing, FP 284
definition list, FP 238
DHTML Effects toolbar, FP 101, FP 102
disk-based web, FP 11, FP 306, FP 317
docked toolbar, AP 8
download time, FP 2, FP 5, FP 125,
    FP 126
drag and drop, FP 17, FP 20, FP 21
drop-down list, FP 243, FP 250, FP 264
drop-down menu, FP 243–244, FP 251,
    FP 264
Dynamic HTML (DHTML),
    FP 100–104, FP 108

E

e-commerce, FP 234
electronic database, FP 237
e-mail link, FP 237. *See also*
    mailto:link.
E-mail Results tab, FP 256
embedded files, FP 130
embedded style sheet, FP 190
estimated download time, FP 194
expanded menu, AP 3
external style sheet, FP 188

F

field. *See* form field.
file properties, viewing, FP 18, FP 25
filename, changing, FP 17
filename, FP 39
files, moving and organizing, FP 17
Filez Web search tool, FP 332
find and replace
    change page banner, FP 80
    global, FP 78–80
flipping, FP 124–125
floating toolbar, AP 8, AP 12
Folder list, FP 7, FP 16, FP 25, FP 51,
    FP 63, FP 264
folder, default, FP 6
Folders view, FP 4, FP 16–19, FP 25
font characteristics, changing, FP 76
font color, setting, FP 179–180
Font dialog box, FP 102
font formatting, removing, FP 75
form confirmation, FP 337
form elements, adding, FP 240–247
form field name, FP 247, FP 280
form field properties, FP 247–255,
    FP 264, FP 280
form field validation, FP 250–255,
    FP 264, FP 280
form field value, FP 247
form field, FP 238, FP 264
form handler options, FP 237, FP 238,
    FP 238
Form Properties dialog box, FP 237
form results, FP 237
    saving, FP 237–239, FP 264
    sending, FP 256–258
Format Painter, FP 76, FP 103, FP 122,
    FP 260
Formatting, copying, FP 82